GROUPS
IN
SOCIAL
WORK

GROUPS
IN
SOCIAL WORK
An
Ecological
Perspective

Pallassana R. Balgopal
University of Illinois at Urbana–Champaign

Thomas V. Vassil
University of Maryland at Baltimore

Macmillan Publishing Co., Inc.
New York
Collier Macmillan Publishers
London

Macmillan Publishing Co., Inc.
866 Third Avenue, New York, New York 10022

Collier Macmillan Canada, Inc.

Library of Congress Cataloging in Publication Data

Balgopal, Pallassana R.
  Groups in social work.

  Bibliography: p.
  Includes index.
  1. Social group work. I. Vassil, Thomas V.
II. Title.
HV45.B25   361.4   82-15283
ISBN 0-02-305530-8   AACR2

Printing: 1 2 3 4 5 6 7 8   Year: 3 4 5 6 7 8 9 0

Dedicated to Our Parents
The Late Professor and Mrs. Pallassana S. Ramanathan
Mr. Vangel N. and Mrs. Kile S. Vassil

Preface

Although the authors of this volume come from different personal and professional backgrounds, they share a number of significant similarities, the most important one being that they both started their professional careers as settlement house workers in Boston. This experience during the formative years of their professional career had a marked impact on their ideologies as group workers. As a result, both share the sentiment that groups in social work, to be effective as an intervention modality, need to include four key dimensions, namely, the individual, the group, the worker, and the agency-environment as interlocking units of equal importance. These four dimensions are often discussed in group work literature, but seldom are they presented as interlocking units. It is in this context that the authors embarked on the project of writing this volume.

Soon after this joint venture commenced, the authors recognized the need of a conceptual framework for organizational purposes. This framework will be complementary to the four group work components and the mission and objectives of the profession within the current societal climate. An ecological framework that emphasizes the interrelationship of the person and the environment seemed to hold promise. Underpinning this framework is the assumption that an optimum degree of integration is necessary between the person and various environments in order to maintain and enhance the problem-solving capacities and growth of constituent members in their own natural environment. The fundamental task for social work practice in groups is to build a culture that would contain within it adequate provisions for its own change.

The ecological concepts have been well articulated in biology, but their explication in social and behavioral sciences is in a rudimentary state. Furthermore, it is difficult to present practice components of groups in social work through the ecological framework on its own because it refers to the study of human behavior in general. Therefore, two other perspectives, namely, symbolic interaction as propagated by George Herbert Mead, and field theory as developed by Kurt Lewin, are incorporated to complement the ecological framework in presenting conceptual and practice components of groups in social work.

The purposes of this volume are three-fold: (1) to present the four dimensions of groups in social work: the individual, the group, the leader, and the agency-environment as equally important and interlocking units; (2) to present key structural and process concepts of small groups as related to the practice of social group work; and (3) to present key strategies of interventions relevant to working with differential social work clientele.

Humanistic and structural approaches in the social work profession have expanded the intervention strategies available to the practitioners in groups, which are applicable to the beginning, middle, and ending phases of the cycle of group work practice. As the assumptive world of problem-definers expands, so will differential use of groups in various settings and under different auspices become altered to meet the challenge of contemporary life. The network of ideas and interlocking content presented in this volume will serve as a springboard from which emergent and various extensions of the use of groups in social work as related to varied client populations may be postulated. That is to say, groups in social work may represent a most viable and effective means for enhancing the life of groups of people, only some of which may be classified as problematic in their everyday functioning.

In the first chapter, a brief overview of the state of the art of social group work is presented. Recent developments in social group work as reflected in the current scene, and projected directions for the future are also discussed.

In Chapter 2, the salient concepts that explicate the ecological perspective are presented, with their relevancy for groups in social work. The works of James Kelly, Alexander Leighton, Eugene Odum, and Herbert Thelen guided the discussion of the ecological concepts. The decision to include concepts underlying this perspective was arbitrary, but the principle guiding this decision was based on the relevancy of this knowledge for social work practice with groups and the authors' experience. To reduce the abstraction of these concepts, appropriate examples have been included. The reader should be aware that these concepts as related to groups in social work are incorporated in subsequent chapters.

The focus of Chapter 3 is an exposition of the symbolic interaction perspective formulated by George Herbert Mead and Kurt Lewin's field theory. These complementary orientations are utilized to explicate further the notion that the group is a mediating vehicle between the internal and external demands that are continually manifested in group processes. The relevance of these two frameworks in clarifying the various facets of member behavior, group processes, and worker interventions is presented by incorporating process recording of a group led by a professional social worker.

In Chapter 4, the four major components that encompass the ecological perspective of groups in social work, namely, the individual, the group, the worker, and the agency-environment, are discussed. Subsequently the interplay between these components is presented in an integrative fashion.

The key structural properties of groups such as assessment, goal formulation, composition, size, programming, and contracting are spelled out in Chapter 5. A model for articulating the ecological concepts with the structural properties is presented in some detail with group assessment and compositional factors. Subsequent application of this perspective to other properties is not emphasized in such depth in order to avoid redundancy. The reader has to bear in mind that similar application can also be implemented with other structural properties.

The focus of Chapter 6 is on examining the salient process components occurring in groups in social work, which include subgroups, scapegoating, group conflict, roles, and norms. Each of these structural properties and process components is examined through their historical evolution and current status. Relevant practice principles pertaining to these topics are presented. The list of these topics is by no means an exhaustive one, but the authors' contention is that the units discussed in Chapters 5 and 6 have significant bearing on determining the quality and effectiveness of groups in social work. This premise is based on and also was confirmed by their students' interests and concerns around these topics. Similarly, in the authors' consultation within the practice community, questions related to these issues were frequently raised.

In Chapter 7, using the construct of group culture, phases of group development are examined. The thrust of this chapter is to delineate that group cultures and member(s) behavior are interrelated. The implication of this for practitioners is that understanding this interrelationship can be useful in devising appropriate interventions. Major theories of group development as proposed by social scientists, including social workers, are examined along three phases—beginning, middle, and end. Also included in this chapter are suggested practice principles as related to group development.

The differential aspects of professional leadership are presented in Chapters 8 and 9. (In this volume, *leader* and *worker* are used as interchangeable designations to imply professional social worker working with groups). In Chapter 8, roles and functions, differential styles and personality traits of the leaders and their impact on leadership effectiveness are discussed. Subsequently an ecological perspective of group leadership based on the formulations of Mead and Lewin, leadership roles as related to the structural and process components, and co-leadership are examined.

The focus of Chapter 9 is on leadership interventions. Generally, interventions in working with groups are discussed in relation to differential phases of group development. In this volume, rather than using that format, structure and process are used as the two key dimensions of groups in social work, to delineate specific intervention strategies. The rationale for this approach is to avoid the problem of overlapping interventions within and across stages of development, but at the same time to distinguish clearly the concrete applications of different strategies. In this chapter, significant interventions in working with differential groups complemented with appropriate case illustrations are presented.

The last chapter of this volume focuses on the issue of education for competence in social group work. Two complementary and unique approaches are presented that are consistent with the ecological perspective, which emphasizes different teaching formats for group work education. This chapter also includes discussion around curriculum development in group work and the empirical role of the group worker.

The topical units discussed in this volume cover key aspects of groups in social work both from conceptual and practical points of view. The conceptual content specifically related to the functioning of small groups in the social environment is relevant for human behavior and social environment and group dynamics/group process courses. The conceptual content about groups in social work blended with topical units of group work practice and differential leader interventions is specifically relevant for generic group work courses. Thus this volume will be useful for both advanced undergraduate and graduate social work students.

The writing of this volume involved many hours of collaborative writing and dialogue in person and over the telephone. Moments of excitement, joys, and frustrations were openly shared, and by the time the volume was completed both authors came to appreciate and respect each other not only as group workers and social work educators but as close friends who share many similar sentiments and values.

In joint authorship, the author listed first is generally considered the senior or primary author. In this volume, it is not so. In the absence of an alternative to reflect that responsibility was shared equally, the authorship is listed alphabetically.

ACKNOWLEDGMENTS

The writing of this volume involved assistance from many people. Although it is impossible to identify all of them individually, we do want to acknowledge our appreciation to all of the social work students in our group work classes at the Universities of Houston, Illinois, Maryland, and Western Michigan. These students over the years stimulated our ideas and patiently bore with us while the ideas presented in this volume were tested in the class.

This volume has profited by the incisive and thorough criticism provided by our esteemed professional colleagues Professors Joseph Anderson, Gerald Euster, and Gary Lloyd. Their instructive criticism helped us clarify and revise many of our ideas. A special note of thanks is also due to Professor Gloria Marek for her helpful suggestions in the formative stage of the manuscript.

Deans Donald Brieland and Francis Itzin provided personal encouragement and support while this volume was being completed. Administrative support through their offices at the School of Social Work, University of Illinois at Urbana–Champaign was instrumental in completion of this work. Dean Ruth Young of the School of Social Work and Community Planning at the University of Maryland also provided timely support.

We want to express our thanks to Emlie Adams, Bob Berger, and Mojie Burgoyne, whose selective reviews of the literature are incorporated in parts of Chapters 5 and 6. Gilbert Greene and Bruce Lane's assistance in preparing the material on Symbolic Interaction and Group Composition are highly appreciated. We also want to extend our gratitude to Clyde McDaniel and Paul Ephross whose co-authored work with one of us is presented in parts of Chapters 8 and 10. We want to thank the Council on Social Work Education, John Wiley Publications, and Meta Publications for their permission to use extended quotes from their publications. We also wish to thank Ken Scott, the Senior Editor at Macmillan, whose continued encouragement in completion of this volume is recognized.

We want to express our sincere appreciation to the secretarial staff at the University of Illinois for their tireless and generous efforts in typing several revisions of the manuscript. Christina Fisher, Jeannette Ingram, Jean Rodgers, and Virginia Peggs deserve a special accolade for going beyond the call of duty.

Special recognition is accorded to Shyamala Balgopal for her expertise in preparing the bibliography and index, and locating references, always under the pressure of time.

Last but most important our "primary groups," which include our wives Shyamala Balgopal and Toyoko Vassil and our children Meena and Anita Balgopal and Kristina, Andrew, and Jonathan Vassil, always stood at our side and readily gave us encouragement, affection, and love. To all of these wonderful and beautiful people our gratitude is affectionately expressed.

Pallassana R. Balgopal
Urbana Illinois

Thomas V. Vassil
Baltimore, Maryland

Contents

**1. GROUP WORK: HISTORICAL OVERVIEW
AND CURRENT STATUS**   *1*

Introduction   *1*
Historical Antecedents   *2*
   Phase One. Up to 1950   *2*
   Phase Two. Decades of 1940s and 1950s   *7*
   Phase Three. 1950s to Present   *8*
Current Status   *16*
Directions for the Future   *17*

2. THE ECOLOGICAL FRAMEWORK   *19*

Ecological Perspective   *20*
Basic Concepts   *25*
Significance for Group Work   *43*
Summary   *47*

**3. SYMBOLIC INTERACTION AND
FIELD THEORY**   *49*

Symbolic Interaction Perspective   *52*
Basic Propositions   *53*
Significance for Group Work   *55*
Lewinian Field Theory   *66*
Lewinian Change Principles   *68*
Significance for Group Work   *72*
Mead and Lewin: A Complementary Perspective   *73*

4. THE ECOLOGY OF GROUP WORK PRACTICE   *79*

The Individual   *79*
The Group   *90*

The Worker *95*
Agency Settings and Environments *99*
Individual/Group/Worker/Agency-Environment:
    Summary and Integration *111*

5. **STRUCTURAL PROPERTIES**   *117*

Structure and Process *118*
Assessment and Composition *119*
  Assessment and Composition: An Ecological
      Perspective *123*
  Selected Practice Principles *129*
Goals *130*
  Goals: An Ecological Perspective *133*
  Matrix for Practice *134*
Contracting *135*
  The Nature of the Group Work Contract *136*
  Contract: An Ecological Perspective *139*
  Selected Practice Principles *142*
Programming *143*
  Rationale for Programming *146*
  Programming: An Ecological Perspective *147*
  Selected Practice Principles *148*
Size *148*
Selected Practice Principles *152*

6. **GROUP PROCESS**   *155*

Subgroups *156*
  Subgroup Development *156*
  Subgroup: Membership and Emergent
      Patterns *158*
  Impact on Group Process *159*
  Subgroups: Implications for Practice *160*
Scapegoating *162*
  Dynamics of Scapegoating *162*
  Scapegoat and Victim *164*
  Scapegoating and Group Process *166*
  Scapegoating: Implications for Practice *167*
Group Conflict *168*
  Positive Functions of Conflict *169*

Conflict Theory Expanded: Implications for
    Practice *173*
Allogenic Conflict *174*
Roles *178*
    Roles: Implications for Practice *182*
Norms *184*
    Norms and Cultures *188*
    Group Norms: Implications for Practice *190*

7. GROUP DEVELOPMENT   *193*

A Theoretical Overview *195*
Stages of Development *197*
The Beginning Phase *197*
The Middle Phase *202*
The Ending Phase *209*
Principles of Group Development *211*

8. LEADERSHIP IN GROUPS   *213*

Leadership: Roles, Functions, and Situations *213*
Leadership Style *216*
Leadership Traits *218*
Leadership: Ecology, Mead, and Lewin *219*
Leadership: Structure and Process *222*
Leadership and Member Role Induction *223*
Co-Leadership *229*

9. LEADERSHIP: INTERVENTIONS   *235*

Warmth, Empathy, and Genuineness *236*
Self-Disclosure *240*
Confrontation *242*
Humor *245*
Exploration *249*
Summarizing *250*
Support *252*
Cognitive Restructuring *253*
Role Playing *256*
Use of Programming *260*
Sequencing *263*

Timing *264*
Partializing *268*
Clarification *269*
Universalization *269*
Modeling *271*
Work with Individuals, Groups, and
    Environment *273*
  Work with Individuals *273*
  Work with the Group *277*
  Work with the Environment *278*

**10. EDUCATION FOR COMPETENCE FOR
SOCIAL GROUP WORK**   *281*

Educating Students for the Practice of Creative
    Group Work *284*
  Education for Creative Group Work *287*
  The Dangers of Technology *288*
  Educational Approach *290*
Structural Approach for Teaching Social
    Group Work *292*
Teaching Technologies *293*
  Developing an Educative Class Culture *293*
  Developing Work Groups *294*
  Integrating the Session *295*
  Practice Interventions *296*
  Integrating Settings and Other
    Environments *296*
  Discussion *297*
Complementarity Between Experiential and
    Structural Approaches *300*
Curriculum Development in Group Work *301*
  Mission and Goals *302*
  Curriculum Content *303*
  Curriculum Format *304*
  Teaching-Learning Format *305*
  Faculty Resources *305*
Inquiry and Group Work Practice *306*

BIBLIOGRAPHY   *315*

INDEX   *331*

1
Group Work: Historical Overview and Current Status

INTRODUCTION

The perplexing and diverse issues facing contemporary society have considerable impact on social work practice with groups. The call for change and subsequent recalibration of policies and practices among major institutions such as the church, schools, public welfare, family, and government reflect a sharp division between the person and his/her environment. Fundamental questions of who the person is what he/she would like to be, and in fact what he/she could be, are affected by a multitude of factors. Affecting stability and opportunity are sexism, racism, interethnic rivalries, unemployment, pollution, deteriorating neighborhoods, and the like.

The existential plight of individuals in contemporary society is due to disjointed and discontinuous relationships among their significant others such as family members, friends and neighbors, colleagues at work, and fraternal groups. Similarly, diffusion between the individuals and significant institutions such as schools, employers, health care agencies and so on play a central role in producing an identity conflict. Combinations of these twin events jointly disturb the rhythm of individuals' competence. In this context, the task for social work practice has been, and continues to be, to ameliorate the relationships and uncertainties between individuals and their environment. This task is accomplished by social workers not only via their own unique professional roles but also through needed collaboration with other human service groups. Irrespective of the means to perform this task, the goals for social work practice remain consistent; the enhancement of human potential and growth, prevention of emotional and social dysfunctioning, restoration of health and well-being, and the rehabilitation of incapacitated individuals.

From its beginning, social work has been concerned both with the person's capacities and the environmental conditions that ameliorate, support, or exacerbate the utilization of the skill abilities inherent in the person. The clearest and most recent statement in this regard has been postulated by Gordon (1979): "The dual focus on person and environment . . . is the distinctive hallmark of social work, setting it apart in perspective from all other frames of reference through which man is viewed." In point of fact, the reciprocal and dynamic interactions and transactions between persons and environment are inherent in the historical moorings of social group work since its inception. A brief excursion into the historical antecedents of social group work is a useful beginning point for developing a frame of reference that is attuned to present-day conditions, opportunities, needs, and constraints. The phases discussed below represent convenient and arbitrarily chosen time frames for purposes of highlighting and describing selected events.

HISTORICAL ANTECEDENTS

Phase One: Up to 1940

Social group work emerged as a response to social problems engendered by the industrial revolution. The dramatic impact of industrialization significantly altered a domestic and agrarian way of life into one governed by machines, production, technology, and bureaucracy. Industrialization also concentrated resources in the urban areas, resulting in immigrants being forced to congregate in these areas for survival. In this transition, many people had to relinquish the accustomed way of life that had served them well for centuries. Bertrand Russell (1951) summed up the case as follows.

> The industrial revolution caused unspeakable misery both in England and America. I do not think any student of economic history can doubt that the average happiness in England in the early nineteenth century was lower than it had been a hundred years earlier, and this was due almost entirely to scientific technique.

In Chicago, Jane Addams was to describe a similar portrait of misery. She noted that thousands of workers were employed in underground sweatshops, living in squalid poverty with inadequate health and welfare facilities.

Toynbee Hall was one of the first settlements developed to address some of these issues related to the new immigrants in London. Other early stalwarts were to be found among institutions such as the YMCAs, Boys Club, and YWCAs. While agency responses and philosophies varied, suffice it to say that attention was directed to help and work with individuals and groups. Their purposes, as noted by Wilson (1976), were to alter "(1) the dreadful conditions under which many people were living; (2) the causes of the conditions; (3) what to do to change the conditions" (p. 7). Some. agencies such as the Ys focused on youth with the expressed purpose of promoting "mental, moral, physical, social, and spiritual welfare" (p. 6).

The settlements provided a major impetus to work with disadvantaged populations, a tradition which underpins community center work in the current scene. Toynbee, with the aid of Canon Samuel Barnett, set up instructional and recreational services for immigrant groups in London; Neva Boyd in Chicago introduced the use of recreational activities in playground groups. Consistent with the yearnings of immigrants in America, it was an accepted pattern among ethnic groups to attempt to construct a social reality through both formal and informal associations that nurtured and sustained their psychic and survival needs in the new land (Handlin, 1951). Settlement houses provided a vehicle for these ethnic groups to exercise their sentiments with the help of resident volunteers.

Over the first three decades of the twentieth century a number of significant concepts emerged. Central themes for working with groups were espoused by Dewey, James, Cooley, Lindeman, and Follett. To the settlement-inspired concepts of nearness and neighborhood, self-participation, and diversity of approaches for problem solving was added the notion of democratic process, which encompassed the method of inquiry. Two other important ideas by Dewey were also introduced. The first was that interaction and continuity are inherent in problem solving and the other was the importance of collectivity. Dewey's (1933) ideas emphasized that experience and thought could be analyzed concurrently and continuously, which introduced the method of scientific inquiry into problem solving. The group then not only served recreational and social action needs, the latter referring to altering salient neighborhood conditions which maintained poverty, but it also served educative and personal development needs. The central idea of self and group striving, both within and beyond the group, emerged.

The potent themes during the formative stage of group work included social participation, social action, the democratic process and learning and growth in the context of the neighborhood (Briar, 1971). In reviewing Coyle's work, Hartford (1964) has noted that up to the 1930s three areas of group work could be identified. They are

> The development and social adjustment of the individual as a person; his ability to deal with others, to cooperate, to contribute to his fellows, to be at home in various kinds of groups.

> The enrichment of the interests of individuals through increasing knowledge and skills, and the integration of these interests into a life pattern of his own determining.

> The development of social responsibility toward the community involving not only the prevention or cures of antisocial behavior but the encouragement of participation in order for social improvement (p. 65).

Two central themes summarized in this analysis are that the group was utilized and initiated on the premise of "normality as a basis for growth" (Hartford, 1964, p. 65), and the group was seen as having potential to serve all strata of society. Early group workers were required to have knowledge of three sets of dynamics, the person, the group, and the social situation. Somers (1976) in reviewing the dominant influences on group work in those early years draws on the philosophy of pragmatism as a major influence. She notes

> (1) The idea that the individual can influence, manipulate, change, or even control his environment; (2) emphasis upon philosophy as the experimental study of the uses of ideas and knowledge, and belief in the effectiveness of ideas and in the potential and power of novel ideas; (3) the emergence and dominance of William James' humanistic view within Pragmatism, and his emphasis upon the individual as central and upon the individual knower as actor; and (4) John Dewey's more socialized philosophical theory that took the form of instrumentalism, which be-

came "both a social theory and a social influence," to the effect that ideas are plans of action, that genuine understanding comes only from direct participation in events, and that intelligence is a major, effective instrument in modifying the world (p. 335).

In spite of the egalitarian intent that pervades the early history of social group work, the historical analysis also raises other significant issues. For example, initially this mode was geared primarily toward: (1) working with stigmatized segments of society, (2) within traditional leisure-time agencies or agencies specializing in services for the deviant; (3) the worker's role was one of educating and enlightening the members as to their problems; (4) the goal was one of assimilation of these "unfortunates" into the mainstream of society.

The initial clients in group work practice were those people who tended to be nonparticipants in the labor force—the physically and mentally handicapped, children under sixteen years of age, senior citizens over sixty-five, substance abusers, social deviants such as juvenile delinquents and adult offenders, the poor, and new immigrants. Anderson (1960) in this context has indicated, "There was a time when certain programs were identified with particular groups in our society. These groups were described as the dependent, defective, delinquent, and the poor" (p. 64). He goes on to say, "Members of certain racial and ethnic groups who are newcomers in our communities face serious problems of adjustments and assimilation. Differences of color, custom, and culture give rise to fears which in turn create tension, hostility, and open conflict" (p. 70).

Wilson and Ryland (1948) further illustrated the emphasis on serving deviant clients by citing the usage of different types of groups. They seem quite egalitarian in giving examples of all age ranges; however, each group is characterized by at least one socially stigmatizing quality, e.g., behavior problems, physical handicaps, old age, housing project dwellers (poor people), blacks, and juvenile delinquents. Hence, the designation of the various clubs, or their nicknames as given by Wilson and Ryland include: "Striving to be like others," "Trouble makers," "Convalescing soldiers face the future," "Program content as a tool for recovery," "The aged find security among their peers." Trecker (1955) also illustrated typical group processes by using as examples groups that were outcast or socially deviant in some way. Lurie (1965) noted, "The acceptable patterns for intergroup relationships were assimilation, in the case of immigrant groups differing in culture and religion, or subordination for nonwhites" (p. 396), and in the same context,

Conover (1965) asked "whether rehabilitative programs and services aimed at social adjustment—in terms of the more serious social problems such as delinquency, modifying deviant behavior, or help with medical, psychiatric, and related problems—are the only ones that should be classified as social work" (pp. 375-376).

In "The Cultural Context of Social Work," Stroup (1957) points out a contradiction in social group work values. While he readily holds to the traditional belief that immigrants must be assimilated, he chides the American people for "remaining statistically, in the gross, monogamous, devoted to the 'free enterprise system,' Protestant Christians, moderate Republicans, and devotees of the efficacy of education" (p. 65). Follett (1942) strongly embraced integration as a means to reduce the tension between differing groups.

For all the talk of democracy, the importance of the individual, and the right of persons to be different, the pervading belief was still "You have a right to be anything you want, as long as you're exactly like me." Those who did not adhere to this were classified as deviant and were the main target for group work services. The efforts of group workers were directed toward facilitating cultural assimilation of their clients within the dominant norms. While assimilation was the overriding objective, questions were raised by some social workers as to whether it should be the ultimate goal (Addams, 1910; Simkovitch, 1936).

The typical clients with whom group workers dealt were in a "one-down" position—both because of the deviancy with which they were associated and the fact that they had problems in adjustment that either required enlightenment or help in solving. Tropp (1972) states this situation clearly.

> In a treatment setting which attempts to use the group method, the user starts from a position of dependency, either having sought help at the point of desperation or having been forced to submit to a helping authority at the point of conflict with society. In the latter case, the user is able to receive help only when he voluntarily accepts the fact that he is dependent upon this help. Being dependent, he must learn to accept the authority, the wisdom and the treatment that is offered him. He cannot successfully extricate himself from the dependent role until he has found ways of coping autonomously, and, in the involuntary placement, has met the requirements that the provider has set for his freedom (p. 18).

This is precisely the position in which many of the clients found themselves; because of their devaluation by society, they were in no position to bargain. Solidarity among oppressed groups had not come into being, and so clients were forced to accept the role of the worker as "teacher"—to instruct them in the error of their ways, and in the methods to correct them.

The importance of the centrality and high validity accorded the worker and his values cannot be overemphasized. Minimal attention was paid to the individuation of participants. The movement toward self-determinism and uniqueness of the individual was further crippled by the participants' lack of bargaining power. Their individual, cultural, and ethnic values were virtually ignored since ultimate successful assimilation into the society-at-large was the prominent goal. As Wilson and Ryland (1948) point out social work was operating from the general stance of "doing for" clients, building character, and "the care of the weak by the strong." Furthermore, the worker influenced this or that opinion, until the client began to "see the light" and slowly came around to the worker's stance. It was assumed that the worker's opinions of right and wrong were intrinsically more valuable than the client's—regardless of background, culture, age, physical, or spiritual characteristics. The workers regarded as successes those clients who conformed to the prevalent social values of the time.

Phase Two: Decades of 1940s and 1950s

The second phase in the development of social group work includes the decades of the forties and fifties. Significant in this period was the advent and influence of Freudian psychoanalytic psychology, which made a dramatic impact on social work curricula. The essential thrust of Freudian thought placed a greater emphasis on emotional conflicts or distress from the individuals' experiences as the major cause for their social dysfunctioning. Due to this theoretical influence, individuals were viewed as inert beings, subject to the influence of their interior struggles among unconscious, conscious, and governing features of the conscience. As a consequence, the worker in the group adopted a more passive interpretive stance, in contrast to an activist problem-solving position that had been developed by Dewey (1933) and others as noted earlier.

During this period the Freudian orientation was highly valued in working with emotionally disturbed children and adults. Social group workers, similar to other helping professionals, regarded the mastery and usage of a Freudian framework as a necessary pathway to becoming a valued and respected professional. Social work curricula placed heavy emphasis on psychoanalytic theory; similarly, agencies required their workers to incorporate this orientation in their practice.

World War II enhanced the thrust toward specialization, as group work was introduced and practiced in medical and psychiatric settings with service personnel. In addition, therapeutic group work was practiced within residential treatment settings. To sustain this newly acquired "status," group workers began to emphasize more and more the curative component in their work. This development signaled a redefinition of behavior as either "normal" or "sick."

With the emergence of the dichotomy between normal and sick, group workers attended to the concept of study, diagnosis, and treatment, which are commonly attributed to the medical model. In this model group workers pay considerable attention to assessing the individuals' functioning and determining the most appropriate means to alter their dysfunctioning. Significant attention was also given to the developmental history of individuals from which the prescription of wellness was derived.

One of the chief contributions of the psychoanalytic movement was a strong emphasis on the potency and expertise of the worker. The major thrust of the group was on the individuals and to eliminate the symptomatology that contributed to their illness. The environmental context of the individual's discomfort was given minimal attention.

During this period, as the psychoanalytic movement was making its mark on group work, traditional group work, as described in Phase I, continued to thrive. The primary adherents of this orientation were located within settlement houses, neighborhood centers, the Ys, and sectarian community agencies. The focus of group work within these settings was on socialization and recreational groups for children and adults. The workers in these settings were more sensitive to the environmental factors and their effect on individuals' functioning. Unlike the psychoanalytic orientation, workers hesitated to assume an omnipotent role. Although community-based workers perceived themselves as competent, their interventions were governed by social work values such as worth of human dignity, nonjudgmental attitudes and democratic principles. In summary, the group and the members both received high attention. The environment also was taken into consideration, but it was limited to the immediate environment of the members. The worker assumed enabling and facilitative roles.

Phase Three: 1950s to Present

In the present context the third phase of the historical development of group work includes events occurring from the late 1950s to the present. The social, intellectual, economical, and technological changes of the past two decades have left group work in a changed position in a rapidly changing world. The country experienced the dreams of Camelot, the glories and frustrations of the Civil Rights Movement, several traumatic assassinations, a halfhearted but appealing War on Poverty, a highly publicized conflict between generations, a rediscovery of race and ethnicity as variables in human affairs, and massive shifts in the economic and educational status of a large part of the American population. The decade that saw the immense tragedy of Vietnam also witnessed abortion law reform, no-fault divorce, pollution alerts, astronauts, the Women's Rights Movement, and the Gay Rights Movement. The decade also saw the rise and fall of an American president. (Ephross & Balgopal, 1978; Balgopal and Vassil, 1979).

Changes in the mood and times were accompanied by significant changes in thinking about group work practice. The differences were articulated on the basis of varied assumptions about the role of the worker, the group members and the content of the group, and the usage of group itself. Social workers proposed three distinct group work models, which have been labeled for convenience as remedial, reciprocal, and developmental. (Papell and Rothman, 1966).

The work of Vinter and his colleagues (1967) at the University of Michigan, assumed within the *Remedial Model,* focuses on the individuals' dysfunctioning and utilizes the group as a context and means for altering deviant patterns. In his description Vinter notes

> This approach to group work practice focuses on its utility in ameliorating the adverse conditions of individuals whose behavior is disapproved, or who have been disadvantaged by the workings of an imperfect society. It emphasizes manifest personal and social problems and the rehabilitative potentials of guided group processes in alleviating these problems. Persons most appropriate as clientele for such service include the physically or mentally handicapped, legal offenders, emotionally disturbed, isolated, or alienated persons, those lacking effective socialization and the like (p. 2).

The Michigan School contributed to specificity and rationality in expert worker planning and executing of change, and a clear focus on the individual as a target point of change. They emphasized attention to institutional and subinstitutional elements towards change as these impinge on member functioning, reliance on a study, diagnosis, and treatment framework based on deviance, role induction, and interaction as major organizing ideas.

Professional expertise of the worker flows through activities such as: (1) worker as central person—object of identification and drives;

(2) worker as symbol and spokesman—agent of legitimate norms and values; (3) worker as motivator and stimulator—definer of individual goals and tasks; and (4) worker as executive—controller of membership roles (Vinter, 1967).

Environmental change in this approach tends to be explicitly limited to organizational and institutional elements that contribute to the individuals' dysfunctioning. While the focus is on the individual who was experiencing difficulty, the approach is proposed as useful for those likely to be affected, which takes into consideration preventive aspects. It needs to be noted however, that in the more complete writings of the Michigan School (Glasser, et. al., 1974) the preventive aspects are not given the same emphasis as the remedial components.

Another dramatic entry in the group work practice arena was the introduction of the *Mediating Model* by Schwartz (1961). Relying extensively on open systems theory, humanistic psychology, and an existential perspective, Schwartz molded the separate themes into a coherent gestalt. The following points explicate the mediating model:

1. People and society have mutual needs which draw them together. Dissonance or interference with these mutual strivings produce conflict. The resolution of conflict occurs when the interested parties confront the dilemmas with all of the available inner resources that they can utilize at the moment. The sources of strength lie in the mutual aid capabilities of both parties.
2. Attention is directed toward the relationship of members in the group with each other, with the worker, and the group as a whole. Indeed it is the relationship among the members that defines the characteristics of the group. In contrast to the actions and reactions of any set of members, emphasis is placed on the continuing and reciprocal transactions of sets of members with each other, the worker, and the group. The process of acting carries with it simultaneously the promise of changing.
3. Emergent goals and actions, based on feelings, assume high priority. There are no *a priori* outcomes devised because it is assumed that intensive involvement by the parties in the current realities will generate their own purposes and means. Within the emergent and work-oriented time frame, client and worker, together and separately, challenge the current problems, honestly, openly, and forthrightly.

4. Basic educative processes are utilized which incorporate partializing, synthesizing and generalizing the thought-feeling and action components of the problem.
5. A general set of professional tasks are posited which include searching for common ground, detecting and challenging obstacles, contributing ideas and feelings, lending a vision and defining the requirements and limits of the worker-client collaboration.
6. No distinctions are made with respect to types and varieties of groups and/or settings since it is presumed that the model has wide applicability. In addition, the parties involved in the helping process include those who have a stake in the problem.

In this model the individual and the group are significant components as is the context for social environment in which the problem rests. The worker's role appears to be facilitative, relying on the power and potency of the mutual aid system to take care of itself (Schwartz, 1976).

The group work faculty members of Boston University under the leadership of Bernstein, introduced a third approach to group work in 1965, which they designated as the *Developmental Model.* In this approach, groups are seen as having "a degree of independence and autonomy, but the to and fro flow between them and their members, between them and their social setting, is crucial to their existence, viability, and achievements." (Bernstein, 1973, p. xii). This implies independent effects of, as well as interdependence among the three variables, namely, individuals, groups, and their social environment.

This model is primarily based on the dynamics of intimacy and closeness between the members over a span of time. The degree of intimacy is taken into account for appropriate worker interventions. Conceptualization of study, diagnosis, and treatment is made at all three levels of individuals, group, and the setting. The knowledge base for this model draws from Erikson's ego psychology, group dynamics and conflict theory. The model includes a very clear explication of the connections between social work values and group work practice.

In describing the role of the worker, Lowy (1965) one of the major architects of the developmental model, has succinctly stated

Like all social workers, the group worker is engaged in exploration (study), diagnosis and treatment. He is concerned with the following components: community, agency, group, individual member, program media (tools), and himself as worker. He has values and attitudes; he has goals derived from his professional and agency identification. He uses knowledge and understanding of these components and brings to bear his skills acquired through training and experience (p. 82).

In essence the group is envisioned as a microcosm of society, and as such represents the rich texture and patterns encompassed in the social reality constructed from the assumptive world of the group's membership. Thought-feeling, sentiments, and behavior are continually assessed and recalibrated as they flow through the interlocking pathways of individual members, group as a whole, the social environment, and the worker. It is postulated that the developmental model is a compromise between the reciprocal, remedial, and traditional approaches (Lowy, 1970).

In addition to the three approaches discussed in the foregoing paragraphs, a number of other formulations to group work practice have also been developed. Roberts and Northen (1976) compiled a volume of comparative approaches to group work practice, and abstracted the salient features that are germane to these formulations. These are the following. (1) All approaches adhere to a strong commitment to the integrity and worth of the individual and to one's right to self-determination; (2) All approaches describe some sort of transactional process between workers and members for establishing goals and objectives; (3) In providing group work services, the agency is considered as essential a component as community sanction; (4) there is a universal agreement that knowledge of group dynamics is essential for effective group work services; (5) In all approaches the major concepts are organized around coping and problem solving capacities of the individual, the differential stages of group development and the relationship between the individuals and their environment; and (6) There is a general consensus that all of these approaches can be practiced within a variety of primary and secondary settings. In addition, all of them profess applicability of their approach to a wide variety of clientele (pp. 369–394).

Despite the above similarities in these formulations, there are certain sharp differences and, according to Northen & Roberts (1976), they are (1) Purpose of applications of the approaches varies from informal education to socialization, normal development, rehabilitation or therapy; (2) Underpinnings of these formulations are rooted in differential theoretical orientations which ranged from those developed by social workers to those of behavioral scientists such as John Dewey and Mary Parker Follett. Some of these approaches were primarily developed from the works of social scientists and existential philosophers; (3) In these formulations there is a sharp difference regarding a definition of an appropriate philosophy of science essential for knowledge building; (4) These formulations differ in determining who is the unit of attention for group work services; (5) There is also difference of opinion as to whether group work services ought to be offered to involuntary clients; (6) There is no consensus as to the agency policies and its impact on group work services.

The authors indicate that the ten contemporary group work theorists pay minimal attention to the following: (1) Feelings and emotions of group members are given little attention for purposes of assessment or treatment; (2) Most of these approaches do not incorporate work with communities as an essential dimension for group work practice; (3) Crucial material pertaining to ethnicity, culture, lifestyle, social class, and gender and how these variables affect group work practice were virtually never discussed in any of the ten approaches; (4) Most of these approaches are discussed for their applicability in working with formed groups rather than natural groups.

In summarizing the formulations of group work practice over the last fifty years, Somers (1976) extracts ten themes. Five of these deal with the nature and dynamics of group work and the other five with the role of social group worker. The themes that mark the nature and dynamics of group work are: (1) Personal and social goals in combination form the basis for group work practice; (2) Group work practice continually evaluates the process of learning and doing in groups; (3) Changes in thought-feelings seem to be related to productive problem solving; (4) Group work has the potential as an effective problem solving modality in a variety of settings with different clients; (5) Group work can change the opinions and actions of individuals and/or groups. Somers, in expanding the persistent themes related to the role of the worker, states: (1) The worker's role includes separate, parallel and collaborative work before, during, and after group sessions; (2) Learning is a process of struggle for the worker; (3) Worker must be an active participant in the entire group experience; (4) Group worker does not have the sole responsibility for the existence of the group; (5) Group worker has to maintain reality focus and evaluate the end result.

Some of the recent thrusts that hold promise for social work education and practice are the practice models developed within Gestalt Therapy, Transactional Analysis, and Behaviorism. These approaches have been making an impact on all the helping professions, and social work practitioners are paying increased attention to these new modes of treatment. In social work meetings, workshops, forums and continuing education programs, these group modalities are well attended.

Gestalt Therapy today as expounded by Perls and others (Perls, 1947, 1951, 1969; Polster & Polster, 1973; Fagan & Shepherd, 1971) is based on a complex interrelated set of concepts from a variety of sources, such as Gestalt Perceptual Psychology, Existential Philosophy, Organismic Psychology, Field Theory, and Psychodrama. The term *gestalt* is a German word with no absolute English counterpart. Initially applicable to psychological studies in perception, it now conveys an approach to the vital components of the individuals' existence—thinking, acting, and feeling. It implies that life and individuals' conceptualized sense of order and meaning of that life is made up of bits and pieces, all connected through their experience over time and processes through emotional and cognitive functioning, which makes sense of it, and is available for utilization in further experience.

In Gestalt Therapy, maturing is the transcendence from environmental support to self-support. The worker aids the clients in learning how they prevent themselves from maturing. Further, it is the aim of the worker to help the clients become aware of and accept responsibility for how they make themselves feel bad by playing games. One of the major concepts of Gestalt Therapy is present-centeredness, which is based upon the premise that individuals encounter ongoing conflicts that are interrelated to the way they are functioning at the present moment. The worker through a variety of experiential interventions facilitates individuals' awareness of their functioning within conflicting life situations. The worker also refrains from making interpretations, but constantly brings the individuals' behavioral patterns to their attention.

Transactional Analysis is a system for analyzing and explaining intra- and interpersonal processes. This therapeutic mode was developed by Berne (1961). His major premise is that individuals are products of social processes, and that they use social processes, outside of their awareness to reinforce self-defeating behavior. Berne proposes that personal change can be maximized through group psychotherapy where the social processes are much more varied than just one-to-one therapist/client relationship. Within the group setting individuals can be confronted when engaging in self-defeating behavior. Once they are aware of their behavior they can do something about changing it and the group provides a safe environment for practicing new behaviors.

Transactional Analysis focuses on present, interpersonal behavior rather than on having individuals talk about their past. This approach holds that change is more difficult when a person just talks about his past and his problem; they need to be actively dealt with and this can best be done in the here-and-now.

According to Berne (1966), there are four major features of Transactional Analysis: (1) *Structural Analysis,* which is a method of anlayzing thoughts and feelings and behaviors based on the phenomena of ego states; (2) *Transactional Analysis proper,* which involves the interactional processes that occur between the ego states of one person and the ego states of another. All transactions can be classified as *complementary, crossed,* or *ulterior.* A *complementary transaction* is one in which the response to a verbal or non-verbal stimulus is appropriate and expected and "follows the natural order of healthy human relationships" (Berne, 1964, p. 29). A *crossed transaction* is an unexpected response to a stimulus. An ulterior transaction is one which involves more than two ego states. When an *ulterior message* is sent, it is disguised under a socially acceptable transaction; (3) *Game Analysis,* this involves examining repetitive patterns of interpersonal behavior of individuals that are problematic; (4) *Script Analysis,* a person's script is one's overall life plan that was initially shaped by interpersonal experiences in the developmental phase of life. It is related to the early decisions and the positions taken by a person in childhood. The role of the group leader is partly didactic, and a teacher, the leader, explains the key concepts and helps the members to discover the disadvantageous conditions under which they made their earlier decisions, adopted life plans, and developed strategies for relating to people.

Behaviorism is beginning to make its impact on social work with groups (Feldman and Wodarski, 1975; Rose, 1977). This orientation locates expertise in the worker who seeks to identify in collaboration with a client, observable and classifiable problematic behaviors in the context of social referents. Conditions for change, such as group cohesion and specific program schedules are implemented to alter dysfunctional patterns and learn new styles. Extension of behavioral principles to the social context in the forms of tokens and other rewards are used to promote desirable and adaptive performances.

The expertise of behavioral group therapists is essential in assessing and devising a treatment plan for each individual group member within the context of the group. Upon negotiating a contract, the behavioral therapist and client calculate the specific elements of the disturbing behavior to be decreased or desired behaviors to be developed. Careful minitoring, often in the form of problem-specific instruments, is used for purposes of providing feedback regarding

15

behavior changes. Other group members may provide assistance and feedback concerning progress throughout the stages of the treatment process.

A variety of structured interventions, drawn from and supported by research evidence, are utilized in order to accomplish change objectives. Behavioral rehearsal, role playing, modeling, didactic presentations, and reinforcement are among some of the strategies employed by the behavioral group therapist. Curricula for change are often designed to incorporate gradations in learning from simple to complex. As members become more involved in the group, they also assume greater responsibility for developing their respective behavioral change procedures. The behavioral group therapist introduces and consistently maintains group expectations to encourage member attendance, systematic analysis of problems, peer reinforcement, and support of member efforts. By judiciously intervening in the kind, rate, and frequency of communicated exchanges between and among members, the therapist implements and maintains therapeutic norms. Modifying interactions for learning and support is accomplished by such means as differential reinforcement (praise, approval, showing interest) and rotating group leadership among members to insure participation and involvement. At times, subjective and diffuse anxiety on the part of members may seriously interfere with goal setting and goal implementation and may also threaten the therapeutic group process. Rational and practical procedures are instituted by the behavioral group therapist, assisted by other group members, to induce a corrective pattern practiced and controlled by the overly anxious member.

Behavioral group therapists have staked a claim to precision and effectiveness in group treatment on the following bases: (1) specifying individual and group tasks; (2) monitoring explicit and desired behavioral changes over time; (3) using expert therapist knowledge and validated practice interventions; (4) providing peer review, feedback, and analysis; and (5) applying feedback from monitoring to correct or support goal changes. Behavioral goal therapy has been conducted with adults and children to assist learning in such problem areas as self-defeating behavior, weight control, assertiveness training, marital conflict, and defiant behavior in institutional settings.

CURRENT STATUS

The early formulations of practice with groups tend to focus more on the group and the environment. In this scheme, the worker was perceived as a role model whose aim was to assist the group members to function within the prevailing societal norms. Interest shifted sharply to the internal assumptive world of the person with the emergence and incorporation of psychoanalytic thought. Vinter and his colleagues shaded the focus on the person toward more specificity within an international theory. In their context precision and expertise were located in the worker, and the group was used as a means to further individual ends.

Schwartz reformulated group work views based on the assumption of expressed mutuality of transactions and interdependence among group members and other pertinent systems. The worker oriented his/her professional functions to a facilitative role. A signal achievement in this formulation was the abandoning of the worker mystique.

The Boston model reintroduced the importance of both the person and group and paid somewhat less attention to the direct impact of the environment. While the worker's orientation includes both direct and facilitative approaches the examples that explicate this model clearly lie in the arena of letting the group struggle with goals and their implementation.

The models based on Gestalt Therapy, Transactional Analysis and Behaviorism are current and have significance for the field. In these models the major focus is on the individual; the group is used only as a context to enhance the individual's current functioning. Similarly, the focus on the environment is limited only to the members' immediate concerns in the group. The leader/worker in these approaches plays a very active role in assisting individual members to gain awareness and/or skill regarding their current functioning.

DIRECTIONS FOR THE FUTURE

The major foci of the individual, group, environment, and worker are essential dimensions which have to be included for effective use of groups as a viable modality of interventions. These components need to be seen as interlocking elements that affect all aspects of group work. Furthermore any new framework with respect to social group work must take into account those factors identified by Northen and Roberts (1976) as relatively absent from current formulations of group work practice. Thus careful attention such as cultural pluralism, natural groups, and the internal world of the consumer must all be integrated into the context of the person's natural surroundings or community. Creating harmony between the public and private worlds of the client necessarily requires attention to both a person's view and the mixed reality to which that view is subjected, validated, altered, or diffused. This applies not only to where one lives, but works, plays, seeks creative expression as leader, follower, and so on.

These considerations correspond very closely to the objectives enumerated in the Report of the President's Commission on Mental Health (1978). A major thrust of this report is to recognize and strengthen the natural networks to which people belong and rely upon such as families, friends, kin, social networks, and others. The objectives provide unique challenges for social workers and other human service professionals together to develop a great appreciation of group membership—not merely as clients but as consumers and citizens who live, interact, affect, and are affected by a multitude of significant relationships through both formal and informal means.

To our way of thinking, the ecological framework hold promise in meeting this challenge. In brief, the ecological framework emphasizes relationships among persons and their social and physical environment. This framework implies that "there are neither inadequate persons, nor inadequate environments, but rather the fit between person and environment may be in relative accord or discord" (Rappaport, 1977). Attention to the connective tissues that hold people together and satisfy or frustrate their needs in everyday life constitutes the organizing theme in the ecological orientation.

2
The
Ecological
Framework

Life does not exist in a vacuum. Loss of identity
means loss of meaning. Forced compromises mean
fragmentations. The never-ending struggles of the
contemporary man!

The history of social group work reflects the profession's response to perceived challenges that appear at different points in time. Solutions have been tempered by advances in social and behavioral sciences as well as shifts in the way that people are viewed and to be understood. Descriptions of several group work models have alluded to the different ways in which clients, the place of the group, the worker's focus and the impact of the social environment are conceptualized. An analysis of contemporary social group work theories concluded that each of the models was incomplete in one way or another. On this basis it is suggested that another orientation is called for that needs to incorporate the spirit, the mood, and needs of contemporary people in a more complete fashion. The ecological framework which emphasizes relationships between and among persons and their environments is a promising beginning to refocus professional social group work practice.

The ecological perspective is simply a way of viewing the four dimensions of practice with groups: member, worker, the group, and the environment. This framework provides an avenue for a broader understanding of the interplay among these four dimensions. It requires a shift from the language of the machine metaphor—viz., social engineering, friction, resistance, equilibrium, force field—to the vocabulary of the organic metaphor—viz., adaptations, development, cycling, transaction, and open, dynamic system (Bennis and Slater, 1968). Process and context take precedence over structural arrangements. Underpinning the ecological perspective is the assumption that a minimal degree of integration is necessary between the person and various environments in order to maintain and enhance the problem-solving capacities and growth of constituent members in their own habitat. The fundamental task for professional practice in groups is to build a culture that contains within it adequate provisions for its own change. This permits the reconciliation of various frames of reference that are represented in the ongoing interrelationships among person, group, and environmental processes.

ECOLOGICAL PERSPECTIVE

Ecology is derived from the Greek work *oikos*, which refers to living in the home or homestead. This definition incorporates the formative idea of natural habitat and related notions of interdependence and continuity. The use of the term *ecology* is generally attributed to biologists and refers to the organized minutiae of daily activities that are part and parcel of individuals' relationships with each other in their community. The actions which govern how people get along come from a combination of ways in which the individuals have managed their lives in the past, and how they anticipate the future. More often than not the small adjustments in day-to-day living represent a fine tuning of more stable and satisfying strategies that have guided their lives. At times of crisis and needs, individuals have to rethink and take time to reorganize their lives and regain a sense of composure. In each of the above situations, changes in the person leave their impression both on himself/herself and on significant others.

Social and behavioral scientists are utilizing an ecological perspective to provide a comprehensive and systematic framework for the study of human beings' social existence. The concept of human ecology is readily associated with the comprehensive nature of the fieldwork of the cultural anthropologists. Kluckhohn (1963) states

> We require a way of thinking which takes account of the pull of expectancies as well as the push of tensions, which recognizes that growth

and creativity come as much or more from instability as from stability, which emphasizes cultural environment.

The ecological orientation is incorporated by psychologists, and in this context Rappaport (1977) notes the following.

the ecological viewpoint should be regarded as an orientation emphasizing relationships among persons and their social and physical environment. Conceptually the term implies that there are neither inadequate persons, nor inadequate environment, but rather the fit between persons and environment may be in relative accord or discord (p. 2).

Kelly (1968) has extensively used ecological principles in formulating preventive psychological interventions. According to his thesis, as the structure and social units vary, one has to make appropriate shifts in models of dealing with disruptive events. He further states that interrelationships between the functions of social units and the participation of individual members become primary targets for interventions. These interventions rearrange the interrelationships between individual behavior and social functions, and also alter the behavior of one social unit or the expressive behavior of any member of the society. In social group work changes in tasks are accompanied by changes in process. The sociologist Park (1961) describes two "ecological" levels in human societies: (1) the symbiotic level that is rooted in impersonal competition; and (2) the cultural level which is based on communication and consensus. These two levels are assembled and expressed in various patterns of social organizations which in turn influence and guide individuals' social functioning. In psychiatry the value of the ecological perspective's comprehensive view of a situation and its capacity to accommodate a variety of theoretical models has been explicated by Auerswald (1968), who indicates that this approach has a distinct advantage over the more segmented and narrowly defined interdisciplinary approach.

Social workers are increasingly incorporating ecological concepts in their practice. Schwartz (1971), utilizing the concept of symbiosis, describes the relationship between the individual and his/her nurturing groups, the relationship which social work attempts to imporve. Germain (1979), stresses that "in an ecological view, practice is directed toward improving the transactions between people and environments in order to enhance the adaptive capacities *and* improve environments for all who function within them" (p. 17). According to her (1973), major advantages of the ecological approach to social work practice are

An ecological perspective contributes scientific knowledge concerning the delicate relationships of human beings to the rapidly changing physical and social environments. At the same time, it fosters a passionate concern for human aspirations and for the development of milieus to promote them. An ecological perspective enables us to reach toward a complementarity between our scientific and humanistic concerns, between cause and function (p. 326).

In discussing the relevance of ecological perspective for social work practice, Hartman (1979) succinctly states

An ecological perspective directs us to understand events and behavior in the context of the many influences and variables that impact upon and have a part in the production of those events and behaviors. It encourages us to focus on the adaptive balance they may exist between living beings and their environments. It leads us to understand and evaluate events and human responses in terms of their contribution to adaptation, integration, and differentiation (p. 240).

Siporin (1980) in a recent article delineates that the ecological framework enables helping professionals to gain a broader perspective, a unitary and comprehensive target for study, including a dynamic understanding of people and their sociocultural-physical environment. He further proposes that as a strategy for assessment, it enables one to appraise consistencies, strengths, complementaries, as well as inconsistencies, discrepancies and conflicts as they affect quality of life. Once an assessment is established on this basis, appropriate interventions can be implemented to fit the person and the milieu.

From the foregoing review it is clear that the promise of an ecological perspective is recognized by academic disciplines as well as practice professions. With this multidisciplinary approach, it is imperative that the foremost task be to delineate the most relevant and operational concepts and principles from this framework. This is an arduous task, but to draw linkages between the individuals and their social contexts within a changing society is the governing principle of the time. Using a hypothetical case illustration, selected concepts and principles underlying this perspective are drawn and discussed.

The Case of the Smith Family in Mapletown

The Smith family is composed of mother, age 38, father, age 43; son Ronnie, age 15; and daughter Nancy, age 11. They moved to Mapletown seven years ago as a result of Mr. Smith's promotion as area manager for a life insurance company. They live in a primarily white neighborhood where most of the families are of their age, income and family size, and are home-owners like them. The surroundings are aesthetically pleasing.

In the Smith family, mother, father, and children get along pretty well. They take time and interest in listening and sharing in each others' joys and sorrows. Although the Smiths on occasion vent differences, they get over them very quickly. They engage in many family-planned activities such as outings, picnics, vacations and the like. A visitor to the Smith house will see a neatly decorated and comfortable, warm home. On weekends it is not unusual for the Smiths to socialize with other families. Similarly the children on occasion invite their friends for parties and overnight visits, an experience common in the neighborhood.

Mr. Smith rides in a car pool in keeping with the energy crisis. He has a number of pleasant associations at work. In the past two years he has been under considerable pressure to increase sales, but has the knack of not letting pressures get to him. Mrs. Smith finds the nearby shopping center convenient for groceries and other household needs. Due to her husband's decrease in sales and to inflation, Mrs. Smith has been selling Avon for the last several months, but finds this work unsatisfying. Both parents take an active interest in their children's education, the P.T.A. and other special events which contribute to their education. The school is of particular interest because families in their neighborhood have been pressured to consider a program of busing for disadvantaged children in order to upgrade the latter's education. The parents also belong to such social organizations as a church social club, fraternal organization and others. The children also participate in numerous extracurricular activities. The Smiths also keep close contact with their extended families on both sides.

In this neighborhood, medical facilities are close enough for emergencies and regular care. A manufacturer wants to develop and build a small parts plant nearby, which is raising some tension among the residents as to the effects it will have on property values, traffic safety, and security. Divided opinion among the residents with respect to other racial groups buying homes is creating unease and tension. The Smith family, their friends, neighbors, and work associates have very strong and disagreeable opinions on the subject. This is making them evasive with each other. In addition the county correctional agency wants to open a group home for recently released youth. Because of his pride and concern for the neighborhood, Mr. Smith volunteers time on the neighborhood council to resolve these perplexing issues. Despite Mr. Smith's reassurance and support, his wife is extremely concerned with the potential changes occurring in their neighborhood. As a result, she is very unhappy and moody. On the recommendation of their minister, she has been going to the local mental health center, where after being seen individually for three sessions she has been participating in a Group Therapy session for six weeks. The sessions are conducted by an experienced clinical social worker.

(Excerpt from Mrs. Smith's Group Therapy Session)

After some initial guardedness, Mrs. Smith has become quite open in expressing her feeling about the changing conditions in her neighborhood. The group has two minority members who have not verbally responded to Mrs. Smith's reactions but considerable tension is evident in the group. For the sixth session, Mrs. Smith became very irate and said that she has been turned down for a job for the third straight time this week. She was open with her anger towards the male members for the advantage they have over women. One of the white male members at that time confronted Mrs. Smith with her own reluctance to welcome racial minorities and socially disadvantaged residents and children to their neighborhood. The worker's comments were directed to appreciate every member's individual needs and wants. He chose to support group safety by not focusing on the confrontation explicitly between the white male member and Mrs. Smith and implicitly between her and the minority members, and others as well. It was not clear what the worker's own stand on these crucial issues was...

One could go on with the process description about the Smith case including Mrs. Smith's therapy group, but there is sufficient data available to examine the situation along an ecological perspective, which follows.

BASIC CONCEPTS

Natural Habitat

Life in the homestead refers to the natural habitat, a central construct in the ecological perspective. According to Odum (1962), the habitat of an organism "is the place where it lives, or place where one would go to find it." The ecological niche is "the position or status of an organism within its community and ecosystem resulting from the organism's structural adaptations, physiological response, and specific behavior" (p.27). The daily life of the Smith family as they go about their business living in their community, interacting with neighbors, work, shopping, school, and so forth are part and parcel of their natural habitat. That is to say, this family knows the streets, the faces, the routines, and expectations of their community, and share their sentiments with other members in their community. Each person when alone or with others knows who she/he is, has a sense of belonging, but at the same time preserves and respects each other's life space. This represents commitment and dependability, which are necessary to maintain everyday life. Group workers have to be aware of the dependable, steady, and natural circumstances in the lives of the group members. For example, the workers will have to know Mrs. Smith's apprehension towards the potential changes in her community. She suddenly realizes that the world around her is going to change, and not in a way to her liking.

Ecosystem

This is any area of nature that includes living organisms and non-living substances interacting to produce an exchange of materials between the living and nonliving parts; that is living organisms and their nonliving environment are inseparably interrelated and interact upon each other (Odum, 1961). This principle of interdependence or reciprocity between structure and function is one of the axioms in the field of ecology (Kelly, 1968). For Quinn (1933), ecological interdependence determines the position of the individual in space and in the division of labor. It furnishes a basic framework for the social structure, but is not social. [On the other hand, he continues] . . . social interaction takes place on a different level. Man the social unit is not a mere living organism, but a person with status. Persons modify one another through communication (p. 568).

Ecosystem is the basic functional unit of ecology, as it includes both organisms and environment, the two essential properties for the maintenance of life. The goal of an ecosystem is to survive and flourish in a healthy, steady state. According to Siporin (1980) and related here for social group work purposes, "an ecosystem consists of people, their life situations, and the well-functioning or dysfunctioning behavior patterns that result from their interaction. This is a problem(s)—person/people—situation unit that is basic in social work thinking, and that is basic to a needed comprehensive approach to assessment and intervention" (p.510).

The principle of ecosystem is evident in two instances in the Smith family. Because of inflation, Mrs. Smith was forced to work outside the home. Her first job is unsatisfactory, and she begins to look for a higher paying job. Similarly, due to the energy crisis, Mr. Smith was forced to participate in a car pool. With spiralling inflation and a growing energy crisis, many such people as the Smiths who had moved to distant suburbia for privacy are now forced to either resort to public transportation, participate in car pools, or move back closer to their place of employment.

Diversity and Continuity

Ecological principles relating to diversity focus on the organism-environment relationship. In essence this means that the range of different types of organisms that can exist within an environment is determined by the capacity of the environment's resources to meet the differential needs of the organisms. Continuity refers to the organism's capacity to function over a period of time despite its encounter with diverse elements. The ecological balance is the functional interplay between the diversity and continuity.

The Smith family, along with the neighbors, friends, and associates, appear to be well-located in their community. Their associations are altogether enjoyable, predictable and continuous, and shared with others, which provides community stability and meaning. This does not mean that there are no troubles and conflicts, since the Smith family have their arguments, but these are tolerable and acceptable. If the members of the Smith family or other community members cannot tolerate each other and store

26

their differences until they erupt in bitter exchanges, their relationships begin to deteriorate. When they cannot tolerate each other, they begin to get defensive due to fears, anxieties, and uncertainties. This can take place on a broader level. In Mapletown, the portent of racial migration, establishment of new industries, and opening of a correctional facility pose considerable stress and strain. At the same time it provides new opportunities for employment, reduction of tax base, and cultural enrichment. Several responses to these events are notable in the case illustration: (1) For Mrs. Smith, the level of tolerance has been exceeded and she reverts to a constricted style of life. (2) For Mr. Smith and others the levels of tolerance are manageable because these people are able to take their concerns to the neighborhood council. (3) For Mr. and Mrs. Smith and their neighbors and friends, evasive responses to several community issues have affected their interpersonal relationships. The result is that they avoid discussing the issues and store their negative feelings. In this context they all have retreated into a protective and noncommitted stance. (4) Covertly the fears of racial intergration and of accepting deviant youths may involve concerns about the future association of their children with the new residents.

Among the conflicts posed as a result of diversity in a number of organisms, two patterns are suggested in the interplay with their environments: (1) When the organisms and their environments are accepting of diversity, the process of adaptation is smooth. (2) On the other hand when the organisms and their environments are not willing to tolerate diversity, their relationship is stalemated.

The concept of diversity can be extended to the phenomenon of cultural pluralism. With the recognition that cultural pluralism is an essential component of the American social fabric, group workers need to be sensitive to diversity as it relates to cultural, racial, and ethnic differences. This sensitivity will aid them in directing their efforts towards members' preservation of their respective heritage, rather than the relinquishing of their identity to assimilate into the mainstream.

Interactions and Transactions

Interaction and *transactions* are terms often used synonymously by social and behavioral scientists to describe communication patterns. But it needs to be clarified that in the present context these terms connote different meanings. *Inter* means "between" and *trans* means "across or beyond."

Transactions refer to negotiations with a variety of systems with which the person has been or may be engaged. Thus, a personality is, in part, the result of an accommodation and/or assimilation of

27

myriads of transactions among a variety of systems that span the individual-community continuum. The person, then, internalizes expectations and role competence (or their converse) from a number of sources of group memberships (assuming groups to include two or more members). These various transactions represent, in the person, an internal committee, which becomes activated through habit or anxiety in new situations.

Interaction as a process implies sequences of action and reaction, much like that of two billiard balls colliding. Transaction refers to the interdependent and resonating aspects of parts in a system. In this view, one can only understand the one part by viewing it in the context of interrelationships with other parts. Spiegel (1971) delineates the differences in the following way.

> *Interaction* describes a process in which entities are connected with entities in a sequence of action and reaction, like billiard balls. The patient unburdens herself to her therapist; the therapist makes an interpretation; the patient goes home and for the first time tells her husband what she really thinks of him; the husband calls the therapist in a rage; the therapist notes that the patient is losing some of her inhibitions but, in the process, may be acting out too much. The focus is on the behavior of each entity rather than on the interplay of all as a system.

> Transaction refers to a web of complex, interwoven systems within a total field such as the metabolic, endocrine, and neuro-physiological processes that maintain blood sugar at a steady level. Because of the chainlike and reverberating effects, with constant, mutual adjustment of subsystem to each other, such processes cannot be appropriately described by reference to the activity of any one organ or structure. All systems are involved in the behavior of all. On this view, structure (an organ, an institution) becomes both the produce of the systems which maintain it and the source (if one is needed) of the activity of some of the systems. The choice of cause or effect is up to the observer—a product of *his* activity—rather than a fixed principle given in the nature of "reality". What is found when the scientist publishes a finding is what he had arranged to look at, because nature consists merely of processes of exchange—that is, transaction (pp. 23-24).

In an ecological perspective of group work, both of the above concepts are essential. When the worker and/or members individualize their attention to one another, the process is interactional. If the focus of attention is directed to the group as a whole or to exhanges among subgroups, then the process is transactional.

The Smith case illustrates some of the ways that ecological perspective can be utilized to analyze the person-environment matrix. The foregoing discussion, though not completely exhaustive, does clarify this stance. Further explication of the ecological perspective is necessary to highlight other significant features of this framework.

Holism

The gestalt of the person-environment configuration connotes the concept of *holism,* which includes the totality of the situation. It also implies that this situation is a culmination of the interplay of a number of variables. This means that observers must view the totality from a multidisciplinary lens to include an understanding and awareness of feelings, perceptions, roles, group memberships, and the like. The complexity of this process is described incisively by Inkeles (1964), with particular reference to the current scene.

> Effective participation in a modern industrial and urban society requires certain levels of skill in the manipulation of language and other symbol systems, such as arithmetic and time; the ability to comprehend and complete forms; information as to when and where to go for what; skills in interpersonal relations which permit negotiation, insure protection of one's interests, and provide maintenance of stable and satisfying relations with intimates, peers, and authorities; motives to achieve, to master, to persevere; defenses to control and channel acceptably the impulses to aggression, to sexual expression, to extreme dependency; a cognitive style which permits thinking in concrete terms while still permitting reasonable handling of abstractions and general concepts; a mind which does not insist on excessively premature closure, is tolerant of diversity, and has some components of flexibility; a conative style which facilitates reasonably regular, steady, and persistent effort, relieved by rest and relaxation but not requiring long periods of total withdrawal or depressive psychic slump; and a style of expressing affect which encourages stable and enduring relationships without excessive narcissistic dependence or explosive aggression in the face of petty frustration (p. 414).

In many ways the above description connotes a sense of balance and rhythm in meeting the obligations and potentiating opportunities inherent in the life process. The dynamic aspects of this "balancing process" for the person is described aptly by Leighton (1959), in his definition of personality: "The acting of a person is considered as a living, self-integrating unit" (p. 17). Thus holism rests on perceiving persons in the context of their relationships with different levels of the environment such as family, friends, work associates, neighborhood and the like. Thomas and Garrison's (1969) definition extends Leighton's ideas and links it forcefully both to Inkeles' description and life in the homestead in the following way.

29

> An egocentric social system is . . . that partially constant and partially changing set of persons with whom ego habitually interacts (and transacts), throughout his life cycle, and the patterns of interactions (and transactions) which define the interrelationships among them (Parentheses ours, p. 320).

It is clear that this orientation transcends the more usual ways of perceiving a person as relating to the family, or to the neighborhood, since the person is viewed in the dynamic context of the societal matrix. It incorporates the notions that a teacher, sister, police officer, or uncle might be most influential to a person. This provides a platform from which continuities and discontinuites in a person's life may be addressed.

The difference between persons' actions in the family, or peer groups, and persons' concurrent relationships to both the family and the peer group is worthy of careful attention since it gets at the heart of the transactional context. Auerswald (1968), notes the distinction in terms of the holistic notion within an ecological model. He captures the shortcomings faced by discipline-specific specialists in the following way.

> Most clinical theorists, planners and practitioners, regardless of discipline, seem caught in the highly specialized sequence of their own training and intradisciplinary experience, upon which they seem to depend for the very definition of their personal indentity. Generally speaking, a situation seems to exist in which the intergration of the cognitive apparatus of the clinician is such as to exclude as a piece of relevant data the notion that his intradisciplinary "truths" which he carries to the interdisciplinary arena, are relative. He most often will hear and understand the notion when it is expressed. But, again speaking generally, he treats it as unimportant to his operations, as peripheral to the body of knowledge he invests with meaning (p. 214).

The vantage point for observing and classifying data with the interdisciplinary approach is indigenous to each discipline. While each discipline may borrow and incorporate concepts from other bodies of knowledge, the metaphors and the language of the discipline remain fairly intact. Ecological approach of holism on the other hand focuses on the properties of the system as a whole. That is, attention is directed towards the connecting links between various subparts of the total gestalt of the phenomena. As a result, the template of the whole is not predetermined by viewing it through any single profession's window, but through the many windows analogous to the reflection of light through a prism. At the operational level it means a number of choice points for intervention emerge which may be assumed by the various helping professionals with a stake in the problem. By viewing the problem in a holistic way, professional intervention may shift in subtle ways to satisfy the idiosyncratic character of the problem template. For example, the concept of a treatment team in hosptial settings suggests the value of the holistic approach. Frequently, the patients may become confused and overwhelmed in their therapeutic relationships and goals when dealing one-to-one with any primary therapist, be it a psychologist, nurse, physician, rehabilitation specialist, or social worker. Oftentimes mixed communication and conflicted sentiments force the patient to choose the path of least resistance as well as clouding his own perception of what it takes to get well. By focusing on team conferences operating under a mandate to collaborate on a rational and interconnected treatment plan, the patient's misgivings can be approached and controlled. In addition, to the extent that the treatment team can develop and accept emergent norms that are germane to its own functioning, then the treatment planning and interventive steps assume a unique character tailored to the patients. In this context, discipline-specific conceptions of the patient problems are transcended in terms of priorities in the quantity and quality, as well as the form and content of interventive strategies. Hence a strong patient-oriented alliance among the team members may be used to advantage for selective treatment purposes rather than insistence on professional boundaries and functions. The same logic may be applied to the professional role functions in organizations or departments as they relate to patient needs.

There are distinctions to be made between holistic practice which refers to generalistic activities and holistic administration, by which is meant the management of team roles in a case. Both have to be considered. The implication for the Smith family is that several intervention roles might be necessary. Attention to Mrs. Smith may have to include attention to family patterns as well. Subsequent interventions may have to encompass community organization strategies.

Adaptation

Adaptation is a key concept in the ecological perspective. For Vaillant (1977) "adaptation is as different from adjustment as art is different from a commercial illustration. Adjustment can be viewed as a snapshot but to view adaptation requires, at the very least, a motion picture camera" (p. 360).

An important principle clarified in Vaillant's work is that various

31

individuals who are similarly endowed with high intelligence, education, life opportunities and so forth, utilize their capacities and environmental resources in a variety of ways that produce different degrees of wellness. Some, for example, transcend the experience of the loss of a loved one through such artistic endeavors as writing poetry. Others favor a resolution through a benign acquiescence to life events and opportunities, while still others drift into patterns of drug abuse and withdrawal. It is not simply the presence or absence of any single "healthy" mechanism that makes the difference, but as Vaillant suggests

> Adaptation must reflect the vigorous reaction to change, to disease, and to environmental imbalance . . .The life circumstance they truly impinge upon health, the circumstances that facilitate adaptation or that stunt later growth—in contrast to fame—are not isolated events. What makes or breaks our luck seems to be the continued interaction between our choice of adaptive mechanisms and our sustained relationships with other people, (p. 368).

Adaptation refers more to the entire fabric of life over time and as it applies to the present. It is probably never complete but represents a series of emergent compromises in day-to-day living with in the governing parameters of general useful patterns of managing one's life. Adaptation has both a temporal element that includes long-term and immediate strivings, as well as an array of skill-abilities, some of which have worked over time and are exercised in current situations. Others must be either developed and drawn from personal archives or emerge brand-new in instances of crisis. These three aspects of adaptation are to be contrasted to a fourth which is a genetic patterning of the capacities inherent in a person at birth and which provides both opportunity and constraints along a developmental arc.

The genetic dynamic viewpoint, such as the developmental model, it not negated but there has to be equal concern about the extent to which social environment makes the difference between mild psychosocial disabilities on one hand or more severe, disabling symptoms for the individual and a burden for the community on the other. One might ask the question: What are the patterns in the community which predispose individuals toward anxiety, depression and apathy, or striving, mastery and competence? Or to ask the question in another way, what is in the neighborhood that is toxic for family A, benign for family B, and potentiating for family C? Adaptation then, implies both growth and change as well as stability and maintenance. In concert with the holistic and multifactorial nature of cause-effect, adaptation must be viewed among variables such as person-person, person-group, person-neighborhood and so forth. Furthermore, adaptation is not a process that resembles a series of logically interconnected steps. More often than not, it is a compromise that includes a trial and error process. One might expect both progress and slippage towards goals. White (1974) notes that "adaption often calls for delays, strategic retreat, regrouping of forces, abandoning of untenable positions, seeking fresh intelligence . . . Sometimes adaptation to a severely frustrating reality is possible only if full recognition of the bitter truth is for a long time postponed" (p. 50).

The character and influence of time as a major determinant in growth and development has been phrased succinctly by Leighton (1959) in the following way.

> The personality of an individual flows in sequence through a large number of simultaneous expressions, like a symphony being played by an orchestra, and there is intergration somewhat parallel to the intergration of wind, strings, and percussion in constituting the total pattern . . . repeated with variations—childhood, youth, maturity, and old age . . . Personality may be thought to have a score also, laid down by the genes, but it is much less specific and its patterning is subject to change while in the act of performing (p. 18).

Adaptation is a complex dynamic process, partly governed by genetic endowment which is both extensive and specific, and which includes the exercise and practice of skills, some accrued through past achievements and others newly emergent as a response either to disturbing demands or to new and potentially rewarding experiences.

The impact of the person and the environment as mediated by the process of adaptation may be characterized in several ways. Weiss (1963), describes the elements of adaptive process as including both elastic and plastic responses. That is, in times of stress, an organism may simply resist the intrusion of an external demand that relates to tolerance of elasticity of the organism to absorb pressure, much like a person undergoing anxiety. Weiss also includes an accommodative element in which the organism simply adopts the change and yields to its consequences, thereby becoming altered in the process. These notions appear to refer to a reactive stance on the part of the organism. A third component is what many have referred to as mastery, striving, or self-expansion. In this situation the person actively engages in the environment, and in the process may alter it to suit his/her needs. Hence, adaptation as a process may include resistance, acceptance, alteration, and transformation with respect to external demand. These same processes have their internal counterparts as well in terms of dealing with subjective perceptions of feeling and moods. Under any condition it is important to recognize that the outcome of adaptive behavior is a product of the internal and external demands.

Competence and Well-Being

It is useful to explore the relationship between competence and well-being. *Competence* refers to the repertoire of skill abilities that a person has been able to use and exercise toward some sort of achievement. Frequently, in the past, well-being and nonwell-being, or more succinctly, mental health and illness have been perceived as opposite poles along a single continuum. Implicit in this view is the notion that if a person isn't ill, then he/she must be well; therefore, mental health is the absence of illness. In many ways this is a stultifying view and probably represented only a beginning point of diagnosis. In effect, the relationship of health to illness has been very difficult to assess.

Studies on the topic suggest a major break with this earlier mode of thinking. That is, it has been suggested that the variables that are related to health and illness may be independent of one another. There is a measure of commonsense knowledge that seems to go along with this point of view. For example, among cancer patients in remission, neutralizing the physical state of the disease does not necessarily mean that the patient is in a sound emotional state. In fact, studies by Bard (1955), Bard and Sutherland, (1955), and Schonfield (1972) have noted that, for whatever reasons, psychological invalidism may continue and govern the life of the patient after the cancer has been arrested.

Bradburn (1969) selected subjective feeling states that people experience in their everyday lives as the foci for study, and classified them simply as positive and negative. He states that

> we found evidence that indeed there do appear to be at least two types of feelings and that the difference between the number of positive and negative feelings is a good predictor of a person's overall rating of his own happiness. Similarily, we expected that these two types of feelings would have an orderly relationship to a person's feelings of well-being or happiness . . . we also found something unexpected and not widely commented on for centuries: the two types of feelings are independent of one another. When we say that they are independent of each other, we do not mean that they can occur simultaneously or that people

34

move from positive to negative feelings and back again in a cyclical fashion. We mean that within a given period of time, such as a week or two, one may experience many different emotions, both positive and negative, and that in general there is no tendency for the two types to be experienced in any particular relation to one another. This lack of correlation means that information about the extent of positive feelings a person has experienced in the recent past does not give us any information on the extent of his negative feelings (p. 225).

The researcher also notes that quantity of affect is not related to the quality of affect. Whether one has a lot or a few positive and negative feelings, self-reports of happiness for each are about the same. Thus, for example, if a person has problems with marriage or on the job, these do not necessarily decrease positive feelings, and vice versa, satisfying involvement with friends and/or organizations does not lessen negative feelings.

Beiser and Leighton (1976) address the same issue with respect to normal people in natural settings to ascertain, in more detail, the correlates of well-being, particularly with reference to the contributions a community makes. From a set of predetermined assets that seemed to differentiate between successful and unsuccessful adaptation, three dimensions were extracted, namely, *negative affects, pleasurable involvement,* and *long-term satisfaction. Negative affect* refers to poor physical health and diminished ability to relate to others. *Pleasurable involvement* refers to ability to secure emotional support from appropriate others, to maintain judicious balance among various social roles, ability to roll with the punches in unexpected situations, an immediate, smooth way of acting in interpersonal situations, ability to plan, sense of personal worth, psychological acumen (ability to size up other people), and participation in community activities such as social clubs, civic groups, and the like, and satisfaction from work. *Long-term satisfaction* depends more on the availability and responsiveness to emotional ties and satisfaction that results from consistent family and community relationships over a period of time. In the latter case, one begins to note a sense of continuity and role harmony that "keeps working." In their study in a rural community, Beiser and Leighton (1976) found that for men, job-related provider roles produce more satisfaction, while for women, interpersonal relationships and participation in informal community activities are more important. In essence, the point is that some sort of integration and balance in a community is a prerequisite for mental well-being and furthermore, that the neutralization of physical infirmities in and of itself may not be sufficient for well-being. The investigators caution that although their findings at this point have heuristic value they need to be subjected to further testing. But the extent to which participation at task and affective levels, expressed in a variety of roles in a community, are important benchmarks for well-being suggests that role opportunities and utilization must be available in the environment, and that personal capacities must be developed for their use. It seems reasonable to suppose that small face-to-face groups offer at least one viable and practical opportunity by which these connections, both for persons and for the environment, can be integrated. The group experience becomes a way station at which members can give up or reaffirm old roles, try new ones, and transfer them to their natural habitat. Further they can also evaluate the features which are considered essential for their well-being back home.

Social Environment

As discussed earlier, habitat comprises an essential context for understanding human behavior from an ecological perspective. However, to apply this concept of habitat to practice situations, group workers will have to be cognizant of life patterns of groups members that include interrelationships with *family, social networks, organizations* and *communities*. From the vantage point of the group members all of these comprise significant elements of their social environment. For meaningful group experience for members, the workers will have to assess how these factors impact on role performances in the group.

Family The function and importance of the family has been stated in various ways by numbers of theorists.

Nurturance, socialization, and educative functions are essential components in the growth and development of children, as well as in the adult members. The distribution and quality of relationships among members in families obviously can produce a wide variety of "types" that have direct bearing on how any one member perceives "self", and, for children, this lays the groundwork for future choices, goals, and actions. In simple terms, the possibilities of distinctive family relations can be dramatized by considering a family composed of three people,—father, mother and infant. Expectations of performances among these three roles can clearly typify a part of family functioning. In addition, however, one also may want to consider other role sets such as husband and wife, or man and woman, each with their own respective attributes, which congeal into a dynamic and striving threesome, or into patterns that may be characterized as of despair, anxiety, and conflict. However the case may be, these roles are continually interacting and transacting in ways which make up some sort of totality—resonating, defending, communicating, deciding, organizing, fighting, supporting, and so on in rather continuous and stable ways. This role complex may change, of course, as more children are added to the picture, and as one can well imagine, the number, type, quality, and distribution of relationships changes as well. For example, if one were to add three children to the above family, the complex of six individuals generates at least fifteen relationships. Hence, one can begin to appreciate the tugs and pulls, opportunities and constraints relevant in this group. In essence, the family as a whole is analogous to the soil from which plants must grow. The web of relationship provides the nutrients from which children form images of themselves.

Families do not exist in a vacuum. The importance of the social and physical habitat in which families reside must be considered. Dramatic changes were demonstrated with regard to family functioning in a residential family camp experience, in which a number of low-income families collaborated in developing a viable "temporary system" away from home (Vassil, 1978). Differences in perception among and between families, adults, children, and staff were noted over a three-week period. Not only do latent and buried sentiments of families reemerge in a safe environment, but for other constituent members as well. For example, adolescents who are perceived as major irritants back home, find room to be most productive in roles as staff. The use of groups was an important vehicle in organizing the therapeutic environment at camp. Group work with families in more complex settings for purposes of neighborhood and community development have been reported as well (Glaser, 1972).

Social Networks Extended family, neighbors, friends, and work associates in special interest activities form an important base for stability, self-worth, and support. Knowledge regarding social networks is relatively new in social work. It seems logical that the variety, number, and quality of role relationships among the social networks would be related to coping and adaptation, particularly in times of stress. Whether or not a network is closed, constricted, expansive, fragmented, or integrated would seem, on the face of it, to be related to a person's role differentiation or constriction, and consequently the life choices that are available and acted upon.

The following questions posed by Somers (1976) illustrate the relevance of the concept of social network for group work practice.

1. Do mothers with whom I work depend upon and receive temporary help from women members of their extended family or neighbors or friends during hospitalization and immediately after returning home with newborn babies?
2. Do older persons with whom I work depend upon and receive regular help from extended family members, or neighbors and friends?
3. Do partially or severely handicapped members with whom I work receive regular help from extended family, friends, or neighbors during periods of noninstitutional care?

In essence, social network refers to the significant people that a person associates with in many ways. Murphy (1976) conceives of network as the effective social milieu in that it refers to those others to whom a given individual is linked in terms of influencing or being influenced by, supporting or being supported by, depending on or being depended upon.

While characteristics that would be useful to define types of social networks are still being developed, a number of aspects may be posed. For example, size of network and frequency of inter-actions among members would appear to be useful. Frequency of interaction suggests that, as in a group, the greater the interaction the greater the cohesion and influence. Large numbers of people would require certain structural hierarchies within a network, perhaps ranked in order of proximity or perceived importance among such groups or members of certain extended families. It is quite likely that whether and to what degree members of networks associate with each other or with certain central persons would be related to such events as supports, information, decision-making, and so on. Glaser's (1972) work on stairwell societies showed that central persons in certain twelve-family stairwell complexes in a housing project received and distributed information to other "followers" that was related to life in their housing unit. The composition of a social network may shift depending on the nature of the situation. For example, a seriously ill family member may draw greater attention and support from extended family and friends than in more normal circumstances. Also types of illness may make a difference, as for example, between cancer and heart attack. Friends and neighbors seem to play a significant role with heart attack patients, (Croog, et. al., 1966), while with cancer patients, a number of variations were seen ranging from close to quite distant patterns, some of which were attributed to the illness (Vassil, 1978). Other possibilities include the overlapping of roles, as when formal work associates may also be informal friends who help with the care of a sick family member.

38

The potency of social network may also be related to ethnicity or social class. Experiences working in low-income neighborhoods suggest that sex-role stereotyping with respect to informal leisure time activities governs the place and purpose of social activities. Men may frequently be found together in a local beer parlor or in sports activities, while women tend to satisfy their interpersonal strivings through phone contact with relatives or women friends rather than with nearby neighbors. In middle-class situations, examples of social networks are fraternal, professional, and special interest organizations for men and women alike.

In a pioneering effort, Bott (1971) concentrated her efforts on the sex-role pattern within married pairs and how these related to significant others outside the family. An interesting finding is that there is greater flexibility among married pairs when their circle of significant others is loosely associated. This finding seems to be consistent with sex-role stereotyping among lower-class or ethnic groups, which permeates and maintains husband-wife roles and expectations along preconceived norms. Attneave and Speck (1974) utilized the network concept in structuring treatment for clients in crisis, based on the assumption that reorganization of member affiliation in the client's natural "life space" is integral to any change efforts. Their work conceptualizes a series of phases in the treatment process pertinent to alterations in the natural network. Knowledge of social networks has implications for group work practice in understanding informal ties to improve the qualitative assessment of a member and/or group, and with forming and involving network members for support in times of crisis. This knowledge can also be used to improve the quality of life in neighborhoods.

Organizations Moos and Houts (1970) studied the environmental effect on individual behavior and found that the interaction between the individual and setting was a more important behavioral determinant than either the individual or setting alone. As part of their research, the authors compared two mental hospital wards. One ward was perceived by patients as high on the dimensions of autonomy, involvement, spontaneity, affiliation, and practicality. The other ward was seen by patients as having little of these qualities. A comparison of the two wards showed that the patients on the "high" ward were more satisfied, self-confident, and less anxious than those on the "low" ward.

This study is just one of many research findings which demonstrate the very important effect that specific organizational climate can have on individual and group behavior. In addition to psychiatric hospitals, the influence of organizational climates has been demonstrated in business organizations, classrooms, and schools, (see for example, Thelen, 1974; Walberg, 1969; Litwin and Stringer, 1968). The work of Barker and Gump (1964) on large- and small-sized high schools demonstrate differences in activities and roles among students. Among their major findings are the following: large high schools offer a wider range of different activities which may produce more vicarious satisfaction among students; in small high schools, there are fewer activity types but greater participation which fosters more satisfaction in competence and cooperation. The importance of space has been studied with respect to individuals and small groups (Sommer, 1959 and Seabury, 1971). The importance of space to social work with groups is obvious. For example, group work with disturbed children is almost impossible in large spaces without a great deal of planning and preparation. Aggressive, acting-out adolescents are extremely challenging when confined to a small room for any length of time.

Organizational support of activities is another important aspect. Redl (1966) sums up the clinical importance of activity structure on member performance by noting: "We have plenty of evidence by now that . . . the very exposure of children to a given game, with its structure and demands for certain constituent performances may have terrific clinical impact . . . (this) goes for many other activities patients engage in arts and crafts, woodwork, outings, overnight trips, cookouts, discussion groups, musical evenings, and so forth" (pp. 87–88).

Neighborhoods and Communities The quality of neighborhood life is another aspect that affects the development of individuals. Gans (1962) and Suttles (1968) offer rich descriptions of the ways in which ethnic and racial ties can merge to produce unique patterns that govern and guide behaviors. In the delinquency area, the work of Spergel (1976), Miller (1958), Cloward and Ohlin (1976), suggest that neighborhood norms are reflected in the response of adolescent gangs. The idiosyncratic relationship between types of gangs and neighborhood norms has also been discussed by Alissi (1965). Spergel's work (1976) on classifying communities was based on comparisons of certain characteristics in inner-city regions. He was able to classify communities as "mass movement," "controlled," "pluralist," and "communal," according to such variables as access to economic resources, mobility patterns, race, ethnicity, and access to cultural values. Additional structural variables in community organization including exchange patterns, resources, auspices, and

40

program commitment were utilized. Differences among these community types with respect to delinquency policies and patterns of adolescent adaptations are discussed.

Leighton's indicators include the following:

1. High frequency of broken homes (physical absence of one parent, or chronic distance between parents).
2. Few and weak associates (few groupings of people formally or informally).
3. Few and weak leaders (no power of influence).
4. Few patterns of recreation (absence of sports, playgrounds, activities).
5. High frequency of hostility (a great number of hostile words and acts directed at each other and outsiders).
6. High frequency of crime and delinquency (assaults, robberies, child abuse, or neglect).
7. Weak and fragmented network of communication (poor roads, transportation, isolation).
8. Widespread ill health (prevalence of accidents, chronicity, other physical impairments).
9. Extensive poverty (severe and prolonged want).
10. Extensive migration (differential loss of people by age and sex categories. Certain groups leave faster than replaced. For example, imagine a neighborhood overloaded with one parent families, young children, and senior citizens).

A disintegrated community, in Leighton's terms, was coined a *collection.* In this type of community one might find numbers of individuals living in the same geographic area but having inconsistent and transient encounters with one another. People may work in the environment but normative community patterns are limited, as for example, (1) against disease—nonaccessible or nonutilized health services, (2) shelter-inadequate clothing, lack of heat, impaired housing facilities. In addition, socialization of preschool children may be inconsistent or individualistic, and the lack of help from socializing agencies such as church or recreation may strain the individual capacities for coping. Hence, the process of disintegration means not only a relative absence of community patterns, which, if present, could improve community functions, but refers as well to an ongoing deterioration of the system.

Leighton's (1959) work led him to the following propositions, which connect striving sentiments (personality patterns) with the sociocultural environment, and fits in nicely with the ecological perspective.

41

1. Sociocultural situations that interfere with sentiments bearing on obtaining recognition foster psychiatric disorder.
2. Sociocultural situations that interfere with sentiments of physical security foster psychiatric disorder.
3. Sociocultural situations that expose a growing personality to defective role relationships foster psychiatric disorder.

A number of examples of sociocultural conditions that can interfere with the emergent and striving personality of people can be cited.

Recognition may be interfered with by skill deficits with respect to activities, lack of caring in the home, or a cohesive set of attitudes that are sensitive to failure and subsequently block out success (the person who believes everything turns to failure).

Cottrell (1976) has also conceptualized the community but in competence and process terms rather than with indicators as Leighton and Spergel have done. For Cottrell, a competent community is one which (1) can collaborate effectively in identifying the problems and needs of the community; (2) can agree on ways and means to implement the agreed upon goals; (3) can achieve a consensus on goals and priorities; and (4) can collaborate effectively in the required action. The similarity of these goals and objectives to the problem solving through groups proposed by Somers (1976), is relevant. In addition to the components requisite to a competent community, Cottrell also lists eight essential aspects for competent functioning; commitment, awareness of self and significant others, clarity of situational definitions, articulateness, communication, participation, conflict containment and accommodation, management of relations with the larger society, and machinery for facilitating participant interaction and decision making.

The sum and substance of the ecological perspective is expressed in the following principle with implications for practice.

1. Events throughout life have potential for generating challenging and stressful circumstances.
2. Stressful circumstances may create psychosocial disabilities which can range from severe to mild or none.
3. Sociocultural event processes can either generate, maintain or reduce the levels of psychosocial disabilities.
4. Patterns of psychosocial disabilities will reflect the imbalance among interactional and transactional processes between person and the environment.
5. Sociocultural events that interfere with a person's cognitive, affective, perceptual, interpersonal and social strivings will tend to foster psychosocial disabilities.

6. A certain amount of integration in a sociocultural system is required to maintain and enhance the problem solving capacities of the constituency.
7. The group is a mediating vehicle between the internal (personal) and external (social-environmental) demands.
8. The group reflects society in the microcosm and incorporates among members their adaptation or lack of it with the environment.
9. Professional function emerging from the ecological perspectives dictates that both process and content reflect the societal diversity (pluralism) particularly as it relates to the work of the group.

SIGNIFICANCE FOR GROUP WORK

The foregoing discussion of the concepts underlying the ecological framework provides a sense of understanding and meaning of a member's life within his/her environment. The primary aim of social group work is to bring about a balance between the members and their environment.

The following section focuses on further exploration of these concepts as related to social group work. For purposes of convenience and explication, these concepts have been sorted into ecologically derived organizing themes which relate to social group work practice.

Group Habitat

In any homestead or habitat there are limited numbers of resources available because "the field" does not belong to any one person, but to groups of persons. While one might argue that each person has inherent capacities for cognitive, behavioral, emotional, social and affectional strivings, "the field" itself may provide limited access to exercise these strivings. Interferences may come in various ways, but it is not hard to visualize that the same institutions which are mandated to help people can also produce adverse effects. Institutional racism and sexism within human service organizations are two examples.

Any number of interrelationships existing in a community may support degrees of merit or inadequacy. Relationships between any two sets of people can be "transient," "unilateral," "parasitic," or "parallel". Under these conditions the exercise of the person's capacities (elaborated in Chapter 5) may be severely constrained and over time can result in a disparagement syndrome. When relationships are cooperative and work-centered, then we think we have the means for rearranging peoples' capacities and experiences in such a way as to produce in them a sense of belonging to a group and of being right in what they think or do. One should not infer from this that a greater number of relationships are likely to generate a personal sense of well-being. In point of fact, a few well-chosen roles may be as eventful as a broad array of roles. In either case it is the exercise of a person's capacities in relationships that is relevant. Although it is difficult to replicate exactly the habitat of each and every member, social group work practiced from an ecological perspective has the potential to provide a realistic microcosm of the members' field. Conflict or diversity in groups facilitates recognition of member differences as a fixed reality. These differences can range along such dimensions as sex, race, ethnicity, economics, and so forth. Similarly the attribute of holism emphasizes the context and content of the group life, thus avoiding the danger of perceiving group members from a narrow, segmented view.

Group Boundaries

Groups are not self-contained. One has to consider the permeability between the group and what influences it from the outside. There are various ways to depict the relationship of the outside–inside. The idea of overlapping group memberships, which refers to an individual's remembered group membership roles, past and present, real and imagined, depicts the permeability of the group boundaries from the perspective of both the individual member and the group collectively. For example, how any one member deals with others and how others deal with themselves is based in part on their successful adaptation to certain roles. Member role patterns are amenable to change because transition points in their lives may induce different needs and requirements. At one point satisfactory member roles may become unsatisfactory because of transitional relationships with extended family. Several examples may be cited to explicate the point. Grandparent involvement in certain cultures may intrude into the family style of a young couple having their first child. Group work services for married couples struggling with issues of culturally induced sex-role stereotyping and self-perceived egalitarian needs between the spouses must continually face the residual pressure of outer group peer relationships with extended families, friends, neighbors, and the like who support the traditional expectations. Similarily, in childrens' groups, how members relate with siblings will affect their interactions with other group members.

The concept of diversity as expressed through cultural pluralism in social group work sensitizes both members and workers alike to concerns regarding their differential role functioning. The concept of adaptation is useful in understanding why and how various members adapt themselves in similar life situations differently. Inherent in this conception is the notion that conflict, or differences among the members, fuels the change process. Conflict within tolerable limits generates creative tension between dependability and uncertainty, between safety and adventure. Psychosocial incapacity occurs when the limits are stretched beyond one's capacity for recovery and healing, or for breakdown and repair to take place simultaneously. Accommodating and containing conflict within reasonable bounds depends on the implicit and explicit agreements that constitute the group culture at one point in time.

Group Resources

At any given time, the resources available for group effort from its membership is bound to be less than the demands covertly or overtly expressed by the group members. In other words, the composite of the resources of individual members and the worker is less than the demands made by the total membership. Due to this discrepency in the resources, conflicts emerge within the group situation. This conflict provides an impetus for the group members to explore alternate means for managing their difficulties.

The resources available in groups rest in the capacities and skills members bring with them, as well as the values, knowledge, and skills that the worker exercises to create group conditions for change. Among members, several resource areas may be identified, namely; *cognitive, perceptual, affective,* and *interpersonal.* Capacities for planning, anticipating, exercising judgment, self-observing, reality testing, insight, and playing with ideas may be grouped as *cognitive.* Tolerating ambiguities, demonstrating openness to new sensations, selective screening of cues are *perceptual.* Feeling pleasure in what one does, a sense of optimism, self-esteem, and expressing humor relate more or less to *affective* states. Capacities of empathy, trust, love toward another, using appropirate sources of emotional support, being dominant when needed, submissive where appropriate, being affiliative but also tolerating periods of aloneness represent *interpersonal* themes. These capacities are not meant to be exhaustive, but descriptions of resources among members at personal and interpersonal levels. The worker, through his/her own values, knowledge, and skills attempts to translate and transform this pool of capacities into a group which may then manufacture opportunities for moving from transient and associative relationships to work patterns.

The group is a complementary and accommodative unit to the members' other available significant networks. For example, a person discharged from a psychiatric institution could benefit by involvement in a supportive group with other dischargees. But reentry in the community requires self-initiation and engagement of personal tasks in relationships with peers, neighbors, family, work associates and so forth. The supportive groups may be used to mediate member capacities to those other powerful and resource-rich opportunities.

Group Exchange

Group exchange implies the transaction and interaction between and among members and a worker within a time frame in a given environmental context. Three dynamic processes elaborate further the idea of group exchange. The internal dynamic refers to the relationship between and among group members such as the affective ties among members. The generative dynamic is defined by the relationship between the members and the worker and includes members' goals, group goals, agency policies, professional values, worker knowledge, and skills. The external dynamic is shaped by the relationship of the group within a given environment, such as the significant environmental climate that bears directly on the group functioning. For example, groups conducted within correctional settings are adversely affected when national media publicizes such inmate riots in prison as occurred at Attica.

Transactions between the members and the group are governed by two sets of paradoxes. Members cannot be in conflict and at peace at the same time. Neither can they express affection and hostility, nor take a chance and be certain simultaneously. In addition, the group can exercise authority in controlling conflict, but in the same process may have to face loss of support from the members. The transactions between these member paradoxes and group authority are probably handled through a series of group cultures that permit or constrain sets of relationships that regulate these transactions. Examples might be cultures of participation, conflict, support, work, and so forth. These combinations represent expansions and alterations in member roles over time as new information is accepted, tried out, and absorbed for expression into new role patterns (Glidewell, 1975).

Group Worker

The major task of the worker in the group is to articulate and connect the three realities of person–group–environment as they are expressed in the group in a shared frame of reference. The development of a shared frame of reference is consistent with the concept of mutual aid that describes desirable relationships among persons as they seek to find meaning in their lives. No utopian state is visualized. A shared frame of reference refers to the utilization of differences and similarities among persons and groups as a springboard to constructing a more acceptable life plan for an individual than is currently available. The moving dynamic is conflict. The nutrient is support, both personal and group. Belongingness, balance, diversity, and continuity are forebears to transitional situations that are accommodated, transformed, and absorbed over time through various psychosocial climates, each producing their own corresponding sentiments. The shared frame of reference is most complete when it is at the same time most flexible in terms of sharing resources and expectations concerning interdependence, dependence, and autonomy.

Worker activity is directed at four sets of relationships, member–member, member–group, member–worker and member–environment. Attention to process and content further dictates a curriculum for action. Legitimation and authority for change emerges through authentic encounters between the worker and members. This represents a shift from earlier conceptions of the worker as cool, detached, authoritative, and attuned to the members' psyches. In addition, instead of limiting worker interventions to conflicts prevalent at intrapsychic and interpersonal levels, conflicts rooted in intergroup or societal levels are considered as the proper domain for practice activity. An example of this is to be found in the conception of "allogenic conflict" which refers to friction or discomfort experienced by individuals because of significant and notable differences among them such as physical, psychological, racial, religious, economic or social (Balgopal and Vassil, 1979).

SUMMARY

In reviewing the pattern of work that encompasses the person–society continuum, it appears that efforts are underway, both empirical and practical, for clarifying the various "clumps" that make up the person's life space. Family, extended family, friends and neighbors, neighborhood, and community are being redis-covered as essential components in growth and development. While the units are different, they are congenial to an ecological perspec-tive that guides our thinking to view the various "niches" and cultures that individuals belong to and rely on for purposes of identity and change. The group as a vehicle for changing has to be adapted to different purposes, degrees of sophistication, organiza-tional settings, type of client problems and so forth.

Meaning and identity of group members represent two distinctly related but somewhat separate ideas. To the extent that there is consonance or dissonance between the two in a person's life, any number of possibilities are open. "Successful" executives and public figures have been known to commit suicide, which suggests a sharp disparity between their public and private selves. Other persons who appear to have low opinions of themselves, a narrow self-identity, even some "lost souls", may find great meaning in one aspect of their lives. For example, prisoners may develop their writing, musical or sports abilities. While there are great variations between meaning and identity, the interplay between the two as expressed in members' private and public concerns, actions, and belief, their collective fusion in one form or another, is intimately related to the habitat in which they live. The natural habitat affirms, reaffirms, or exacerbates distinctions between the two which can lead to well-being or unhappiness. The rich tapestry and fabric of these twin ideas is better expressed by philosophers and writers, than by social scientists. Their importance for social work practitioners is the ex-tent to which the goodness of fit between the person and the natural habitat offer significant means and choices by which the fullest potential strivings of individuals may be realized.

Interactions and transactions are process constants. Cooperation, and conflict among human beings is inevitable in life. It is not conceivable that a person's complex of needs, wants and desires can be attained in a social vacuum. Survival, satisfaction and self-development are assured through interdependence. This is not to say that interdependence reflects equality. On the contrary, in the web of similarities and differences among people, various patterns of cooperation may be required such as superior–subordinate patterns of autocracy, compliance, counterdependency, and egali-tarianism. In addition, interdependence is not to be confused with autonomy or independence.

Autonomy or independence finds expression in choices and

opportunities for membership in a variety of groups. The major focal point for consideration by the practitioner in groups is: what are the potentiating and constraining opportunities for independence and interdependence in the natural and formed associations in the habitat for the promotion of well-being, restoration, prevention, or rehabilitation?

Interaction and transactions among human beings, it must be assumed, will create their own inherent social order. The multiplication and transformation of this dynamic generates and reflects the tension between innate strivings and some sort of organized patterns.

One may extend this rather simplistic view of development to include neighborhood and community. Informal and formal groupings such as transitory, cliques, networks, work teams and the like represent some of the associations likely in the span from person to environment. Whatever the situation it seems inescapable that growth and arrest are intricately connected to participation in an array of small groupings. The task for group work practitioners is to facilitate the members' struggles in achieving both a social and personal identity. In addition, professional workers have to assist group members in utilizing a variety of resources, including the group, to integrate themselves within their life space. Contributions from the natural, behavioral, and social sciences have resulted in the formulation of an ecological framework as presented in this chapter. This framework is useful for group workers in factoring out key elements in their practice such as membership, the agency, the worker and the environment. Symbolic Interaction Theory as formulated as Mead and Field Theory developed by Lewin are two promising approaches that can complement the ecological framework especially in developing practice components in work with groups.

3
Symbolic Interaction and Field Theory

In the 19th century, the problem was that God is dead;
In the 20th century, the problem is that man is dead;
In the 19th century, inhumanity meant cruelty;
In the 20th century, it means schizoid self-alienation.
The danger of the past was that men became slaves.
The danger of the future is that men may become robots.
(E. Fromm, 1963, p. 101)

In our contemporary society individuals are engaged in a never-ending struggle to find meaning in their existence. It is paradoxical that despite all the technological amenities and modern conveniences available to them, individuals are experiencing a heightened sense of loss and worthlessness. Some have turned to the teachings of Eastern philosophies and religions to find a meaning for existence. A diversity of other paths to spiritual peace are being explored to satisfy the inner needs of one's self. The meaning of the external side of one's self is largely determined by how individuals interact with their significant others and, based upon this interaction, how they are perceived by others and how they perceive themselves. The emergence of self and how it is influenced and determined by the significant others are among the basic tenets of symbolic interaction theory. This school of thought directs attention to processes that govern conduct between two or more persons, or between persons and referent groups that are seen as important. The concept of role taking and perceived signals that guide expressive and responsive behavior in the form of verbal and nonverbal cues, represent key elements of this theory.

SYMBOLIC INTERACTION PERSPECTIVE

Since George Herbert Mead's lectures on symbolic interactionism at the University of Chicago beginning in 1893, this orientation has been extensively developed, discussed and researched by social and behavioral scientists. This school grew primarily under the influence of pragmatism, which emphasized attitudes and meanings for one's behavior. The focal point was the self or personality as influenced by interaction with the society.

Symbolic interactionists stress the relationship of self and society and how they influence each other. This theory offers a perspective in understanding the individuals in primary and other groups, from both psychological and sociological points of view (Balgopal, Munson, Vassil, 1979). Symbolic interaction is the attitude one has towards oneself, the perception one has of others' attitudes towards him/her, and the way they communicate and share meanings around these perceptions.

The term *symbolic interaction* is defined by Herbert Blumer (1978) as "the peculiar and distinctive character of interaction as it takes place between human beings. The peculiarity consists in the fact that human beings interpret or 'define' each other's actions instead of merely reacting to each other's actions" (p. 97). Blumer (1969), has summarized the basic position of symbolic interactionism in the form of three premises: (1) "Human beings act toward things on the basis of the meanings that the things have for them." (2) "The meaning of such things is derived from, or arises out of, the social interaction that one has with one's fellows." (3) "These meanings are handled in, and modified through, an interpretive process used by the person in dealing with the things he encounters" (p. 2).

According to Mead (1934), all group life is essentially a matter of cooperative behavior. In discussing Mead's Social Psychology, Meltzer (1978) states that in order for human beings to cooperate, it is essential to have a mechanism so that each acting individual:

(1) can come to understand the lines of action of others and (2) can guide his own behavior to fit in with those lines of action.

Mead holds that a human being cannot develop a self except in relation to others. According to him, the self emerges concurrently with the ability to take roles. He focuses both on the internal as well as external interactions of an individual and how they affect a person. Mead further stresses that symbolic interaction is both the medium for development of human beings and the process by which human beings associate and interact with each other. In view of his interest in the dynamic processes of social interaction rather than the static structure of social organization, Mead perceives the individual as an active and thinking agent rather than a reacting and passively responding organism. (Mead, 1934).

Rose (1962) contends that the symbolic interaction school is based on the following assumptions: (1) Man lives in a symbolic environment, as well as a physical environment. (2) Through symbols, man has the capacity to stimulate others in ways other than those in which he is himself stimulated. (3) Through communication of symbols, individuals learn huge numbers of meanings and values and hence ways of acting—from other people. (4) The symbols and the meanings and values to which they refer do not occur only in isolated bits, but often in clusters, sometimes large and complex. (5) Thinking is the process by which possible sanctions and other future courses of actions are examined, assessed for relative advantages and disadvantages in terms of the individual's value system, and chosen for action.

Several major ideas are highlighted in Mead's seminal work and are explicated further by his successors. They are identity, meaning, process, thinking, and development. The common thread that holds these ideas together is that self-identity is a continuous and emergent process that is embedded in dialogue, reflection, and actions with significant others.

BASIC PROPOSITIONS

Basic propositions of symbolic interaction theory have been succinctly presented by Manis and Meltzer (1978), and these are

1. Distinctively human behavior and interaction are carried on though the medium of symbols and their meanings. This proposition implies that human beings do not typically respond to stimuli, but assign meanings to the stimuli and act on the basis of the meanings.

2. The individual becomes humanized through interaction with other persons. Human beings become capable of distinctively human conduct only through association with others. We are not born human, then, but become human. Human nature, mind and self are not biologically given; rather, they emerge out of the processes of human interaction. Interaction with others is seen as giving rise to the acquisition of human nature, thinking, self-direction and all other attributes that distinguish the behavior of humans from that of other forms of life.

3. Human society is most usefully conceived of as consisting of people in interaction. This proposition emphasizes the processual nature of human society in preference to the more common metaphors of social structure, social organization and social system. This theoretical orientation recognizes that individuals act and interact with larger networks of other individuals and groups. Some of the networks are far removed from given individuals in time and space, and yet have an appreciable impact on them. Nonetheless, the organization of any society is a framework within which social action takes place, not a set of complete determinants of the action. Such structural features as social roles, social classes, and the like set conditions for human behavior and interaction, but do not cause or fully determine the behavior and interaction.

4. Human beings are active in shaping their own behavior. According to symbolic interaction theory, human beings have some degree of choice in their behavior. Given the ability to select the interpret stimuli—rather than to respond immediately and directly to whatever stimuli are present—and the ability to interact with themselves, humans are capable of forming new meanings and new lines of action. This proposition points to the fact that the socialization of human beings both enmeshes them in society and frees them from society. Individuals with selves are not passive, but can employ their selves in an interaction that may result in behavior divergent from group definitions.

5. Consciousness or thinking, involves interaction with oneself. When one thinks or engages in "minded" behavior, one necessarily carries on an internal conversation. One makes indications of things to oneself, sometimes rehearsing alternative lines of action. This process involves two components of the self: The *I,* a spontaneous and impulsive aspect, and the *Me,* a set of internalized social definitions.

The human being is a social being. Only through the use of

socially derived symbols in interpersonal activity, which duplicate that activity, can the individual perform such unique functions as abstract and reflective thinking. These modes of thought help individuals to designate objects and events over a period of time, without having direct experience of the things to be learned.

6. Human beings construct their behavior in the course of its execution. The behavior that emerges from the interactions within an individual, according to many symbolic interactionlists, is not necessarily a product of past events or experiences. Human beings are, at least in part, participants in creating their own destinies. This does not mean humans have complete free will.

7. An understanding of human conduct requires study of the actor's covert behavior. If human beings act on the basis of their interpretations or meanings, it becomes essential to get at the actors' meanings in order to understand and explain their conduct. However, it needs to be recognized that no amount of simply observing behavior from the outside will provide an understanding of actors' views of their social world, and hence an understanding of their conduct. (Manis and Meltzer 1978, pp. 6–9.)

The foregoing set of propositions of symbolic interaction theory by Manis and Meltzer describe images of human behavior, the social setting within which such behavior occurs and the relationship between human behavior and its social settings.

SIGNIFICANCE FOR GROUP WORK

The nature of human interaction is determined by internal factors, such as self-perception based on past experiences, thoughts and fantasies. It is also determined by environmental variables, as for example prevailing attitudes and beliefs on race relations over which individuals have very little control. Ethnic minorities of color often are stigmatized by the dominant society as inadequate and content with their inferior status. The labeling of a group of individuals as deviant is caused by the larger society's inability to support alternate value systems that are in conflict with the dominant values and norms. Although in group work the influence of environmental factors have been recognized, there is minimal evidence of how interventions implemented within the professional context have taken these factors into account. Frequently the pressure for conformity leads to the individual's development of a marginal social identity, and interventions are directed to overcome this marginal identity without taking into account the factors which contributed to this development.

A major theoretical concept of symbolic interaction is social process which has significance in understanding the interplay between individuals and their environment. Humans as intelligent and self-conscious beings are viewed as constantly changing through interaction with their environment. Their collective actions can affect the structural elements of society, which in turn, brings about changes in role relationships. From this perspective, process is a dynamic idea which assumes an action-oriented concept of society. Process and actions constantly create, support and alter person-roles in society as, for example, the changing roles of ethnic minorities and women in an institutional context.

The concept of reference groups based on symbolic interaction perspective also has a great deal of relevancy for present-day group work. Shibutani (1978) has defined a reference group as

> that group whose outlook is used by the actor as the frame of reference in the organization of his perceptual field. . . . Of greatest importance for most people are those groups in which they participate directly— what have been called membership groups—especially those containing a number of persons with whom one stands in a primary relationship. But in some transactions one may assume the perspective attributed to some social category—a social class, an ethnic group, those in a given community, or those concerned with some special interest (p. 111).

Reference groups may be perceived as an audience consisting of real or imaginary members. It is an audience before whom individuals attempt to retain or enhance their standing. In discussing the relationship between individuals and their groups, Sherif (1967) stated

> that human interaction in a pattern of reciprocities is not the same as the behavior of the same individual in isolation. As a rule, the actual behavior of the person is not what he might have done in isolation, but what he does as affected, modified, and even transformed within a pattern of reciprocities in which he has a particular place (p. 20).

Individuals hold simultaneous membership in different groups. Mills (1967) has indicated that in our society each individual belongs on an average to five or six groups. The group worker, to understand the meaning of a member's interaction within the group context has to have an appreciation of the various reference groups to which the member belongs, and also the nature of his/her membership. For example, John Davis, a married man with two sons, an architect, is a member of a therapy group in the local mental health clinic. He is very active in the local chapter of the American Society of Architects and is the treasurer of that group. He is on the Board of Directors of the Little League, which he helped to organize in his community. He is also an active member of the choir group of his church, and along with his wife, is a regular member of a bridge group. Whatever John's problems are that brought him to treatment, knowledge about his membership in various groups provides the worker with a sense of his competence in many different areas. Subsequent to this data the next step for the worker would be to explore the quality and meaning attributed by John to these relationships.

Symbolic interaction has heuristic value in providing a methodology for understanding member behavior and analysis of the group process. For example, arriving late for a group session could have a number of meanings for a member, such as "I am sufficiently high-powered that I can come and go as I please," or "I am really angry with this group and that is why I am arriving late," or "I have other important things in life than just coming on time for this group." The member's late arrival and the ways it is perceived by other group members will be a determining factor in how they relate to him (Sampson and Marthas 1977, pp. 135–136).

Another implication of symbolic interaction theory to group work is that the meaning for one's behavior is a result of their interaction with others. Meaning does not exist prior to or separate from one's interaction with others. Meaning emerges through interaction in small groups. As discussed earlier, the meaning of behavioral characteristics of individuals are better understood as aspects of social interaction. The others confirm or refute the behavioral patterns in question. The following examples of group interaction clarifies this proposition.

> One member of the group seems to lack initiative; he always waits for others to take the lead and get things going. Our response is to ignore him, let him remain silent, and to take on the initiative ourselves.
>
> In another group, one member always seems to be the scapegoat, the butt of everyone's jokes or anger. Whatever group she enters, people automatically give her this scapegoat identity. People resent any efforts she makes to change from being the scapegoat.
>
> A group of recent cardiac patients contains one man who complains that since his attack he feels that there is little reason for him to go on living; he can't do any of the activities he used to do, especially around

the house, where he has become almost a helpless invalid because everyone does everything for him.

In each of these examples, we have one person who seems to possess a particular characteristic or a consistent way of behaving: a passive man without initiative; a scapegoat; a helpless invalid. It is easy for us to attribute this characteristic to something within the person. So we come to think of the man as "being" passive, as lacking any initiative, perhaps even as being a bit ignorant or uncaring. We think of the scapegoat as having "the kind of personality" that grates on others' nerves, as someone who deserves to be ridiculed and joked about. We think of the cardiac patient as being a helpless invalid, as one who has no contribution to make and so must be totally cared for. According to the symbolic interactionist model, what we have failed to consider in each case are the ways in which the person's behavior has its meaning confirmed through the actions of others, how others' responses establish the person's characteristics.

Remember, it is the responses of others that complete the social act initiated by the person's gestures and which thereby render it meaningful. Thus the man in the first example does not have the passive qualities independent of the ways others treat him. If his behavior lacks initiative and he seems to be passive, we must examine the ways in which the responses of others help confer this meaning. Indeed, other people's response of ignoring him and taking on the initiative themselves clearly helps to sustain his identity as one without initiative. Likewise, the cardiac patient is not a helpless invalid nor the woman a scapegoat without others in the setting (e.g., the family, the group) to confirm these characteristics. (Sampson and Marthas, pp. 139–140).

Another key concept of symbolic interaction theory for group work is self-identity. A person's identity refers to his/her perception of who he/she is, the self-concept as a social object. Identity not only locates a person in a social world of other persons, but it also involves roles and action that place them within a social network. Identity formation of individuals is an ongoing process constantly influenced by their significant others. It is in this context that the process occurring in groups can be analyzed along the symbolic interactionist frame of reference, which will give an understanding for the worker of how particular members are perceived by their fellow members. Perception of others can be effectively used in assisting the individual member to gain understanding and awareness of themselves.

This perspective emphasizes the individuals' functioning within and across differential role sets in a group. For example, counterdependent aggressive suggestions from others can be viewed as an attack on self-esteem. Rather than acquiescing to the implied threat, an angry counterattack preserves, for the moment, the self-image of the defender rather than the victim. From the vantage point of the worker, attention to the specific exchanges between the defender and aggressor roles provide insight into the group process. The worker also has a stake in the situation, as a participating "self". These three roles—members, worker, and significant others—evaluated on the basis of role expectations and actions are an example of the analytic utility of the symbolic interaction perspective. The application of this perspective in understanding group process including member behavior is presented in the following record (Greene, 1979).

Excerpt from the Eighth Session

Date: Wednesday, August 19, 1978
Time: Approximately 6:45 p.m.
Setting: Mental Health Institution operated under state auspices.
Subsetting: Group Therapy Room in the outpatient building. This is an outpatient group therapy session with five group members in addition to the group worker.

Group Members:

1. Kevin. age: early 40's, slender, blonde hair, approximately 5'10", married, white, male; employed in a gas station; in the group in order to overcome fear of heights and to control temper.

2. Tony. age: early 50's, heavy set, dark hair, approximately 6'1", married, white male; retired heavy-equipment operator, in the group due to anxiety, depression, insomnia, excessive anger and poor interpersonal relationships.

3. Steve. age: middle 40's, average build, 5'8", white male, married; employed as an accountant, in the group due to anxiety, depression, difficulties in decision making and tolerating stressful situations.

4. Bill. age: middle 50's, slightly obese, approximately 6'1", white male, married, retired on disability, previously employed in electronics, in the group due to anxiety and depres-

---

sion related to family problems and difficulty accepting disabilities and retirement.

5. *Jim.* age: middle 60's, slender, approximately 5'11", white male, married; employed for past 25 years as automobile salesman and approaching retirement in the near future; in the group due to anxiety and depression related to family problems and coming retirement.

6. *George.* age: 31, average build, 6'0", white, male, single; M.S.W., experienced group worker.

Background:

The group sessions are held once a week on Wednesday evenings from 6:00–7:30 p.m. All the group members are outpatients having had brief periods of hospitalization at one time or another. The group members come to the sessions to discuss problems they have been having and in the process receive feedback, support, or confrontation from the group members and the worker. Also, group members make therapeutic contracts for specific personal change whenever they so desire.

Group Norms:

Informal, individual self-disclosure, some risk taking, high degree of mutual trust and support.

Prior to this interaction the group members had been taking turns discussing what positive changes they had made during the previous week. After doing this the worker asked the group if anyone had anything specific they wanted to do for themselves during this particular meeting. Kevin then spoke up.

Actual Process Units (U)	*Interpretation of Process Units (What the Interactant is Really Saying)*
U1: *Kevin.* I have a couple of things I need to get off my chest.	I'll feel better after sharing some experiences and/or feelings with you.

Actual Process Units (U)

U2: *George.* How will you feel after you get them off?	What is your purpose for doing this?
U3: *Kevin.* Well, I feel bad about one of the situations. It's one of those that you don't look for but you can find yourself in. I didn't react the way I might have reacted 4 or 5 months ago.	I didn't really have much time to decide how to respond. I responded differently than I normally would have and I am not sure I did the right thing.
U4: *George.* So how will you feel after you share with the group by getting this off your chest?	You still have not stated your purpose clearly.
U5: *Kevin.* I think I'll feel better by letting them experience the way I handled it. I feel bad about it in a way. But I'll feel better by sharing it with the group.	I am ambivalent about the way I handled the situation. I feel good about it in a way and bad about it in a way. I hope to resolve these ambivalent feelings by sharing it with the group.
U6: *George.* Anything you want from the group specifically?	What do you really think you need to resolve these ambivalent feelings?
U7: *Kevin.* I want some feedback.	I want the group members to tell me whether I did the right thing or not.
U8: *Kevin.* First, on the positive side. I'm continuing to work on headaches and fear of heights. George has helped me with this. My headaches are better and I'm taking less medication than before. Hopefully, the headaches are diminishing and I'll overcome that. Now for the situation I found myself in yesterday. I went to the grocery store to cash a check and the store has a policy that you can't cash a check there unless you buy something. A man in line in front of me was asked by the young woman who approves checks if he was going to purchase something. He immediately blew his top saying, "Goddammit, I trade here all the	I am asking some definite changes that I do feel good about. I am more in control of a part of my life that I previously did not have any control over. So, even if you think I mishandled the situation I'm getting ready to tell you about, at least you won't think of me as a totally inadequate person.

61

time and I don't need to buy
anything." He was cussing up a
storm. I felt sorry for the young
girl. I purposely kept my back
to him at first and finally turned
around and looked at him. This
guy was really overbearing. I
could've really called him some
names. Four or five months ago
I probably would have said
something just to get him to
take a swing at me. And he was
bigger than me but I used to
never worry about that. But I
felt like pounding the hell out
of him. Knock him down and
kick the hell out of him. And
I'm still angry about not doing it.
I'd like some feedback on this.
I didn't say anything (*to the
guy*). The guy turned around
and saw me looking at him. So
the girl approved his check
and then he immediately left.

I did not approve of the way this guy
was behaving. I wanted to do something about it but didn't know
what to do.
In the past I knew what to do and
would have done it.

In the past I knew that I was a
brave person. When I was angry
at someone, I was not afraid to
tell them.
I'm still a brave person. I wasn't
afraid of the guy. I just wasn't
sure that my former way of responding was the best way. This
time I chose to do just the opposite
and not say anything to him.

U9: *George.* Is there anything
about this incident that you
are feeling good about?

Are you feeling good in any way
about choosing to experiment with
responding in a manner different
from the past?

U10: *Kevin.* I guess I'm feeling
good that I didn't blow my
stack. Now this is where
Tony comes in.
(*He is addressing Tony, a
member of the group who also
has much difficulty controlling
his temper.*)

I feel good knowing that I can be
in control of myself despite my
strong feelings. If I can do it,
so can you, Tony. It is possible.

U11: *Tony.* Kind of hard to stand to
take that stuff. . .

I would have trouble controlling
myself in that situation.

U12: *Kevin.* (*interrupting Tony*)
Well, it really wasn't any of
my business. I'm not a police
officer.

By looking at the situation in this
manner (which is a different way
of viewing it), I can rationally
analyze my response and more
easily control myself in the future.

U13: *Tony.* You hate to see someone abused who is innocent.

I'm not so sure I'm going to accept
your rationalization.

Actual Process Units (U)	Interpretation of Process Units (What the Interactant is Really Saying)
U14: *Kevin.* I really felt sorry for for the girl.	It was not easy for me not to say something and take up for the cashier.
U15: *Tony.* Whenever I'm in a situation like that, its hard for me to keep my mouth closed too.	I don't rationally analyze situations like that and I know how you must have felt.
U16: *Kevin.* I found out, I couldn't, hardly do it—but I did and I don't know whether I did it to . . . I mean it made me feel like a coward or something, in that respect.	With great effort I changed one of the problem behaviors that I wanted to change in group therapy and the end result is loss of self-esteem. If I received some compliments for my change, my self-esteem will be restored.
U17: *Tony.* Yeah, you would want that man to say something to you. That's the way I feel about it, even though it's not your responsibility or your place.	I'm starting to realize that there were alternative ways to respond and to view the situation.
U18: *Kevin.* I don't know, I guess I didn't look too good when he turned around and looked at me, because he just picked up his money, turned around, and left. I never said a word. I decided I'd just look at him. I felt like this wasn't the type of character you could say, "Hey, you're getting out of line."	I gave the man a reason and opportunity to say something to me.

My assessment of this guy was that if I had said something first there really would've been a fight. So if there was going to be a fight between us, he would have to initiate it. |
U19: *Steve.* It took a lot of strength not to say something.	I think you did the right thing and you are not a coward but a person of strength who is in control of himself. So here's the feedback you wanted.
U20: *Bill.* Do you want my positive feedback?	I'm not so sure you really want to hear that what you did was right. Is this what you want to hear?
U21: *Kevin.* Yes, I do.	I really do want to feel good about what I did.
U22: *Bill.* I see, I recognize the change in you.	I can tell that you have changed for the better since coming into the group.

Actual Process Units (U)	Interpretation of Process Units (What the Interactant is Really Saying)
U23: *Tony.* I want to say I admire you for being able to control yourself.	I think what you did was quite an accomplishment and a change like this is a desirable goal for me.
U24: *Kevin.* I appreciate that. I look forward to the day when one of you can tell me the same thing that you acted the same way (*pause*), Tony. (*All the group members then laughed.*)	I am no longer feeling ambivalent about how I responded to the guy and I now have my positive self-esteem back. And now that I know that what I did was OK, I want you, Tony, to have a similar goal and when you accomplish it you can have the positive experience I had by sharing it with the group.
U25: *Steve.* Tony, you told us recently about how you handled a situation differently.	(Steve coming to Tony's rescue.) Don't be so self-righteous, Kevin. I'm not going to let you, Tony, off the hook because you have already proven that you can change and exercise control.
U26: *Kevin.* Yes, I had forgotten about that.	I don't want to discount your achievement, Tony.
U27: *George.* So you have handled some things differently, haven't you, Tony?	I want to reinforce your accomplishments.
U28: *Tony.* Oh yeah, definitely.	Thanks for the recognition.
U29: *George.* I want to check something out with you, Kevin, about your asking for feedback. Sometimes when people ask for feedback, the hidden message is, "I want to hear feedback that agrees with the decision I've already made about what I did."	Were you already feeling good about what you did but not going to trust your feelings and assessment until you received verification from others?
U30: *Kevin.* The thing is, I don't know whether I made the right decision or not.	I wasn't sure whether I was justified in feeling good.
U31: *George.* What kind of feedback were you really wanting?	Were you wanting to feel good about what you did?
U32: *Kevin.* Really, I guess I was wanting what I got.	I really did want to feel good about handling that type of situation differently, not feel angry and like a coward.
U33: *George.* OK.	

At this point, Kevin went around to each one in the group giving them positive feedback about changes they had made. Then the focus moved to a different person and a different problem.

From the above illustration it appears to be clear that Kevin came to the group session with an intention to check out with fellow group members his previous day's experience. The worker seemed to have his own notion about Kevin's intention or purpose to participate in the group session. But he did not intervene based on his implicit understanding, but rather focused on the present. Although he was confrontive, this was again in the context of the present, and focused on Kevin's needs and requirements from the group (Process Units 1–7). This worker strategy encouraged Kevin to self-disclose and share his experiences with the group.

In Unit 9 the worker raised an exploratory question to reinforce Kevin's examination of his behavior. This intervention not only facilitated Kevin's self-evaluation, but he was able to transfer a new meaning of his behavior to a fellow group member, Tony. Subsequently, Tony began to appraise his own self, (Process Units 10–18).

In the Process Units 19–25, it is evident how the group members play the role of significant others in giving positive feedback to Kevin and in return he becomes the significant other for Tony. This process also exemplifies the interplay and fusion between personal identity and social identity. Kevin began to have more positive feeling about his own behavior (personal identity), and when this was confirmed by his fellow group members (social identity), he shifted his role in the group situation from that of a receiver to a giver (Unit 25).

The worker retreated to the position of a silent but attentive audience (Units 9–28). But when it became evident to him that Kevin was quite open and secure about changes in himself, the worker confronted Kevin with the original perception about his intent for this revelation in the group (Unit 30). This reconfirmed for Kevin the emergence of a desired self in the social situation of treatment.

Consistent with the symbolic interactionist perspective, the worker focuses on processes in the immediate present which lay the groundwork for purposive self-evaluation in the presence of attentive significant others. The emergence of the desired self in the social situation of the group is demonstrated in the shift from personal identity to social identity. The transfer of meaning inherent in the role transition is consummated when the actor reverts from receiver to giver—and assumes the role of a significant other for fellow group members. This approach can be utilized in appraising the role performance of members in action and structure appropriate interventions to facilitate the resolution of the members' concern.

LEWINIAN FIELD THEORY

Field theory emerged out of a new conception of reality spurred by bold and innovative developments in the physical sciences. In contrast to Newtonian mechanics which stressed the simple cause-effect relationships between two events or particles, field theorists maintained that "the distribution of forces in a given environment determine what an object with certain properties will do in that environment," (Deutsch, 1968, p. 413). As employed in the social sciences, the assumption is that "the properties of any event are determined by its relation to the system of events of which it is a component," (Ibid., p. 414).

The field theoretical notions developed in the latter part of the nineteenth century served as a springboard for Lewin's ideas (1936, 1951). The basic proposition underlying Lewin's approach was that behavior was a function of the person and his environment. Behavior of every kind, such as thinking, striving and the like, was considered the product of a field of interdependent and resonating events. The totality of the field at one point in time was conceptualized by Lewin as the life space or psychological environment. The relevant elements in a person's life space were those that were experientially significant to the individual. Hence, to understand a person or group, one must of necessity understand the subjective world as the individual perceives it. In addition, events in the "here and now" take precedent over the past and the future. This is not to say that past events and future expectations are unimportant, but that their effects are more indirect. While all three perspectives, past, present and future, are considered, the present is by far the most important in reference to a person's behavior.

Lewin used a number of dynamic concepts such as tension, valence, force, barriers, region, and paths to further explicate his idea of motivation. The person-environment matrix may consist of a number of regions which may refer to activities, thoughts, ideas, places, etc., and which may be located internally within the person or externally in the social environment. For example, in the context of an athletic event, two major regions in the life space of adolescent boys might be the press of the activity itself and its demands, together with the skill-abilities of each of the players. The connection between the sport and the boys which produces some sort of regulated behavior is called the path. Sometimes the connection between any two regions is not evident, as for example, when a group cannot figure out how to deal with a particular problem. In this case, one may postulate that there are barriers to solutions, which are, for that moment in the group's life, unseen. The extent to which a group or person responds or strives toward a particular activity (a region in itself) characterizes the idea of valence, which has also been described as the combining power of an element. The concept of valence is intimately related to concepts of tension, force, and locomotion. The interrelations are discussed by Deutsch and Krauss (1965) in the following way.

> Lewin states that a system in a state of tension exists within a person whenever a psychological need or an intention (sometimes referred to as a quasi need) exists. Tension is released when the need or intention is fulfilled. Tension has certain conceptual properties: (1) it is the state of a region that tries to change itself in such a way that it becomes equal to the state of its surrounding regions, and (2) it involves forces at the boundry of the region in tension. A 'positive valence' is conceived as a field in which the forces are all pointing toward a given region of the field (the valent region that is the center of the force field), whereas all the forces point away from a region of 'negative valence.' The construct 'force' characterizes the direction and the strength of the tendency to change at a given point of the life space. Change may occur either by a locomotion (a change in position) of the person in his psychological environment, or by a change in the structure of his perceived environment (p. 38).

Tensions or felt needs (real or imagined) provide the source of energy, but attainment of a goal and, release of tension, requires a connecting point (path) to an activity or object which is available for satisfaction. Locomotion toward the goal-object requires both thinking and doing.

Implicit in the notion of life space, regions, tension and the like are a set of other characteristics which are akin to a systems perspective. For example, interdependence, dynamic balance among elements, and the steering function of feedback among system parts and the whole are consistent with a systems framework. In essence, it appears that the internal world of the individual or group represents the gestalt of the person and his environment. What fuels the system is conflict or tension which is a constant among and between the parts and the whole.

A system in balance represents a dynamic equilibrium between internal (person) and external (environment) pushes and pulls. In a group, this would be reflected in the opposition between individual versus group demand. Barriers to a solution, such as when choices for alternative actions are not available to the group, produce discomfort and conflict since the ambiguities tend to increase among the part–whole relationships. For Lewin, the general approach, as in action research, was to utilize the scientific method of inquiry for arriving at intelligent, informed decisions.

One of the features of Lewin's thinking is the concept of overlapping situations. In commonsense terms, this refers to a person's overlapping membership in various referent groups which in fact, may be a source of tension (for example, John Davis illustration). The imbalances faced in role conflicts constitute one of the driving forces in group life. The method of inquiry as an approach to greater choices and alternatives sets in motion a reconceptualization of various roles, that completed assumes a vitality of its own. The process does not stop, of course, since the imbalancing and tensions among a number of regions (internal and external) constantly provide the impetus for change.

LEWINIAN CHANGE PRINCIPLES

Underpinning the principles and based on the field theoretical perspective is the assumption that change must affect the person's thought-feeling-actions. In any circumstance, the "whole" person must become involved in the process. Principles of change as delineated by Benne (1976) are helpful in understanding the operation of Lewinian Field theory.

1. The processes governing the acquisition of the normal and abnormal are fundamentally alike.

Implicit in this principle is the idea that processes described as pathological may well be necessary aspects of personal growth. The arbitrary distinction between normal and abnormal tends to overlook the reasonable expression of idiosyncratic responses to particularly stressful circumstances. Acting-out adolescents in a disintegrated neighborhood are not necessarily pathological. In fact, these responses are quite likely survival-specific and essential, given the options.

2. The reeducative process has to fulfill a task which is essentially equivalent to a change in culture.

Changes in culture mean changes in expectations. Individuals and groups are more likely to alter their behavior when conditions of safety and experimentation are present. Member changes in groups are often resisted by close associates outside the group, who would prefer the status quo. In this instance the cultural change is incomplete because expectations in two different and related contexts are at cross-purposes.

3. Even extensive firsthand experience does not automatically create correct concepts (knowledge).

Effective change emphasizes the actual experiences of new principles of learning through human efforts at constructing a new reality. The spirit and method of inquiry, which are the best that we have to arrive at something called the "truth," must accompany change processes. Feelings, perceptions, values, and commitments of participants comprise the data to be processed in applying the method of inquiry.

4. Social action no less than physical action is steered by perception.

Lewin's emphasis on perception, particularly as it is embedded and expressed in the person's assumptive world is a focal point for change. Alterations in the way a person perceives himself and the situation are necessary correlates to learning. In social work groups, the use of feedback and authentic expressions of concern are two of the benchmarks for change. In addition, to the extent that a group member can direct positive sentiments toward other members and the group as a whole, the propensities for self-modification increase. Implicit in this principle is the application of sensitizing experiences for social action, which is consistent with Lewin's interest in both the person and the environment.

5. As a rule, the possession of correct knowledge does not suffice to rectify false perceptions.

This principle underscores the point that the laws governing perceptual, cognitive and affective processes are not necessarily the same. As a result, the "whole" person must be involved in any collaborative efforts toward problem solving. Forming a "protective envelope" in groups encourages the active exploration and alteration of charged areas in a person's life and emphasizes the validity of precognitive levels of experience. For example the worker and the group can suggest realistic options, which a member accepts, but does not believe.

6. Incorrect stereotypes (prejudices) are functionally equivalent to wrong concepts (theories).

Habitual beliefs are accompanied by an explanation as to the correctness of their existence. Only experiences which command the complete involvement of the person can lead to giving up of an original set of ideas and behaviors. In groups, concensual validation by other members work to produce enough ambivalence so that a person might question previously held and important notions. Self-experimentation and persistent application of self-inquiry and self-observational processes in the public culture of the group are the necessary steps toward releasing encumbering modes of behavior.

7. Changes in sentiments do not necessarily follow changes in cognitive structures.

This principle refers to the independence, noted earlier between processes of changing cognition and those related to action. The separation and compartmentalization between actual and ideal behavior or feelings may, indeed, produce more discomfort (as for example, a guilty conscience), which also acts to postpone appropriate conduct. The antidote to this division in the assumptive and behavioral world is personal involvement in facing and acting upon choices that pose alternatives to previously undesirable actions or value sets. To put it succinctly, the more that authentic feelings are invested in a problem, the more likely changes of a person's actions will follow. Hence, public actions must be in touch with private feelings and not sealed off from the reality of life in the group.

This principle also entertains a number of ideas and concepts that are most attractive. The norms of a reeducative group must include those embedded in the method of inquiry and participation in framing problems and working out solutions, open and honest communication, and subjecting ideas and hesitancies to empirical test. Others may be posited as well, such as focus on the psychological present, esprit de corps, norms favoring innovation and novelty, egalitarianism, and authenticity (Miles, 1968). The development and utilization of these norms underlie the use of a group

70

approach by which individuals alter their thought-feeling-actions. In addition, members begin to address their work in the group as entailing reduction of tensions which emerge out of role conflicts, real or imagined, that present themselves out of their membership in various other groups. This issue speaks to the point of overlapping group membership and neatly summarizes the breadth of potential experiences necessary if one is to traverse the individual–societal continuum in the group. This is an important point because the group members must incorporate into their private culture those requirements for satisfactory participation in the relevant societal world around them. It would seem that the fabric of the group culture, apart from the facilitative and scientific norms mentioned earlier, must include experiences that may have input for member roles outside the groups such as citizen, volunteer and the like. Of course not every group experience has to meet all of these requirements that together form a platform for adaptation to the broader society.

It seems reasonable to state that the problems members contract to work on in groups include relationships that extend beyond their intra- and interpersonal sphere. This suggests that current issues of racism, sexism, and the like, apparent and potent in the broader relevant society, require some attention for both members and professionals (Balgopal and Vassil, 1979). In this way, the enculturation process begins to incorporate and address the individual–societal continuum.

8. Acceptance of a new set of values and beliefs cannot usually be brought about item by item.

In contrast to approaches that focus either on skill training or sensitivities to feelings, or even to cognitive restructuring, if one is to consider changes in all three areas, it would require a growth principle that encompasses and orders the configurational gestalt of thought-feeling-actions. This is consistent with the principle of alteration of the three components as being invested in the same process, even though the laws governing each may be different. This leads to the tentative proposition that changes in each of the three areas may represent complete acts in and of themselves. But it is by moving back and forth between thinking-feeling-doing that a principle for change underlying all three may be incorporated. The presentation of these types of possibilities simply confirms the generative and imaginative qualities of the field theoretical perspectives as developed by Lewin.

SIGNIFICANCE FOR GROUP WORK

Systems and phenomenological approaches are blended in the foundation of field theory. The method of inquiry is viewed as an essential tool in changing the psychological life space of individuals or groups who are motivated to do so. Implicit in the Lewinian view is the point that change requires alterations of cultures that persons are bound to. These cultures, in turn, may traverse the individual-societal continuum as experienced by persons, for example in groups. Change processes described by Lewin as the unfreezing, shifting, and refreezing of forces that oppose and balance each other in a dynamic equilibrium are directed toward recalibration of cognitive-affective and action behaviors. Learning or growth is reflected in changes between and among the part–whole relationships. The consistency of changes depend on comprehending and acting on the underlying assumptions or models gleaned through the change process.

Lewinian Field Theoretical concepts are further implicated in group work by analyzing the key process components in the outpatient group session presented earlier.

The participation patterns of the members demonstrated that an image of the group as a group has been formed. Based on process comments between and among Kevin, the members and the worker, norms that describe group level sentiments include perceptions of safety, trust, agreement to listen, willingness to risk self-disclosure, and mutual respect. In addition, a measure of ambivalence was manifested through Kevin's possible setting-up (manipulating) the group members to tell him what he wanted to hear. This is an example of negative valence in that there are oppositional sentiments between the individual and the group. These oppositional sentiments are also shared by other members. For example, despite the workers' attempt to explore Kevin's ambivalence, no other member was willing to pursue the topic. This suggests that despite a supportive, empathic and risk-inducing climate, members are still cautious and guarded with respect to open confrontation. To the extent that their personal life space is still protected, work still remains to be done to "help unfreeze" this negative dynamic. The worker astutely recognizes this norm and backs off from promoting member confrontation at this time. Had he not done so, the members' discomfort may have polarized the group into a self-protective unit.

Another feature that connects the internal processes of the group with external behavior may be conceptualized as the issue of overlapping roles. Kevin acted so as to alter his previous public behavior, which formerly would have resulted in a heated clash with someone he perceived as overly antagonistic. The reenforcements and support he received in the group for thinking first about the consequences of his behavior before acting, suggests that, in Lewin's term, he had reconceptualized the problematic situation. At this point, despite some ambivalence, Kevin's self-righteous behavior has been contained. At the group level Kevin's sharing of his modified behavior serves as a model for other members to emulate.

MEAD AND LEWIN: A COMPLEMENTARY PERSPECTIVE

The work of Lewin and Mead is instructive in clarifying and articulating the connections between part–whole relationships in groups, as for example, with concepts such as roles and norms. The conception of self-development in and through primary and secondary groups was a central theme for both Lewin and Mead. Processes of cognition and perception were emphasized as they were manifested in the context of contemporaneous circumstances as individuals sought to orient their activities to events that they faced or anticipated. The existential moment also meant a psychological fusion between the past and the future, consistent with their ahistorical focus. Adaptation over time, a major organizing theme in the ecological perspective, complements the Lewin and Mead formulations by adding a developmental perspective for group work practitioners, that enhances the holistic approach common to these orientations.

Private, unconscious, affective components are not excluded in the thinking of Lewin and Mead although they have been less emphasized. Manis and Meltzer (1978) pointed out that

> Present-day symbolic interactionists have followed Mead in overlooking the role of the emotional component in human behavior and interaction. The affective aspects of the self, personal relationships, and large-scale social phenomena are so thoroughly ignored, except in consideration of "emotional contagion," in the area of collective behavior, as to suggest an unacceptable image of human beings as purely rational. In partial extenuation of this oversight, however, has been an occasional concern with the sentiments, those emotions which Cooley characterized as entailing sympathy, or role-taking. Thus, Erving Goffman and Edward Gross and Gregory P. Stone have analyzed embarrassment, Kurt Riezler has written on shame, and Cooley's concern with self centered upon self-feeling. It is nonetheless true of symbolic interactionists, as of most other social psychologists, that they have given scant attention to such emotions as love, hate, anger, joy, and sorrow (pp. 438–439).

With respect to the unconscious domain, Manis and Meltzer (1978) stated that

> Closely related to the preceeding stricture is another that concerns scanting of the irrational aspect in human behavior. It is difficult to find a considered discussion of the unconscious in the writings of the symbolic interactionists. The few references tend to renounce the concept without substituting adequate explanation. There is no reason to assume that the perspective cannot accommodate unconscious phenomena, obdurate though they may be. Just as different levels of awareness are recognized for symbolic interaction and nonsymbolic interaction, so can they be recognized for conscious and unconscious (as well as subliminal) processes of behavior (p. 439).

Cartwright's (1959) presentation of Lewinian theory takes into account internal processes. Quoting Leeper, he noted

> The question is therefore, whether we should define cognitive processes, perception, thinking, concept formation and the like in terms of *conscious* processes, exclusively, or whether we should say that consciousness may be present or absent, as the case may be, and that all these processes are to be defined in terms of these other functional relations.
>
> It seems better, therefore, to avoid norm definitions and to say that cognitive processes include all the means whereby the individual represents anything to himself or uses these representations as a means of guiding his behavior (p. 68).

Internal needs and tension states represent Lewin's concern with the internal dynamics of personality. He used the concept of valence, which refers to a unique and differential attachment to the "field of action" as a way of signifying the connections between a need and the context in which it took place. This connection is a useful bridge to understanding group-relevant aspects of personality.

Lewin's work was centered on the individual and his relationship within the life space. Emphasizing the intentional and purposive aspects of group, the field of focus includes not only relevant aspects within primary or secondary groups, but also the particular environment within which the group was located. For Lewin, the way a person subjectively perceived the "life space" in which he/she was enmeshed was an appropriate target for study and action.

Mead's point of departure was social interaction. Persons in interaction with one another constructed an emergent reality which was fashioned by overt as well as nonverbal behavioral actions such as body movements, facial expressions, tone of voice and so forth. These activities resulted in a definition of the situation within which meanings were attributed and expressed. Meanings include cognition, valuations, and feelings, both private and public. These processes were manifested through role taking, which shapes a self-identity based on how one perceives and responds to communication emitted from significant others, which is incorporated into the term, the "generalized others," or "community of attitudes" (Turner, 1974 p. 155).

According to Dunphy (1972), "The generalized other becomes the basis of the individual self and is the means by which the individual incorporates external reality into his own developing patterns of behavior" (pp. 11-12). The concept of the generalized other suggests a more inclusive social interactional field than Lewin's concept of the field which has been used to sharply demarcate the gestalt of the group in concepts such as "atmosphere", "climate" and so forth. However, it is possible to utilize the concept of "typical" members in a group as a special case of the more general "generalized others" as a way of articulating group relevant sentiments. In terms of generalized others as referring to reference groups, Lewin's concept of overlapping group memberships as potent forces for behavior appears to be a way of explicating the potency of referent groups into the group sphere. In this analysis, it would seem that there are at least two "fields" for consideration in small groups, the person's subjective perception of the group life space, and the more inclusive social interactional field (Bales and Cohen, 1979).

For both Lewin and Mead, the emphasis was on how, rather than why, a person does what he does, which represents a different shift from personality theories accounting for person behavior in groups. That is not to say that theories of understanding "why" persons respond in the way they do are not feasible. In point of fact, assessment of role patterns and content may produce insights into the affective and private world of the individuals from which the dynamics of group relevant aspects of personality can be formulated or articulated with other theoretical models (Stock and Thelen, 1958). Society and the self, for both Lewin and Mead, are connected through the group processes. The group relevant aspects of functioning, which includes the private and public worlds of thoughts, feelings and actions, real or imagined, are rooted in transactional processes which may provide pathways for developing a social psychology of human dynamics that is in harmony with an ecological orientation. Mead's theorizing, especially in its role-taking aspects lends itself to specificity in terms of action and paves the way for descriptions and assessment of problems based on role functioning or dysfunctioning. Lewin's concept relative to the life space or gestalt, which can be interpreted to refer to the group-as-a-whole is more difficult to pin down, but norms can be helpful in delineating different types of "group cultures". For both Lewin and Mead, the interactional processes are always in motion and account for the dynamic aspects of groups. Bonner (1959) stated the complementary and dialectic between Lewin and Mead in the following way:

> The basic concept in this view, whatever terminology is used, is *action-in-a-field*. . . . In the human individual, who always lives in a group, it is *symbolic interaction*. In group behavior it is an *intricate net* of *symbolic interaction*. When the group, finally, is complicated, as it usually is, by cultural demands or expectations, the behavior consists of *sanctioned* forms of symbolic interaction (p. 19).

The upshot of the foregoing suggests that each person in a group has awareness of each and every other person. The awareness entails perceptions of others not only from the self-perspective, but from the perspective of all the others. These form a field that influences member behavior in the sense that they behave "as if" the gestalt is a deciding factor. Hence, the behavior of individuals is determined by the structure of their interrelationships. To understand the various patterns that occur in the group requires an interdisciplinary focus for study that would include psychology, sociology, and cultural anthropology.

Group behavior may be explicated by threading some of the concepts described in the foregoing analysis. Anticipation or expectancy can be related to role perception, which, in turn, leads to role taking. From role perception to role enactment or performance is a small step to more complicated processes of role differentiation, role complimentarity, role conflict and so on. Communication through symbols provides the context from which meanings are elicited and guide action. Bonner summarized the point.

> By virtue of communication, anticipation, role behavior, and symbolic interaction people form common perceptions of one another and of the situation in which they interact. When they see the same object or event in very much the same way, they are able to work in unison toward the same goal. When they have no common perspective, they work at cross purposes, and their relationship is conflictual rather than consensual. Especially clear in this analysis is the role perception-and-enactment function in which each person assumes a clearly structured psychological activity toward the others (p. 37).

From the foregoing comments, the ways for examining part–whole relationships appears to include perception, roles, and norms, the latter concept meant to describe the gestalt of the group, group climate, or group-as-a-whole. The practical import for social group work practitioners is that assessment can be specific with respect to a member's particular role performance problem. Role dysfunctioning, of course, can be an admixture of the strain between ascribed and achieved roles and personality. The alteration of role dysfunctioning may be targeted either in the person's behavior or in significant others in the environment who contribute to the member problem. Attention to member attributes, interaction, and to the social context presupposes no single conception of etiology although the social interactional field is an important point of departure. The work of the group which the worker must address then is based on personal, interpersonal, and social demands. Another important practical point is that the worker is a most important figure in the interactional field, not only as expert, but as member and person among other roles. As a practical matter for assessment, this means that the group at all times represents a mixed reality that continually needs clarity in order to formulate structures and process tasks for work.

4
The Ecology
of
Group Work
Practice

The focus of this chapter is to examine and discuss further, the four key components of group work practice, namely, the individual, the group, the worker and the agency-environment. Each of these is examined separately, followed by a discussion of the transactions among them.

THE INDIVIDUAL

The dynamics of the individual development are best represented by the developmental tasks and issues related to age and process-specific stages of life cycle. Maladaptation is present when persons fail to outgrow the dependent needs of childhood, or to achieve a reasonable compromise between autonomy and discipline, or have inadequate options in the role models with which they identify and so forth. When these latter conditions are coercive and continuous, then the person customarily moves from a citizen to a client role, and thereby becomes eligible for group work services. The individual's problems violate or strain certain pertinent standards and expectations by those who have a stake in the situation. In many cases clients who receive services have virtually no say as to the relevancy or the mode of services offered. It is infrequent that this involuntary status is recognized. Usually they tend to be labeled as resistive and hostile clients. This dynamic is manifested through subtle and nonrational cues transmitted by the worker through a well-intended but limited perceptual screen, as manifested by incidents of institutional racism and sexism.

The crucial variable affecting the individual's induction into the role of client-group member is the manner through which he/she is perceived by the worker, fellow group members and the agency. It has been stressed that the group members seldom voluntarily seek group service through social agencies. The situation is compounded when group workers limit their involvement to formed groups with clients, rather than working with them in their natural groups and settings.

Attention to the involuntary status of the members and how they affect practice has been minimal, although there are exceptions (Briar and Miller, 1971; Yelaja, 1971; Etzioni, 1961). The involuntary induction of individuals into client-member roles is often associated with authoritarian settings. Etzioni has succinctly identified three categories through which processes of involuntary induction are instituted:

1. *Alienative Involvement.* In this category, the members seldom share the worker's values and often are hostile to compliance with agency and worker expectations. Examples of these are inmates in correctional institutions, members in substance abuse programs and children in remedial centers of learning.

2. *Calculative Involvement.* This category encompasses a quid pro quo orientation that is nested within a win-lose situation. The members knowingly permit themselves to be "taken in as members," and in the same process maintain control over the situation. For example, spouses of alcoholics will often "play the game" of group membership in selected treatment programs. In reality they are extremely hesitant to give up their control over their partners. In many ways nonuser spouses are quite facilitative in maintaining the user's drinking pattern.

3. *Moral Involvement.* When there is a complementarity between member and worker expectations, the involvement of the member is manifested in a high degree of cooperation and commitment to mutually shared expectations. Both workers and members are clear of what each has to offer and to work on. According to Etzioni, "Moral involvement designates a

positive orientation of high intensity" (1961, p. 10). Married couples who seek and accept the terms of assistance in the resolution of their marital difficulties illustrate this point.

This raises the general issue of dysfunction, membership, and practice. Several reasons can be posited for a limited perspective on service. In the first place the turmoil of the past two decades brought into question the caretaking and therapeutic functions of social workers who were charged as being agents of social control. The profession's response was to encourage agency and workers to move closer to and into the communities where clients lived. Secondly, humanistic psychology and existential philosophy placed greater emphasis on the active, searching sentiments and a sense of immediacy in a person's life. Each person has not only the right to determine his/her destiny, but also to have access to needed resources. Furthermore it needs to be recognized that individuals are basically creative, industrious, and caring. It is often circumstances beyond their control that force them into unacceptable behavior. A third contributing factor was the overemphasis on and limited suitability of the psychoanalytic mode when applied to social problems. Distinctions between "normal" and "abnormal" had become blurred through the widespread use of analytic metaphors as manifested in the overextension of the illness model. For example, parents whose emotional resources are drained due to chronic illness of their children in inadequately heated homes are not subjects for therapy.

Challenging the stereotypes of clienthood generates the impetus for reexamining and revalidating the uniqueness of the person. Appreciation and sensitivity to limitations imposed on person-capacities which may be buried under an oppressive station in life, cast a new approach to well-being and illness. As was suggested in earlier chapters, a person's satisfaction with life reflects both quantitatively and qualitatively more positive than negative experiences. When there was sufficient continuity and accumulation of good feelings over time, another important increment was added to well-being. In simple terms, two individuals may worry pretty much the same way, but one may be much happier because of his/her involvement with family, friends, and activities.

Individual Capacities

Group members need to be seen first as individuals with inherent capacities for adaptation and change. Our view includes capacities that encompass internal, interpersonal and sociocultural functioning which are consistent with the ecological perspective. Table 4–1 below lists the particular capacities that delineate in more detail the three dimensions noted above. The purpose and the intent of these capacities are to provide workers with benchmarks by which to assess potential skill and abilities of the person and the facilitative or curtailing processes in the habitat which relate to the exercise of these capacities.

Table 4-1: Description and Discussion

Table 4–1 designates a catalogue of person-capacities which refer to "those abilities that the individual may be helped to draw upon . . . in order to deal with his current situation" (Ripple, 1964,

TABLE 4-1.
Member Capacities*

Internal	Inter-Personal	Social
(a) *Cognitive*	Empathy	Role Adaptability
Intelligence	Authenticity	Role Integration
Logical Reasoning	Warmth	Role Embracement
Intellectuality—	Trust	Role Distance
(Ordering, simplifying, and classifying)	Ability to reciprocate	Role Disparity
Planfulness	Social Competence	
Creativity	Flexibility—to be	
Insight & Awareness	assertive, submissive	
Self-identity	or affiliative when	
Anticipation	appropriate	
(b) *Perceptual*	Intimacy and Isolation	
Tolerance of ambiguity		
Openness to new experiences		
Selective Awareness		
Discriminating cues		
(c) *Affective*		
Spontaneity		
Sense of pleasure		
Sense of competence		
Sense of humor		
Sense of optimism		

*Capacities included in the table are drawn from the works of social and behavioral scientists such as Bruner, Erikson, Piaget, White, Leighton, Rogers, Mead and others.

p. 28). Abilities may also be construed as resources that the individual brings to a situation, although the degree to which any are exercised will depend on life patterns and opportunities. Three major dimensions noted in the table are *internal* (or personal), *interpersonal* and *social*. *Internal* represents aspects that are to be viewed from the "skin-in," so to speak. *Interpersonal* refers to relationships between and among individuals, and *social* encompasses person-behaviors or roles that are manifested in wider contexts. The intent of the list is to provide guidelines by which the transactional set between and among the three dimensions can be explicated into a descriptive configurational pattern that presents a picture of the member(s) eligible for group services. How the gestalt relates to the particular problems to be addressed in the group is essential in determining and developing group purposes and goals. Each of the three dimensions will be discussed briefly.

Internal

The internal dimension encompasses cognitive, perceptual and affective states. Cognition is primarily a conscious activity that pertains to "a process of knowing, a getting to know in an idea context rather than simply "perception," which is the sensory part of the process" (Bales and Cohen, 1979, p. 195). Both cognition and perception may be regarded as being located at the "tip" of personality. Affective states include more temporary and short-lived feelings and emotions (joy, fear, anger) which are likely to turn up in many different blends. These are distinct from moods which are more enduring and thematic and not so easily related to specific events. Determinants outside the field of consciousness may affect the exercise of capacities, but group workers are less likely to direct their efforts specifically to inferred unconscious urges.

Cognitive Native intelligence, logicality or reasoning ability and intellectuality may be reasonably assumed to cluster together. Intelligence refers to genetic endowment although environmental conditions surely affect its character. Group work is a valuable tool in enhancing the social and personal functioning of individuals who exhibit impairment of intellectual functioning due to organic brain disorders, brain injury or retardation. Intellectuality refers to abstractional processes such as ordering, classifying and simplifying events. The ability to use the "rules of reasoning" in resolving contradictions or, in simpler terms, to make sense of competing information is referred to as common sense. Putting ideas together in ways that make sense, in ways that are orderly and time-oriented, may be termed planfulness. One observes this in the abilities of individuals to develop goals and specific subgoals or steps needed to complete actions. When individuals get stuck in one groove of thinking about a topic or problem and see no solution in sight, a "time out" period and return to the problem may provide what Bruner (1969) calls an "effective surprise," a fresh solution that may appear obvious only after it has been found. Through some sort of internal process, the "pieces" of the problem have been recombined in a way that structures a solution. Capacities for novelty and flexibility require an ability to play with ideas. The exploratory theme in playfulness is likely to be related to creativity and insight and the logical manifestation of these processes in planning for the future are probably interrelated. Creativity is distinguished from insight in that the latter applies to self-knowledge. These strivings are often within the goal contexts of members and workers in treatment and growth-oriented groups since one important attribute of these groups is to assist the individuals in clarifying their perception of personal assets and liabilities and recalibrating their application in new and acceptable ways.

Anticipation, or looking forward to events has been cited as having a profound influence on human functioning (Leighton, 1959). Anticipation may be positive or negative, accurate or inaccurately perceived depending on other factors in the personality or in the person's life space. Anticipating that one has respect from peers in what one is or does is often a precursor to authentic behavior in group work, particularly to expressing and accepting negative sentiments. When negative feedback is persistent in an environment, then anticipation and imagination are diluted in their potentiating aspects. People who have to continually face the drudgery and frustration of a powerless existence may gravitate to a state of disparagement and the consequences of alienation and anomie. Anticipation is a powerful sentiment that can be revitalized or used for socialization purposes in a variety of groups. Appropriate reality testing is interrelated with anticipation at least in terms of accuracy. For example, excessive expectation can lead to failure, as can continued misplaced efforts to alter circumstances that cannot be modified. A sense of identity suggests both consistency and continuity in the way one knows oneself. Cognitive mapping or "knowledge about the environment in the forms of what-leads-to-what" (Hilgard, 1964, p. 71) refers to a more or less complete representation of the operating characteristics of the real world such as the value systems of which one is a part. Suggested in this concept is an understanding of the gestalt of events that are patterned in meaningful ways and that guide one's behavior. A sense of belonging to something greater than one's self addresses the moral base of one's existence, of being right in what one is or does. An important aspect of recognizing the pathways and topography of one's life is the frame of reference that is used to make these judgments. This, of course, is related to the concept of reality and requires workers to discriminate patterns of behavior based on their context. For example, dropping out of school for youth may well be an acceptable pattern in certain neighborhoods. Yielding to the inevitable in most circumstances may be a sign of flexibility.

Perceptual Perception refers more to sensory processes such as taste, sight, hearing, and so forth which provide trigger mechanisms for other processes. Openness to experience and sensations means that, at the very least, a person is aware of the stimuli (Rogers, 1964). This is an important attribute for group membership if members are to expand their coping repertoires. In that context, and in problem solving efforts in general, it seems reasonable to assume that ambiguity and uncertainty are relative constants. Inability to tolerate uncertainty constricts one's options and narrows a person's world view. Some consider learning for uncertainty a major life task (Jaques, 1970). Whenever old habits, nonrational, rational, or irrational are to be changed, or in instances of lost opportunities or mistakes, a sense of loss of anchoring points needs to be accommodated, a common phenomena present in most of group work practice. Limits to the task, whatever their source, are the initial step that provokes uncertainty and the attendant anxiety that accompanies it. There are other features to uncertainty, of course, such as lack of knowledge about how to proceed, or knowledge of the steps but not of the consequences of the public aspects of the action. The "worry work" that usually accompanies the psychological processes in preparation for problem resolution (major decisions, exams, and so on) is another example of a feature associated with uncertainty.

Selective awareness, or its opposite, selective inattention refers to ignoring things that do not matter and sorting out those that do. Sometimes persons do not attend to significant events for reasons that may or may not be obvious to the individual involved. The psychological dynamic of blocking is an example of this phenomenon. In another instance, groups may assist individuals in knowingly taking on roles that are foreign to their character. For example, adolescents may learn from their "gang" to act "cool" in the face of situations that normally would provoke them. Selective awareness in conjunction with anticipatory socialization is a valuable educative and reeducative tool in group work. Selectively attending to events then may be used for purposes of maintaining security (Sullivan, 1953).

Cues are signals for action and may be blatant or intimated as, for example, when a group worker looks expectantly at a group member for a response to a topical area related to the members' concerns. A person's definition of the situation is often dependent on cues that are emitted back and forth between and among individuals, either verbally or nonverbally, directly or indirectly. The potency of subtle cues affecting participation patterns in interactions has been noted in a study by Duncan (1972) who identified six turn-taking cues such as body movements, tone of voice, facial expression and so forth, that are relevant for smooth interpersonal exchanges. It is not hard to visualize that self-centered persons might have difficulties in discerning these among significant others. Perceptual attributes would appear to be abundantly modifiable, sharpened, or even desensitized as the need may be in group work practice. The definition of the situation, from members and workers' points of view is a perceptual field that encompasses both individual and social realities. Perceptions seem amenable to alternations in groups because they are inseparable from much of what occurs in group participation. In the cognitive-perceptual realm, sensitizing participants to characteristic patterns of responses to self and others creates a formidable set of observation and action skills. These are useful for self-change, for training others, and for inducing social change in organizational contexts through group methods.

Affective The third aspect related to internal sentiments emphasizes feeling states, particularly those that are expressed verbally or nonverbally as reaction to events. Competence at the subjective level refers to pleasure in functioning or a feeling of efficacy, according to White (1963). This feeling is intimately connected to self-esteem which is a product of reflective self-appraisal which leads to self-respect. The sense of satisfaction, inherent to be sure, emerges from doing a task well. Feelings of efficacy, then, are based on self-approval and acceptance.

Spontaneity is more or less a "thrusting out toward new experience" (Leighton, 1959, p. 25), or an urge toward engagement with events and objects outside of one's self. It is probably more of an admixture of cognitive and perceptual processes than simply a feeling state, but it is included here to highlight the sense of unabated urgency that is represented.

The sense of pleasure may be defined as the ability to enjoy one's self, and it also refers to a more enduring state than only temporal satisfaction. Excitement at being associated with valued activity, or expressions of happiness that events are going the way one would like speak to other facets of this attribute, which has also been designated as pleasureable involvement (Beiser, 1974).

Humor has been noted as mature adaptive mechanism by Vaillant (1977). In relationship to other individuals, humor has the quality of producing pleasant affects and often is a vehicle through which uncomfortable situations can be handled. In this context, humor can serve the function of relieving tension. On the negative side, humor can also be used to direct aggressive feelings toward another and create more problems than it solves. The ability to laugh at one's past mistakes is another sign of positive adaptation. Optimism and hope may be synonymous terms manifested in feelings that unexpected events, whatever they may be, will turn out favorably. Hope represents more of a desire and is often accompanied by anticipation and expectations. Feelings of faith in change are marked by individuals' spirituality rather than rationality.

Support and expressions of these attributes among group members are evident to practitioners who have assisted ex-mental patients to plan and implement their initial leisure-time activity in the community; with parents and children who have co-participated in athletic and social events that are an uncommon experience "back home"; or in the planning and implementation of special programs on festive holiday occasions. The importance of these types of activities as they are worked out in small groups are a common occurrence in institutions, community centers, mental health centers, and so forth.

The internal or personal dimensions are representative of what is often meant when professionals speak of meeting personal needs in groups. In any event, the utilization of groups to fulfill personal need has to be based on the curtailing or enhancing processes in the environment.

Interpersonal

Interpersonal relationships in dyads, triads and more extensive forms are ever present in the maturing personality. Self-identity becomes shaped, altered, and validated through continuous interactions with peers and others within and across generations. Empathy, trust, and abilities for mutual give and take are necessary components in developing smooth and relaxed associations throughout life. The more these attributes are constrained, the more difficult it is for individuals to perceive themselves as others see them, and the more self-alienated a person becomes within their own sense of identity. Without adequate capacities for these attributes, it is very difficult for individuals to engage in meaningful relationships with other group members. In such cases, specific group programs that are directed toward training individuals in these abilities may be useful, as for example, with certain patients who exhibit psychotic patterns.

Observations of the ways in which individuals deal with interpersonal sentiments of superiority, subordinancy and egalitarianism provide useful data on group-relevant aspects of the personality, as do expressed or wanted needs for inclusion, control and affection (Schutz, 1958). Social competence entails having an effect on others through engagement in real give and take, and in this regard is different than competence as self-appraisal. White's (1963) conception of social competence, then, refers more to the social origins of the self as they are manifested in acts of receiving and giving help, affection, ideas, opinions and so forth. The ability to love is a very complex idea and in a broad sense, refers to committing one's self to another person or persons. The act of giving love, in an idealistic sense, stems from a position of neither wanting nor seeking a return of favors or "gifts" offered. In practical terms, being "there" when one is needed, engaging others with words, smiles, and actions that convey positive regard are expressions of love. In an existential view, it also means sharing and risking one's humanness in the process, and exposing vulnerabilities which may invite rejection.

Flexibility in interpersonal relationships includes the ability to manifest and shift capacities for closeness, for yielding to others if necessary and also to be dominant if the situation calls for it. One other aspect needs to be considered, namely, being able to tolerate periods of being alone, which Rayner (1978) has noted as "intrinsic to sure self-feelings and integrity" (p. 51). The latter point is closely related to autonomy that is essential for independent judgments. The concept of flexibility should not be construed to mean that any one person ought to have equal proportions of these capacities. There are innumerable blends of these aspects, but taking cognizance of their manifestation, or absence, is useful for assessment and surely appropriate and manageable in group work.

Social

Social functioning, the third major dimension refers to a summary of patterns that have accumulated over a period of time and that are manifested with continuity and sufficiency in day-to-day living. There is the added consideration that the variety, complexity, and quality of person-roles and situations that have been experienced add up to a satisfaction with life. Terms such as role harmony, embracement, integration and adaptability, applied to either a wide range of roles or just a few well-chosen ones, describe a set of sentiments that underpin and guide actions in certain and uncertain situations.

Adaptive social functioning means the utilization and application of an individual's task and affective strivings with friends, family, in the community, and shifting, if need be, along the developmental life arc. It means satisfaction in planning and living one's life in work, with the family and elsewhere, and to achieve many of the things one wants to do. These satisfactions, which must be understood against a background of more positive than negative experiences, also include long-term benefits which are continually manifested in easygoing interpersonal relationships.

Role changes are part and parcel of development over the life trajectory. Young adults, for example, are faced with tasks that include selecting a mate, starting a family, getting started in a career and locating a new congenial social group in the process. In contrast to an adolescent, the young adult must embrace roles such as worker, citizen, taxpayer, parent and provider. With the addition of one child to the family, the number of interrelationships change sharply. Among the most relevant are man-husband-father, woman-wife-mother, and each of these transacting at different levels with the child in dyadic or triadic combinations. It is not hard to visualize additional role engagements with the addition of more children. Family patterns during these years are shaped by decisions regarding economics, childrearing, leisure time, community and marital pairing, particularly as they are manifested in dependent, interdependent, and independent sentiments. In midlife, to extend the example further, the major tasks shift to issues that include the polarities of young/old, destruction/creativity, masculine/feminine, and attachment/separations (Levinson, 1978). These polarities reflect major decisions that lead to a modification of previous roles as man, father, woman, mother, citizen, provider and so forth. In many ways, the midlife transition represents a looking backward and forward.

The thrust of this example is three-fold. In the first place, transitions in life may be accompanied by role shifts. The way that earlier experiences are handled sets the stage for later problem resolutions. These role shifts are accompanied by modifications of earlier practiced person-capacities, which are likely to be validated through membership in a variety of small face-to-face encounters, some more temporary than others. Finally, the reaffirmation of identity at each particular transition point may succeed or fail in varying degrees. New psychosocial competencies, role differentiation, role fusion or role disparity are concomitants of the change process and all are amenable to validation. Extensions, or reorientation in small groups, and understanding the potential of group work to the life arc defines the opportunities for professionals to apply the group modality for multiple purposes.

The import of these dimensions, namely, internal, interpersonal, and social, point to a holistic conception of people in context, as revealed in the choice points and processes that forge a self-identity. These attributes are to be viewed as continually in motion, sometimes clustering one way or another; at other times reordered to fit new situations. In terms of work with groups, these attributes must, of necessity, be related to the particular and specific problems or purposes for which individuals seek services. For the worker, they signify constellations or patterns of thought-feelings and actions that can be amended in the structure and process of the group. The list included in Table 4–1 itself is arbitrary and not exhaustive, and the gestalt is more relevant than any single item. Their relevance is intended for heuristic purposes and as guides to understanding members' participation in groups.

THE GROUP

As discussed in Chapter 1, the historical development of social group work illustrates a dialectical process of thesis, antithesis and synthesis. The initial thesis of group work was the amelioration of the social environment by working to eliminate generalized group dysfunction. Goals of improved social conditions and social betterment were approached through the social action and social change efforts of neighborhood groups and settlement houses. Although these groups were a "collection of individuals," the focus was upon the group as a whole and its relationship to its social environment. In terms of the individual-group-environment complex, the environment and groups' needs were assessed as primary and the individual members' needs were assessed as secondary. The emphasis of this relationship can be illustrated as an ENVIRONMENT-GROUP-INDIVIDUAL complex. For all the emphasis on democratic principles, the uniqueness and importance of the individual, and the right of an individual to be what he/she chooses, the prevailing belief was "you have a right to be anything you want, as long as you are exactly like the rest of us." Thus those persons who did not abide by this principle of conformity were readily classified as deviants and became the focus for group work services. In this context, the group was used to effect change in the members through the process of assimilation and acculturation.

In the 1960s a major shift in the focus of group work resulted in maintaining the focus on the individual, but also reemphasized the importance of the group and of the social environment. Major sociocultural-political developments recognized that diversity is a given fact within the normative structure of a pluralistic society. With this ideological shift, group workers began to pay increased attention to the individual's relationship to the total environment. Another aspect of this shift was the movement away from focusing only on dysfunctioning aspects of the individuals, but also providing group work services to maximize the individuals' potentials. The human potential groups, sensitivity training, T-groups and others illustrate the adoption of the new goal of enhancing the general functioning, in addition to the more traditional goal of eliminating specific dysfunctioning. Thus the general goals of group work includes both improving normal functioning and neutralizing the abnormal dysfunctioning of individuals. This synthesis reemphasizes the importance of the group and environment within the individual-group-environment complex which can be illustrated as an INDIVIDUAL-GROUP-ENVIRONMENT complex. Within the ecological perspective of group work all three, individual, group and environment are seen as interdependent, and equally important parts. However, it needs to be stressed that the worker has to determine which component or components at a given time needs the major attention. When an individual member comes to a group session and reports feeling depressed because of some personal tragedy, the worker has to channel the group's resources and energy to assist the member. Similarly, when the total group is encountering some difficulty, the focus of interventions will have to be directed to the total group. For the same context, if the group as a whole or some members within the group are violating certain environmental norms, the worker has to assess the situation and if needed, intervene on behalf of the environment.

As presented in Chapter 2, the ecological perspective of group work aims at creating a better match between the coping behaviors of the individual and the qualities of the impinging environment for the purpose of creating growth-inducing and environment-ameliorating transactions. In other words, the focus of the group is to produce growth in the individuals as well as improve the social environment.

The importance of using group at this point of interaction between the individuals and their environment is aptly illustrated by Lewin's (1951) identification of common problems associated with groups.

> A change toward a higher level of group performance is frequently short lived; after a 'shot in the arm,' group life soon returns to the previous level. This indicates that it does not suffice to define the objective of a planned change in group performance as the reaching of a different level. Permanency of the new level, or permanency for a desired period should be included in the objective (p. 228).

Although Lewin was discussing behavior *within* groups, one can carry this further to the importance of group members being able to not only grow and change their behavior within the group, but to be able to incorporate this new behavior into their repertoire after they leave the group and return to their own environment-habitat.

Differential Use of Groups

Human groups exist in order to meet such needs as affection, nurturance, recognition, belonging, influence and the like. While these pertain to personal needs in the contexts of others, exchanges among members in terms of competencies, skills, ideas, feelings and so forth, provide a basis for anchoring, extending, or altering a concept of one's self as well as significant others. The members of a population thus depend on one another, either directly or indirectly, for their well-being. Goldschmidt (1972) notes the importance of groups in society in the following way.

> While it is not accurate to say that a society is merely constructed of social groups . . . it is proper to say, (1) that all societies involve a multiplicity of groups; (2) these groups are structured so as to interrelate; and (3) group structures and group interrelations are essential for the operation of all social systems (p. 167).

Transitions in group and intergroup relationships occur throughout the life cycle. Shifts are discernible in adolescence when peer groups occupy a powerful strategic and referent position that may match the family in terms of affecting one's identity striving (Merten and Schwartz, 1967). In the transition from adolescent to adulthood, movement from peer group to near group to bridging groups that pave the way for participation in broader community activities are fairly common. At the neighborhood level, citizen participation and improved competencies are manifested in shifts from transitional and episodic groups to associative and work groups. The powerful effects of the absence or reduction of group linkages are evident when individuals move to another community or in the case of retired citizens.

The linkages between and among groups constitute the broad application of the principle of mutual aid. When there is deterioration or diffusion in the processes within, between, and among groups, then people begin to feel the effects of alienation. In a practical sense, the therapeutic communication (Ruesch, 1961) that is part of daily life may dissolve and be replaced by hostility or distancing. Alienation may be viewed as not only a distancing from the self that is manifested in a lack of openness but also to a shallow time perspective, lack of a future orientation and reactive to external reinforcement. Mutual aid then may disappear in conjunction with forces of attraction, social comparison, feelings of lack of power, and status loss.

In noting the relevance of small groups to the larger community and the attendant processes that govern opportunity, stability or incapacity, Glidewell (1972) states that

> The actions of larger forces is the community act through resources interchanged among small face to face groups—dyads, triads, families, neighborhoods and work groups.—Decisions are not sufficient unless they are reinforced by the actions of many of the small face to face groups which are the basic implementing social component of the community—families, neighborhoods, classroom, work groups, church groups, recreational groups—(p. 216).

The simpler associations, intimacies, personal exchanges and loyalities present in small groups make them powerful referent groups through which well-being or illness may result. The dissolution of these linkages produce stresses which break the productive rhythms of life and are likely to lead to neuroses, psychoses and other unwanted effects while they also do not permit healing and recovery to take place. At this point, professionals are called upon to develop temporary systems, which operate to rebuild and reorient processes of adaptation. Whether these temporary systems are based on formal or informal and natural groupings, experience shows that even within institutions and between institutions and the individuals' natural habitat, discontinuities and duplication in group-relevant aspects of living frequently confound pathways to mental health.

The new competencies gained through participation in groups in selective and closed settings leads to the next step, namely, reintegration into the person's natural habitat. New competencies also imply shifts in one's conception of self, of status and power, at least as perceived in the helping context. Returns to other settings and situations suggest a redistribution in the interrelationships with the other persons. For this reason, linking change at one level to another is an important consideration, whether it be an unruly child in a classroom, a discharged mental patient into the neighborhood, a halfway house in an urban district, a depressed mother back into the family patterns, a cancer patient back to work, adolescents discharged from residential treatment settings to their neighborhood and so forth. It would seem that new competencies are likely to be short-lived if the other relevant systems are not also given attention.

This line of thinking implies that a differential use of groups is necessary to restore, maintain and reshape the ecological balance necessary for an acceptable standard of living to both the reintegrated member and significant others. Therapy groups in hospitals need to be integrated with interdisciplinary teams who are charged with developing treatment regimens, with discharge planning groups, with socialization and activity groups for patients in the community and perhaps reinnoculation groups for those who are experiencing distress at some point in their community tenure. Other types of groups can be posited. Orientation groups to prepare patients for membership in therapy groups, preparation groups for families moving out of or into new neighborhoods, family life education for those facing the stress of life transitional crises, and so forth are additional examples of the ways in which groups can enhance, restore, or maintain the quality of life. These are consistent with the purposes of social group work as formulated by the Committee on Practice of the National Group Work section of NASW in 1964. According to the committee:

> The social group work method is used to maintain or improve the personal and social functioning of group members within a range of purposes . . . for corrective purposes when the problem is in the person of group members or in the social situation or both, for prevention where group members are in danger of dysfunction, for normal growth

purposes particularly at critical growth periods, for enhancement of the person and for purposes of education and citizen participation (Hartford, 1964, p. 5).

Applying the group modality for different purposes and in different settings satisfies the requirement in the ecological perspective for a unitary and holistic approach. In connecting competencies earned through group experiences to factors in the environment in which groups are located or as competencies to be used elsewhere, we begin to appreciate the threads that form a viable network and life space, that can provide necessary supplements of therapeutic communication to validate and reaffirm an individual's identity.

THE WORKER

The group worker role has been profoundly influenced by change in perceptions about people. Rather than being perceived as an inert being simply reflecting the intrapsychic struggle, an individual is viewed as influencing and being influenced by his/her social environment. The role of the workers and how they intervene within group work context is discussed in depth in later chapters. In the present context, the significant changes in the social and behavioral sciences and their influence on the current perception of the worker within an ecological perspective of group work practice are explored.

One of the major shifts in the social and behavior sciences is from a Freudian conception of human-beings as passive and re-active to that of self-actualization as developed by Maslow, Rogers and others. The concept of the individual as passively influenced by the balancing or rebalancing of internal forces has shifted to the concept of a striving organism actively engaging, influencing and being influenced by the environment which includes significant others (Balgopal and Vassil, 1979). As discussed in Chapter 3, the symbolic interaction perspective aids the worker in understanding how group members are influenced by their respective significant others. Similarly when group members develop a sense of identity with the group, fellow group members as well as the worker may emerge as significant others for them. Recognizing this shift, the worker may appropriately use self and the group to aid the member in question. The following example clarifies this point.

David, age 22, a graduate student, was a member of a group which was meeting under the auspices of the campus student health center. David's reasons for participating in the group was that he was feeling very depressed and was unable to concentrate on his studies. He had virtually no friends or any social life. He went home every other weekend. His parents who were supporting his studies usually gave him his expense money during his home visits. In the group sessions, David began to express his anger towards his parents for treating him as a child; and he especially did not like that they used their financial support to control him. The group members were quite supportive of David and agreed that his parents were indeed treating him as a child and that they were using financial support as a manipulative device to control him. (All of the other group members, also students, were between the ages of 19 and 26. Some of them were getting partial financial help from families but all of them also were receiving some sort of fellowship or were working part-time). After one of his visits home, David came to the session and was extremely upset over how his parents tried to control him. At that time one of the group members, Kevin, became quite vocal and told David to stop being a baby and grow up. Kevin was joined by other fellow members especially by Nancy, Pam, and Billy who all pointed out that David needs to grow up; as a graduate student, why is he so dependent on his parents, and so on. David became quite upset, but was not verbally responding to the confrontation of other group members. Pam then said to him that he is nothing but "Alex Portnoy." David at this juncture became very emotional and started crying. He then went on to say how lonely he is, and also how scared he is to meet people and make friends. His reason for going home was that at least he won't have to sit in his room alone and be depressed. With this revelation it appeared that the group members had emerged as significant others for David. The worker asked David whether he wanted any specific thing from the fellow group members and to this David said yes—*their acceptance*. When the group members were asked whether they can give anything specific to David, a number of them including Kevin and Pam invited him to join them in some social activities during the coming weekend . . .

Continual experiencing through interaction is the sine qua non of group work. The broad objective is to increase both the self-awareness and the assessment of individuals as they anticipate and engage in new situations. A secure member is one whose personal frame of reference is adequate and valid, who initiates action in his/her own behalf and avoids some of the demands that he/she cannot or do not wish to meet. At the same time such members are unequivocally engaging the internalized demands made upon them by significant others (Thelen, 1950). In the case illustration, it is evident that through confrontation with group members David gained awareness in his own behavior or at least was able to verbalize his own role in his present predicament, and was thus able to be receptive to the assistance offered by fellow group members.

Another change has been the shift from groups in which an emotionally detached worker offers introspective insight and feedback to the group, to those of experiential process where the worker is actively engaged in growing with and through other group members. The worker's reflective stance towards the group process is interwoven with his/her own feelings, reactions and needs. This shift in the worker's role is a topic of much debate. The psychoanalytic or Freudian model of group treatment is often set up as a "straw man theory." The worker who hardly responds and is preoccupied with maintaining "objectivity" is ridiculed. But, reflecting on one's own stance toward the group process and member interaction, without influencing the group to focus on the worker's own personal needs or overwhelm the group with his own conflicts and struggles is an arduous task. Often workers find themselves in a predicament, not knowing whether to be detached or reflect their own feelings. In other words they experience conflict between maintaining objectivity and becoming too subjective. What is an appropriate degree of objectivity and inappropriate degree of subjectivity is difficult to assess. However the concepts of role distance and role embracement from the symbolic interactionist perspective can aid workers in appraising their roles within group work situations. "To embrace a role is to disappear completely into the internal self available in the situation, to be fully seen in terms of the image, and to confirm expressively one's acceptance of it. To embrace a role is to be embraced by it" (Goffman, 1975, p. 124). In role distance, the person performs the role, but resorts to behavior to keep one's self from embracing the role. Frequently the distance is maintained through behaviors such as nonchalant competence, avoiding interaction on the same level, making jokes and so on (Munson and Balgopal 1978). Stebbins has developed two other kinds of role distances—major and minor role distance (1975). "Major role distance refers to the attitudes and behaviors that occur in highly threatening situations, while minor role distance develops in moderately or slightly threatening situations" (Munson and Balgopal, 1978). The following case example illustrates a worker's response based on major and minor role distance, to a member's statement of suicidal threat in a group session involving seven other emotionally disturbed members.

Near the close of this group session, Mary said she again felt the desire to do away with herself. These same kind of feelings had previously resulted in her hospitalization. She felt that a rehospitalization would not help, refused to consider that as a possibility, and admitted that during her last hospitalization, she had to struggle against taking a razor blade and slashing her wrists while on a weekend visit home. She was over-wrought because she felt "going back to the hospital would not help and nothing was going to change at home." The group members were at a loss to help Mary. The group seemed to be looking to me to say or do something. I remember feeling like saying, "You know there is a strong possibility Mary will do away with herself before we meet again next week. We might not ever see her again. I hope this is not the case, but it could happen. Does anybody want to say anything to Mary in case we don't see her again?" What I have learned about working to keep people from doing harm to themselves and others prevented me from acting on my true feelings, and the only genuine recourse I felt I had in the situation. My values and feelings were in conflict. Instead of acting on my own feelings, I feebly encouraged Mary by saying, "See you next week!" (Munson and Balgopal, pp. 409–410).

In the above illustration, the worker participated in a major role distance to deal with an extremely sensitive issue. If the worker would have moved to a minor role distance and reacted within his/her own true inner feelings, there is a possibility that the entire situation could have been different. The other group members would have been able to express concern for Mary and demonstrate that there was genuine regard and caring for her (Munson and Balgopal, 1978).

Group work is a process of human engagement, in which the development of self in relation to others is important. And in this regard, it is increasingly stressed that the worker also has to be genuine and authentic and allowed to grow. Authenticity is de-scribed by Levitsky and Simkin as a "state of individuation, of truly being one's self" (1972, p. 252). Krill (1966) contrasts au-thentic man with his opposite—the self-enslaved, cowardly, inau-thentic man. According to Krill, the inauthentic man is one who views himself/herself as a completed, set and secure person. A person who feels righteous about his/her "good saved self." The inauthentic person's life situation is completely fixed by early deterministic forces, because he lacks faith in his own potentialities and capabilities. In existential terms, an authentic person faces up to one's own distorted hopes and expectations of life, comes to grips with the world as it is, and finds a place for oneself as honestly as one can. The authentic person is one who gives meaning to one's life, and to the lives of others by accepting realistic "giv-ens", and lives in accordance with them. Krill further stresses that to be an authentic human being, one has to be always in a process of change, of becoming, of venturing forth and unfolding one's potentialities.

Authenticity for the group worker can be explicated as the appropriate blending of professional closeness and distance. "In the objective mode, the worker maximizes the professional closeness and personal distance, while in the subjective mode, personal closeness and professional distance are maximized" (Munson and Balgopal, 1978, p. 408). The facilitative worker behavior of authenticity through nonpossessive warmth, and empathy foster interpersonal relationships among members, which in turn lead to trust, respect and commitment to interdependence. Guided by sensitive listening and feeling, honesty and genuine caring, the worker can influence the development of a "protective envelope" or interdependence through which successful work can be accomplished. It is likely that the facilitative cluster will induce forces toward self-disclosure, and in turn conflict as described by differences in overlapping group membership which one can expect will be projected onto other members. In addition, the manifestation of the struggle between need for security and work may be expressed in a variety of ways by different group members. The worker through clarification, experimentation and authentic use of himself/herself can facilitate in establishing a group climate in which members can take risks and begin to share their struggles.

The worker's activities are directed towards specific responses and actions, overt and inferred, as expressed by David (in the foregoing case illustration). The processes of self and other perceptions and evaluations which lead to behavior are manifested in the dialogue between and among the members and the worker, which compliments the symbolic interaction perspective. However, two other points are noteworthy. In the first place the members act "as if" the group agreement is to confront David. This illustrates Lewin's concept of the gestalt of the group as a whole. In addition to the theoretical and practical components of the worker's role, another aspect emphasized by Lewin needs to be recognized, namely the empiric or research/investigative role. The method of inquiry is relevant and necessary for evaluative purposes and expanding knowledge in theory and practice.

AGENCY SETTINGS AND ENVIRONMENTS

Historical events and societal changes have forced the profession to review its earlier approach to client services based on a methodological perspective (Specht, 1977). The profession's response to charges of conservatism and control was to reassert and reaffirm its historic mission as centered within the neighborhood and community to which its functions were directed (NASW, 1971). This matched the philosophic stance of social work which was rooted in closeness to the citizens who required its help. Social work educators reconceptualized the practice haze so that a variety of professional activities were dictated by the inbalance between the person and situation (Bartlett, 1970). These events have provided the impetus for developing and formulating a unifying framework for professional purposes that encompasses many transactional sets between person and environments; between significant actors and specific settings. The work of Gordon (1979), Germain, (1979), and Meyer (1979), have articulated the major themes that characterize an ecological orientation and which has its counterpart in current formulations of the goals and objectives of the mental health movement (President's Commission on Mental Health, 1978). New conceptions however do not necessarily lead to new policies or practice. As Lloyd (1978) succinctly points out

> It is conceivable that social work could become an instrument of social change in the future. It is not such an instrument presently. Instead, professional focus remains on individual functioning (perceived within an organismic or systemic context) and on services to ameliorate, stabilize or modify problematic situations. The overriding concern is growth and development of individuals within the constraints of institutional and normative limitations. Given the pace of status revolutions, social work values and knowledge lay behind change in the wider culture. The politics, culture and governing bodies of the profession grapple with yesterday's problems while trying to remain au courant through rhetorical pronouncements (p. 51).

These considerations raise serious questions about residual agency sentiments that limit professional function to a single methodological base. Indeed, the ecological perspective would require a concerted effort to develop and implement a holistic approach, perhaps population and geographic-specific. This approach would encompass multimethod practice applied for purposes of amelioration, prevention, restoration or promotion of well-being. It is in this context that the utilization of one method of service, group work, needs to be considered as part and parcel of an organizational context.

Social group work is generally practiced within an institutional framework which intermediates between the person and potentiating or curtailing environments in an organized fashion. Mental health clinics, hospitals, schools, community centers, correctional institutions, residential treatment centers, public assistance, family and child welfare agencies and, YMCAs and YWCAs typify some of the contexts in which the groups as a method of social service delivery is offered. Variations among agency practices in the use of groups reflect differences in historical development, social science thinking, professional concerns, and philosophic orientations and assumptions about the human condition. Organization ideology, policies, goals and complexities are other factors which influence group purposes, foci and structures such as size, composition, type of clientele, leadership and interactional patterns. Resources such as time, space and manpower are additional considerations that have to be taken into account in the practice of group work.

Klein (1972) notes that the phrase, "use of the agency", has several connotations.

> "It conveys the ideas that are associated with the influence of setting in practice. These include the structure of the agency, its social climate, the congruent or dissonant messages that it sends, the willingness of the agency to permit a particular kind of practice, the compatibility of the other services in the agency with the group services, and whether the agency policy and operation evidence belief in and support of social group work." (p. 273).

Two hypothetical examples may be cited which demonstate the various influences of agency policies and organization complexity in group practice.

Large Psychiatric Hospital

In a large psychiatric hospital, the practice of groups was utilized for a patient population composed primarily of male patients diagnosed as chronic schizophrenics, undifferentiated type. Services to this population were organized through various interdisciplinary teams composed of psychiatrists, nurses, social workers, rehabilitation specialists and psychologists. Departmental autonomy and levels of authority among the various disciplines compounded the treatment regimens which were supposed to be holistic. The time and duration of meetings, place, composition of groups, type of leadership and orientation, goals and resources available were further complicated by the different orientations and assumptions of authority within the respective disciplines. Interdepartmental rivalries precipitated the role disparity concerning treatment directives and patient responsibilities. For example, some group meetings were held in large auditoriums, which violated the sense of togetherness and security that a group must develop as part of treatment. Other patients were administered drugs just prior to group meetings which interfered with treatment objectives. At times, new patients were added to the group by well-intentioned physicians, but without proper preparation. Confidentiality was violated on occasions when maintenance personnel performed their duties while a therapy session was in progress. To further complicate the situation, patients were often unable to avail themselves of their primary therapist's time. Followup procedures that should have resulted from emergent group therapy goals were often lacking. These contingencies posed formidable barriers with respect to treatment contracts, goals and expectations. Inconsistencies within a hospital service system can complicate a patient's reentry into the community. Interferences within hospital treatment programs designed to help patients learn societal competencies can handicap their adaptation in after-care facilities. Large bureaucracies rely on procedural routines and specializations as a method for orderly and predictable service, but it can be seen, from the above examples, that institutionalized procedures can severely interfere with professional practice.

Community Center

In a small neighborhood community center governed by policies that encouraged independent and creative professional efforts toward working with children, adults, families and community groups, emphasis was placed on natural groupings and on a set of assumptions that maintained equal concern for problems and opportunities within the context of the neighborhood and beyond. Supervised and trained volunteers were assigned to work with children and youth based on interests expressed during family registration periods. Special services to children and youth of concern to parents were the responsibility of trained professionals. The security-inducing atmosphere of the agency attracted other adults and families with problems. Referrals from other agencies for both children and families provided another source of client population. Treatment orientations included recommended participation in community groups which were developed in order to foster patterns of leadership that would congeal normative behavior within the neighborhood. For example, school-referred truant children would be assessed on the basis of parent-child-school relations which might also be the domain of other parent groups working to recalibrate school-neighborhood relationships. A decentralized and person-neighborhood centered orientation emphasizing "nearness" to the community clearly reflected a human relations approach that optimized choice points for intervention. On the other side of the ledger, overlap of services and functions among staff workers also complicated interagency relationships. Referred children and families often were among the most difficult to work with and absorbed a great deal of the staff's time and energy. Limited access to the environmental resources located in other community institutions and some negative attitudes were formidable barriers to group practice. For example, group work with post-hospitalized mental patients, or older delinquent groups that included preparation for employment was thwarted by lack of concern among employing agencies. Thus, the transition to citizen roles of the constituent members was restricted.

These two hypothetical examples represent polar types of agencies ranging from bureaucratic multidisciplined to single discipline, decentralized community centers. Differences in size, complexity, "assumptive world," extra-organizational and environmental climates, types of clients, member-worker roles and so on have their impact on the group services offered.

Recent attempts to conceptualize and articulate the present realities in terms of organizational context for group work practice have emphasized certain common themes which have been sorted into discrete categories called *transitional* and *social conflict* (Glasser and Garvin, 1976). The social functions of these organizational orientations may be described in broad terms as *socialization* and *resocialization*. *Socialization* refers to preparing and introducing people into their social roles as well as helping them experience creative and expressive needs. *Resocialization* is directed at integrative services aimed at assisting individuals in psychosocial adaptation. Settlements and community centers typify the socialization aspect, while mental health centers, family service agencies, sheltered workshops might represent the latter. Special provisions in a transitional category are entered for individuals who are in a state of "normlessness". Rap centers, encounter, and marathon groups typify this development. Institutions that are mandated to govern the lives of constituent members—such as residential treatment centers and correctional facilities—represent another aspect of the social conflict category.

These distinctions are useful in sorting out the context of service, type of service, clientele, technologies and so forth and in that sense represent an addition to correct conceptions. Cogent arguments, however, have also been articulated for the point of view that agencies may perform functions that include several of the above categories, simultaneously. Deferences in this regard have been noted in the foregoing work as well. Indeed, in various community-based agencies such as settlement houses or community centers, what has been described as "socialization" is an integral part of a treatment plan, directed at psychosocial adaptation. Street work with delinquent youth is an example of the fusion between the two. The danger in separating categories of service (social-ization, resocialization) by types of agencies is that it may re-new old themes concerning "special" and "traditional" agency settings which are contrary to current sentiments regarding holistic and multidimensional practice. It is important to restate that there is only one helping process which entails a number of methods for enhancing and sustaining client capacities for various purposes. Further articulation by types of service, environmental and agency setting, group structure, process, purposes, goals, outcomes and so forth can be very helpful in sorting and refining practice theory. The differential use of groups in multidiscipline as well as single discipline agencies would suggest that in the future an emergent fusion of social work traditions with respect to group work prac-tice is inevitable.

A Conception for Agency Functioning

Current trends and future prospects seem to indicate that social work practice in groups will be used for many purposes within a single agency or department in a large bureaucracy. The question that requires further consideration is how agencies might adapt to an expanded unit of service which is likely to cause strains in their organizational character. In this sense, there may be many ways to organize services and manpower in order to deal effectively with a variety of contingencies. Surely, the needs of individuals and their natural habitats are sufficiently complex and shifting to require selective and different agency responses. There need not be inherent and stubborn contradictions between work with delinquent youths, a tenants council, the Junior Chamber of Commerce and veterans organizations.

Let us now turn to an alternate viewpoint that attempts to lay the groundwork for agency functioning in complex and shifting condi-tions. If the group worker, portrayed as a tough-minded problem-solver, has been characterized as standing midway between change and certainty, no less can be said about the agency positioning between order and disorder. The same society that mandates agency functioning also contributes its share of the problems. Hence, the agency is placed at the vortex of competing claims and counterclaims. Agency policies, objectives, resources and constituencies reflect divisions and diffuseness of society in general. Indeed it is the way in which these competing claims are handled that defines the value of the agency to the community and to society.

Three organizing concepts can provide useful bridges by which to attempt to understand, clarify, and grasp the potentiating aspects of agency functioning. These concepts are leadership orientation, innovation, and temporary systems.

Leadership Orientations Institutional norms prescribe certain role functions that are clearly in line with societal expectations or an agency wouldn't be in operation very long. These norms which govern both substantive and procedural aspects of staff duties, both departmental and interdepartmental in more complex settings, are important because they certify routines and expectations that culminate in dependability. Positions and tasks in an organization include lines of authority, responsibility, expectations, accountability procedures and so forth. For professional staff, the job functions are underpinned by values that affirm the dignity and opportunity for individuals to fulfill their potentials throughout the life arc. There is another side of the coin, of course, which differentiates what has been termed the nomothetic dimension from the ideographic (Getzels et al., 1968). In the latter dimension, the individual need dispositions of the person in the role is emphasized. Individual worker interests, capabilities, and desires represent a goal orientation in an organization that is intimately related to the agency products or services, and stands apart but related to institutionally imposed norms. The third leadership orientation posits a function that must connect the other two components. That is, the limits and resources available—which include skills, feelings, opinions and other person-capacities together with budgetary requirements, space, time credibility and so forth at the organizational level—must continually be confronted so as to make intelligent application of the strengths of both to the problems at hand, both long-term and short-term. This orientation is less pure than the other two and has been described by Getzels and Thelen (1960) "as an integrated structure of ideas about the way in which cultural, institutional, group, and individual factors interact and, in the process of interaction, change and bring about change" (p. 81).

No utopian state is intended or visualized in this perspective. The intended image we wish to present is of a system continually in motion and grappling with complexity and dissonance in dealing with current realities. Indeed the point is that leadership, a representative concept, and action are continually being defined and revalidated according to situations. It also means that agencies must be creative and innovative instruments for change in the community. This leads to the second organizing concept, that of innovation.

Innovation Certain qualifications are necessary in explicating the idea of innovation because if that is all an agency did, it would soon be in trouble. No agency can survive very long or maintain its credibility simply by being innovative because that is only half of the equation for change. The other half, previously referred to as dependability, predictability, certainty, orderliness and so forth, is required to maintain a judicious balance in an agency's operation. There is plenty of evidence in studies of the diffusion process to suggest that a significant number of other actors (agencies) who have a stake in the situation will respond in ways that ensure responsibility, (Rogers and Shoemaker, 1971). When an innovation is accepted, these same actors or agencies are quite likely to ensure its implementation: Hence, in the formulation, and as part of the essential leadership function of optimizing transactions among resources at person and institutional levels, there must be a continual dialectic between innovator and what may be termed as the defender role. That is, the role and function of critic has to be built into the agency processes. As an example of this, the use of the method of inquiry is one way of assuring premature closure as well as community-composed criteria that are available for internal and external (public) scrutiny.

What complicates the task, if we accept the description of the agency as positioned at the vortex between crosscurrents of competing claims between person and institution, are the various salient publics or constituencies to which it must attend, respond, alter, yield, ignore or whatever the case may be. The constituencies refer not only to other social welfare agencies, both public and private, but client constituencies as well. The overlap between staff and board or executive specific constituencies is not likely to be great. Taking a slightly different but relevant view, the agency must take the position that freely accepts cultural goals without necessarily accepting the form, structure, and methods, by which they are translated into solutions (Merton, 1966). Health services that are essential but are not accessible for constitutent members of a community are not terribly useful. The same argument for ineffective services may apply in those instances in which services are accessible but not utilized for various reasons.

There are many types of constituencies represented in agency processes, often appearing as invisible participants in the goal formulation stage of work with groups. Schools want children to be readjusted; employers want dependable and responsible workers; policy and criminal justice systems want youths to be obedient and law-confirming; children want places to play; parents want help with child rearing; politicians want nondemanding constituents; maintenance persons want neat, tidy families and so on. Competition for space, time, and staff resources complicate the picture. Executives responsible to Boards of Directors who represent broader interests and values including professional and business interests, want economy, efficiency and accountability that is in harmony with their notions of social and political realities. From this brief exposition it can be seen that the raw materials for an agency "product" are diffuse and powerful.

If one accepts the point that various publics such as other agencies, constituencies, institutions and other complex person–community processes place constraints and limitations on an agency, the intermix among them presents opportunities as well. The trick is to figure out how these can be managed judiciously and at the same time maintaining credibility with those very same agencies whose support will be necessary for implementation. An examination of the ingredients that constitute the innovative process are to be found in the characteristics of temporary systems.

Temporary Systems Among the most salient characteristics of agencies in the innovative mode are (1) capacities for being in touch with a wide variety of other systems including relevant constituencies external to the organization; (2) a sense of venturesomeness and comfort with occasional marginal roles with respect to significant others; and (3) an ability to manufacture and act upon different roles that are required in different circumstances. The recurrent features in temporary systems, as noted before include novelty, newness, experimentation, egalitarianism, present-centeredness, authenticity, and task focus. These attributes together with judicious application of the method of inquiry as problem-solving methodology, make up the rules of the game, as it were. The authority for changes are group-inspired rather than by the personal charisma of any one individual. In addition, temporary systems are defined as oriented toward changed individuals, programs, or organizational structures. Small face-to-face groups are a special case of temporary systems, as for example when compared to classrooms. Certain phenomena characterize groups designed for change induction purposes. Miles (1964) noted the following.

> These include increased energy devoted to the accomplishment of novel, significant, focused, internalized, shared goals; effective, controllable procedures for achieving the goals; esprit de corps, group support, and mutual identification with peers; high autonomy and spontaneity, with freedom for creative experimentation, along with norms actively supporting change itself; higher-quality problem solving via increased communication among participants and fuller use of member resources; active meeting of members' needs for autonomy, achievement, order, succorance, and nurturance; high involvement and commitment to decisions, followed by group support for implementation after the termination of the temporary group's life (pp. 655–656).

A number of roles have been identified for community change, namely, initiations of change, experimenters who are willing to try it out, adaptors who are willing to use it with certain modifications, constructive critics, facilitators who focus attentions on orderly processes and occupy mediator roles, fact finders, reality testers, and the uncommitted (Klein, 1968). These roles are also applicable to small working teams and other groups and are examples of the group's ability to manufacture and introduce roles for high level functioning.

The most potent type of group is one that has built into it the means for its own change which is implied along the descriptive attributes of change-inducing temporary systems. The dialogue between change and dependability creates problems as well as opportunities and processes of role differentiation and implementation also imply a lot of work and struggle. For new decisions, policies, plans and programs to emerge, which are analogous to new competencies, continued linkages with other systems are necessary. These relationships are reciprocal to be sure. This means that agencies may be either recipients or initiators of change and the process will be further complicated by multiple group memberships. However, the guidelines presented in temporary systems properties are useful in applying professional skills to whatever arrangements of groups are available for inducing change at various levels. There is one other important consideration that needs to be noted. An innovative stance may be aptly utilized at a number of choice points, as for example, (1) original contribution; (2) among a converging band of initiators; (3) part of a later and larger circle of those planning for action; (4) inclusion in a legitimating body that approves the project; (5) as implementors, and (6) evaluators (Klein, 1968). It must be stressed that these bench marks are not to be conceived as mechanical insertions in a calculus for change. They are suggestive, as with attributes of small working groups as temporary systems, of an approach that can be useful in dealing with the holistic approach inherent in the ecological perspective. The emphasis on process does not negate either content or judgment, but places it in the context of conditions that may be necessary for developing a resilient, shifting and continually emergent and validated generalized frame of reference between and among agencies, various publics, and constituencies.

Organizational Contexts and Working Groups

The notion of a working group has to be connected to organizational contexts in order to clarify its utility both for assessment and as guides to action. The following diagrams adapted and modified from a schema developed by Getzels and Thelen (1960, p. 80), depicts the centrality of the group within an organizational context.

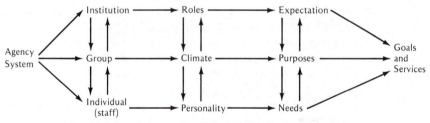

Figure 4-1. Community Values, Beliefs, Constituencies.

The diagram places the agency and its internal organization in the context of various constituencies and sets of belief systems. The group (staff meeting, decision-making bodies and so on) is designated as a mediating instrument through which institutional and personal interests are processed and coordinated into services. The features of temporary systems are to be cultivated and operationalized within the group climate. Competing claims and crosscurrents of special interests come to the attention of working groups by way of linkages of the organizational participants in various other groups. Instrumental and expressive cycles that pertain to shifts in the group process and structure also generate particular constellation of roles that are related to different organizational contexts and ultimately to services offered by way of groups.

It is important to note that no safe middle ground is advocated as an ideal way to resolve competing claims or innovative efforts. Emphasis on institutional norms or personal predispositions is analogous to organizations that exhibit such different characteristics as highly bureaucratized to storefront operations. Examples that illustrate the range of organizational contexts might include, in order of decreasing complexity, the following: correctional facilities, psychiatric hospitals, residential treatment centers, child care settings, mental health centers, family service agencies, settlement houses, community centers, runaway shelters, rape crisis centers, spouse assault agencies and so forth. Each organizational design is reflected in role patterns which dictate interactions and transactions among and between staff, departments, clients and so forth. The relationship between organizational complexity, staff autonomy, control and procedures has been shown to affect constituent members' responses in a variety of settings both within an institution and in the community. (Moos, 1974). It is more reasonable, given the variety of settings, to perceive the parameters of the working group as oscillating between institutional and perhaps control requirements to the more intimate spontaneous and informal patterns that are person-centered. At some point, of course, an excess in either direction may go beyond the pale. Strict control produces as many problems as reliance on idiosyncratic behavior. Within these two broad parameters however, working groups can confront and challenge the complex realities to forge innovative and/or dependable solutions to person–environmental needs.

While the working group is one major feature of an innovative organization, it by no means is to be construed as the only one. Staff, executors, and other professional departments interchange in many other groups such as committees, task forces, informal social groupings, citizen groups and so forth. The impetus for change may come from any one of multiple groupings. Indeed, the working group requires challenges from the "outside" so to speak, because they constitute the "work" of the group. The emphasis on personal interchanges are important because they keep the organization in touch with the sentiments of significant others; although, as an adaptive solution, one has to put up with lack of foresight. This is common among storefront and other small, and creative agencies which also have to grapple with overlap and a "crisis" every day. Reliance on rules and regulations as an adaptive solution produces a loss of resiliency that may also cause hostility and frustration among staff at the expense of certainty, although overall purpose is fairly well maintained. Working groups that emphasize a mix between external and internal demands, and that depends on the authority of the group, may get stuck in a groove of thinking that sidetracks them from long-range goals and outcomes. Tenants councils and street work with youths are examples of the latter. The point of all this is that present and emergent realities need to incorporate and welcome input from diverse and often contradictory sources. Such is the nature of the challenge presented in the ecological perspective.

INDIVIDUAL/GROUP/WORKER/AGENCY-ENVIRONMENT: SUMMARY AND INTEGRATION

The ecological perspective is anchored in the interrelationships between and among persons and their natural habitat, which includes many types of specific environments. Utilization of the assumptive world that underpins people in relation to the environment dictates an expanded view of the unit of service or the case, as has been explicated recently by Meyer (1979). Basing her argument on an epidemiological orientation which refers, in social work, to the incidence and distribution of psychosocial adaptations, she noted that

> How is this way of thinking about practice different from past ways of thinking, and what is involved in an epidemiological orientation? By thinking "hospital floor," for example, rather than "twenty cases," or by drawing a boundary around an arena, certain phenomena or conditions of life, the related variables within this boundary can be explored and assessed, and whatever methodology or model of practice suits the defined need in front of us can be chosen. . .

> In child welfare, for example, a boundary might be drawn around a certain number of city blocks or, in rural areas, around a certain number of square miles. Within that area, all the components of child welfare transactions would be located—natural parents, child, foster parents, group home, crash pad, counseling center, homemaker service, day care center, administrative office, and so on. That is a child welfare "case"! (pp. 269–270).

The assessment procedures always require matters of judgment and perhaps ideology as well, but the holistic emphasis presents a challenge for social work practice that can serve as a unifying orientation for the profession.

The construct of temporary systems, such as the small face-to-face group, can be used as a bridging principle by which to interconnect

111

accommodations between the individual and the environment. The intervening influences such as community and institutional processes can be channeled by agency functioning, both substantively and procedurely, to optimize the quality of life at the same time that dependability and foresight are enhanced.

Person and homestead, a central organizing theme in ecology, means that people need each other to survive and grow. Individuals exchange affections, skills, and ideas not only in small face-to-face encounters that are more likely to be temporary than permanent along a life trajectory, but also accept and negotiate these encounters according to pathways that are embedded in family, ethnic, and community belief systems.

We have noted that life events never seem to sit still for too long. Either a new child enters a family, job changes occur with new career opportunities that entail relocation as well, a close associate or family member gets sick, economic shortages curtail leisure-time pursuits and so on.

Common sense and experience indicate then that change is fairly constant and pervasive, although more often than not in the miniscule and manageable rather than catastrophic. Advancing age alone inevitably presents and creates opporunities and constraints. For example, young children tend to take events as they are; at adolescence and beyond, one takes a longer look at the future; from mid-life onwards, individuals look backward and forward, more often than not to reaffirm their identity, but also to resteer it to coherence if need be. Surely, these considerations indigenous to time, age, process and specific events along a life arc present unique opportunities for group work.

Reviewing the trajectory of life at whatever cross-sectional moment, the give-and-take among all the interrelationships one encounters have a certain consistency, otherwise one's identity would be in serious jeopardy. In other words, to the extent that the habitat provides ego-enhancing opportunities for the exercise of person-capacities such as judgment, intelligence, planning, thinking, feeling, permitting trust, love, recognition, and so forth, then one can surmise relatively smooth, but not unencumbered growth patterns. Dependability is necessary for these capacities to become forged into an acceptable life course. When an individuals' expectations are in line with the shared expectations of others, then life can be suitable and satisfying. Under these conditions, unanticipated events may be perceived as challenges rather than insurmountable obstacles. When, on the other hand, there is social injustice, then all the dependability in the world can not equate with the time, effort, energy and investment a person has made to reach his/her goals. Individuals, no matter what their capacities, have different thresholds of tolerance for stress. Sometimes a person tends to certainty, at other times to adventure. When the limits are stretched beyond one's capacity for dealing with discomfort, recurrent patterns of hostility, withdrawal, defensiveness, counterdependency, or law-violating behavior can lead to disparagement and toxic states. This is not to say inherent sentiments for striving, achievement, mastery, acceptance, satisfaction, belonging, status, and being right in what one is or does are missing. Rather, the point is that they are buried and hidden. At points of generative conflict or debilitating stress, temporary systems such as small groups, formal or informal, natural or formed, are important modalities for service. Whether for corrective purposes, for growth and enhancement, for restoration or rehabilitation, small groups are an inevitable and eminently useful target point for addressing quality of life issues both in a temporal or developmental basis.

In a more limited sense, small groups provide opportunities for self-change. The capacities cited earlier in Table 4–1. that describe individual sentiments can be altered, exercised, recalibrated or augmented in intimate face-to-face encounters. Change carries with it a new set of competencies which include alterations in power and status, however miniscule they appear to be. Reorganization of sentiments in small groups are related to role complexity and status inequality. There have to be interchanges among leadership and followership patterns in broad terms or else the best competencies may wither if self-conceptions are continually aggravated by larger sets of community forces. Returning to the small groups, reorganization and differentiation emerge as some members direct, others follow, implement, or critique either in pairs, triads or larger clusters. These behavioral patterns may shift off course, at least in their expression as different members attempt new roles. The complexity of organization also requires setting priorities in delaying immediate achievement, of checking reality with the status quo, of seeking a willingness to experiment and seeking alternatives and compromise. Issues of control and conflict are springboards for reassessing developmental horizons and in the process, differentiations become a powerful and acceptable norm. At the same time. these sentiments, group-relevant aspects of personality development, may be upsetting to others in the environment who might prefer to keep their community, families, citizens or constituents unchanged, or else they themselves have to accept differences in their own behavior. For this reason, linkages within and between significant others who have a stake in the problem have to be engaged. Thus, the target for change shifts to other groups in other contexts, concurrently, or later as the case may be, and perhaps permanently when it comes to institutional change. These considerations are most apparent when children are discharged from institutions and return home; when ex-mental patients are trying to reintegrate into the world and family, work, and social activities; when inmates demand self-governance in institutions; when challenges are raised for group homes that house exceptional children or adults; or when reconstituted drug abusers return home to family and friends. Even under the very best of conditions, newly earned psychosocial skills may produce very little return and may have to be continually fought for if more powerful segments of the community judge unfairly, harshly, and hold back the necessary resources for maintaining an acceptable order in the lives of those who have been labeled deviant. When institutions insist on compliance and conformity that disconfirm personal development, then the return to disabling patterns may be expected. It is for this reason that agency functioning must encompass a holistic and a realistic approach to enhancing and maintaining the quality of life. The argument is not for innovation at any cost. The perils and weaknesses of this stance have been cited as producing maverickism that outstrips credibility. The point of view advanced is that agency functioning can profit from utilizing a temporary system (staff meeting) that fully applies and is responsive to its unique qualities, and in so doing is responsive to institutional, societal, group and personal interests. In such a case, the various indigenous and salient constituence that are represented by various staff, executive and board interests are allowed to emerge. These many transactional and competing sets that oscillate in the group from institutional control to personal interests, also broaden the range of choices for action. Again, the ability of the small working group to forge a coalition of actions as it reverberates between task and expressive demands, represents a powerful vehicle for addressing change and progress.

Professional function straddles the middle ground between order and disorder, between freedom and constraint. Underpinned by values that guide activity toward the optimal functioning of individuals, of mutual respect, dignity and opportunity as inherent human rights, professional workers have to be tough-minded problem-solvers, challenging the obstacles as well as supporting the competencies necessary for exchange and productivity between and among individuals and groups. The ameliorative potential of small face-to-face groups becomes the working arena for facilitating dependency, interdependency, and autonomy between the person and environment. To prevent superficial eclecticism, the three roles that accompany professional activity, namely, theoretic, empiric, and practice, must be inseparable parts of professional work with groups. These three roles are necessary to safeguard and operationalize the values inherent to the social work profession. They are connected to a conception of practice that maximizes conditions, opportunities and resources among and between individuals in their habitats.

The integrating threads of persons, groups, worker, agency-environment are essential understandings from which assessment and utilization of groups begins and proceeds. This perspective, which attempts to equate the importance of these four components, seeks to identify and clarify continuities and discontinuities in group service patterns directed for a variety of purposes, with different populations. Group therapy, for example, with Chicanos in prison may very well be counterproductive if it does not engage the constrictive and opposite sentiments of control expressed through administrative and staff actions within the institution. In addition, developmental aspects of Chicano culture relative to male roles and responsibilities and how these contrast with the role of inmate need attention. Perhaps consciousness-raising groups responsible for programming that is culture specific is a more realistic use of groups, as might also be self-governance opportunities. Discharge groups that are in harmony with expectable opportunities and roles available and viable in "back home" situations are another example of the principle of continuity of service. A holistic approach presents these challenges.

Similar considerations can be applied to work in low-income and disintegrated areas. As mentioned earlier the development of a "stairwell society" in a public housing project was intimately related to street work with delinquent youth and other such programs. Utilizing a small-group approach for organizing tenants' self-help groups produced new leader-follower patterns among a number of small quasi-autonomous stairwell groups that eventually led into a community-wide tenants organization. Constituent members of the community, through social organization, were able to develop and complement a set of agreed upon norms concerning time, place and program for adult and children's leisure-time activities. Support for a teen lounge, for example, enabled heretofore "left out" adolescents to plan, develop, and implement a rather complex adolescent service with the assistance of adult volunteers. Eligibility for and continuance in the program governed by a rather loose federation of several adolescent groups, reinforced expectations of behavior that were pro-social, such as respect for property and others' rights, tempered use of alcohol, using discussion to resolve differences, and anticipating and avoiding situations that could produce violence. In terms of the groups, the processes that differentiated leadership among the youth groups also produced leadership among the adult groups. In both cases differentiation of member roles unsettled a powerful community norm that "everyone is in the same boat."

Professional service is not meant to guarantee a palliative for constituent members. However, the differentiation process also generates roles that need to be fulfilled by other members and, indeed, this is the case where skilled professionals provide the leadership. In both sets of groups, personal, interpersonal, and social factors are continually engaged, and in that process, generate forces for the dependability and conflict that are part of and linked to community patterns. From this transactional sets, a generalized frame of reference is continually shaped, lost, altered, and maintained. Processes of repair and breakdown occur simultaneously. It is when they do not, that serious consequences may ensue.

The holistic approach provides the necessary framework that clarifies and reaffirms professional social work practice in groups as encompassing reformist and meliorative functions, as well as promoting well-being or rehabilitation at the point of breakdown.

5

Structural Properties

In the ecological framework of group work, groups are perceived as a system which interfaces between the individuals and their environment. This framework is based on the premise that there is a direct relationship between social work groups and the members' natural environments. Although it is not always possible for the social work groups to be similar to each and every member's natural environment, attention needs to be given to ensure that these two dimensions complement one another. Group workers have to acknowledge that they are not the end all for all the needs of their members and that groups are only a facilitative mechanism to assist in gaining awareness and developing the skills to manage the members' internal and external struggles. The ecological framework can enable the workers to help map the member's total relevant situation, provide knowledge about the various social networks and support systems operating in the members' environments, and how these could be mobilized effectively in helping to meet the members' needs.

Workers' interventions that are guided by the symbolic interaction perspective enables the members to explore and understand uncomfortable differences between their personal and social identity.

When there is a notable discrepancy between these two perceptions, the individuals' functioning is jeopardized. These can range from difficulty in family relationships, peer relationships, to work situations. Lewinian field theory emphasizes the dimensions of motivation and life space to the symbolic interaction perspective.

In this chapter the key structural properties of group work such as assessment, goal formulation, composition, size, programming and contracting are discussed with select references to the ecological, symbolic interacton, and field theory perspectives. A model for articulating the ecological concepts with the structural properties is presented in some detail with respect to group assessment and compositional factors. Subsequent application of the model to the other properties is not emphasized in depth in order to avoid redundancy. This list of structural properties is by no means exhaustive, but includes those which have a bearing on determining the quality and effectiveness of group work practice. Each of these properties is examined through processes of historical evolution and current status. In each section of this chapter a list of practice principles is presented to clarify the impact of these properties on social group work practice.

STRUCTURE AND PROCESS

The dynamics of action in work with groups are frequently described in general terms such as group structure and group process. Both of these components are interrelated and interdependent and have direct bearing on the outcome for individual members as well as for the total group. Group process refers to both the present, "here and now" happenings within a group session, and the interactional and communication patterns among the group members and the worker. In essence, the phenomenology of the actions, what occurs in both the public and private world of the members, is the process. The attempts to account for the process, to explicate, describe, and understand it—requires the use of contructs such as roles, interaction, size, composition of the groups, and so on, which serve to partialize the reality into communicable symbols. These are called structural components or properties. They are not structures as one might think of when we use words such as buildings, tables and chairs. The structural properties or components within group work are used to describe and analyze group events, happenings, in short—the group process. The relationship of group structure and group process is most crucial for the worker. Professional leadership can alter one or the other or both to influence or modify the behavior of group members, or other dynamics within the group. For example, the worker could change the task which could affect what is happening in the group. Or he/she could change the structure of the group by adding new members, or

118

change the location of the group. These factors obviously affect the member's interaction with each other, with the worker, and with the group. Attention to process refers to the expression of thought-feelings between and among members and the worker. This would include listening to each other, the ways in which members think about, act and respond to each other's comments, including emotional reactions. The emphasis is clearly on the "how" of interaction, as well as on the inferred expressed meaning or "hunches" that each message contains. A characteristic and persistent arrangement of actions and reactions by any one member may be conceptualized as a role pattern.

ASSESSMENT AND COMPOSITION

The properties of group assessment and composition refer to the issues of (1) how the members of a group are determined, and (2) how potential or acting group members may affect each other and the group as a whole. According to Hartford (1972), groups basically emerge in one of the following styles.

1. Groups may be self-composed, such as family groups, street gangs, patients in a psychiatric ward, and so on. In these instances, the members determine who will be incorporated into their group.
2. The members may individually choose to be part of a group on their own initiative, such as parent-effectiveness training groups, personal growth groups, and so on.
3. Membership for a group is determined on the basis of a specific characteristic, need or problem of individuals who happen to be in a given location at a given time, such as probation officer's caseload, patients on a certain ward of a hospital, and so forth.
4. An agency or worker may determine the composition.

Composition of therapeutic groups has been extensively discussed in the literature; however, writers have frequently taken a rigid stand on who should be included in such groups. These stringent selection criteria often emphasized the negative aspects of the individuals, thus barring them from membership in therapeutic groups.

Beginning in the forties and well into the fifties, group composition was mainly concerned with factors that would not be considered an asset for the total group process. A majority of these factors noted a rather negative and conservative approach to the study of group composition, with emphasis on the differences instead of its attributes. In a search for a systematic method of composing groups, Redl (1951) came up with what he calls, "a few very basic principles of group life," which are as follows.

1. The way a group is composed must not be left to chance; it may be of very great importance for the kind of group life that will develop and for the effects the group will have on some of its members.
2. Some of the most dangerous mistakes we can make in group composition lie in the direction of three group psychological principles:
   a. We must not ignore the possibilities of 'contagion.' Children put into a group in which they do not belong will either become serious disturbances to the group and to discipline, or they will suffer grave damage through exposure to the wrong group life.
   b. We must not develop blind 'germophobia'. In other words, the fact that one youngster is 'worse' than others in itself does not mean he will wreck the group or cannot be worked with. There are ways of combining his or her needs, under skilled group leadership, with the needs of the total group.
   c. We should however, watch out for the danger of 'shock effect.' If Richard is too far from the behavioral level of the rest of the group, serious neurosis may be developed through an intolerable conflict within him, constantly stirred up by wrong placement (pp. 186–187).

Wilson and Ryland (1949) focused on a number of factors related to composition. These factors included groups with different ages, intellectual range, educational background, social experience, occupational range, social class and composition as to sex. Their opinion that the worker needs to be attuned to individual differences in order to totally understand the success of group composition, is illustrated as follows.

Since each individual brings with him into his group not only those qualifications which are like other people's, but also those which are different, the universal factors of difference among groups are found in the unique personality of each of the members who compose them. Successful development is closely related to the worker's understanding of these factors, of difference and to this ability to use their effect in the groups which he serves (p. 138).

For Bach (1954), four personality criteria for exclusion in the group consisted of a "patient's insufficient reality contact, his culturally deviant symptomology, his dominant character such as the chronic monopolist, and the psychopathic deviant." "Environmental criteria refers to the state of realistic difficulties in the actual life situation of patients" (p. 18). Bach used the example of divorce as an environmental crisis and goes on further to say that, "a crisis in the social environment naturally absorbs the attention of the patient involved in it, but this is not the best time to attempt insight. Another reason for excluding patients under acute environmental goings on detracts the group's attention from the here and now interpersonal relationship" (p. 23). This seems to be a far cry from where we are with respect to pre- and post-divorce groups, families of burn patients, and other treatment groups which respond solely to a specific environmental crisis.

Frank and Powdermaker (1953) focused on members who dropped out of treatment groups and came up with criteria for group composition which was somewhat different than had been experimented with previously. They drew up specific attributes for effective group composition. These include: the patient's ability to be openly aggressive or competitive with peers, the ability to tolerate aggression from others, and the ability to reveal weaknesses. These writers had embarked on new territory for the understanding of group composition. They committed themselves to the task of more sharply defining and more effectively using the aspects of clinical evaluation, and psychological tests that had been found helpful in predicting behavior in those groups which had been carefully scrutinized under their new criteria.

Schutz (1961) studied group composition based on the concept of compatibility in terms of three basic interpersonal needs: inclusion, control, and affection. He stated that

> Various indices of compatibility were computed for pairs of people, based on the characteristic ways in which they expressed behavior in these areas and how much of each kind they wanted from others. From these considerations two kinds of compatibility are computed, one based on a notion of need similarity called interchange compatibility. These two types of compatibility can be computed for each of the three areas of validity for composing productive, cohesive groups desirous of mutual interaction. (p. 275).

In the last decade, behavioral attributes have received more attention. Bertcher and Maple (1974) state: "Descriptive attributes were once thought to be most useful in selecting group members. However, research has shown that behavioral attributes, which indicate how an individual interacts with others, are much better predictors of an individual's behavior in a treatment group." (p. 187).

Group workers are now beginning to turn toward the idea of what makes a group work, instead of what goes wrong. Both Frank and

Powdermaker and Schutz had given us a good start as to possible positive factors that aid in the group process through the interaction of mutually identifying group members. The purpose of the group plays a vital role in the structure of group composition; in addition to affirming the principle of compatability and complementarity. In this context Northen (1976) has indicated

> The composition of formed groups is related to the purpose of the group, and the needs, problems, and personal and social characteristics of the members . . . Knowledge of the factors that influence the participation of members is used by the worker to determine which ones seem most crucial to the purpose and anticipated content of the group (p. 135).

Common questions to be answered in composing groups are the following. Will the person benefit from this group? Will he/she be able to participate? Will he/she interfere with the realization of the purpose of the group, and the needs and purposes of others? Klein (1972) has suggested nine principles for composing social work groups which seem to be among the most useful criteria up to the present. These are

1. Compose the group so that there is homogeneity with regard to the developmental task.
2. Compose the group so that there is heterogeneity of coping patterns and defenses.
3. Compose the group so that there is balance and at the same time so that it is weighted toward the positive.
4. Compose the group so that there will be both stimulus for interaction and movement toward change in behavior.
5. Compose the group so that levels of remission are not very different.
6. Assess and predict the probable role behaviors one can expect each potential member to enact.
7. Avoid bringing people into a group when their behavior will be palpably ego-alien to any other member . . .
8. For groupwork to be a treatment of choice, the members must have some degree of social hunger.
9. For groupwork to be indicated, potential members must be able to communicate with others in the group in a meaningful way (pp. 60-63).

Klein brings out an important point as he talks about the criteria for groups and their relation to group composition. The purpose or goal of the group may find itself being hidden in the group if the composition of the group is too far out of line with the desired or expected outcome. "Whatever the criteria used and whether by worker, staff, or group itself, the important point to see in consideration of group composition is that some scheme for determining composition may lead to more predictable outcomes in the uses of groups for specified goals," (Hartford, 1972, p. 137).

Two other important components of group composition that need to be dealt with by the worker are the heterogeneous and homogeneous groups. Heterogeneous groups have a wide range of personality traits whereas homogeneous groups have shared symptoms. The desired objective of the group may point in the direction of the need for a specific type of group. Depending on the objective, heterogeneity may be used in order to have social diversity or homogeneity in order to have social similarity (Hartford, 1972). Yalom (1975) uses heterogeneous groups for conflict areas and homogeneous groups for ego strength. There appears to be a general clinical sentiment that heterogeneous groups have advantages over homogeneous groups. Homogeneous groups, are believed to "jell" more quickly, to become more cohesive, to offer more immediate support to the group members, to have better attendance, less conflict, and to provide more rapid symptomatic relief. But experience seems to indicate that homogeneous groups, in contrast with heterogeneous groups, tend to remain at superficial levels and are an ineffective medium for the altering of character structure.

The type of group is partially determined by the anticipated total group effectiveness, which is what each individual and worker brings to the group. As Bertcher and Maple (1974) pointed out

> Effective groups tend to have interactive, compatible, and responsive members. Interactive members like each other.
>
> Responsive members are interested in helping each other. Research indicates that a group often is more effective if members have homogeneous descriptive attributes and heterogeneous behavioral attributes. Common descriptive attributes help foster interactiveness and compatibility: . . . Heterogeneous behavioral attributes on the other hand, increase the chances that members will be constructively responsive to one another (p. 193).

Assessment and Composition: An Ecological Perspective

The impact that a specific group has upon the development of group members is determined by two factors: (1) the nature of the group and its environmental context; and (2) the nature of the interactions which occur within the individual–group–environment complex. The ecological framework of group work utilizes an intimate understanding of the nature of the individual–group–

environment complex to facilitate the growth and development of not only the individual within the complex, but of the entire complex.

The ecological framework for assessment and composition of social work groups can be constructed around three principles of ecology presented by Kelly (1970). These principles state that (1) within an ecosystem there is a cycling of resources and energy; (2) the environment affects the styles of adaptation or diversity found within its influence; and (3) functions within an ecosystem are interdependent. The following components of these principles have relevance for organizing group assessment and composition.

1. Resources and Energy
2. Diversity
3. Organismic Relationship of Interdependence

Resources and Energy

An examination of the concepts of resources and energy indicates that "resources" is a broad category of environmental components needed by an organism; energy is one of these needed resources.

Resources are of two types, those whose increased availability stimulate their increased use and those whose availability does not influence such usage. When resource availability is high, increases in the availability of the resource has a diminished impact on the system to the point where an optimal level is reached, beyond which there is no beneficial effect and the possibility of the occurrence of detrimental effects exists.

Energy as a resource is defined as the capacity for acting or being active; and it is described as existing in two forms, an active form (kinetic) and an inactive form (potential). Energy in an ecosystem can move toward the production of entropy, or disorganization of the system, decreased interactions, and lower levels of active energy; or, it can move toward synergy, the increased organization of the system, increased interactions, and heightened levels of active energy.

The context of the group work situation as an ecological complex provides a structure from which the worker can efficiently organize his/her perceptions of the resources and energy dynamics of the group. For example, an energy pattern may develop from a supporting group member to another who needs support in order to work out a problem. The conversion of group support energy may be efficient if it stimulates the member to begin to work on the problem or inefficient if it is met with a discounting or denying behavior. Finally, the level of energy found in specific types of group interactions and the impact that this has upon the types of group interactions the group seeks is important for data organization. A group may remain at a high level of conflict if conflict as a "food" of the group has a high energy or nutrient value.

Diversity

Ecological principles relating to diversity appear to focus on the organism-environment relationship. Species diversity within an environment depends on the area, geographic isolation, richness of the environment, and the ecological diversity. In essence this means that the range of different types of organisms that can exist within an environment depends upon the capacity of the environment's resources to meet the different needs of the organisms.

In order to translate the ecological principles of diversity into the context of the groupwork situation it is necessary to look closely at what diversity means in the group context. Biological diversity indicates the number of different species which are able to exist within the range of conditions found in a given environment. Within the group context a similar diversity can be identified in the number of different people who exist within the immediate environmental conditions of the group. However, in addition to this immediately visible interpersonal diversity, there is an intra-individual diversity, or a range of differences within a single individual group member, and what might be a range of diversity brought to the group from the differing environmental backgrounds of the individual group members. This is an example of Lewin's principal of overlapping membership. Thus, when considering the diversity of any group, it is important to consider the total range of differences which includes the diversity of the individuals within the group, the diversity of the external environments brought to the immediate group environment by its members, and the diversity of characteristics found within each individual group member.

Within the group context the potential for expressed differences is dependent upon the total range of diversity and the degree to which the immediate group environment can support the range of uniqueness. The "inhabitability" of a group for any one individual is dependent upon the level of tolerance that the group has for his/her entire realm of individual differences. Further, the predictability of the group environment, that is, its tendency not to exhibit drastic fluctuations in its tolerance range, will have impact upon the level of expressed diversity found within group interactions. Group environments which allow the accumulation and expression of differences in individuals facilitate an increase in the alternative choices and behaviors available to its members for coping with problems and obtaining need satisfaction. This increases the overall stability of the group. Accommodated diversity which allows an increase in the organizational complexity of a group is likely to have an impact on the group's efficiency.

Greater choices and options in a group are associated with more complexity, which also allows for greater collegial participation and support in trying out new behavioral patterns.

These principles relating to diversity within the individual-group-environment complex of the groupwork situation outline the framework with which the groupworker can organize his/her perceptions of the diversity of the group. Data relating to the total range of diversity within the group can be organized within the three levels of group diversity, interpersonal, intra-personal and social. What this implies is that both quiet and active members in a group complement each other by not competing for group resources. When they can exchange and incorporate portions of each others skills both profit. Furthermore, these competencies can lead to greater satisfaction in their day to day living and working habits.

Interdependence

Organisms living within an ecosystem establish relationships of interdependence with other organisms. These relationships have impact upon the structure and functoning of the total system and upon the structure and functioning of the individuals within the environmental system. Five basic types of species interrelationships have been defined by the biological scientist (Knight, 1965). Two different species that are not affected adversely or beneficially by close association are defined as having a relationship characterized by *Neutralism. Commensalism* is the term used for a second type of relationship in which one organism definitely benefits from the association, but the other is neither beneficially or adversely affected. *Parasitism,* on the other hand, implies a relationship in which one organism extracts essential materials from a host organism. This relationship benefits the parasitic organism but adversely affects the host organism. *Obligatory Mutualism* (Symbiosis) indicates a relationship in which two different organisms must remain together in order to survive. In this relationship both organisms benefit; however, both are also limited by the fact that they must remain together to survive. *Non-obligatory*

Mutualism describes a relationship similar to Obligatory Mutualism in that both organisms benefit; however, in this relationship neither organism must remain with the other to survive.

The above relationships describe the nature of direct interrelationships found within the ecosystem. There are also indirect relationships within such living systems. The variety of functional roles filled by the organisms within an environment and their interdependent functional relationships provides the basis for indirect relationships of interdependency. This means that impact upon one part of the group and its relevant environment affects all other relevant parts of the group.

The translation of these biological principles of organismic relationships of interdependence to the context of the individual–group–environment complex of the group situation provides the groupworker with a valuable organizational framework. The groupworker can use the concepts of autonomy and dependency to classify data which indicates the degree to which individuals need others within the group as the source of growth-inducing energy. An autonomous individual within the group would be a person who is highly self-motivated, who identifies those aspects of his/her self which need to be worked on, and who takes the initiative to make his/her own growth- and change-producing inner connections. The dependent individual is one who relies heavily upon the group for the energy and stimulation to grow and change. A person who needs a great deal of group support and stimulation or relies totally upon the groupworker to provide the inner connections that lead to growth could be classified as a dependent individual. An interdependent individual will fall somewhere in between these two poles. These characteristics, as applied to the group situation, are ideal types and as such are not found in pure form in the group.

The general level of dependency of an individual within the group that is identified by their position on the autonomy–dependency continuum can be looked at in more detail if the specific types of direct interrelationships they are involved in are identified. The concepts of Neutralism, Commensalism, Parasitism, Obligatory Mutualism, and Non-obligatory Mutualism provide the group worker with descriptive terms that can be applied to the specific interrelationships of the individuals. In a relationship of Neutralism, ideally two group members are not directly involved. This does not mean that there is a lack of any involvement, rather a lack of direct involvement. Commensalism within the group would describe the relationship in which one member utilizes the support, insight, or personal resources of another member without that member being affected by the relationship. A parasitic relationship can occur when one group member obtains benefits from manipulating or using another person in a way that is detrimental to that individual. A person who "puts down" another group member to boost their own ego could be classified as a type of parasite within the group, as could a person who emotionally drains another's supply of caring and support without replenishing that supply. Obligatory Mutualism is indicated when two or more individuals within the group form an interdependency that is necessary for their survival in the group. This type of relationship is illustrated by the victim-rescuer relationship and the sado-masochist relationship in which both parties are dependent on the other for their existence. Non-obligatory Mutualism is perhaps the goal of an effective groupwork situation. In this relationship the involved individuals benefit from the relationship, but are not dependent upon the relationship for survival. An exchange of support and understanding, shared mutual experiences and feelings, and other mutually beneficial interactions which do not tie the participants together in a dependency relationship are examples of this type of relationship. The distinction between this type of interdependence and the dependency of the obligatory mutualistic relationships is important. The dependency of the obligatory mutualistic relationship indicates the necessary continuance of the relationship for the individuals' survival; while the interdependence of the non-obligatory mutualistic relationship is more accurately described as a cooperative relationship necessary for obtaining certain benefits but not necessary for survival.

Indirect relationships within the group originate from the same principles that apply to living systems. Change or disturbance in any member of the group will directly or indirectly affect all other members because of the functional and structural interdependence of the members' group involvement. This indirect effect may take the form of a delayed response. An incident within the group to which a member does not become directly involved may cause a response from the individual at a later time due to the time necessary for that person to integrate the meaning of that incident into their own personal structure. Indirect effects may take on an amplified nature. An experience affecting one person may have an amplified effect on another person who reacts to that stimulus within the context of the other influences impinging upon him. Experiences which repeatedly occur within the group may have an amplified effect on the members of the group because of the cumulative nature of the reactions or because a tolerance threshold is exceeded. A groupworker who repeatedly uses conflict to

128

deal with the group or a group member who repeatedly assumes the victim role may solicit amplified responses from the remainder of the group which has grown increasingly hostile to these stimuli or which suddenly releases built-up reactive emotions. Multiple, distinct group experiences can have an interactive effect which amplifies or diminishes their intensity. A conflict situation within the group which would normally be expected to create an intense group reaction may have a relatively minor effect on the group if it follows closely behind a series of different conflicts which had drained the group or lessened the impact of conflict on the group. Similarly, if an intense conflict is followed by a humorous situation, the humorous situation may take on an amplified impact because of the release of tensions created in the conflict situation.

From the foregoing discussion, the principles of resources, energy, diversity and interdependence have implications for assessing needs that relate to group composition. Member capacities as presented in Chapter 4 are useful in elaborating person, interpersonal, and social characteristics of potential group members. An overriding principle is that the potential for change in groups is enhanced when differences are harnessed for work through interdependent efforts. Individual differences are not lost in the process but are expanded to the end that the member's goals have beeen reached.

Selected Practice Principles

1. Group assessment and composition are structural properties of group work which are based on the perception, organization, and interpretation of personal, interpersonal and social data. Data perception and interpretation are obviously necessary for group formation and the groupworker's anticipated functioning within the group. However, there is also need for an efficient means of organizing perceptual data so that effective interpretations can be made. An organizational structure for groupwork data must be comprehensive in its capacity to organize the total range of information derived from the formative groupwork situation and flexible in its capacity to accommodate the application of a variety of theories to give meaning to this information.

2. The use of intake procedures or pre-group preparation sequences remain important points for initial assessment.

    Among the strategies that can be used are interviews, psychological testing, and diagnostic groups which are important methods of collecting initial data pertinent for group formation.

However, this data should be used only as a guide in understanding the member. Subsequent assessment of the members
in the group should be modified on the basis of their patterns
of group participation.

3. Assessment is based on an understanding and evaluation of
member capacities as they are manifested in their day to day
living. Implications of this principle are that member attributes
have to be organized in the context of their significant personal, interpersonal and social activity patterns, in combination
or separately. For example, assessment of a member as "passive-
aggressive" is not sufficient or appropriate unless this pattern
is related to specific contexts such as "passive-aggressive in
dealing with family and/or work associates".

4. Specificity of members' needs is necessary in order to formulate the common purpose of the group. Implications of this
principle are reduction of initial member anxiety and uncertainty, supports processes for mutual interaction and provides
a mandate for worker activity.

5. Members' homogeneity in purpose and heterogeneity in coping
patterns provides the impetus for work in the group. What this
principle means is that differences stimulate interaction and
similarities keep it in bounds. In addition, member differences
are resources for exchange in the group work.

6. Group composition should be sensitive to the environmental
climate regarding attitudes towards racism and sexism. This
principle does not contradict cultural pluralism nor does it
make it automatic. For example, residents of socially integrated public housing projects may not tolerate group work
services provided in mixed groupings.

GOALS

Traditionally, goals in social group work were formulated by the
worker, whose actions were guided by the agency's policies. Lowy
(1970) identified five major sources of goals in social work with
groups: (1) social work values; (2) goals of settings in which social
work with groups is practiced; (3) goals of the group; (4) goals of
individual members; and (5) goals of the social group worker as a
member of the social work profession, as a change agent, and as an
employed staff member of an agency. Despite Lowy's identification of the differential sources which affect goals in group work,

the frequent debate still continues whether goals of individual members supercede that of the goals of the total group.

A brief review of how goals were perceived in social group work indicates that until the 1960s, although the benefits for individual members were mentioned, the major focus was on group goals. Assimilation and integration were seen to be valuable ends by the profession, along with the socialization of the individual members. These goals were to be accomplished by focusing on group interaction, group process and the use of the worker as an agent of society. The group was perceived as the "collective conscience" having the resources and potentials to influence the individual members' "deviant behavior". This idea is clearly evident in the writings of pioneer group work theorists.

Wilson and Ryland (1949) stated, "most social agencies serving groups have two purposes in common: (1) to help individuals use groups to further their development into emotionally balanced, intellectually free, and physically fit persons; (2) to help groups achieve ends desirable in the economic, political and social democracy" (p. 61). Coyle (1951) indicated, "the group worker enables various types of groups to function in such a way that both group interaction and program activities contribute to the growth of the individual, and the achievement of desirable social goals" (p. 466). She stressed that social workers use relationships in groups as a means to individual growth and development but always in relation to the larger goals of helping the individual to move in the direction of acceptable behavior where society is concerned. Trecker (1955) indicated almost the identical goal: "fundamentally the purpose of social group work is to bring about the highest possible development of human personality, dedicated and devoted to the democratic ideal" (pp. 67-68). Phillips (1957) stressed that both individual and group goals can be met simultaneously; however, group or social goals obviously takes precedence. The major focus of group work is on socialization of members.

In the 1960s a major shift occurred. Differences began to be looked at as a positive factor both in groups and in a democratic society. Groups were no longer seen as an experience solely for the socially deviant, but as valuable experiences for all people. These factors influenced the change of focus from the group to the individual. Rather than taking a stance of "curing the sick," group workers began to see the importance of providing an atmosphere for "meaningful personal experiences" for the members of their groups.

Konopka (1963) stated, social group work "is a method of social work which helps individuals to enhance their social functioning through purposeful group experiences and to cope more effectively with their personal, group or community problems" (p. 29). According to Vinter (1965), "Group work is a way of serving individuals within and through small face to face groups in order to bring about the desired changes among the client participants" (p. 715). While this shift from group goals to individual goals was occurring, some group workers continued to stress that both could be met simultaneously. Northen (1969) emphasized that goals are seen as a combination of the influence of the agency, individuals, and groups as a whole. "The social worker participates in the group system to influence the way in which the members work toward facing and solving their problems—those of the individuals, the internal system of the group, and the wider environment" (p. 11). Hartford (1972) also shared similar views. According to her, goals are to be perceived as a combination of agency goals, worker goals, individual goals, and group goals. Usually these goals are ordered in some way as to produce the primary and secondary goals which can later be changed or renegotiated as the group progresses.

As seen in Chapter 1, the goals in the different models of social group work emphasized differential units of the group. In the remedial model group, goals are usually formulated in relationship to the individual member needs. The worker's main function is to focus on the need of the individual member who has a problem in his/her social functioning. Recipients of group work services are those who are unable to adapt to conventional social roles (Vinter, 1974). In Schwartz's mediating model (1961), goals are directed toward the relationship of group members with each other, with the worker, and the group as a whole. He focuses on the relationship among members that defines the characteristics of the members. In this model, emergent goals and actions are based on feelings. The major focus is on the creation of an atmosphere which would allow for reciprocity between group members for a meaningful interaction which will fulfill their respective needs. In the developmental model the goals are deduced from diagnosis of the group and the individual member based on the stage of group development and his/her interests, needs and aspirations as a group member (Lowy, 1970). In this model, the feelings and sentiments and behaviors of the group members are continually appraised in relationship to the group process and the total functioning of the group along with the worker's own sentiments. All of these factors are taken into consideration in formulating the goals for the group.

Goals: An Ecological Perspective

In the ecological framework there are four major sources of goals. Their significance is highlighted at two points in the beginning process (intake and contract formulation). Goals are also located in the agency, the worker, individual members, (or subgroups where there are prior friendships and other associational patterns among members), and the "group itself." The term *group* is used here to mean the cognitive-affective map or mental image of groups in the minds of both workers and members. An exception might be noted in the context of natural groups or primary groups such as families and gangs where the group is already formed. The basic ingredients of the group-to-be are assessed at intake, an exploratory and fact-finding dialogue between member(s) and worker. This can include the initial outline of the contract, a rather important structural component which is used to designate a meeting of the minds between the worker and members concerning expectations, offers, promises, and agreements within the context of problems, purposes, and relationships. (This will be discussed in depth later on).

The sources of goals in ecologically based group work suggests that there can be congruence or incongruence among all or between some of the four components; individual, group, worker and agency-environment. Furthermore, member goals can be both avowed (meaning what they say) and unavowed (what they don't express and may or may not know about). This suggests that both overt and covert forces are operating at any one time among all four components. In other words, some combination of public and private behavior is ever present. Similarly social group work goals may be short-term or long-term. However, it needs to be pointed out that professionals who hold to an existential point of view would argue the importance of only the immediate goals.

Individual members may want to join the group or may be referred to social group work services to deal with such areas of concern as problems in their relationship with family members. Individuals may want to participate in groups but may be not able to express this explicitly. Furthermore, social work groups also have antithetical goals that may shift from time to time. For example, the group may want active direction from the worker but at the same time want to make their own decision—a feeling which they may not be able to express. Agencies also have goals which are a significant factor in work with groups. The agency controls the worker's scope and legitimacy. For example, in a department in which there are psychiatrists, clinical psychologists, and social workers, a psychiatrist may recommend the client for group and supercede worker objection for that client in the worker's group. In custodially oriented and/or bureaucratic organizations the norms and values of group work may be antithetical to the formal organization. Similarly, goals of group work in an interdisciplinary agency setting might often be influenced by the needs of other professionals. For example, the goals of a group conducted in a school setting may be influenced more by the teachers than the youngsters who are participating in those groups.

In summary, the goals in social group work come from differential sources and they all affect the overall goals. What the worker needs to be aware of is that goal formulation in an ecological framework is a process and not a static phenomenon. What this means is that it is an ongoing activity affected by all four components. Furthermore, the chances of goals being accomplished will depend upon whether they are clearly stated and understood by everyone concerned including the individual members, worker, and the total group. Furthermore, the goals need to be stated in behavioral terms so that periodic evaluations of the status of goals, whether they are achieved or not, could be evaluated.

Matrix for Practice

Choice points for practice principles that are suggested in the foregoing discussion on goals are summarized for purposes of clarity in the following matrix.

GOALS
(ambiguous/specific)
(avowed/unavowed)

Sources of Goals	Immediate	Short-Term	Long-Term
Member(s)			
Group			
Worker			
Agency/ Environment			

Figure 5-1.

The matrix illustrates the factors that a practitioner must take into consideration in the goal formulation process. Elements of time, specificity and public avowal of goals can be used to clarify issues of congruency, or lack of it, among the four major sources of goal. To illustrate the use of the matrix, we shall focus briefly on agency/environment as a choice point for its influence on goals.

One of the objectives of community mental health centers is to assist the client to make an optimal adjustment as soon as possible. In this regard short-term group work services may be offered as a treatment modality for clients in various crisis situations such as the loss of a loved one. The purpose of the groups is to help the clients deal with themes of dependency, loss and sundry ambivalences, and to learn to use old and new resources for current and future functioning. Inherent in short-term services are specificity of goals, clarity, and other concrete worker activity. However, there are a number of other factors which can complicate the stated purposes. The agency-based nature of the services may preclude a number of potentail members. Also members with limited verbal skills might feel alienated. Due to the cost efficiency factors, workers may be required to form groups larger than desired and inconsistent with their skills and comfort. Contingencies such as these must be taken into account and reconciled during the goal formulation process.

CONTRACTING

During the past decade, the social work literature has abounded in discussing the need for contract as a key concept for effective social work practice (Maluccio and Marlow 1974; Croxton, 1974; Seabury, 1976). Although there is almost universal agreement at the present time concerning the desirability and necessity of the contract, no such universality of agreement exists with regard to its exact nature and terms. However, the gaps separating the various theoretical positions are microscopic when compared to the gap between theory and practice. All too often the social work contract is viewed in simplistic terms whereby it is reduced to a fee for services arrangement. Essential elements are likely to escape notice or be dismissed as unimportant. As with dissatisfied marriage partners who awaken one day to find that the vows they took ten years ago served only to mask the fact that their expectations about marriage were tragically dissimilar, failure on the part of the worker and the client to consider crucial contractual elements may also result in confusion, hostility, and ultimately, "divorce" (Croxton, 1974).

The shadow of the medical model still stretches long and dark over group work practice in spite of the fact that this model has been widely rejected as being inappropriate. The ego aggrandizement attendant upon assumption of the role of "expert" is often too tempting for the worker to resist, with the result that the members are forced to assume the complementary roles of ignorant and passive recipients of wisdom and instruction. Even worse, the worker-member(s) relationship may be seen as analogous to that of artisan-raw material, with the worker as sculptor whittling and chipping at a malformed lump of rock until its appearance gives him/her pleasure. Contracts in group work by and large remain vague, unstructured and nonspecific. They are ill-defined and in part tend to serve the worker's hidden agenda (Croxton, 1974).

The Nature of the Group Work Contract

We live in a contractual society. All manner of goods and services are acquired with the contract as a necessary intermediary, and many of our activities and relationships, such as driving a car and getting married, are governed by contracts. On a broader level, it can be seen that the existence of society itself is based on contractual agreements between individuals and groups that ensure cooperation and mutual interdependence.

From the legal standpoint, a contract is "a promisory agreement between two or more persons in which there must be subject matter, consideration, and mutuality of agreement" (Corbin, 1963, p. 2). While this is also true of the group work contract, the latter differs from the legal contract by virtue of being fluid and dynamic. Allowance is made for the fact that situations and people change over time, thus necessitating periodic review of previously formed agreements. Also, failure to live up to designated responsibilities in the group work contract does not result in fines and imprisonment, as is so often the case with violations of legal contracts.

The material in the social work literature that focuses on the contract generally emphasizes its importance in motivating the client toward more active participation in the entire process of assessment and goal formulation. Social work practice maintains that client participation is necessary to assure the success of therapeutic intervention, and that the client should be included in deliberation about the problem and planning of tasks to be undertaken in problem reduction. Maluccio and Marlow (1974) stated that "It is logical to extend the concept of 'maximum feasible participation'

in policy-making and planning to direct and personal interaction between social workers and clients whether the latter are individuals,
families, groups, or communities," (p. 28), and that "the client is
emerging from his traditional roles as a passive recipient of service
to an active, self-determining person who cooperates with the
worker more and more consciously and deliberately in the helping
process" (p. 29).

Besides enhancing member participation, contracts can also be
used to reduce members' level of anxiety. By spelling out precisely
the needs, expectations, and limitations involved, the member(s)
can establish workable boundaries and will feel more comfortable
by obtaining some familiarity in his/her new situation. The contract
can be used in numerous other ways, as outlined by Maluccio and
Marlow (1974).

> The use of a contract can help facilitate worker-client interaction, estab-
> lish mutual concerns, clarify the purposes and conditions of giving and
> receiving service, delineate roles and tasks, order priorities, allocate time
> constructively for attaining goals, and assess progress on an ongoing basis
> (p. 28).

Various definitions of contract and necessary components of a
good contract have been specified by a number of writers. According to Klein (1972) a contract is an agreement, both verbal and nonverbal, between the client and worker about the purpose of the
endeavor and the way in which they will work together. Goldstein
(1973) stated that a contract is "the organized set of explicitly or
tacitly understood ways in which the interactors in a system agree
to carry on their business" (p. 137). Croxton (1974) presented contract as an agreement between the worker and members which must
address itself to (1) mutuality of understanding concerning ultimate
goals (product); (2) reciprocal obligation relating to the helping
process (specifications); and (3) ultimate expectations (terminal
behavior).

From the above definitions two basic parts of the contract can be
deduced—the establishment of the ground rules and the delineation
of tasks. Establishment of the ground rules is the first step in
negotiating the contract. This phase determines the need of service
for the member(s), the roles of both worker and member(s) in their
relationship, the amount of involvement required of both, the extent to which interaction may be carried, the degree of power held
by both parties, and the possibility of renegotiation or termination
of the contract by joint agreement of the participants. This is the
process part of the contract.

The second part of the contract, delineation of tasks, spells out the strategies to be used, who is to perform what tasks, and responsibilities in the performance of those tasks. This part also focuses on mutual goal-formulation. This is the task or purpose half of the contract.

There are several necessary components to a contract that make it a valid and forceful tool in the worker-member relationship. These have been expounded by numerous writers. Sulzer (1962) maintained that a contract must always be "modifiable by joint agreement," explicit in order to prevent misunderstandings, and must clearly state the nature of the relationships (p. 271). Dinoff et al., (1972) stated that the contract must actively involve both parties, should be written in the early stages of interventions, should specify terms accurately, must be perceived as fair, and must be reasonable. The contract will not be a contract if it is not agreed upon mutually without pressure being exerted on either party, whether internal or external to the relationship. The contract must be renegotiable in order to allow for later changes of perception in either the relationship or accomplishment of goals. The contract must be explicit and specific to make sure that there is no room for misinterpretation. The contract must carefully delineate the nature of the relationship so as to ease anxiety and prevent dependency of usurpation of authority. The contract must be perceived as fair by both parties to promulgate effectiveness in the relationship, and the terms of the contract must be reasonable in order to prevent frustration and disillusionment in the outcome of the therapeutic endeavor (Seabury 1976). Operationalization of the social work contract requires a firm understanding of the terms of the concept together with an appreciation of how the contract takes shape over time within the helping process.

With regard to the unfolding of the contracting process in the group over time, Croxton (1974) enumerated several phases—prior conditions, the exploratory phase, the negotiation phase, the preliminary contract, working agreement, secondary contracts, and termination and evaluation. Prior conditions refer chiefly to the agency setting in which treatment might take place. Here the purpose and guidelines of the agency constitute limitations on the contractual deliberations of worker and member. During the exploratory phase, worker and member engage in orienting behaviors around expected role relationships and agency function. The negotiation phase involves becoming increasingly specific about mutual expectations and norms of behavior. The preliminary contract is often a simple agreement between the parties to try out the process and see how it goes, while recognizing that the client may need to experience the therapeutic relationship for a longer time in order to gain necessary knowledge about what should be done next. Consensus is reached concerning the nature of the problem, treatment goals, and means in the working agreement. It is understood that the agreement is dynamic, not carved in stone, and that it can be altered by the mutual consent of the parties involved. Secondary contracts are formed which define obligations among the various members in the group. In other words these agreements involve only certain members and/or the worker. An example of a secondary contract is when members A and B agree to point out their respective behavioral incongruencies. The final stage is contract termination, which allows the participants to evaluate their progress. It is here that the member(s) and the worker take a look at each treatment goal they had established and see to what extent their goals have been attained. It should be understood that these phases don't always follow in strict order, nor are they one time only affairs that can be disregarded after their first appearance. It may be necessary to initiate the process several times within the course of treatment.

Contract: An Ecological Perspective

Despite the numerous positive aspects of the contract, it would be a mistake to consider it a panacea; it is also subject to limitations and potential abuses which must be taken into account. Beall (1972) for example, focused on the dangers of entering into contracts with members prematurely, before sufficient background information has been gathered. Such contracts impede the future work of the practitioner and member(s) and may very well result in failure. Seabury's (1976) work, concerning possible negative aspects of the contract, listed a number of limitations. He mentioned that it is difficult to negotiate contracts with the involuntary clients that make up a significant percentage of social work clientele. In addition, not all clients are capable of participating in formulating the terms of a contract, for example, young children, developmentally disabled persons, and psychotic individuals. It is also difficult to establish contracts with multiperson client systems when members of the system cannot reach consensus regarding goals, and contracts with individual members may contradict each other. Other limitations of contract formulation within group work include member(s) capacities, worker competencies, agency resources and environmental climate. Sharp imbalances among one or a combination of the four components of group work may set the stage for abuses of the use of contracts.

It should be clear by now that while the contract may be necessary for the attainment of group work goals, it is hardly sufficient. Just as it is possible to violate the spirit of a law while religiously following its letter, it is also possible to follow a cookbook type contract procedure and at the same time subvert its very purpose. What is suggested is that the only way to ensure that the contract formation process is actually contributing to a positive outcome is to view the process in the light of our highly touted though largely ignored social work values. The values of human dignity, self-determination, nonjudgmental attitudes, and democratic beliefs will remain attractive but meaningless abstractions unless they are continually operationalized within the therapeutic/helping relationship.

Although, all social workers believe in the worth and dignity of the individual as a concept, it will be worthwhile to examine this value in the present context. One of the key values accepted and supported by the social work profession is that each person is a unique individual and he/she has to be accepted and respected for what he/she is. With the growing acceptance of cultural and social pluralism, diversity of lifestyle and beliefs has to be sincerely accepted and not merely tolerated. Thus adherence to this value implies that group workers will have to be sensitive to the uniqueness of each and every member of the group. Even when they find themselves diametrically different in beliefs and lifestyles to member(s), they will have to be certain that advertently or inadvertently they do not discount the member(s)' inherent dignity. Compton and Gallaway (1979) raised another problem confronting the social workers and that is of striking a balance between classifications and the responsibility to respond to persons as individuals on the basis of common characteristics. In social work intervention, the merits and demerits of the use of classification has been frequently debated, but is still commonly used. Workers need to be aware that they do not direct their focus of interventions to the classification category in which the clients fall, but rather work with then as unique individuals. Appropriate strategies of interventions are not arbitrarily determined but active involvement of members is essential, bearing in mind their inherent dignity as human beings.

Self-determination refers to the belief that people have the potential to decide their own destiny, that people are basically good, independent, and industrious, and they should have the choice in determining their own lifestyles insofar as possible. Within the context of formulating a contract, this value expresses itself in the willingness of the workers to seriously consider the aims of the member(s) including exploration of the various alternatives implicitly and/or explicitly available for them. "It is fraudulent to think of self-determination without alternatives" (Compton and Galaway, 1979, p. 131). It is easy for the worker(s) to superficially act respectful while listening to member(s)' opinions and ideas on alternatives which they secretly dismiss as unsophisticated and irrelevant. The virtual omnipotence implied by the medical model is at this time likely to rear its ugly head as the workers use their position of perceived authority to manipulate subtly the expressed wishes of the members until their goals have been unrecognizably recast into the *a priori* goals of the worker. In such a case, the mutuality is only apparent, as we are in reality dealing with a process of "psuedo-mutuality" in which at least one and maybe both participating parties have been deceived. Mutuality does not preclude unique individual competencies and abilities between worker and member(s). What it does mean is that despite such differences, in order to work together the parties concerned have to maximize strengths, and be sensitive to each others' needs.

The question of nonjudgmental attitudes arises in connection with the establishment of both goals and procedures. The contract can function as a safeguard insofar as its existence can make it more difficult for the worker to lapse into rampant subjectivity. The workers who find that their values are incompatible with their member(s) can bring this up within the context of the contract and try to arrive at a different mutual agreement that will be satisfactory to both. Without a contract, there is the possibility that the worker would become more and more judgmental, thereby jeopardizing the working relationship.

The concept of democratic values in group work practice bears little relationship to political notions of democracy. In group work, the rights of the individual take precedence over the rights of the majority. "Each man occupies a position of equal importance to the society. No irrational means of discriminating against them is acceptable" (Schniderman, 1974, p. 46). This distinction becomes crucial in group content, since it is not acceptable to make contracts with any members of the group who disregard the rights of another member. The worker needs to bear in mind that each of the member's needs are important. Otherwise, group work intervention becomes a cruel deception that perpetuates injustice.

What does it mean for a worker to say to a member, "I care for you," when he/she doesn't bother to form a contract with this client? What does it mean for a worker to form a "psuedo-contract" with this client, a "contract" that is bereft of any trace of the social work values so loudly proclaimed on the battlelines? What it means is that group work carried out under such conditions is merely one more victimizing part of society, issuing yet more promises that can't be kept. For unless the group work endeavor is based on a valid, mutually derived contract that is thoroughly informed with social work values, the worker is engaged in the cruelest kind of victimization—perpetrating a hoax under the guise of offering help.

Selected Practice Principles

1. Contract formulation is a systematic and planned activity. For example, this process includes different phases, each of which needs articulation, negotiation commitment and periodic evaluation.
2. For contracts to be effective and meaningful, adherence to professional values is mandatory. No one member's rights can be infringed upon at the expense of another's needs, such as physical and emotional security for the members.
3. Contracts must include responsibilities as well as consequences for violating the terms of the agreement by any of the concerned parties. It is not sufficient to outline the responsibilities and the consequences inherent to the contract without implementation of either one. Nonperformance with respect to any of the terms vitiates the contract, wholly or in part depending on the circumstances. For example, physical violence may require immediate termination, whereas unreported absenteeism may require judicious confrontation.
4. Contract formulation includes procedural as well as human relationship components. Terms relating to the former include the following; time, place, duration, number of sessions, fees, attendance, memberships, confidentiality, privacy and so on. Some of the terms relating to human relationships and expectation of participation include mutual respect, honesty, and authenticity.
5. Contracts have to be stated in explicit and clear terms. For example, a well-formulated and explicitly stated contract will protect the group from sabotage by members whose excessive personal needs may at times impinge upon the groups' goal-directed activities.
6. Punitive usage of the contract as a control measure to satisfy either the worker and/or agency goals should be avoided. Similar contracts should not be used to mark worker limitations. An example would be a worker's retreat into the role of an "expert" when his/her behavior is challenged.
7. Process of contract formulation should have options for sec-

ondary agreements involving certain members and/or the worker.

PROGRAMMING

From the beginning, the use of programs and activities has been a major structural component of social group work. Initially, this departure from the traditional reliance on verbal discussion similar to that of casework was perceived by the social work profession with skepticism. Programs and activities were synonymously linked with play and recreation and thus group work was criticized for not living up to the expectations and standards of the helping professions. Group workers however, justified their use of programs and activities as systematic and planned strategies which were very effective in assessing member and group needs, and in determining their developmental stage. Programs were presented as a tool to be used by the group worker, in other words it was a means to achieve an end rather than an end itself. Thus, group workers in the settlement houses and other neighborhood centers went beyond simply organizing pleasurable activities, although "having fun" as a group goal was by no means ruled out. Programs and activities were seen as intervention strategies to achieve goals, whether they were focused on the individual or the group, addressed to rehabilitative or normal developmental purposes, or generated by the worker, the group members or the agency.

Programming in social group work has been explicated in various ways. Klein (1972) defined *programs* in the broadest terms which include everything that the group members do. He distinguished activities from programs and according to him, the former included such things as crafts, dramatics, and games. Northen (1969) used the term "action-oriented activities" to describe planned, structured interactions in the group. Middleman (1968) used a broader perspective by employing the term "nonverbal content" to describe those interventions whose primary intent is directed toward overt behavior of group members. Nonverbal content, may in fact, contain verbalizations of discussion, role play, or drama, but the focus is on behavior rather than verbal expression of thoughts or feelings. Both Northen and Middleman use the concept of program to imply those activities which emphasize "doing" rather than "talking."

Vinter (1967) refined the definition of *program* in group work, by clarifying that the concept of program loses meaning when it is used to refer to all of the social interactions and processes engaged in by the group. According to him, program is a general class of group activities consisting of a series of social behaviors. These behaviors are guided by meanings and performance standards from the larger culture. In program activities, there is a typical pattern, a sequence, and a conclusion of some sort. Program includes use of and interaction with physical objects. Vinter noted that games, athletics, music, and crafts are the usual program activities. Such things as discussion, role playing, drama and story telling, however, all have programmatic aspects.

In social group work, the debate along the "doing" and "talking" continuum is still going on. As stated earlier, Northen (1969) favored the term "action-oriented activities," and takes an approach that falls toward the talking end of the continuum. She also placed heavy emphasis on discussion as a means of achieving group goals and objectives. For her, action-oriented activities are a preferred method when group discussion has failed or been minimally effective. Action-oriented methods are to be employed only as a means of facilitating the discussion which must always follow the activity. Programming in Northen's view has relevance "for young children and people, whatever their age, who have low tolerance for or lack of ability to communicate verbally in effective ways" (pp. 138–139).

Middleman's (1968) position on nonverbal method in working with people fell at the "doing" end of the continuum. Nonverbal activities are seen as nearly complete within themselves. Growth, change, and development occur during the activities themselves regardless of any verbal follow-up. This is not to say, as Middleman is quick to point out, that there is no discussion or verbalization during or after the nonverbal activities. Rather, it is to emphasize that program activities have rehabilitative and growth-enhancing qualities of their own and discussion occurs as a supplement to doing.

Whittaker (1975) made the distinction that whereas a talking-based process may be effective with adults and, to a lesser extent, with teens, program-type activities are most effective with children. The younger the group of children, the larger the part that should be played by program activities. However, he warned that activities should not be used as a reward that is conditional on performance but employed on a regularly scheduled basis. Whittaker responded to criticism made by practitioners who have experienced problems in use of programs with children, and clarified that the problem lies in ineffective and inappropriate use of programs rather than in any inherent flaw in theoretical formulations. Group overexcitement is perceived as a result of selection of age-inappropriate activities, and confusion is due to the lack of proper planning. Whittaker saw a dangerous trend in the excessive utilization of program activities by certain agencies which overemphasize development of socialization skills in young children. Often children spend their day on buses with other children, in day care or nursery school, in after-school groups, and in neighborhood play groups informally organized by their parents. There is a danger in that some children are seldom left alone. Solitary play and fantasy as well as socialization activities are necessary for both cognitive and affective development, and thus the group workers have to structure program activities which would provide opportunities for both solitary play and/or parallel play.

While most authors take a position somewhere along the talking-doing continuum, Shulman (1971) proposed an alternative way of looking at the group process. He presented a "mixed transaction model" of human interaction. In his view talking and doing are not really separate, but together they are part of a series of exchanges or transactions between individuals or groups of individuals. Thus the task of the group worker is to facilitate mutually productive transactions through all mediums that are available to members. Shulman's conceptualization has merit in that talking has a nonverbal aspect closely related to the doing involved in planned program activities. The other side of the coin is that doing may be seen as a behavioral manifestation of cognition which is an integral part of talking. Talking and doing are intertwined and should both be used to achieve differential goals.

Traditionally programs and activities have been used in working with children or selected adult populations such as the developmentally disabled. However, with the explosion of the human potential movement of the 1960s, interest in programs and activities drastically increased. Some exciting and powerful games to enhance group members' awareness of themselves as well as to facilitate their interactions with each other were suggested by some of the pioneers of this movement (Levitsky and Perls, 1970; Schutz, 1967; Gunther, 1971). Unfortunately, with the greater acceptance of the movement and as growth groups become a vast profit-making phenomena, a number of shrewd entrepreneurs exploited the situation. They not only produced movies like "Bob and Carol, and Ted and Alice," but also mass-produced the do-it-yourself-kits of home activities and parlor games. This introduction of commercial kits had a dual effect on programming and activities in group work. Those original skeptics of this component of group work became doubly critical about using any kind of activities within group work. On the other hand, there were those who were enamored of all the new games and equated worker skill and competency with knowledge and ability to possess a neverending supply of new, stimulating games and activities.

Rationale for Programming

Middleman (1968) stated that the developing child learns a sense of self through doing activities. A recognition of "I do" precedes awareness of "I am." A rationale for use of program activities, according to Middleman, can be found in the writings of educators Jerome Bruner and Maria Montessori. Bruner theorized that people learn through active stimulation of the musculature system in addition to the more passive mode of cognition. Learning occurs through three systems; through manipulation and action, through perceptual organization and imagery, and through the symbolic apparatuses of cognition and language. Social group work often is a form of education and all three systems of learning should be engaged. Montessori contributed a similar notion that cognitive learning is enhanced by stimulation of all the senses.

Kernberg and Ware (1975) described several functions of play. Through play one is able to obtain pleasure at a minimum of risk. If he/she is provided with certain kinds of activities, it is possible for the participant to test out new roles such as moving from passive to active forms of interaction. Play has a cathartic effect in and of itself and it is possible to gain a sense of mastery over anxiety, at least temporarily. Kernberg and Ware reiterate concepts of Erik Erikson and Jean Piaget who have written about the function of play. Erikson sees children's play as a means of mastering reality through model creation and planning. Adult play is seen as a temporary stepping out of reality-imposed limitations. Piaget sees a dual function of play. Because environment acts upon the individual, play provides an opportunity for the adaptation of self to reality. Also, because strength of the self through expression of emotions acts upon the environment, play provides practice in the adaptation of reality to the self.

Konopka (1963) described play as the work of the child; it is the child's occupation. Through play children learn to express feelings and thoughts of fear, anger, and love. For the adult, play is a re-creation of capacities; a kind of creative work. Activities provide adults an opportunity to tell without words. Play, according to Konopka, is a way of changing feelings and attitudes through experiencing.

Schutz and Seashore (1972) formulated a rationale for use of nonverbal exercises. They see group members as being caught up in

146

a pathological cycle of helplessness and withdrawal. The group has to break this cycle by facilitating movement into a growth cycle of personal action. Whereas the child requires non-verbal activity for normal development, the adult needs programmed exercises to increase awareness of resources in others and in the self that he/she cannot readily see.

Program activities may be used to address various purposes of the social group work processes from the viewpoint of the worker, the group member, and the sponsoring agency. In Vinter's terms (1967) program activities can be used by the worker as an indirect means of influence over the group process. Konopka (1963) visualized program activities as being particularly useful for group members who have difficulty to engage in group discussion. Whittaker (1974) detailed the use of program as an aid to the worker in individual diagnosis, group diagnosis, treatment intervention, behavior management and reinforcement of discussion.

Programming: An Ecological Perspective

The foregoing discussion of the use of programming and activities clearly reflects that the use of these components is aimed at the understanding and functioning of all aspects of the group members. Programming as a shared activity accords an opportunity for group members to cooperate as well as compete with each other. Cooperation and competition are the two societal dynamics which influence the functioning of all individuals. By introducing appropriate programs and activities, group members can be provided with a testing ground to assess themselves as cooperative and/or competitive individuals.

The verbal mode of intervention is not always effective with certain client groups. Some ethnic groups as well as clients from lower socioeconomic classes often hesitate to engage in verbal disclosure of themselves. In such situations, use of programming and activities can be very effective as a facilitative device. In other words, programming can be used to facilitate group participation among members who are blocked by ethnic and class differences. Similar experience has shown that men are considerably more guarded and hesitant in opening up in groups than women. With the use of programs one can reduce their apprehensions toward involvement in groups. One can go on with similar examples, but it is apparent that programming and activities complement the ecological perspective of group work, especially the concepts of holism, diversity, competence and adaptation as they relate to group members.

Although the value of programming as a viable structural component of group work is recognized, it is imperative that the worker is cognizant of the following points. For a program to be effective the members should be involved in its planning and operation. The right to the exercise of free choice is a legitimate social work value and this must be adhered to by the worker. Prescribing program activities only on the basis of worker- or agency-perceived objectives is to be avoided. Members' decision to participate or not participate must be respected. The worker should also participate in the activities introduced in the group. Shulman (1971) saw the worker as having equal status with the rest of the group. We also believe that effectiveness of any given activity should be tested before it is introduced in the group. Selection of program should be in relation to the group's developmental phase. Whittaker (1975) suggested activities requiring low cooperation be programmed in early stages lest group members be asked too much too soon. He elaborates that, in later stages, activities can be selected to deal with issues of the fight or flight response to anxiety, of power and control or of autonomy and self-determination.

Selected Practice Principles

1. Interventions in social group work should be extended beyond verbal modes to include use of activities and program.
2. Decision to use programming should be a joint endeavor between the parties who have a stake in the issue.
3. Programs can be used to modify group process.
4. Programs have to be differentiated according to member(s) needs, skills and interests.
5. Evaluation of the impact of a program group member(s) needs to be conducted after its implementation.
6. Programs should be used as a means to achieve an end determined by all four components of group work.

SIZE

There are two types of groups that fall under the domain of social group work: natural groups and formed groups. Natural groups are internally developed and their size is often unconsciously determined. Rarely are naturally formed groups larger than seven members (Steiner, 1972). This natural limit on group size reflects its impact on group dynamics and member preferences. Geographic location also influences the naturally formed groups. Hare (1976) indicated that size of naturally formed groups of rural adolescents usually consisted of three members, whereas group size among urban adolescents generally was four or five members. This discrepancy in size between the rural and urban groups may be due to the physical distance and lack of easy availability of transportation for the rural youths.

Although it is increasingly recognized that group work has to direct its efforts toward both natural and formed groups, by and large such efforts are directed to working with formed groups. Formed groups are those which are formed for a specific purpose. Size as a determinant variable on the effectiveness of such groups has been extensively studied. Research has shown that size has an effect on members, group goals, worker role and so on.

The maturity of the group members needs to be considered in relation to the size of the group. Very young children are often baffled and confused in large groups. Northen (1969) indicated that young children become overstimulated and confused in large groups. They are more comfortable working out their problems within fewer relationships and through cooperative efforts. Latency age children need a small group so that they can have security while they attempt to master the situation. Older adults seem to have difficulty concentrating or becoming involved in large groups (Kalson, 1977).

Members' socioeconomic background also affects how they relate in groups. "Children from large, economically deprived families often are not ready for the intimacy of a very small group" (Northen, 1969, p. 100).

Group size also affects interaction among the members. In a small group, each member has more demands on him/her to become fully involved in the group's communication network. As group size enlarges, the communication network is also affected. In large groups, such a communication network is very complex. With the increase in group size, members have less time available to them to express their thoughts and feelings. In a large group, the members have a large number of relationships to maintain. The number of potential relationships increases with the increase in group members. Hare (1976) postulated that the number of possible relationships grows more rapidly than the growth in the group size. He proposed the following formula for assessing the number of relationships that are possible in groups:

$$X = \frac{N^2 - N}{2}$$

When X = number of symmetrical relationships

N = number of individual members.

Using Hare's formula, in a group of six members, fifteen relationships are possible. Whereas a group of fifteen members will have one hundred and five relationships.

Member satisfaction is also affected by the group size. Members of groups larger than ten members indicated numerous dissatisfactions with their groups. Members indicated that large group activities were poorly organized; the group did not function favorably; there was lack of coordination; there was insufficient time to verbalize and the group time was poorly used (Steiner, 1972). Members of large groups also perceived the group as too hierarchical, centralized and disorganized (Slater, 1958).

Smaller size of group also affects member satisfaction. Members of a small group have difficulty in tolerating conflict and they avoid discord. Slater (1958) described small groups as tense, passive, tactful and constrained to work together in a satisfying manner because of a fear of alienating one another. Slater's description of the necessary conditions for maximum satisfaction needs to include the following: the group has to be large enough to allow members to express positive and negative feelings freely and make aggressive attempts at problem solving, yet small enough so that regard will be demonstrated for the thoughts and needs of other members; large enough so that a loss of a member will not destroy the group and small enough so that a loss of a member cannot be ignored (p. 138).

In smaller groups members interact with each other with greater intensity, but with the increase in size it is difficult for group members to make their unique contribution to the group process. In this context Hartford (1972) stated

> It could be concluded that if individual participation, satisfaction, and engagement of the group members in a process that will bring about change in themselves is the aim of the group, obviously it must be small enough for each person to be heard and to contribute, and also to feel the impact of the group upon his beliefs and behaviors. However, groups should not be so small as to over-expose members or to provide too little stimulation (p. 162).

Group size also has bearing on other aspects of group process such as emergence of subgroups. With the increase in size of the group, there is higher chance for subgroups to occur. Cartwright (1968) in discussing group cohesiveness implied that larger groups tend to be less effective due to more absenteeism and member turnover, thus lessening attractiveness of the group for the member.

Group size also affects the role of the worker. Northen (1969) indicated that "as groups increase in size, there is a tendency for more communication to be directed toward the worker rather than toward other members" (p. 99). According to Hare (1962), "The leader in the group of five will have more influence on the group decision than the leader in the group of twelve" (p. 239). For Hopper and Weyman (1975), the leader of a larger group faces difficulty in balancing individual and collective needs of the members and thus he/she tends to formalize the various activities.

Organizational functions of the worker also are influenced by group size. Large groups tend to experience a greater degree of laughter and joking (Hare, 1976). In larger groups members tend to become more self-benefitting and feel freer to exploit the group (Hambruger, 1975). As the group size inflates, the severity of the results of alienating a single member becomes less intense (Slater, 1958). Due to these negative aspects of member(s) behavior, the worker is forced to assume more control of the group.

Regarding the optimum size of a group, Klein (1972) noted that although five to seven members are ideal, these numbers require that all members regularly attend all sessions. Hartford (1972) stated that the number five appears frequently as the optimum size, but unless the group is mandatory or compulsory, there is always the possibility of absenteeism and this factor should be considered in planning group size. She suggested two more than the minimum as a good number for treatment groups.

Hare (1962) also seemed to agree with several others that size five is the optimal size for most groups:

> Size five combines the characteristics that: (1) a strict deadlock is not possible with an odd number of members; (2) the group tends to split into a majority of three and a minority of two, so that being in a minority does not isolate the individual but allows him sources of gratification; and (3) the group appears to be large enough for the members to shift roles easily and for any individual withdrawal from an awkward position without necessarily having the issue resolved (pp. 243–244).

Shostrom's (1972) stand regarding the size of therapeutic groups was very clear when he warned potential members that

> Never participate in a group of fewer than half-dozen members. The necessary and valuable candor generated by an effective group cannot be dissipated, shared and examined by too small a group, and scapegoating or purely vicious ganging-up can develop. Conversely, a group with more than 16 members generally cannot effectively be monitored by anyone, however well-trained or well-assisted (p. 473).

Slater (1958) indicated that groups of four to six are most satisfying to members, while groups larger than six tend to encourage too much aggression, competition and inconsideration. Golembiewski (1962) enumerated that groups of fewer than four expose their members too much and they feel tense and constrained to express their attitudes and feelings. Although Yalom's (1975) observation regarding size of therapeutic groups may not have complete consensus, it summarized the various implications for treatment outcome.

> My own experience and consensus of the clinical literature suggest that the ideal size of an interactional therapy group is approximately seven, with an acceptable range of five to ten members. . . When a group is reduced to a size of four or three, it often ceases to operate as a group, member interaction diminishes, and therapists often find themselves engaged in individual therapy within the group. Many of the advances of a group—the opportunity for broad consensual validation, the opportunity to interact and to analyze one's interaction with a large variety of individuals—are compromised as the group size diminishes (p. 284).

Selected Practice Principles

The foregoing discussion clearly reflects that group size has been extensively studied by small group theorists and practitioners. It is also clear that group size is a very significant structural property in group work and it has bearings on differential aspects of the group work process. The question that has to be answered is what is the optimum size?

It is evident that when two small group theorists and/or practitioners get together to discuss the optimum size of a group, they may end up with three of more opinions! The point is that group size has to be determined by a number of crucial variables and there is no one particular magical number that can be proposed as definitive.

The following practice principles are helpful in determining group size.

1. *Size is related to demographic characteristics of members.* Age, socioeconomic, cultural milieu all have a bearing on size. For example, a children's group will have to be considerably smaller than the adult group.
2. *Size is related to the interaction desired.* This principle implies that the smaller the group the more demand there will be for each member to become actively and fully involved in the group. Smaller groups also demand intimacy on the

part of members. In forming a group of members who are very threatened by closeness to others, such as certain mentally disturbed clients (schizophrenics—paranoid type), a small group must be avoided.

3. *Size is related to individual member needs.* The smaller the group the greater the chance of meeting member needs because there is more flexibility in directing group efforts.

4. *Size is related to interaction with the worker.* If direct interaction is not always desired between the worker and members, the group can be smaller. By increasing the size, the interaction between the members and worker can be increased.

5. *Size is related to worker comfort.* This refers to the degree of comfort the worker feels in the group. Unless the worker is comfortable, he/she will not be cognizant of group processes, member(s) needs and so on.

6. *Size is related to shared leadership or co-therapy.* When groups are led by two or more workers, the size of the group also should reflect the increase. Otherwise the ratio of worker-member will be disproportionate and both leaders will experience discomfort.

7. *Size is related to initial mortality rate of the group.* Size of the formed group should initially include a couple of members more than the desired number. Experience reflects that dropout rate in formed groups is considerably higher than in the individual mode of intervention.

8. *Size is related to group dynamics.* Size does affect dynamics such as subgroupings, coalitions, decisionmaking and so on. If the goals of the group are to sensitize the members to these processes, then the group size has to be bigger.

9. *Size is related to space and time.* The size of the group will depend on where the group is meeting and whether the space is adequate for the group. Duration of the sessions will also have bearing on the size. Having shorter sessions for large groups will prove to be a frustrating experience for everyone concerned.

10. *Size is related to agency policies:* This principle implies that agency policies such as agency finance and worker caseload have direct bearing on the number of members served in groups.

6
Group Process

Group process refers to all the happenings within the group, and to the interactional and communication patterns among all members, between some members, between all members and the worker, or between some members and the worker. According to Luft (1963), group process "refers to an inference about the meaning of behavior in the group. Behavior may be verbal, as in discussion, or non-verbal as in keeping silent or facing a particular person while addressing the group" (p. 8). Whitman (1964), defined group process as "the dynamics, emotional developments and unfolding affective patterns of the group" (p. 310).

Group process also includes the happenings which are often categorized as group dynamics and which encompass interactional units such as patterns of subgroups, cliques, coalitions, conflict, cohesion, group norms, group roles, decision making and so on. The process component in this chapter is examined along the symbolic interaction and field theories as dicussed in Chapter 3.

Lewin's field theory holds that behavior is the result of a field of interdependent forces. Thus, to analyze group process, it is essential to bear in mind that both individual and group behavior are parts of a system of interrelated events. An individuals' behavior is always derived from mutual relationships between the concrete individual and concrete situation. Thus to appraise the behavior of any unit, be it individual, group or large agency, one needs to study the unit in the context of the total field. The main thrust of field theory is that "an individual's behavior is a function of the 'life space or field', which consists of the person and his environment viewed as one constellation of interdependent factors operating at a given time" (Northen, 1969, p. 15). Thus behavior depends neither on the past nor the future, but on the present field, and needs to be understood in the context of here and now (Marrow, 1969).

Human groups are organismic in nature and are constatnly undergoing change. This change is due to the internal dynamics and/or external—environmental conditions in which the groups operate. As seen in the previous chapter the structural properties are vital components of group work and can be effectively controlled by the worker in achieving the desired goals. Similarly process variables also affect the functioning of the group, thus impacting on the effectiveness of group work. However, the major difference between these two components of group work, is that the structural properties can be managed by the worker. For example, the worker can determine the size and composition of groups, but when it comes to group process, it is not always possible for the worker to control all the group happenings. This is the major reason why the terms, *guide* or *direct*, rather than *control* are used in discussing worker activities related to group process. Group process is a fluid force that is constantly undergoing change. The worker has to be aware of what is transpiring within the group and must direct or guide the group accordingly.

In this chapter the key process components of group work such as interactional patterns, group norms, role and culture, subgroups, group conflicts, scapegoating and group development are examined. Similar to the structural properties, the process components are first reviewed, then discussed in the context of ecological group work practice and subsequently their implications for practice are presented.

SUBGROUPS

Subgroup formation is a common occurrence in a group work situations. This dynamic has significant implications for the individual members, total group membership and the worker. The presence of a subgroup affects member(s) and worker behavior thus impacting on the total group process. The formation of subgroups and their impact on group process are varied. For a comprehensive understanding of this process component it is examined along some of the frequent questions raised by small group theorists and group workers.

Subgroup Development

Both group and individual forces contribute to subgroup formation. Among individual members certain similarities enhance the possibility for a bond to occur. Some of these similarities include physical attraction, attitude similarity, values, congruence, and personality characteristics (Shaw, 1971).

Group size is also a highly influential factor in the formation of subgroups. Phillips (1973) claimed that larger groups tend to foster subgroups with divergent goals. The converse of this premise is that when the group is small enough to permit direct communication, it is more likely to retain unity.

The group situation elicits its own dynamics which produces fractionalization. Initially group members turn to each other for cues or approval, especially during self-disclosure. From this inter-personal pattern subgroups emerge within the group, whether due to feelings of attraction or repulsion, interest alignments or antago-nisms (Hartford, 1972). According to Yalom (1975), subgroups in therapy groups arise from the belief of two or more members that they can derive more gratification from a relationship with each other than in relating with the total group.

Members in formed groups, in the initial phase to ward off anxiety, tend to bind together with fellow members who have simi-lar needs and goals. For example, if a group goal is defined as self-awareness, member(s) who fear group experiences which would entail lowering of old defenses may seek out other group members with similar apprehensions. Thus, certain members bind together into a self-supporting subgroup which functions as a safe haven for them.

Subgroups are sometimes formed due to member(s) discontent. This discontent could be directed toward the total group itself, the group experience, or towards the group worker for having brought them into an "unpleasant" experience. Member(s) in these situa-tions form subgroups to either sabotage the total group or to de-fend against closeness. Yalom (1975) indicated that subgroups are a manifestation of a considerable degree of undischarged hostility in the group, especially towards the worker. Members unable to ex-press their anger and frustration directly toward the worker, release these feelings obliquely by binding together.

Bennis and Shepard (1956), based on their research on human re-lations groups, proposed a theory of group development. In their theory these authors noted that in initial stages of groups, mem-bers' interaction is affected by uncertainty and/or ambiguity re-garding what to expect from the group experience and each other. The interaction is classified into two catergories: dependent and interdependent. Dependent interaction is affected by members' orientation towards authority and how the power issue is handled in the group. The interdependent interaction is determined by the members' orientation towards each other including personal relationship. Both these dynamics have significant implications for formation of subgroups, for example, because of the ambiguity of the group purpose two opposed subgroups develop around the issue of leadership and group structure. In the subsequent phases of group development, different subgroups reemerge around the issue favoring or opposing close interpersonal relations among group members.

Co-therapists who lead groups may at times inadvertently promote subgroup formation (the fan club syndrome). This is apparent when certain groups' members are subtly and perhaps nonrationally encouraged to align with one, or another worker. Such clustering may be due to conflict between the two workers. It could also occur in those situations where certain members perceive vicarious pleasure in keeping the leadership divided.

Subgroup: Membership and Emergent Patterns

Group members with strong personality characteristics tend to stimulate subgroup formation. In other words, influential or dominant members tend to coalesce with more passive group members (Hartford, 1972). In discussing personal influence and power, Redl (1949) introduced the concept of behavioral contagion which has relevance in understanding subgroup formation. "Contagion is the pick up of behavior from the individual to another when the originator has no intention of having the others follow him" (Hartford, 1972, p. 267). Polansky and others (1950) found that group members of high status are more likely to influence other members. The implication of this is that some group members adopt the behavior, values, and lifestyles of those members who are perceived as having more prestige or power in the group.

Subgroups can emerge at all phases of group life. As seen earlier in the formative phase of group development, members may bind together for purposes of security and to ward off anxiety generated by the new experience.

The middle phase, sometimes designated the work phase, can also have subgroups. These are formed through affective ties between members who share and experience similar life situations. In this phase, certain members cling together, each incorporating a significant aspect of the other's life as their own. Subgroups in this phase tend to be supportive to members and not necessarily limited in providing security within the group context. They also function as a support system for the members in handling their respective life struggles.

158

Another interesting observation is that members in the work phase are more likely to shift subgroup allegiances based on the issue at hand than their experiences in an earlier phase.

In the ending phase of the group, subgroups are formed as a means to assist members in dealing with their separation anxiety from the group. Just prior to terminating a successful group experience, members accept the termination of the group reluctantly, and as a substitute, form subgroups to maintain their meaningful experience.

Impact on Group Process

As seen from the foregoing discussion, subgroups are formed for varied reasons. This naturally has bearings on what happens in the total group.

Workers rarely bring a group together with the desire to have subgroups emerge. Although during the composition process workers consider whether or not certain members would be supportive of other fellow members, they do not explicitly aim for the formation of subgroups. However, when unplanned subgroups emerge, group interactions and worker interventions are affected. For example, if a subgroup is formed to express hostility towards the worker to challenge his/her authority, then the workers' behavior is different than when another subgroup emerges as a unit to provide support to the worker, especially if the subgroup assists him/her in neutralizing the hostility directed by the former subgroup.

Subgroups have impact on members in different ways. Some join subgroups as a means of protection, but this membership dynamic may also constrain the individual to be assertive and is costly to their personal identity. The result of such instances is that needs of subgroup members are met only if they are accepted and supported by other subgroup members.

Subgroups also raise the issue of loyalty. That is, whether member(s) should be loyal to their subgroup or to the group as a whole. For example, member(s) face a dilemma in how to interact freely without violating the confidence of their subgroup members. Balgopal and Hull (1973) indicated that secrecy pacts between members or between members and the workers can be a resistive and hindering factor in the group's movement.

Inclusion and/or exclusion from a subgroup can be devastating for group members. Yalom (1975), in this context said, "Exclusion from the subgroup also complicates group life. Anxiety associated with earlier exclusion experience is evoked which, if not discharged by working through, may reach disabling levels" (p. 335).

Subgroups can also have positive effects in achieving group goals. When more than one subgroup emerges in the group, the worker by appropriate direction, can channel the competitive and aggressive energy within these groups in order to meet the desired goals. In other words, existence of multiple subgroups generate the requisite resources which can be used to involve all members in the group process.

Subgroups: Implications for Practice

The emergence and existence of subgroups is inevitable. Subgroup dynamics have relevance for several aspects of work with groups, namely: the meanings they have for members and the inter-member dynamics within each subgroup; the relationship of types of subgroups to the dynamics of the group as a whole; the interrelationships of subgroups to each other; and the shifting patterns of subgroups in the group development.

Each of these points of choice inform the worker's selection of actions. In cases where superior–subordinate patterns are evident in any one subgroup, the needs of the participants are designated, and may further clarify their particular problem areas and coping patterns. When there is a stand off between subgroups, as for example, between assertive and counterdependent types, then the worker has to formulate an intervention which will create a bridging group. In other instances where a dependent and affiliative subgroup is locked into a recurrent defensive position, worker actions have to be tailored to alter the group norms so that submissive behaviors can be respected. The use of select structural properties can be useful in designing practice principles for subgroup dynamics.

1. Subgroups can facilitate and/or hinder group process. This implies that while subgroups meet certain members needs and group cohesion, they may impede other group goals. For example, subgroups that enhance closeness and sharing promote group support, but they also can negate member individuation.

2. The terms of the contract can be applied to affect the process. For emergent subgroups that impede group process, the worker can clarify the dynamic by asking for a reappraisal of their actions based on the group's prupose and member expectations.

3. Subgroups can be complementary to secondary contracts. Secondary contracts involve agreements between select members. For instance, in an alcohol abuse group, members who are concerned about "falling off the wagon," might form a mutual coalition to monitor and support each others' goals for abstention.

4. Use of size affects subgroup process. Subgroup dynamics are likely to be more potent in larger groups. If group cohesion is an important goal, then the worker will have to limit the size to support group affiliation.

5. Group composition can be used to promote or discourage subgroup formation. Situations in which the uniqueness of any one member is in marked contrast to the rest of the group can produce stress for the member. For example, one male in an all-female group, or one minority person of color in an all Caucasian group would be contrary to the best interests of the total group.

6. Programming can be used to alter subgroup dynamics. Requirements of different activities are useful in bridging subgroup differences. When the group process is stalemated by several competing subgroups, the worker can introduce an activity to utilize the competitiveness for group cohesiveness. In a latency or young adolescent group, dissident subgroups can be challenged to work toward a common goal, such as raising money for a group outing.

   Activity structure can be manipulated to create safe positions for marginal members in the groups. For example, timekeeper or scorekeeper roles are relatively innocuous roles which require minimal competition, but at the same time involve the members in the group activity.

7. Subgroups can be instrumental in accomplishing multiple group tasks. In task-oriented groups, the division of labor necessary to produce a group product may be organized through specific groups based on members' interest and skills. For example, patients in an after-care mental health setting who decide to prepare a holiday meal need to be helped to organize their energies in terms of planning, buying, preparing, and serving the food.

8. Group life span can contribute to subgroup formation. Groups which are designed to meet for a long period of time are more likely to promote pairing phenomena.

9. Worker styles is relevant for subgroup dynamics. For example, a controlling leadership style, well-intended, overt, or

subtle, can generate negative sentiments manifested in passive–aggressive pairing.
10. Environmental climate can be instrumental in voluntary or involuntary subgroup formation. An example of involuntary subgrouping is when members engage with a few others despite negative sentiments (car pooling). Under conditions of perceived external threat, members, may put aside individual difference for the short-term benefits of a joint action.

SCAPEGOATING

The term *scapegoat* originated in the Old Testament Book of Leviticus. It referred to a live goat over whose head Aaron confessed all the sins of the children of Israel. The goat was sent into the wilderness, symbolically bearing their sins on the Day of Atonement. In current usage, a scapegoat is a person or group bearing blame for others. No one appears to be left out of the process of scapegoating. It is found in dyads, families, work units, groups, local communities and the society at large. Scapegoating is used to justify all sorts of social relationships ranging from wars and interpersonal conflict to everyday life. This is a very common occurrence in group process and the group worker has to at all times keep abreast of its operation in the group. If necessary steps are not taken to contain the process of scapegoating, the experience can be devastating for the victim and the persecutor(s).

Dynamics of Scapegoating

Social and behavioral scientists have contributed to the growing knowledge of the scapegoating process, as they sought to understand the nature of prejudice in the wake of World War II, McCarthyism and the early days of the Civil Rights Movement. It is clearly a process which is actively present in our lives and frequently is not a destructive presence. Coser (1956) indicated

> In aggression against substitute objects, however (as in witchcraft or any form of scapegoating), though the original relationship is safeguarded by channeling aggression away from it, a new conflict situation with the substitute object is called into being (p. 44).

The most prominent theory to be found in scapegoating is based on Freud's psychoanalytic theory. The term *projection* is only one of the defense mechanisms that the ego uses to defend against perceived danger. This defense is used in the scapegoating process and was defined by Freud to be present when an individual attributes a wish or impulse of his own to another person. The person who uses projection extensively has an impaired ability for reality testing (Brenner, 1974). Although it is opposite to projection, since it incorporates rather than expels, *identification* or *introjection* is another defense seen in the scapegoating process when the victim assumes that role. Anna Freud (1936) extended this particular defense by adding the idea of the identification with this aggressor. The individual identifies with a frightening authority figure since he/she can find no other rational way of acting.

Bion's theory of group in the late 1940s was influenced by the concept of identification with the aggressor. He was also particularly interested in Melanie Klein's projective identification theory which implies that individuals project parts of their personality which they have split off from themselves (Bion, 1970). According to Bion, projected identification in groups is manifested through three processes. First, during the dependency state, the group attempts to force the worker to take responsibility for the group. In doing this, the group attempts to seduce the worker (leader) by presenting one of its members as "sick"; this is accomplished through the scapegoating process. If the worker refuses to accept responsibility for the "sick" member, the group crucifies him/her like a Messiah. Subsequently, in its search for a new leader, the group begins pairing of two members to reproduce for the group. When this fails, since it is another attempt to avoid responsibility, the pair is scapegoated. During the fight—flight behavior, the group fights with one of its members to preserve itself (Bion, 1961, Rioch, 1970).

The theory that aggression is directed toward a member of the group who would not retaliate has been applied to small groups. According to Schulman (1956), the member chosen as the scapegoat "serves as the object of aggressive acting out in an attempt to alleviate the tensions generated by preoccupation with hostility" (p. 204). This hostility is caused by a problem which the group members cannot and will not focus on (Thelen, 1954). Such a problem was seen as anger towards the worker/leader, or the struggle for group cohesion.

Scapegoating in the fifties was analyzed in terms of prejudice and redirected hostility. The major theorists of the decade agreed on the nature of the problem, but did little to enhance the practitioners' skills in dealing with it.

The 1960s brought about a great many social changes. The theory which was evolving concerning scapegoating became more complex and sophisticated. Two major ideas emerged, the first being recognition of the function of scapegoating in the family group.

> In the relations of family and individual, the family seeking to rid itself of a felt threat inflicts emotional damage on a member, but this member retaliates and also damages the family. Each defending himself against the other's urge to blame and punish (Ackerman, 1966, p. 78).

Ackerman (1966), proposed that there are two kinds of family prejudice. Private intrafamiliar prejudice becomes displaced and translated into public forms of prejudice against color, religion or ethnicity. This he saw as circular, because public forms of prejudice aggravate the tendency of private prejudice or scapegoating in the family.

The second major development in scapegoating was the combination of the following two ideas. Some authors had been saying that scapegoating was partially caused by "unconscious emotional factors within the victim" (Northen, 1969). Others argued that scapegoating emanated from the group members. The reconciliation of the two approaches led to the notions that "all such group-member conflicts are two-way transactions" (Shulman, 1967, p. 39).

Major contribution to scapegoating theory in the 1960s came from the family therapy movement. Scapegoating was so frequently observed that workers were forced to take a closer look at the dynamics involved, especially as they related to the inherent mutuality among all components of the family therapy context. By the 1970s this mutuality became the focus for much of the theorizing surrounding this dynamic. Feldman and Wodarski (1975) postulated, "Scapegoating behavior clearly involves social interaction between one or more individuals and their peers, (and) has etiological components at both the individual and group levels of analysis" (p. 88). The group as a unit was recognized as playing a major part in assigning people to roles in order to meet certain needs, or as an expression of "the group's psychological conflict, climate or culture" (Klein, 1970, p. 73). The static nature of the scapegoating role was eschewed and more emphasis was placed on the group process of which scapegoating was simply one state (Hoffman, 1971).

Scapegoat and Victim

A great deal has been written about the victim of scapegoating. His/her personality traits, behavioral attributes, unconscious motives and social awkwardness have all been discussed in the attempt to predict and clarify a potential scapegoat's behavior. The role of scapegoat is a personal role within a group, in addition to the conventional or institutional role (Northen, 1969). The individual is said to have failed to develop socially acceptable adaptive responses due to deficiencies which are habituated. Thus, an individual persists in making the same social blunders and becomes identified as socially incompetent. He/she repeats the *faux pas* in each new group situation because such behavior is familiar and comfortable although it fails to elicit positive responses from others (Klein, 1970).

The scapegoat often has difficulty in recognizing the nonverbal cues which facilitate interaction in a group. He/she appears gauche to the other members when he/she asserts his/her own opinion with no awareness of the subtle nuances which have transpired earlier. His/her participation lacks the control other members desire and he/she is punished for such behavior (Beck, 1974).

The scapegoat has been described as having a history of putting oneself into potentially harmful situations. Such behavior shows a lack of adaptive learning (Garland and Kolodny, 1973). The scapegoat also adapts to the situation through negative attention, customarily denies the pattern of persecution or that he/she seeks it. If the scapegoat recognizes a bad situation, he/she disclaims any control over it. Further, adaptive responses are generally projection, resignation or helplessness (Garland and Kolodny, 1973). Feldman and Wodarski (1975) indicated that

> Scapegoats tend to express relatively weak commitment to group norms, contribute negligibly to the performance of basic group functions, express low liking for peers and are attributed extremely low social power (pp. 189–90).

The scapegoat's role is due in large part to the role expectations of his/her peers. As discussed in Chapter 3, the reference group plays a major part in molding a member's expectations and behavior. For scapegoated individuals, reference groups may include peers, family and group members.

Ackerman (1966) proposed that in scapegoating, there is a persecutor who uses special prejudice as a vehicle for attack on a victim. In addition, he suggested that there is also a "healer" who rescues the scapegoat. This healer may be the worker but at times it could be one of the fellow group members, and an example of the protective function of subgrouping.

Scapegoating and Group Process

The sources of tension that lead to scapegoating in groups are adaptive attempts to control the effects of conflict. The group makes an irrational compromise which results in the distortion of the emotional life of the group. The roles within the group become rigid and prejudicial, the result being the occurrence of scapegoating. The prejudice can be directed horizontally, vertically or diagonally, such as male against female, young against old, white against black, power against passivity. There is an allegiance to a particular set of values, and norms, which are organized irrationally around the process of scapegoating.

Stigma according to Goffman (1963) is "the situation of the individual who is disqualified from full social acceptance" (preface). Individuals stigmatize others to confirm their normalcy and adequacy. The group member who is selected as the scapegoat symbolizes the conflict and draws off the tension which is expressed nonverbally in the group. Since the group is unable to scapegoat the outside community, it selects a scapegoat inside the group to maintain its equilibrium. Frequently, the scapegoat is the member having the lowest status in the group. In this context it needs to be recognized that frequently by establishing a scapegoat the group maintains an equilibrium and channels group tension through the victim. Thus, the internal conflicts for the other group members are controlled and unminimized. In other words, it serves as a "personality stabilizing system" for all members of the group (Northen, 1969; Bell and Vogel, 1960).

As mentioned earlier, scapegoating occurs within a group when there is anger toward the worker which the members are fearful of expressing. The style of leadership has a dramatic affect on the behavior of the members. White and Lippitt (1960) indicate that autocratic leadership results in aggression against scapegoats. According to Lewin (1948), in autocratic groups the members cannot obtain a higher status and the group scapegoats a member in order to obtain the desired higher status. Thelen (1954) suggested that some leaders give tacit approval to such actions.

Coser (1956) postulated that need for group cohesion is a contributing factor to scapegoating in a group. According to him, the small group cannot deal with internal conflict and hence punishes expression of dissent with exclusion. The primary aim of the group is to maintain its own structure and it therefore searches for enemies within and without on whom to focus their united animosity.

The selection of the scapegoat is sometimes related to the source

166

of tension in the groups. If the group norm is achievement-oriented, then the individual who does not achieve or achieves too independently may violate the group norms, and thus may be cast as a scapegoat (Bell and Vogel, 1960).

Scapegoating: Implications for Practice

Social roles, personality needs and interpersonal processes combine to form a unifying theme in the dynamics of scapegoating. Based on this premise the following selective practice principles can guide worker behavior.

1. Scapegoating is a cyclical process which is rooted in group processes, group structure and group development. This implies no one member or subgroup serve as the permanent target. Furthermore, shifts in process and overtime demand may create pathways for other members to assume this function. Both affiliative and achievement-oriented members may be subject to ridicule under the right conditions, most often when there is great disparity between their needs and group sentiments. For example, member suggestions "to get to work" may be summarily rejected if the group is comfortable in maintaining the status quo.

2. Etiology of scapegoating can be centered in perceived threats to the members, to the group, or social environment. Threat to a member's self-esteem or status can give rise to competitive feelings which are projected on to vulnerable peers. Group-perceived threats from sources in the environment may trigger ridicule and harsh attacks which are displaced irrationally on the external source. For example, Caucasian youngsters may ridicule ethnic minority youngsters as a means of handling their apprehensions about an up-and-coming athletic contest.

3. Worker reactions and scapegoating dynamics may be correlated. For example, member(s) or worker's ambivalence to handle face-to-face confrontation may lead to choosing convenient targets to mask their own inadequacies.

4. Scapegoating can serve as a safety valve to maintain group balance. Feelings of anger and frustration are common phenomena in groups. When these exceed the tolerance level of the members, the need for ventilating their feelings against a common target produces release from the pent-up emotions.

5. Rescuers of scapegoats are likely to end up as victims. What this implies is that altruistic members who move to protect scapegoated members may be victimized as substitute scapegoats.

6. Scapegoating can be masked through patronizing behavior. An example of this dynamic is when members of a dominant group mask their true feelings toward oppressed members.
7. Competitive processes are more likely to create scapegoat roles. The implication of this principle is that under highly charged competitive situations, members seek to identify weaker members as scapegoats to guarantee their own success.
8. Scapegoating necessitates differential worker roles which are present-centered. The worker has to sustain, support, clarify, mediate, and neutralize the member–group–agency–environment process that maintains or triggers scapegoat dynamics. Helping groups face their discontent, creating and supporting new role patterns for their victims, neutralizing explosive situations by anticipating and being ready for their occurrence, are all practical ways in which to deal with victimization.

GROUP CONFLICT

Whenever two or more individuals interact with each other over a period of time, differences are bound to emerge. However, these differences are frequently disguised or discounted. Some of the reasons being; one party does not want to challenge the power or authority of the other for fear of reprisal or negative consequence; the parties may not be sure of themselves and their stand on issues which have given rise to the differences; and recognition of such differences is perceived as a threat to the relationship. In addition to these reasons, individuals are often reluctant to confront around interpersonal difference as we are conditioned to not dispute over differences. There is a possibility that differences around issues, opinions, priorities, values, needs and so forth can escalate into conflict.

In our society, conflicts are perceived as unpleasant and hostile differences between and among two or more parties. Conflicts are regarded as dysfunctional, disruptive and damaging to any relationship. This attitude is clearly confirmed through expressions in our everyday speech: "Don't upset the applecart"; "Don't open Pandora's box"; "Let the sleeping dog lie"; "Don't open a can of worms"; "Sweep it under the carpet"; "Don't let the skeletons out of the closet"; "Let it be"; and so on. The prevailing societal value is on maintaining the balance, homeostasis or equilibrium. But the paradox is that our society also emphasizes growth, progress and excellence, none of which can be attained by maintaining the status quo. Change is an absolute must for growth, which is not only bound to disrupt the balance, but at times give rise and/or recognition to conflict.

The ecological perspective recognizes that to achieve a balance within a system, conflict is inevitable. Conflict is not regarded as dysfunctional or negative, but frequently seen as a necessary contributing factor for progress. A similar position has been expounded, for quite some time, by social and behavioral scientists. The seminal works of Cooley (1918), Simmel (1919), Follett (1942), Lewin (1948), and the expanded contributions of Coser (1956), Bernstein (1965), and Deutsch (1973), have great significance when recognizing the positive functions of conflict within a social group work context.

Positive Functions of Conflict

Coser (1956), in discussing the functions of social conflict, indicated that in the early days of American sociology there was a great interest in conflict as a social process. Conflict was seen as a fundamental and constructive part of social organizations. Cooley (1918) stated: "The more one thinks of it the more he will see that conflict and cooperation are not separable things, but phases of one process which always involves something of both" (p. 19). After the two World Wars, such writers as Talcott Parsons (1949), and other contemporary sociologists viewed conflict as primarily disruptive, dysfunctional, and as a "disease" (Coser, 1956). Parsons and his generation were interested in the conservation of existing structures rather than progressive change in the social order. Lewin (1948) developed a contradictory attitude toward group conflict, at times emphasizing the positive functions of conflict and then, the dysfunctional aspects of conflict. According to Coser, sociology moved away from identification with social reform and toward a more neutral scientific position in relation to social change, with the additional components of working for industry and government. The trend in sociology away from emphasizing conflict was indicative of what occurred in our society during the postwar years.

"Contradiction and conflict not only precede unity but are operative in it as every moment of its existence . . . There probably exists no social unit in which convergent and divergent currents among its members are not inseparably interwoven," wrote the noted social theorist Simmel (1919, translated, 1955). Coser (1956) derived a number of basic propositions based on Simmel's classic theories and reversed the theme of social conflict from that of dysfunction to one of positive adaptation and adjustment of social groups. "Commitment to the view that social conflict is necessarily destructive of the relationship within which it occurs leads . . . to highly deficient interpretations" (p. 8). It is only through the expression of differences that it is possible for a group to define its common values and interests. As areas of disagreement are explored, areas of agreement become crystallized. At the group level, conflict may lead to enhanced understanding and stronger relationships among members; differences are aired and not allowed to remain submerged. Conflict provides stimulation. Social conflict may have consequences that increase, rather than decrease, the group's ability to successfully solve problems which emerge in that group. Group workers such as Bernstein (1965), Follett (1942), Northen (1969), Klein (1972), and Wilson and Ryland (1949) considered conflict to be an inevitable occurrence which has potentially functional and constructive aspects as well as dysfunctional and destructive ones. This is the general position that most of the social work literature embraces today. Conflict can contain both positive and negative potential at many levels of interaction. The way in which group members resolve and manage conflict is crucial to the survival of that group. The opportunities of the group worker to influence the handling of conflict vary considerably according to his/her attitude toward conflicts.

In propogating the constructive use of conflict, Follett (1942) noted: "As conflict—difference is here in the world, as we cannot avoid it, we should, I think, use it. Instead of condemning it, we should set it to work for us" (p. 30). She suggested three patterns of conflict resolution: (1) domination, (2) compromise, and (3) integration. Domination is a victory of one side over the other. In compromise "each side gives up a little in order to have peace, or, to speak more accurately, in order that the activity which has been interrupted by the conflict may go on" (p. 30). In integration, the goal supported by Follett, neither side gives up anything essential. A new solution is created into which both positions fit and are respected; the conflict is truly resolved.

In his paper on conflict and group work, Bernstein (1965), suggested that social workers present a mixed picture in their ability to handle conflict. Bernstein elaborated that Freudian psychology makes conflict a central construct in understanding how people develop, feel, and behave. According to this theory, people are viewed as constantly living in conflict and, by their very nature, they are unable to escape it. However, the general social atmosphere tends to give conflict a place of lesser importance. Many social workers rate conflict as a highly negative value. Bernstein cited that in "The Teaching of Values and Ethics in Social Work Education" written in 1959, Muriel Pumphrey listed words used by her resource people according to their positive or negative values. Conflict appeared under the heading of "Words Representing Disvalues" (p. 54). Apparently, conflict was regarded as dysfunctional in relation to social work values.

The attitude of the group worker toward conflict can vary. The worker may regard conflict as unpleasant, undesirable, indicative of immaturity, and perhaps even as a reflection of his/her own inadequacy. The worker having this attitude toward conflict may attempt to prevent and even to suppress conflict in groups. This feeling would be conveyed to the members who might adopt a sense of shame or inadequacy concerning actions which express or confront conflict. Another position might be that conflict is somehow an unfortunate concomitant in this stage of the group's development, but that this unpleasantness is a temporary evil and real functioning will emerge as soon as this stage has passed. At the other end of the spectrum, the worker may venerate conflict as an ideal state as Coser did, or the worker may realize that conflict has its terrors but it none the less offers magnificent opportunities for growth.

Northen (1969) defined the essence of conflict as difference. In the conflict situation there are three basic elements: (1) there are two or more identifiable focal units or parties; (2) the units perceive incompatible differences in needs, goals, attitudes, values, or ideas; (3) there is interaction between these units around the differences. Hostility is the emotion often associated with the behavior of conflict. Conflict refers to contradictory, incompatible emotions and impulses within a person on the intrapersonal level. On the group level, conflicts arise out of the interpersonal conflicts of individuals, differences in the members' goals and values, their motivations and interests. Conflict can also be caused from the divergence between the values and norms of the group and those of certain segments of the community of which the group is a part. These differences in goals, values, and norms are caused by differing socio-economic resources and life experiences.

Thelen (1954) noted that the most important feeling to be expressed and dealt with was aggression. Without aggression there is "slavish dependence." Every new gain in maturity has to be fought for and every planned change requires aggression to carry it out. He did not equate aggression with hostility. A decade later Bernstein

171

(1965) viewed hostile and aggressive feelings in groups as normal. It is better to permit the group to ventilate hostile feelings and rid itself of these feelings. Groups tend to reflect the kind of early experiences of its individual members. Most individuals and groups have feelings about authority; consequently the leader must be sensitive to the nature of the hostility and determine the real reason for the hostile and aggressive behavior.

Similar to Bernstein, Coser and Northen also have referred to realistic and unrealistic conflict. Realistic conflict is tied to a rational goal, the conflict concerns the means of achieving that goal. Realistic conflict offers "functional alternatives as to means." The end is relatively fixed, but the means is chosen in terms of what will be most effective in reaching those ends. Unrealistic conflict does not arise from clear issues. It springs from the irrational, emotional process of those involved. Frequently the parties are unaware of the emotional process that has motivated them in the struggle. Most conflicts have rational and irrational elements, being both functional and dysfunctional at the same time.

Wilson and Ryland (1949) suggested that conflicts and their solutions become the central core of any activity of any group. According to them, conflict can be resolved in any of the following ways or combinations thereof: elimination, subjugation, compromise, alliance, and integration. They also agreed with Follett that integration is the highest achievement of group life.

Bernstein (1965) added another framework for conflict resolution. His pattern of resolution focused more on how the conflict is handled by the group members, which he listed in a hierarchy, starting at the lowest level.

1. *Physical violence*—the attempt to beat the opponent into submission.
2. *Verbal violence*—the attempt to belittle the opponent, to make him look ridiculous, and to marshal the feelings of the group and others against him.
3. *Subtler verbal contention*—the attempt to belittle and undermine the position of the opponent without violently attacking it.
4. *Finding allies*—the attempt to line up others to support one's position, which tends to be a power play.
5. *Seeking an authoritative decision*—the attempt to find someone, probably the group worker, who will say definitely who is wrong and who is right.
6. *Creating diversion and delay*—the attempt to displace attention on something other than the conflict.
7. *Respect for differences*—a desire to understand how the opponent sees the situation, to collect and head the needed facts, and to attempt to think rationally about the conflict (pp. 60–62).

The positive functions of conflict are succinctly summarized in Deutsch's (1973) following statement.

> Conflict has many positive functions. It prevents stagnation, it stimulates interest and curiosity, it is the medium through which problems can be aired and solutions arrived at, it is the root of personal and social change. Conflict is often part of the process of testing and assessing oneself and, as such, may be highly enjoyable as one experiences the pleasure of the full and active use of one's capacities. In addition, conflict demarcates groups from one another and thus helps establish group and personal identities; external conflict often fosters internal cohesiveness (pp. 8-9).

Conflict Theory Expanded: Implications for Practice

Although the functional and constructive aspects of conflicts have been recognized by group workers, the foregoing review of literature indicates that this recognition is only on a limited level. Reasons for discomfort with conflict previously mentioned range from a long-standing argument about the influence of structural-functional theory on American sociology to the heritage of the Protestant tradition in the Western world.

The psychoanalytically oriented group workers have focused on the intrapsychic conflicts which members bring to treatment. These include the conflicts one experiences due to unsuccessful resolution or completion of the different stages of the human life cycle. This conflict is referred to as nuclear conflict which lies at the base of personality, and stems from the earliest phases of life (Durkin, 1964). Intrapsychic conflict which emerges in the therapeutic relationship between the member and the worker has been studied under the phenomenon of transference and countertransference. The works of social group workers cited earlier have focused on interpersonal conflict within the group process, which emerges between and among constituent members. The sensitivity training, encounter and other human relations groups received their impetus from the works of Kurt Lewin also focus on interpersonal conflict.

The group workers of the present, similar to their predecessors, focus on the two levels of conflict: the intrapsychic and interpersonal. At this juncture it is suggested that to be an effective worker, one will have to be aware of the conflicts on another level which members bring to treatment. This third level of conflict is designated as allogenic conflict. Allogenic conflict is defined as friction or discomfort experienced by individuals due to significant and notable differences between them. The differences can be both on implicit and explicit levels and further can be physical, psychological, racial, ethnic, economic or on other social and institutional levels (Balgopal and Vassil, 1979; Balgopal, 1980).

Allogenic Conflict

Group workers typically deal with issues such as authenticity, dependency, counterdependence, and so forth, which relate to both intrapersonal and interpersonal conflicts within the context of the group. Allogenic conflict refers to quite a different situation. It presumes that member allegiances to groups based on sex, age, religion, ethnicity, race, and the like are in themselves part of the stresses and strains of contemporary life. Thus, the development of the social self as described by symbolic interaction theorists is intricately meshed with, and defined by, both identification as well as potent experiences with various types of reference groups. Small group processes typically focus on individual and interpersonal dynamics. What tends to be left out are the conflicts engendered by intergroup tensions in the wider society. The effects of these intergroup tensions constitute part of group work, and in fact, focusing on personal and interpersonal material exclusively may be counterproductive with reference to allogenic conflict. The importance of antecedent group experiences has been most clearly stated by Birnbaum (1975) who noted that

> It now appears fallacious to assume that a change process involving interpersonal experiences based on contact and emphasis on human similarities will significantly influence the complex feelings and prejudices which are rooted in group identifications (p. 342).

The construct of allogenic conflict, defined as member group identifications and intergroup tensions needs to be placed into a theoretical context that is applicable to small groups. The following propositions begin to spell out the theoretical matrix.

1. The group is a vehicle through which internal and external demands are in reciprocal and continual interaction.
2. The internal and external demands are intricately interwoven within the interdependent matrix of person-group-and-society.
3. Conflict among these elements provide the grist for work in the group.

The person-group-societal interdependence and conflict are neatly summarized by Thelen in the following way. In broadest terms, "human behavior represents the efforts of human beings to work out the problems from their overlapping membership in various internalized groups" (Thelen, 1950, p. 5–29).

If one accepts the idea that membership in various types of groups during an individual's life leads to an internalized set of thought-feeling-actions, that these are potent influences, and that the social self is in part a function of overlapping group membership, then it is reasonable to consider the effects of these potent membership groups in group work.

Given the relationship between the potency of overlapping group membership and the reflection of society's problems within the interactional matrix of the group, then the content of discussion becomes an important consideration. That is, rather than focusing exclusively on the process behind what is said, the content itself becomes a springboard for group work. One could argue that the emphasis on process may become a defense or escape from highly charged content. This point of view raises a number of issues which need to be considered by the group worker.

Group Phases A number of social work theorists have described stages of group development which typically lead to greater cohesion and from this to an examination of personal and interpersonal issues that are surfaced in the context of mutual respect, self-differentiation, and a group culture which permits risk taking, change, and practice of new behaviors. Phases with respect to groups that focus on intergroup tensions are somewhat different. Birnbaum (1975) noted three: noncohesive, cohesive, and anti-cohesive or divisive, in that order. The noncohesive phase refers to awareness and revelation of primary and secondary group influences (the "who am I" issue). The cohesive phase refers to intermember recognition and appreciation of ethnocentrism. The anticohesive phase refers to exploration and confrontation of the constituent members' present feelings. This point of view apparently contradicts the expectations of developmental processes in regular group work. However, the goals for dealing with allogenic conflict are somewhat different. One cannot expect empathy, trust, and positive regard to be able to satisfactorily deal with issues that have a formidable historical development. The best one can hope for is that persons will realize the limitations and clarify their own commitments and perceptions of the extremely complex variables involved in intergroup tensions. It may not be necessary to love one another in order to work together. As Birnbaum (1975) noted, "It involves a realistic recognition that the effects of group differences can be understood, lived with and controlled, but never dismissed or eradicated" (p. 346).

175

Leader Self-Disclosure and Authenticity Ordinarily the group worker will self-disclose under appropriate conditions and even then in small doses. Worker-directedness is necessary in the early stage of group work to permit group processes to develop. However, with allogenic conflict, the worker may have to make his/her biases explicit at the very beginning in order to allay suspicions that he/she is somehow "above" the issues. The point is that cultural as opposed to personal and interpersonal transferences are to be encouraged.

Process vs. Content A major issue with allogenic conflict is whether or not the worker emphasizes process or content in the work of the group. In terms of group process, the worker raises questions within his/her own "assumptive world", of the following sort, what are the underlying meanings and feelings with respect to what is being said by whom and why now. However, process comments slow up groups, in addition to focusing the work on interpersonal and intra-personal issues. Allogenic conflict requires dealing with the content itself, and thus process comments may detract and legitimize avoidance of intergroup differences which are real, potent, and current. Hence, the emphasis in dealing with allogenic conflict is with potentiating, debilitating, and maintenance of specific forces that undergird racial, ethnic, sex, or other differences.

"Here and Now" vs. "There and Then" While experiencing in the present has been and is an important principle in regular group work, allogenic conflict requires the encouragement of the "there and then" influences precisely because the historical stereotypes need to be examined and confronted. This raises a related issue with respect to worker knowledge. Not only must the worker understand and utilize some of the process skills but, in addition, must have a broad behavior-science perspective of the various arguments and theories underlying intergroup differences. The worker functions as a guide, expert, and in many cases, a group member with his/her own biases and viewpoints which are to be expressed.

Reeducation vs. Therapy Dealing with allogenic conflict would seem to be closer to reeducation than classic therapy. However, one could expect a certain amount of personal growth among members as they learn and become aware of the heretofore unrecognized choice points which they have made, or must face. There is much to be said for the security and courage that is attendant upon the validity and adequacy of a personal frame of reference that permits

176

self-initiation and action on one's own behalf, and an avoidance of demands and pressures that one does not wish to meet.

Problem Solving or Clarification As such, no problems are solved in the strict sense of the word. It is more likely that, at best, one may expect clarification of issues. Members may have a fuller appreciation of how they see themselves, how others see them, and how they perceive other groups. There may be less identity change than identity stabilization and crystallization.

Group Composition As in regular social work groups, heterogeneity among members would seem to be most important, especially around differences in ethnicity, race and so on. Members would also need to be able to articulate points of view, stand up to counter pressure from other members, and have the capacity to expand and rethink their world views. In addition, there needs to be adequate capacity for dealing with the uncertainties that are bound to persist once the group experience has terminated. It seems reasonable that member dyads representing various "groups" would be required for mutual support.

Professional Values Allogenic conflict poses a number of professional value issues germane to group work practice. One will have to ask the hard question of professional identity and skills vis-à-vis the ethnic and other differences and expertise that workers bring with them. Perhaps this will lead to specialization in terms of working with specific populations. Are there in fact ethnocentric configurations of thought-feeling-behaviors that need to be welcomed, sharpened, and conceptualized for teaching and practice?

The most pressing issue, for group work practice is whether or not allogenic conflict can be dealt with at the same time interpersonal and intrapersonal aspects are considered. Discussion of some of the issues has taken the stance of presenting polarities and emphasizing the differences between regular and allogenic conflict. At this point, and intuitively, it seems reasonable that all three forms of conflict be included as part of group work practice. Granted that the balance between content and process is fraught with difficulties, as in the direct and open role of the workers, however, one of the goals of group work, is learning to live with and deal with uncertainty, at cognitive, affective, and behavioral levels. Furthermore, one of the major goals of social work is to enable clients to cope with, and contribute to, a pluralistic community. The issues raised by conflict are most pertinent to this goal. Given this, the group workers can utilize a variety of techniques (role playing and other exercises) to develop a group culture that enhances the uneasy but necessary equilibrium between process and content.

The major goals of group work practice are to facilitate tension reduction and eventual resolution of conflicts experienced by clients. It is believed that in addition to conflicts on intrapsychic or interpersonal levels, conflicts on allogenic levels also fall within the domain of social work practice. To elaborate this point further, let us take a specific example. One is quite aware of the struggle a woman has to go through in our society, within its social, economic and political structure, in attempting to achieve equality with her male counterpart. When a woman group member reveals her frustration and struggles in a social work group situation and aims some of her anger and anguish at male members, her needs are often negated or minimized. Often workers and fellow members in their own "supportive" way dodge this issue and say that the group is not in a position to handle societal inequities. In some instances this woman's feelings are interpreted as due to the Freudian syndrome of "penis envy." Conflicts on these levels do affect an individual's functioning and have to be dealt with in social work groups. The conflict between personal identity and social identity does affect one, and this needs to be recognized by group workers. To deal effectively with allogenic conflicts, the workers will have to be aware of their own values on such vital issues as human sexuality, sexism, racism, ethnicity and so on. They will have to be aware of their values and value conflicts in relationship to prevailing societal values. The workers must also be willing to share their values as well as allogenic conflicts in order to create a dynamic process of values clarification that can often be the initial influence for change on the part of the member.

ROLES

Problems in the definition of the role concept are pervasive in social science literature. Shaw and Constanza (1970) note the difficulties.

> Role theory is a body of knowledge and principles that at one and the same time constitute an orientation, a group of theories, loosely linked network of hypotheses, isolated constructs about human functioning in a social context, and a language system which pervades nearly every social scientist's vocabulary. (p. 326)

For this reason, it is important to develop precision about its definition and use.

Linton (1938) offered one of the most quoted definitions and makes distinctions between status and role.

> A status, as distinct from the individual who may occupy it, is simply a collection of rights and duties . . . (A) role represents the dynamic aspect of status. The individual is socially assigned to a status and occupies it with relation to other statuses. When he puts the rights and duties which constitute the status into effect, he is performing a role (p. 113–114).

Bonner's (1959) definition builds on Linton's work.

> Role per se cannot be defined for as such it has no existence. It derives its meaning from the status of the person who "occupies" a role. Status (also called position) and role are inseparable. It is a set of rights and duties, as Linton pointed out. These rights and duties determine the individual's "place" or position in the group or community . . . A role, on the other hand, refers to the action performed by the individual who holds a certain status, in anticipation of others' expectations. (p. 375).

Thus, two notions are developed by Bonner, that of a person-in-a-position, and that of action or behavior. Biddle and Thomas (1966) have further clarified role conceptions. For them "there is one universal common denominator, namely, that the concept (or role) pertains to a particular person," (p. 29). The authors then go on to extend the role concept into a person-behavior matrix as the most precise way in which the concept of role can be viewed. Position can be used to refer to any subset of individuals grouped together as the basis of a socially recognized catergory. When put in the context of a group, these could include group member, group worker, and typical member. The designations, when connected with perceptions, neatly contain some of the most important ingredients in working with groups.

The particular content of the roles within these three sets may be abstracted from the work of Benne and Sheats (1948) who formulated three member role classifications as functional to problem solving groups. They are group task, group building and maintenance, and personal roles. These designations are quite similar to the instrumental and expressive categories developed by Bales (1950). Items such as "asking questions," "initiating ideas" describe task roles; "sharing feelings," "smoothing out disagreements" relate to maintenance roles; "ignoring others," "goofing off" represent idiosyncratic behaviors. Bales' theorizing (1955) led him to suggest that instrumental and expressive forces are always at work in groups. The interplay between these two forces produces a cyclical orientation that becomes expressed in two problem solving activities, those dealing with group solidarity, or innerevents. These problems result in role differentiation which present solutions to each of the problems depending on the stage of group development. Thus, when a group is working on a task, i.e., planning an agenda for a meeting, it is postulated that, at some point, social-emotional roles will appear, either by way of joking or friendly by-play that will pull the group into the gravitational field of expressive forces. As the task forces become dominant, it deprives the social emotional force of actualization and, in so doing, triggers the release of the task force.

The construct of roles is useful for assessing an individual's tendencies in a group, and provides the worker with a means for understanding the person. The determinants of behavior which describe the particular role pattern must be observed through relationships between the person and significant others, including the group leader. A dependent role pattern might include the following descriptive member attriibutes.

- Gets upset when held accountable for his/her ideas.
- Avoids uncomfortable situations through humorous asides.
- Yields immediately when interrupted by other members.
- Shows concern about what the group leader thinks of him/her.
- Expects group leader to suppress conflict or handle antagonistic members.
- Willing to go along with what the group wants to do.
- Asks for unnecessary help.

The central dynamic in this pattern appears to be a preference for security rather than self-initiative.

A conflicted role pattern would include sentiments that are markedly different from the above. Conflicted members are more likely to

- Perceive that the leader is just like any one else.
- Impulsively express feelings toward other members.
- Prolong or intensify a particular point.
- Ready to take sides in an argument.
- Suggest ideas opposite to the group leader.
- Take criticism as a personal attack.
- Offer advice when it is not solicited.

The dynamic in this pattern suggest self-control as against group control.

A more enlightened role pattern that emphasized personal and interpersonal striving might be described in the following way.

- Suggests ideas when the group is stuck.
- Engages in real give and take with others.
- Builds on others' ideas.
- Reminds group to stick to its purpose.
- Accepts and follows other member's and group leader's ideas when he/she doesn't know what to do.
- Risks embarrassment by sharing honest opinions.
- Invites and supports comments from other members.

These role patterns reflect the dynamics of a person in relationship to other members and the group leader. The particular attribute can be related to task, maintenance, or person aspects in a group, each representing a type of problem that the group must address. In group work practice, each of these three are continually being evaluated for their relevance to ongoing work between group, interpersonal, and personal learning.

General terms describing role patterns such as dependency, conflict, and striving are not meant to provide a complete picture of what the person is, simply because events in groups shift so quickly and may elicit different responses among members. An individual may prefer to be obstinate under certain conditions, cooperative under others and so forth. Recurrent features become more predictable and useful when they are pinpointed to certain specific problems which bring the members to the group in the first place. Even then, careful observation is necessary to ascertain under what conditions, and with whom does so and so behave in certain ways. Assessed tendencies may shift from time to time, or take different forms over time, depending on the work and transactions that are pertinent. Dependent responses may be a sign of maturity when one doesn't know what to do, or defensive if they are underpinned by personal fears of exposure. When nonassertive members can relax their needs to self-protect, and criticize another members' domineering tactics, then we see a shift of diagnosed tendencies that lays the groundwork for a revised and meaningful set of internalized expectations. Shifts in one role pattern mean shifts in perceptions and action of significant others as well. When these complementary activities can be depended upon by the participants, then the context of the actions has become content for the relevant members and the group.

Roles: Implications for Practice

1. Roles are to be conceived in terms of relational aspects. No single recurrent behavioral pattern stands alone but must be viewed in the context of continuous and ongoing actions with other members. Members who are disposed to argue or backbite constantly need reinforcement and stimulation from others who supply the means for its occurrence. The major actors in a group work situation are the members, typical members, and the group worker.

2. The current role behavior patterns are useful only to the extent that they are related to the problem under consideration. It is a disservice to members to categorize them forever with one designation simply because one is not in a position to know all there is to know about a person.

3. Diagnosed role patterns, even when related to problems, may not necessarily be viewed as dysfunctional. For example, dependent behavior (accepting direction from the leader) may help move a group along when it is not sure of what it's doing. Conflictual or assertive tendencies are useful when addressed to confusion over the group's purpose. In addition, the workers task is, on certain occasions, to bridge or interpret one set of tendencies to another simply to enhance exchanges. Flexible behavior, which refers to using different adaptive strategies to situations, means that dependency and assertiveness have their uses, and in their implementation, members can learn from each other. This is an example of the principle of mutual aid.

4. Roles can be usefully distinguished in terms of task, maintenance, and personal aspects. Each of these categories represent a set of activities that can reasonably be expected to occur in groups. Some members are more in tune toward the purposes, ideas, plans, and actions in groups. Others are comfortable with supporting, sharing feelings, recognizing others contributions and so forth. At times members have to "tune out" for short periods so that they can reassemble their thoughts, feelings, and relative position. It is not infrequent that members shift among these three categories depending on the events that are transpiring. Nor is it likely that the shifts will take place in equal amounts, quantitatively or qualitatively.

5. Task, maintenance and personal roles are related to the types of work that the group must consider. Rationality, and ability to plan are necessary ingredients to meet task demands. Attention to feelings (vague and specific), as well as honest and authentic interchanges are correlated to what may be termed maintenance work.

Personal frustrations are likely to require more intimate pairings so that they can be talked out. Attention to each of these role categories is useful to organize the strategies of the group worker.

6. Actions that the worker takes are addressed to relationships between and among members and the worker, because it is in this context that roles are shaped, maintained or altered. The worker may interpret, reinforce, create, or neutralize role patterns in groups. When roles are missing, as for example, in those situations where the group has gotten stuck in a dead end, the worker must clarify the purpose or address the resistance to move the group ahead. In those instances where certain members attempt to dominate and steer the group, the worker must attend to provide pathways for other inputs. Role behaviors that enhance cohesiveness, striving, facing and dealing with discomfort, trying out new behaviors and so forth, deserve support and compliments. Women members in a marital couples group are to be supported publicly (in the group) when they assert their views against opposite sentiments that favor male prerogatives for speaking. Interpreting different role patterns between and mong members is important; it enhances members' understanding of each other. When *counterdependent* members begin to appreciate the dynamics of apathy among other members and vice versa, then the knowledge may serve to relax the depressive anxieties each may raise in the other. Particularistic and designed role exercises are a useful strategy by which role enhancement can be managed.

7. Role differentiation (more than one role) and role complexity (greater breadth in one role) are desired states in developmental group work. This refers to the point that desired and agreed upon change objectives may require learning to act in a number of new roles or simply expanding and modifying a few well-chosen "old" roles. The extent of change can be sequenced and applied through progressively more complex situations that are consonant with the expectations outside the group. It is possible to visualize assisting a scapegoated ten-year-old boy to full-fledged group membership by sequencing timekeeper, manager, referee, and competitive role through the recurrent use of programs such as tag team wrestling matches.

8. In situations of role changes, parties for whom the change has relevance must be attended to. This means that responses, perceptions and expectations are *inextricably* interwoven between and among participants who have a stake in the problem. Changing frequently means giving up an old pattern that is infused with meaning even in situations of duress. Usual ways of responding are

dependable. Attendant themes of loss and apprehension are likely to be present in any form of change. Consequently work with mothers, parents or families of children in activity group therapy, as well as with teachers in school-related problems, needs to be considered. For example, security in dependency is lost to some extent when one becomes assertive. There are also more likely to be *confrontations* and aggressive counterresponses to assertive behavior. Hence, giving up the old for something new raises other issues, such as a potential shift from a subordinate-superior role set to peer relationships.

9. Role perceptions and actions are valuable choice points for assessment and treatment. The relationship between perception and performance is complex, and affective states are likely to intervene in the process as well. Public acts of performance are valuable for assessment because they are observable. Furthermore, they are subject to alteration, practice, and renewal. Perception, which guides action is more inferential and subject to errors in assessment.

NORMS

It is difficult to conceive of stability in groups in the absence of standards or rules that govern behavior. These regulatory mechanisms are necessary because, as Bonner (1959) pointed out

> While there may be no explicit standards present in the early interactive phases of group formation, a set of norms soon develops, giving the interactive structure a degree of stability without which it could not long function as a group . . . . these standards, or norms, serve as frames of reference for the behavior of one individual in his relations to other individuals. When an individual becomes a member of the group, his membership is determined by the fact that he accepts, at least provisionally, the reference frame of the group. He does not behave as he pleases, and he does not satisfy his motives arbitrarily . . . . one cannot explain the similarity of behavior of people in groups on any other ground (p. 50).

The work of Sherif (1936) and Asch (1955) represent pioneering efforts in the study of group norms. In the Sherif study, subjects, under different conditions, were asked to judge the movement of a stationary dot of light in a dark room. When tested alone, each subject developed a personal standard regarding the movement of the dot. The personal standards were replaced by group standards when the subjects were placed in a group meeting for three sessions and the experiment repeated. Differences between group standards of the three groups were noted and attest to the uniqueness of each group. Clearly, however, group standards replaced individual standards. The potency of group standards was demonstrated again, in another experiment, when subjects were tested alone after first having to develop a response in group meetings with several other persons. It was demonstrated that subjects maintained the group-derived standard.

Asch devised an experiment whereby subjects would view two sets of cards: one set containing a vertical line, and the second set containing three lines of unequal length, one of which corresponded to the line on the first card. The object of the experiment was to see if several members, "coached" to give a deliberately inaccurate response regarding the correct matching of lines on both cards, would affect the response of one "naive" subject who was the last to respond after hearing (but not discussing) the answer of the others. While most "naive" subjects discounted the accurate responses 37% of the time, the other "naive" subjects yielded to the group pressure and gave the wrong responses. The yielders demonstrated a powerful need to conform. Both of these experiments demonstrate the controlling and constraining influence of group-derived standards on individual behavior.

Norms can be defined as shared expectations or ideas which lie behind their manifestation as behaviors. Homans (1950) defined a norm as "an idea in the minds of members of a group, an idea that can be put in the form of a statement specifying what the members or others should do, ought to do, are expected to do, under given circumstances" (p. 132).

Cartwright and Zander (1960) addressed the issue regarding the sources of normative formation in groups. The noted "(a) Membership in a group determines for an individual many of the things he will learn, see, do, think about and so on . . . , (b) an individual may act like others because they are attractive to him and he wants to be like them, (c) a person may behave in a manner similar to the rest of the group because he fears punishment, ridicule, or rejection by the members unless he does act as they do" (p. 139).

Norms are ideas that guide behavior, are related to membership, are based on degrees of *attraction* that a person perceives in the group for their (normative) *potency*, and are maintained through sanctions such as ridicule, self-guilt and so forth.

The extent to which members accept or reject the influence of a group as exercised through the interactional network is related, according to Yalom (1975) to how cohesive the group is. In a review of research on the positive effects of group cohesion, he notes that members are more likely to influence and be influenced by others, more willing to listen, participate more actively, endure more stress, and express differences.

Northen (1969) cited other functions which group norms may entail. In the first place, responsibility for enforcing agreements is shared by the group rather than any single member, thereby enhancing cohesiveness. Secondly, while norms can facilitate the group in achieving their objectives, they also can serve as obstacles, especially if cohesion and closeness become ends in themselves. Groups that are very friendly and sympathetic can also be overprotective. There are positive functions to deviance in groups that relate to normative patterns, particularly in clarifying the group boundaries. When a group member violates a norm, the definition of the norm and the sanction become clearer, a point also noted by Cartwright and Zander. For example, new members introduced into a group that has met for some time have to be socialized to learn the rules of the game before their active participation is welcomed. New members are expected to assume a rather passive and subdued role as part of their breaking in period. When their activity exceeds other members' expectations, such as prematurely commenting on others' experiences, giving advice, or offering opinions, other members may freeze them out by withholding communication, by staring, or by simply not responding. Another facet of normative sets is that even in those situations where the expectations are fairly evident and clear, as for example in terms of self-disclosure, one still has to evaluate the quantitative and qualitative limits of too much or too little, and the expressive forms which are tolerable.

While group norms provide the necessary framework for achieving group and member goals, variability in their development and acceptance is to be expected and welcomed. Dependability and certainty can lead to pressures for uniformity that may satisfy needs for comfort and reassurance but they can also stifle change. When members play it safe, do not exhibit strong feelings, and emphasize politeness at the expense of disagreement, their resistances to work have to be challenged. More positive manifestations of pressures to uniformity occur when members share and communicate empathic concern for each other such as exchanging feelings and ideas that are pertinent to the problem at hand. However, in both instances, the impetus for work or change arises out of expectations or thought-feelings that are violated. Without conflict, then, there is little likelihood for change. And the intermember differences, real or imagined, portray variations in each members frame of reference, that, for better or worse, hold the person together and give a sense of meaning to his/her life. These differences are more powerful when they involve beliefs, in contrast to attitudes or opinions which tend to be more superficial. Members, for example, who are self-starters, expressive, competitive, or counterdependent are not likely to sit still for too long in a situation that rewards passivity. It is more realistic to consider that, in general, conflict and cohesiveness exist side by side and not in quantitatively equal amounts. Cohesion produces the necessary protective envelope that relaxes defensiveness and enhances communication. It is a necessary platform on which conflicts, and norms favoring their expression, can emerge. It is for this reason that retreats to rigid and *unyielding* points of view can be successfully managed.

Variability in the development and acceptance of group norms is to be expected. Whenever a number of people commit themselves to work together in a group for whatever purposes, one can expect life to become very complicated. Personal inclinations, past experiences, processes of affection and disaffection, ranking others as a result of social comparisons, all dictate divisions and alliances. These are manifested in variations in the quality and quantity of participation which influences the extent and seriousness to which members are listened to, ask questions or give opinions, feel threatened or comfortable and so forth. These factors play an important part in the development, syntheses, and alteration of expectational sets that govern group behavior. For this reason, it is difficult to conceive of group norms at any one point in time being accepted by all members. A more reasonable position is that a norm attains group potency when more than half of the members are willing to abide by it. If several members consistently arrive at a group meeting late, or there are consistent interruptions of others' opinions, and these behaviors go unchallenged, then one may presume that an expectational set has been accepted, at least for the time being.

Group norms also vary in the scope and expression of behavior that is tolerable, and the limits may shift at different points in the groups' life. Silent members may manifest their involvement in a nonverbal way which signifies a commitment to the group. Members who express a bored, disaffected stance are likely to elicit less favorable responses than those who demonstrate attentive listening. In addition, even attentive listening over a period of time may violate expectations that verbal and emotive participation is a requirement and a commitment to the group work. The rewards that members perceive, elicit, and express that encourage the fostering and continuity of certain norms can be provided in various ways. Receiving and sharing respect, affection, and support between and among members enhances feelings of togetherness in addition to validating a person's conception of self and the reality of the group. In those instances where mutual help seeking and help giving behaviors are exchanged, such as ideas and skills, these norms of complementarity and reciprocity may converge to add impetus for further individual development.

While groups develop a set of expectations that regulate the internal activity of the members, they are not isolated from the environment in which the group exists. Adolescent groups that exhibit patterns of fighting, hostility to institutionally based authority, or truancy, often are in harmony with normative patterns in their community. The "reward" for truancy might lie in the personal needs for membership in a peer group, or acceptance by older youths or adults. Even though truancy and antisocial behavior are perceived as destructive, they are not useless since the capacities and security of individuals are dependent on them to some degree. Oddly enough, law-violative norms are often reinforced through opposite sentiments expressed in other community relationships such as teacher–pupil, policeman–citizen, clergy–parishioner and so forth. Conflicts such as these are likely to be present in the content of work with group and for that reason dictate a course of action that includes group environmental relationships.

Norms and "Cultures"

Clusters of norms may be used to describe a system or group-as-a-whole. Reference to normative sets and their variant development constitutes major foci for group workers in assessment and intervention. Terms that have been used to designate systemic or gestalt states include "atmosphere", "climate" and "culture". The notion of group "culture" has been defined by Thelen (1968) to mean

> the set of agreements through which the group controls its operation. Thus, if a group has a "set toward incouraging members to participate in its leadership, the cultural shift is likely to be the development of the agreements necessary to implement this policy. . . . through experience, the group spells out in practical language the "meaning" of its beliefs about method, authority, justice, and other values (p. 282–283).

The use of the term "culture" to represent a group's normative set is essentially functional. Indeed, there are many definitions and conceptualizations of the term culture as demonstrated in a sizeable book on the subject by Kroeber and Kluckhohn (1952). In this volume the concept is meant to convey the way of life a group develops as an adaptive pattern to recurrent problems that emerge as a result of member exchanges.

It is necessary to point out that the term "total group" is intended to mean more than the sum of the individual members, a point noted in Lewin's work. The "more than" points to aggregate characteristics that are not only different from, but often not found in the components alone. Group culture is defined in terms of agreements that exist for a group at different points in time, or at one point in time, such as a single meeting. Groups are often described as cooperative, competitive, happy, sad, anxious, tight, buoyant, edgy and the like. In each of these situations, certain group-shared sentiments or agreements operate as controls for the expression of behavior on the part of some group members.

The language to describe group cultures is an important tool for group workers because, in addressing communication to the "group", one is actually referring to normative related patterns. Examples of statements that would describe a dependent group culture for example would be: group members' decisions are never final until approved by the group worker; when members disagree, the worker steps in to settle the argument; members prefer to abide by the rules rather than raise questions; and so forth. Hence, as these brief examples indicate, statements describing relationships between members, members and the worker, and both with the group, are ways in which a group culture can be described and related to what the worker observes and assesses in the process of framing an intervention.

The group culture at any one point in time may interfere with, or promote, goal-centered behavior within the group. In a broader sense, the culture mediates between person-centered indications and environmental demands, as for example with program activities. The ingredients of a "successful" culture have been identified by Yalom as change mechanisms, and by Miles as properties of temporary systems. In either case, these properties or mechansims describe a set of norms that the group worker attempts to develop for purposes of change in growth. Discussion, conceptualization, and specification of group norms have been the object of study by various group theorists. Redl elaborated on the significant props of a therapeutic milieu and how they can stimulate childrens' behavior. White and Lippitt (1960) identified elements in various

189

atmospheres (democratic, laissez-faire, autocratic) that *correlated* with leadership styles. Bales' theorizing (1955) led him to develop a methodology for measuring specific member acts that represented instrumental and expressive *forces,* reciprocally influential in a cyclical fashion, in groups.

These states, according to Bales, represented two different problem-solving activities which were expressed in the appearance of certain roles. Stock and Thelen (1958) investigated the types of cultures as they were manifested in subgroups, groups-as-a-whole, and other membership patterns. More recently, Feldman (1974) described and assessed interrelationships among several normative sets and member behavioral patterns. Silbergeld et. al., (1977) have developed an instrument to assess psychosocial cultures in adult helping groups.

The work of these theorists suggest that the group-as-a-whole, a normative set, relates to other structural features in groups such as leadership, subgrouping, program and so forth. They also point to the importance and emerging empirical interest in discovering a set of relationships between part–whole relationships.

The relevance of generalized others, defined as "most persons" in a group to self perception has been demonstrated in a study by Miyamoto and Dornbusgh (1956).

With a little imagination, one can connect role perception or performance patterns, group cultures, program activities, leadership and so forth. The dimensions of cultures, roles, and program activities have been designated as major elements in the development of groups (Vinter, 1967). Identifying, describing and developing normative sets is important for assessment and treatment of the group-as-a-whole and for diagnosing relationships of member tendencies and actions to the gestalt.

Group Norms: Implications for Practice

1. Norms are ideas that are manifested in various behavioral patterns among members, the worker, and the group.
2. Norms are necessary in order to guide and govern group behavior. More than half of the members must accept a norm for the potency of the group to be realized.
3. Group norms are more potent when there is a sense of cohesion or attraction to the group.
4. Norms favoring security and change are essential for group work. *Orientations* which emphasize only one of the normative sets are likely to produce polarization. The relevance of a

normative set is to be evaluated on the basis of the needs of members and the group.

5. Normative sets in groups are related to prevailing community sentiments. Consequently the relationship of the group norms to the environment must dictate the worker's course of action in the group.

6. The degree of acceptance and alteration of a group standard will vary from deep rooted beliefs to superficial opinions or attitudes. The latter are subject to greater expression and change than the former.

7. Deviance or *variations* among members help define the normative set as well as the scope of tolerable behavior.

8. Norms cannot occur without *sanctions,* which may be manifested in direct or indirect ways in the form of guilt, exclusion, or confrontation.

9. Norms may vary from one single meeting, within a meeting, or over a series of meetings.

10. Alteration in normative sets is *inextricably* related to goals, members capacities and intermember patterns as manifested in subgroups, roles and other dimensions. Normative sets, however are a unique emergent reality which contribute significantly to the quality of the work of the group.

7
Group Development

The construct of group culture is a convenient springboard by which to discuss and examine group development. The point of view to be advanced here is that it is easier to justify broad phases of development designated as beginning, middle, and end than it is to specify with any precision an orderly arrangement of phases that occur over time. A review of various formulations of group development suggest a clearer perspective of special problems and issues at the beginning and ending phases. On the other hand, it is also possible to elicit major themes, patterns or cultures that are common among various theorists, and it is our contention that these cultures are recurrent, nonlinear, and emerge continuously in processes of cycling.

The question of orderliness and lineation have been raised by social work theorists. Garland et al. (1965) are not sure whether their stages or frames of reference are normative or descriptive and note that earlier stages may reappear at later points in time in the group's developmental history. Northen (1969) states that

> Actually, no group moves along in an orderly sequence, but progress is made unevenly with steps forward and backward and then ahead to a new level of consolidation of gains. Most groups are in transition somewhere between identifiable stages of development (p. 190).

Sarri and Galinsky (1967) note that

> Periods of progress, however, are often followed by periods of regression. . . .Although the group may experience several 'revisions' and appear

to revert to earlier stages, different dynamics can be expected in each of these regressions and progressions because of prior experiences. Repeated challenges to the leadership structure often occur, as do attempts to revise norms, purposes, tasks, or operating procedures (pp. 83–84).

It appears then that not only might earlier stages appear at later times, but that their form and content will be manifested in more complex patterns due to successive experiences in the group.

While each culture can be described qualitatively, they are not likely to emerge in any "pure" form but in various blends that remain to be described precisely. Cycling of recurrent cultures can occur over time, and at any one point in time, such as a single meeting (Bales and Strodtbeck, 1956). Their presence or absence, in whatever combination or form, will vary with respect to type of group, purpose, setting, goals, leadership, subgroupings, content and so forth. Indeed, the major task of the profession is to discover concommitant variations among cultural configurations and other pertinent structural and process variables. This point of view is consistent with Hare (1976) who notes that

> The assumption that the group moves from phase to phase when a sub-group or leader is able to carry the movement needs to be documented by further research, since previous observers do not discuss the process of development in any detail; rather they simply observe that one phase follows another (p. 111).

What is missing are the methodologies used by participants and worker to move from one stage to another. The requirements for elucidating, describing, and classifying the processes have several implications for practice. The first is that concomitant variation of group cultures, roles, leadership, conflict and the like can lead to a theory of change which can inform assessment. Second, the partic-ular strategies used by practitioners at various choice points in the process can lead to a classification of process-situation strategies that will frame the foundation for a theory of practice and conse-quently to enhancement and teaching of skills. The work of Lewin and Mead, particularly in terms of culture, goals, roles, conflict and so forth, is instructive in elaborating the how and what of process from which the "why" of assessed part–whole relationships can be inferred. To the extent that shifts in part–whole relationships can be described, then principles of change and of human behavior can be inferred as well.

A THEORETICAL OVERVIEW

The construct of culture applies to the totality of the group-as-a-whole at one point in time, or at different points over time. The characteristics of a group at any moment may be described in terms of normative sets, which typically refer to implied or explicit agreements among the group members even in the formative stage Golembiewski (1962, p. 228). Common agreements in groups are acquired through processes of opinion exchange, discussion, conflict resolution, decision-making and interpretation of others comments which incorporate both covert and overt aspects of communication. The unique systems of understandings in a broader sense reflect a bridging of the various individualized *assumptive worlds* that contain intrapersonal, interpersonal and social roots. The group, or *emergent reality*, that forms as a result of member–member–worker interactions and transactions assumes a potency of its own when members begin to pay attention to perceived sanctions or opportunities that refer to expectations of significant others.

The group as emergent reality represents a mediating vehicle between the transactions of persons (internal) and their environments (external). The term *psychosocial* incorporates these different levels of conceptualization which are also to be found in other orientations to the study of human behavior and small groups. According to a survey by Thelen (1959), the interactionists (Bales, Homans) suggest internal (expressive) and external (instrumental) dimensions. Organizational theorists (Hemphill, Stogdill) cite informal and formal aspects. Psychoanalytically oriented theorists such as Redl, Bion and Slavson emphasize genetic modes of adjustment to external demands through some form of central state (ego) functioning. Sociometrists (Jennings, Moreno) postulate forces of attraction and repulsion which delineate members' social space in terms of *psyche* (spontaneous, personal) and *socio* (task, impersonal) networks. Lewin cites the field of forces which impinge on a person's life space as situated in both the situation and the person interface. Mead notes the dialectic between the "I", which is spontaneous and unguided, and the "me" which represents the incorporation of significant others to self-development. Common to these approaches are the ideas of psychological and social-environmental dimensions which are in reciprocal and constant interaction as well as representing two different sets of needs. The group acts as a mediating vehicle for these twin needs, those that are person-centered; and those located beyond the person and in the situation. Both these sets of needs have to be dealt with and represent social work's interest in both the individual and the group, sometimes referred to as two sets of clients (Shulman, 1979). These inner and outer directed needs also signal the possibility of conflict and tension which emerge when processes or authority and intimacy interlock. The purpose of social group work is to set up conditions whereby these opposing polarities can be examined consciously and guided by purpose.

These twin needs represent dialectical forces which are always in a state of tension, such that the appearance of one, sets up counteracting responses from the other. Hearn (1958) used the terms of *organization* and *de-organization* to describe the two competing themes. The former suggests a pull toward conformity and groupness while the latter corresponds to individual interests. The push-pull phenomena has also been termed as centrifugal and centripetal forces by Schwartz (1971). Common group tasks and demands counteract the individuals' separate and idiosyncratic goals and desires. It is possible to incorporate the construct of culture to these twin forces. For example, an overemphasis on common tasks and rules might describe a constrictive, overconfining and highly organized group. An overshift in the opposite direction that favors individuality can be termed labile which reflects loose, possibly affective, and idiosyncratic behavioral patterns in groups. A third type of group can be described as integrative, which refers to a balance between individual and group centeredness. In this configuration one might expect a balancing of formal and informal, or socio and psychic group processes rather than an emphasis on either one or the other. The blend of these two processes corresponds not only to different participant skills, but practitioner strategies as well.

Each of the three distinctive and pure group states has relevance for individual behavior both in terms of constraints and opportunities. That is, for each of the cultures, group relevant aspects of personality, or valences, will trigger different responses among individuals. Thus, for example, dependent members may be frustrated by an integrative state, and assertive and self-striving members, individually or in the group, would likely find it frustrating when dependent members recommend that the group adopt the leader's point of view.

The upshot of this discussion is that group cultures and individual(s) behaviors go hand in hand. Furthermore, the construct of cultures can be related to other concepts such as roles, decision making, subgrouping and so forth. Each group cultural configuration represents a qualitatively more complete picture of group process than any single variable such as roles. The impact of this for practitioners is that these interrelated concepts provide a framework by which part–whole relationships can be assessed and intervention strategies developed and implemented. Whether or not shifts in cultures are signaled by the emergence of particular subgroups, internal leaders and so forth would constitute a major advance in predicting group behavior. Finding concommitant variations within group relationships clearly addresses and emphasizes the importance of the empiric role in practice, a point of view shared by others as well (Northen, 1969, p. 49).

STAGES OF DEVELOPMENT

A stage, according to Northen (1969), "is a differentiable period or a discernible degree in the process of development, growth, or change" (p. 49). The value of stage theory which typically describes developmental bench marks over time is to guide the worker in forecasting probable future scenarios, setting objectives, organizing perceptions for assessing meetings, and inducing a sense of optimism that comes from preparation and mastery of likely responses to various stage specific events. The danger, of course, is in forcing observed and experienced group processes into a set of preconceived stages that may not fit precisely. It is for this reason that stages be conceived in terms designated as beginning, middle, and end, and that pertinent themes be identified which can recur in various combinations. This approach leaves the door open for more precise and empirically derived developmental patterns that can form the base for further testing in a variety of groups, purposes, and settings.

In order to extrapolate common factors and themes along a developmental arc, Table 7-1 has been prepared as a summary of major theories of group development specifically chosen to include social work and social science efforts.

The Beginning Phase

The beginning phase of work with groups includes three subsets of activities or themes that are related to membership issues of initial engagement and continuance in the group. Pre-group refers to activities and sentiments that lead to the first meeting. Exploration and involvement start with emergent processes in the initial meeting which continue and develop into other themes over several early sessions, depending on type of group, purpose, setting, membership,

TABLE 7-1

Models of Group Development: Equivalent Stages

Garland, Jones, Kolodny (1965)	Sarri & Galinsky (1967)	Hartford (1972)	Northen (1969)	Tuckman (1965)	Mills (1964)	Mann (1967)	Glidewell (1975)
	Origin	Pre-Group					
Pre-Affiliation	Formative	Formation	Orientation	Forming	Encounter, Testing Boundaries & Modeling Roles	Initial Complaining, Premature Enactment	Prudent Exploration, Involvement
Power and Control	Intermediate I Revision	Integration Disintegration and Reintegration	Exploration and Testing	Storming	Negotiating an Indigenous Normative System	Confrontation	Conflict
Cohesion	Intermediate II		Problem Solving	Norming			Solidarity
Differentiation	Maturation	Group Functioning and Maintenance	Solving	Performing	Production	Internalization	Work
Separation	Termination	Termination	Termination		Separation	Separation	

and so forth. Each of the three subsets will be described briefly. (The terms *subset* and *cultures* will be used interchangeably.)

Pre-Group   Prior to a first meeting, a series of interconnected activities must take place to lay the foundation for group work. Excellent descriptions and delineations of the tasks and issues have been presented by several social work theorists. Hartford (1972) for example uses the term *pre-group* which includes private and public aspects. Northen (1969) classifies the initial task as planning and intake processes. Garland et al. (1965) employs the term *pre-affiliation* while Sarri and Galinsky (1967) describe preliminary issues as occurring in the origin phase. There are a number of common issues that can be extrapolated from the work of these theorists. Following is an attempt to synthesize the most salient factors.

Prior to a first meeting, a conception of the necessity and utility of a group experience has to be framed in the worker and/or agency assumptive world. Usually, the worker's knowledge of a particular client population derives out of the worker's personal experience, the agency's accumulated wisdom based on service evaluation, or through relationships with other professional staff (referrals) in the same or other agencies. Converting the wisdom staff may have about clients to an ironclad rationale for group as a treatment modality is not particularly easy for several reasons. While there is accumulated evidence that suggests group as a treatment modality "works" (Bednar and Kaul, 1978), whether or not groups are more effective than individual treatment is still an open question (Meltzoff and Kornreich, 1970; Bednar and Lawlis, 1971). Nonetheless, consideration of group work as an expeditious and promising treatment modality may be applied to acting out adolescent groups in a housing project; patients discharged into the community from medical, psychiatric, or residential treatment settings; parents of anorexic children; parents of premature infants; neighbors advocating for a change in services stemming from public auspices and so on.

Other relevant factors follow from the initial conceptualization. After developing a client population, consideration must be given to type of problems, compositional variables (size, age, sex, ethnicity, client capacities, and so on), type of group (short-term, long-term), type of participation (voluntary, natural, formed, involuntary), membership (open, closed) and corresponding agency characteristics that will support or limit the nature of the experience, such as fees, priorities, time, space, and so forth.

Interviewing methods typically are used to assess client capacities, initiate role induction, preparation, goal setting, contracting, and finally to notification of time, place, and date of first meeting. Clients undoubtedly will exhibit ambivalences regarding asking for and receiving help which may vary with age, type of problem, social class, ethnicity and other factors. For example, most helping relationships encompass feelings related to affection (expressive) and task (instrumental) requirements within the helping systems. Needs related to authority and intimacy, particularly as these characteristics may be perceived to reside in the helping persons, are likely to contaminate the client striving for self-sufficiency. These needs are likely to be exacerbated by fears based on uncertainty about what it is like to join with unknown members for purposes of learning or change, despite careful efforts by the worker to build positive expectations.

The conclusion of pre-group work and issues ought to culminate in a sense of optimism between worker and client so that the group modality can be a beneficial experience. Following notification of the time and place of the first meeting, another set of dynamics emerges in the clients' initial encounter with one another.

Exploration Member participation in first meetings is often colored by cautious exploration. The initiation of new sets of relationships with perhaps seven or more other members and a group leader is fraught with uncertainty. Perceptions and appraisals of others are based on the member's previously developed schemata and methods for dealing with new situations. Innocuous and sometimes diffuse conversations (Northen, 1969; Hartford, 1972) can mask approach-avoidance patterns (Garland et al., 1965), which are tempered to locate areas of common concern and interests within the group. The selective awareness is based on a societal frame of reference, since at the moment, it is the most relevant. Seeking and giving information, talkativeness, and tendency to present oneself in the most favorable light are part and parcel of the search for meaning. Questions such as, "what can I give, get, accept or not accept and from whom," reflect initial ambivalences and sorting out experiences about one's niche. The fragmented information that is available, given the tentativeness of initial comparisons, may enhance tensions and lead to reactions of dependence on the leader, silence, self-sufficiency, self-consciousness, checking reaction of others by tone of voice, posturing, gestures and so forth. Sometimes, the anxiety may be displaced by complaints (Mann, 1967) and gripes about "outside" affairs. Attempts to define the situation through mutual exchange of information are directed to overcome and cope with the anxiety of newness (Tuckman, 1965).

The initial meeting may also signal the beginning frustration of two basic and fundamental motives, namely, achievement, effectance or control, and affection or nurturance (Glidewell, 1975; Mann, 1967). Subsequent meetings tend to exacerbate the effects of these twin motives which lie not only within each member, but in the position and function of the group leader. Issues that are raised relevant to this increasing pressure lead to another set of dynamics that may be subsumed under *involvement.*

Involvement There are several other designations that are synonymous with *involvement* (Glidwell, 1975). The heightened anxiety results from a greater appreciation and consideration of what it means to be a member of a group. Often perceived as threatening, this subset has been characterized by Mann (1967) as premature enactment; by Mills (1964), as testing boundaries and modeling roles. Members may face the question of whether or not they should take a chance on a new behavior when the odds for success are low and for failure or embarrassment and confusion are high. Tolerance levels among member interactions are likely to be stretched as well, although not evenly. The preconceived notions members start with in the initial meeting are not meant to have lasting value. Both convergent (closed) and divergent (open) thinking may be manifested in what Mills calls "explorer and experimenter roles." Other emergent roles may be "silent critics as supporters," "overt challengers," and "the aloofly self-sufficient." Superficial pairing is an important tension management device as a response to unsettled feelings. Finding common ground with another provides opportunities to relax and check reality under relatively benign conditions (Northen, 1969).

Glidewell's (1975) explanation of events occurring in the involvement subset, or culture, focuses on the concepts of decentering and risky shift, followed by a reduction in uncertainty. Briefly summarized, Glidewell states that the members increasingly come face-to-face with two frustrating yet necessary motives in groups, namely, achievement or performance, and affection. As uncertainty increases, given the demands of the group and membership, some members are likely to experiment with ways to deal with the incipient uncertainty and thereby take chances as a way of managing a new situation. As they do, cognitive dissonance is reduced by a developing rhetoric that there is more to be gained by risk taking than caution. Sampling of safe outcomes by those who take chances tends to validate the risky shift and thereby generates less uncertainty. This is not to say that all members will experiment at the same time, but that there are likely to be some. In point of fact,

201

this expectation is built into the contract at the pre-group stage. The decentering occurs as a first step in the trial and error process and is propelled by members' striving sentiments to tackle new situations when old (tried and tested) schemata are not quite applicable. The approach-avoidance dynamic then, represents the dialectic between the polarities of exploration and caution and may be considered to continue throughout the life of the group although manifested in other ways as different problems emerge.

The Middle Phase

The middle phase in group development corresponds to decisions members make concerning their commitment to and capacities for change. It may also be called the work phase which is signaled by what Benne (1964) calls the shift from polarization to paradox; by Bales (1953) as the tendency for groups toward equilibrating a balance of forces between task and socioemotional polarities; by Bennis (1964) as oscillation between authority and interdependence; and by Bion (1961) as work-emotionality dynamics. The accent is on polarities that are in constant and reciprocal interaction throughout the life of a group and represent fundamental and simultaneous problem-solving dimensions. In simpler terms, the members are continually faced with decisions and choices in such issues as: foresight or spontaneity, dependability or uncertainty, peace or conflict, dependence or interdependence, me (the member) or them (the group). Each of these competing authorities correspond to different sets of skills, and members may assume various roles depending on their capacities and predispositions. For example, pairing and counselor type roles correspond to affective and stable vicissitudes, while negotiating, assertiveness, asking questions and probing for the "why" are more task-centered. Tuckman's (1965) stages reflect this shifting dynamic over time, as do Northen (1969), and Garland et al. (1965). A shift into the "middle phase" means that these polarities are to be transcended by members, rather than being stuck in one or the other. That is, members must come to grips with the realization that these conflicts are always present; it is through struggle and intelligent choices that we may resolve them. This latter point reflects the transcendance or "working through" phenomenon.

The "middle phase" is signaled by members realization that, in point of fact, they are in charge of their own lives, which also requires necessary changes that they've contracted for. While the expectations have been outlined in the beginning through the contract, the meaning of this hits home in what Garland et. al. (1965) call normative shock. The essence of the normative shock, a transition stage, suggest that time-honored norms, whereby members have a right to receive clear instruction and the worker the duty to supply clear answers, are violated (Glidewell, 1975). The legitimate power of the member to demand answers is dissolved and the ensuing authority vacuum manifested by the worker induces this situation. The dissolution of expectations means that members have to seek from each other the type of help and guidance that they need. Hence, certain members may try to fill the authority gap; others may provide skilled social aid. On the other hand, members with strong safety needs would be reluctant to take initiative in the face of assertive and perhaps competitive demands from other members. The heterogeneity of group membership permits the taking on of roles that can also provide for complementarity such that member A gives and receives certain type of help (ideas, feelings, and skills) from member B whose needs may be quite opposite. Conflict occurs when members' needs begin to interfere with one another, as when two members have needs to dominate. Thus, stability and conflict are ever-present, a point noted by Northen (1969) in quoting Simmel (1955),

> contradition and conflict not only precede unity but are operative in it at every moment of its existence. . . . There probably exists no social unit in which convergent and divergent currents among its members are not inseparably interwoven. (p. 40)

The concept of mutual aid (Shulman, 1979) corresponds to those moments and events in the group when there is a high exchange between and among members in terms of thoughts, feelings, ideas, and skills. When various polarities are being confronted, used, and transcended, then the mutual aid system is operating at its peak, a condition which is described by various theorists as performing (Tuckman, 1965), differentiation (Garland et al., 1965), group maintenance and functioning (Hartford, 1972), maturation (Sarri and Galinsky, 1967) and work (Glidewell, 1975). A unique feature of this phase is that closeness is based not only on the genuine affection between and among members, but also on the recognition that other members have something of value to exchange. These major themes—conflict, intimacy and their conversion to mutual aid (differentiation)—encompass the essential dimensions in the middle phase.

Challenges to the existing structures between and among members and worker precipitated by the normative crises and manifested in power struggles are noted by both Garland et. at. (1965) and Sarri and Galinsky (1967). Resistance to constituted authority and amplification of petty annoyances between and among members has been described by Tuckman, (1965) as storming. Glidewell (1975) asserts that power struggles that emerge out of the authority vacuum represent an increased differentiation of member capacities and interrelationships that are no longer based on peripheral values. The shift is from a member's personal authority to a stance of plausability referring to the observations and opinions of other members. At the same time, psychological safety is reduced and members strive to lessen the anxiety through tension relieving devices such as changing the subject, harmless conversation and so forth. Northen (1969) and Hartford (1972) cite interpersonal disenchantment, expressed in withdrawal, anger, and personal bickering as part of the testing dynamic. Other sentiments include value conflicts, personal and interpersonal ambivalences, and power struggles between and among members and the worker.

The costs of conflict are exceedingly high because they threaten the existence of the group. At some point, and in order to contain the conflict, members reach for closer and more relaxed tension-relieving devices such as supporting another's idea, more attentive listening or self-disclosure, which sets the stage for shared regard (Northen, 1969; Hartford, 1972). This includes the recognition of a multiplicity of skills and capacities among the collectivity that holds promise for dealing with the group member issues. It is evident that the schemata associated with assimilation are not enough, and incipient themes of cohesion, affection and solidarity begin to emerge. Interpersonal attraction is important for an emergent set of norms to develop that can assure dependability, sharing and interpersonal regard. This is necessary in order to relax defenses that can exacerbate conflict and lead to escalation and stereotyping antagonisms. Cohesion sets the stage for cooperation in resolving personal, interpersonal and group conflicts (Deutsch, 1973). This point of view is shared by Mills (1964), and Mann (1967), both of whom cite the paradox of group revolt and shared regard. Mann's thrust is in terms of subgroup dynamics whereby one subgroup tests its autonomy against the leader and another prefers to coexist and maintain intermember sensitivity and attraction.

For Mills, the central member questions are whether or not they can and/or have the capacities for change. Factionalism in the group protects both the innovator and the status quo. Closeness is regarded as important for its own sake, at the same time members struggle with guilt feelings over the revolt and the necessity for making their own decisions.

Residual elements stemming from the group revolt tend to carry over into the cohesion subset. The major emphasis, however, is for self-revelation among members, heightened interpersonal involvement and a feeling that the group is a unique entity (Garland et. al. 1965; Sarri and Galinsky, 1967). Cooperation is preferred over argumentative and idiosyncratic behavior, although these are accepted for what they are. There is greater attention paid to personal feelings in the here and now, and an ability to postpone judgments on each other (Tuckman, 1965).

Glidewell (1975) raises the intriguing point that solidarity is based not only on greater degrees of attraction and perceived similarity among members, but also on the recognition that there are complementary differences which are useful for personal change. In this regard he notes

> Each participant, because of his different resources, supplies another with motives, feelings, or skills which the other could not supply for himself; esteem motives in exchange for safety motives, supportive affection in exchange for prudent apprehension, instrumental skills in exchange for expressive skills. But the demands of the climate emphasize the homogeneity, de-emphasize or indeed deny the complementary heterogeneity. . . . in a climate of solidarity, differences in status, power, and competence are left implicit or overtly denied (p. 163)

The homogenizing effects of group and member loyalities and mutual support provide a secure base for self-esteem. However, underlying differences are suppressed and one can expect these personal needs to reemerge. The major difference is that their reappearance is lodged within the context of a protective envelope. The shared regard and expectations also relax aggressive defenses to the extent that some members will do something unexpected and cycles of exploration, involvement, and conflict will be regenerated, probably in shorter cycles and within a greater sense of safety. When this occurs, then the next subset, potentially the most productive and designated as the mutual aid system, emerges.

The designation of this period, as seen in Table 7–1, clearly point to a flexible group system in which members are respectful, assertive, supportive and interdependent. Common to the theories of Northen (1969), Hartford (1972), Sarri and Galinsky (1967), and Garland et. al. (1965) are the emphasis on work and exchanges of skills; feelings of security and freedom; mutual give and take; a sense of intimacy with one's self and the group; marked degrees of personal and interpersonal empathy; experimentations; valuing novelty and newness; acceptance of individual idiosyncracies; affirmation of one's place, and of being right in what one is and does. The emphasis on competence and mastery is stressed by Tuckman (1965) who calls this stage, "performing." Diagnosis and assessment of problems, individual or group, take precedence over giving up on an idea, thereby suggesting the utilization of the method of inquiry for problem solving (Mills, 1964). Goals may be viewed more realistically in terms of the amount and type of change possible, which also leads to the discovery of one's incompetence (Mann, 1967). However, these limits are not considered disabling as they might have been had they occurred earlier in the group's history. Both conflict and cohesion are used to enhance exchanges of feelings of difference for individual and group work. Regression to earlier subsets is likely to reemerge but only in the context of greater learning and individual growth, as members reassess their personal investment and commitment. It is interesting to note the similarities between the implicit norms underlying the events and dynamics of this subset, and those that characterize temporary systems (Miles, 1968) and change mechanisms (Yalom, 1975) in therapy groups.

Further Considerations of Work

It is useful to explore the meaning of the construct of work since it describes the efforts of the middle phase. Schwartz (1971) uses the construct of *work* to mean "an output of energy directed to certain specific tasks" (p. 8). He further differentiates work into the preparatory "tuning in" phase, followed by beginnings, then work itself, and terminating in the final period of transitions and endings (p. 13). While Schwartz emphasizes the utilization of the term over the entire helping process, the major business of the group, when members get to the hard and difficult change period, is classified as the work phase. Glidewell's (1975) definition of work is "the continuing input, exchange, transformation, absorption, and output of resources" (p. 165). Glidewell further describes this phase as a continual and reciprocal cycling of various climates such as prudent exploration, involvement, conflict, and solidarity. The essence of work includes norms of complementarity and reciprocity, the latter signifying a measure of value and fairness in the exchange process. Furthermore, these phases or climates are ever-present, although occurring in shorter and shorter cycles in the work phase. It is the movement through cycles which enables more resources to be developed and exchanged. This is an important point because it means that cycles do not appear in any simple linear fashion but in various combinations and for that reason, justifies the utilization of broad categories of group development rather than the natural succession of unique phases as expressed by Dunphy (1964). Each of the cycles sets forth certain roles such as pairing in the beginning phase (exploration), negotiation (conflict) and support (cohesion) in the middle phase.

Jaques' (1970) conception of work is more person-centered but is important for describing elements that correspond to the change process that are to be supported in groups. In its most general sense, Jaques considers work as the "mental energy or effort expended in striving to reach a goal or objective by means of the operation of the reality principle, and in the face of the demands of the pleasure principle" (p. 80). Discriminations, judgments, and decisions must be made in the context of tolerating uncertainty. The demands or tasks to be accomplished present their own structures or boundaries while the discretionary content, such as judgments or choices, or application of a person's skill-capacities reside within the person. Jaques redefined his conception of work to include person-centered and task demands. Thus, work "is the exercise of discretion within externally prescribed limits to achieve an object which can be reality tested, while maintaining a continuous working-through of the attendant anxiety" (p. 82).

Jaques enumerates six stages to the process of work. Simply put, they are as follows:

1. A relationship is established with the objective.
2. An appropriate quantity of mental energy is allocated to the task.
3. A mental schema or hunches are developed on how to perform the task.
4. Concentrating on the elements and pieces of the task.
5. Gathering, linking, and synthesizing the elements in the task.
6. Making a decision and commiting one's resources to it.

These stages do not occur in simple linear fashion but are continually cycled in various combinations. Jaques points out that investment in any task is correlated with psychological vulnerability such that the greater the investment, the more chances one takes. Furthermore task complexity, self-knowledge, and the projected amount of time are all interrelated to what might be called the preliminary bonding process. Scouting and exploratory activities enhanced through conflict promote a loosening of the pieces of the puzzle which are then cognitively restructured so as to gain mastery over the problem. The final, and important step, is to subject the product to public scrutiny after new procedures have been framed, accepted, and implemented. The relevance of these recurring stages pertains to the fit of a member's work into corresponding group themes and worker activities which shall be considered in the next chapter.

Stock and Thelen's (1958) conception of work derived from the work of Bion. They noted that

> Experiences in training groups have led us to the recognition of two fundamentally different modes of group life. One is emotional, and is characterized by collective action, not listening, high feelings, contagion, and disorder. The other mode is sober, reflective, and orderly; members listen to one another. Bion recognized these modes and called them respectively "emotionality" and "work" (p. 6).

Stock and Thelen defined work to include the rational aspect of group life that is related to other emotional needs expressed in certain basic assumption cultures that are both shared and cyclical. By basic assumption culture is meant an emotional state theorized as a need among members expressed in an "as if" assumption—that is, members may be in tune with, reacting against, or acquiescing to, a shared perception about the group as a group. For example, in dealing with the issues of relationships to the group leader, members may respond as if it is the leader's responsibility to guide them or give directions. This phenomenon could be labeled a dependency culture. For these authors, and in contrast to Bales, every event in a group is composed of both work and emotional components. In relation to other theorists with regard to work, Stock and Thelen are more specific. Consistent with other theorists, the ideas of tensions and bipolarities are expressed.

These conceptions of work suggest a number of characteristics that provide a qualitative description of the process. Ambivalence, struggle and floundering are suggested, as members deal with the anxiety and uncertainty present in change. Convergent and divergent modes of thinking and feeling both in terms of self and significant others are manifested as responses to the tendencies toward recurring oppositional sentiments at task and affective levels. Personal and interpersonal sentiments are reflected in dealing with anxiety within one's self and induced by others. Periods of relief following conflict reflect attempts to deal with both work and emotionality. Themes of loss, dependency, confusion and embarrassment lead to trial and error experimentation. Personal and interpersonal self-esteem are acquired with mastery of the problem that completes a segment of the change process.

These events predominate in the middle phase and reach fruition in what has been termed by social work theorists as maturation, differentiation, group functioning and maintenance, or problem solving stages. Other theorists use designations such as performing, production, work, and internalization. (See Table 7-1.)

The Ending Phase

The middle phase of group development, particularly mutual aid, emphasizes the exchange and interchange of ideas, feelings and skills between and among members and the worker. Taking chances, using conflict, and depending on others in a supportive climate is the context for change. In shorter and shorter cycles, patterns or climates of exploration, involvement, cohesion and conflict resonate to produce more work and learning, although not equally among all the members. To the extent that part–whole (member-group) relationships have changed, then the members may have experienced and internalized a principle for change, which also represents a modification of the contiuum between and among the cultures of the member, group, and environment.

Endings and transitions are the time when the group prepares for termination. Members look back at the past and forward into the foreseeable future as a way of finding and reaffirming the meaning of their group experience. A number of diverse themes have been reported which encompass the dynamics of termination.

Denial Convenient sidetracking and forgetting that the end is near is a common phenomenom (Garland et. al., 1965; Hartford, 1972; Northen, 1969). Members simply proceed in their deliberations and act surprised when the inevitable deadline arrives. Putting the idea out of mind neutralizes the anxieties and uncertainties associated with endings and preserves the myth that the end will disappear.

Ambivalence Inherent in the dynamic of ambivalence is anger which may be expressed directly or indirectly between and among the members or toward the worker (Northen, 1969; Mills, 1964). Sarcasm, minor irritations, and stubbornness over minor points typify this dynamic. Sometimes the members continue their dialogue as if the worker were not present. The roots of ambivalence are also to be found in feelings of doubt and uncertainty with respect to the future. While the group as a microcosm can be viewed as incorporating the stable and diffuse elements of society, the special nature of the protective envelope permits interpersonal sensitivities that make the experience slightly different. Frequently, clients ponder questions such as "can I make it on the outside," or "where will the backup and understanding be if I fail." The right to fail in a protective setting hardly corresponds to consequences in the real world. Who is to say that the members' special and learned sensitivities will be rewarded by others' actions? In point of fact, others may become irritated with the hard-earned changes that members are justifiably proud of and display. Ambivalence can also be directed toward the worker for other reasons. Feelings may be expressed that the worker should have known that the members couldn't accomplish all they wanted to do. As a consequence, members may perceive that the worker tricked them (Mills, 1969).

Loss and Mourning Themes of loss and mourning commonly associated with separation anxiety may trigger feelings of abandonment which are sometimes manifested in tardiness and absenteeism (Hartford, 1972). These feelings may precipitate withdrawal of affect as a means by which more vulnerable members disengage, particularly those who have been badly hurt in the past (Northen, 1969; Mills, 1964; Mann, 1967). Another response is nihilistic flight as a way of countering anticipated feelings of rejection (Garland et. al., 1965), and which, in turn, serve to weaken the cohesive bonds of the group. Experiences with latency age groups of children who have undergone severe rejection in their families (chronic absent or distant parents) demonstrate patterns of hyperactivity and diffuse anger as a means of neutralizing remembered feelings of abandonment. On the other hand, this dramatizes the significance and meaning of the group attachments.

Sadness and depression are other temporary states (Hartford, 1972, Mann, 1967). Members may regret that they didn't have enough time to raise other issues and as a consequence may renew their efforts to complete unfinished business. Feelings of envy that other members have learned more than they have revitalize social comparison processes that are accentuated in the early group phase (Garland et. al. 1965). Another way of responding to loss is demonstrated in overdependency and clinging to the worker (Hartford, 1972). It is not unusual for loss to precipitate a "social hunger" pattern which can lead to expressions of praise and charismatization of the worker. This behavior represents a regression to an earlier phase where deification of the leader is regarded as an antidote to depression (Slater, 1970). Among low-income groups, the "halo effects" of a group experience are so powerful that termination may be extended for weeks or months after the last meeting.

Review of Positive Experiences Members are quite likely to report on something that they've learned as a result of the experience

(Garland et. al., 1965; Mills, 1964; Northen, 1969; Shulman, 1979). Talking about changes and evaluating the experience seems to dilute the group bonds as new issues are raised that are to be faced in the future. This dynamic points to the nature of ending as transitions, such that new learnings also produce new challenges and constraints. In addition, recapitualization and review of accomplishments lead to a recognition that change represents partial successes. Furthermore one's incompetencies are clarified and must be accepted as well.

Memorialization A final meeting may be symbolically memorialized through a party, taking pictures, exchange of addresses and so forth. The event encapsulates the struggles, yearnings, and accomplishments of members and reaffirms the uniqueness of the experience. The coexistence of joy and sadness, of new beginnings and new rhythms consummate in a remembered event that recedes into a referent group worthy of use in the future.

The presence of these dynamics dissolves the bonds of solidarity and consequently the manifestation and intensity of conflict. Exploration and involvement themes are forecast into preparation for anticipated events after the group is over. Distillation of earlier processes are infused with meanings that are also shaped and refirmed by proximate concerns, more than the various group contexts in which a problem was addressed. Membership in the group becomes a part of the members' "internal committee". The content that has been learned from context becomes a springboard from which the ongoing processes of shaping and reshaping one's identity continue in other life circumstances.

PRINCIPLES OF GROUP DEVELOPMENT

1. Group development is characterized by recurrent patterns that continually spread over the life of the group. These patterns can be identified as exploration, involvement, conflict, cohesion, and work.

2. Cycling as a process defines recurrence. Patterns reappear not in linear fashion but in various combinations and vicissitudes. Each of the patterns elicits a unique configuration of thoughts, feelings, and actions which may or may not be in harmony with sentiments raised by other concurrent patterns. For example, feelings of security can either block or assist search behavior.

3. The occurrence and distribution of the patterns can conveniently be grouped into beginning, middle, and ending phases of group life. Exploration and involvement, partially determined by

pre-group expectational sets, include members decisions about wanting to engage and to continue. Competing sentiments of distance, closeness, and risk taking are manifested in members testing each other out, searching for an acceptable niche, at the same time exploring and charting new territory.

4. Conflict, cohesion, and work encompass events and processes that depict the middle phase. The decision to change is foreshadowed by members struggles and acceptance regarding personal and group responsibility for producing and utilizing the necessary resources. Expectations regarding reciprocal and complementary activities shift from the worker to the members. Confronting issues of safety and uncertainty, foresight and spontaneity lead to corresponding shifts among members' expectations toward each other. Expressions of personal concern for each other counteract the annoyances and disagreeable thoughts and feelings that are produced. A beginning sense of mastery emerges as members begin to use each others' skills, opinions, and resources to handle heretofore uncertain events. For the first time members begin to visualize how the process elements (context) can be incorporated into content which reinforce the commitment to work.

5. The process of work represents a mutual aid system through which emergent problems raised by the continuous cycling of patterns are handled. Acceptance of the norms of mutual regard, novelty, experimentation, authenticity, inquiry, and effort demonstrates that the polarities represented among the patterns are less obstinate and are being transcended. Conflicts regarding intimacy and authority which encompass disturbing thoughts and feelings are used to expand personal, interpersonal and group perspectives, each representing a level of work. Struggle, uncertainty, anxiety, floundering and divergent thinking often accompany the work process which is completed when the troubling elements of the problem are synthesized into a new thought-feeling-action patterns. Flexibility among superior, subordinate, and peer roles signifies a growth experience which merges interdependent, dependent, and autonomous needs.

6. Group termination is marked by a transition from the rhythm of work to disengagement and preparation for the future. Earlier themes of loss, dependency and ambivalence are revisited and coexist with feelings of satisfaction and recognition of limited but worthy accomplishments. As members look backward and forward, the group experience is memoralized and affirmed as a reference point for negotiating the future.

8
Leadership in Groups

The topic of leadership in groups has been extensively discussed and analyzed by social scientists and practitioners. A review of the literature reveals that this phenomenon has been studied along three key dimensions: (1) the role and functions of the leader in the context of the group (leadership tasks); (2) the differential styles of leadership and their effect on the group as a whole and on individual members; and (3) the personality traits of the leaders and their impact on leadership effectiveness. The debate over the issue of the ideal strategy for conceptualizing leadership in groups is still current. In this chapter each of the three dimensions is examined briefly. Subsequently an ecological perspective of group leadership based on the formulations of Mead and Lewin is presented. Following this overview, leadership in groups is discussed in relation to the structural and process components of group work as described in earlier chapters.

LEADERSHIP: ROLES, FUNCTIONS, AND SITUATIONS

Tasks and maintenance group functions have been designated as two fundamental problem-solving activities in groups. The construct of roles is helpful in organizing and describing categories of behavior that leaders may perform in assisting groups to manage and harness these two competitive and complementary problem-solving activities. When leaders ask questions, initiate ideas, make plans, call for action, interpret and clarify member behavior, then they are ex-

213

ercising task functions. When leaders share feelings, encourage cooperation, foster spontaneity, negotiate differences between members, then their actions are designed to solidify group relationships.

Roles in groups are closely interrelated with member relationships and situations. In this regard, it is useful to explore these two characteristics in more detail. McDaniel and Balgopal (1978) have conceptualized this facet of leadership as the situational/interactional dimensions.

Interactionists assume personality differences, and assert that there are four important aspects of group interaction that explain the leadership role: (1) role differentiation (including leadership) is part of a group's movement towards its goal of satisfying individual members' needs; (2) leadership is a concept applied to the interaction of two or more persons, and the leader's evaluations control and direct the action of others in accomplishing common goals; (3) the leader's evaluations are products of perception and emotional attachment; and (4) this leads to a set of complex emotional relationships which, in turn, explain the leadership role (Gibb, 1958).

Leadership can be described as a push-pull phenomena which is a function of the dominance-submission relationship among people. Pull may be seen as imprinting, or when one generates in another the enthusiastic desire to follow. Push may be seen when the leader plans or anticipates action and the followers find themselves in predicaments in which they are dictated to and urged to implement behavior they very much dislike (Cooper and McGaugh, 1963). A combination of the two may be seen in a leader who both dictates and compromises, or vice versa.

Fiedler's (1965) ideas for selecting and training leaders are that it is easier to modify or change one's rank and power than it is to change one's personality. Consequently, improvement in the effectiveness of leadership can be accomplished by obtaining an accurate diagnosis of the group-task situation and by altering the leadership context (i.e. group composition).

The situational dimension implies at least five categories of behavioral determinants: (1) the structure of interpersonal relationships between and among leader and members, (2) the group syntality or the quality of the structure (integration, cohesiveness, solidarity, and so on), (3) characteristics of the larger social context or society in which the group exists and from which the members are drawn, (4) the physical conditions, and (5) the task with which the group is confronted (Gibb, 1958). Emphasis is placed on relationships among leaders-members and their external or social settings. These social settings may be small groups, communities, institutions, political organizations, and business organizations.

The *situationists* assume group dynamics and consider external factors as important determinants of a formed group's efforts toward goal setting and goal achievement. Leadership here is directed toward organizing the group and its goals. The minimal social conditions which permit the existence of leadership are (1) a group (two or more persons), (2) a common task (goal-oriented activities), and (3) differentiation of responsibility (different members have different roles). While there are many more situational factors, these are the minimal ones that will allow for the emergence of leadership. A leader, then, is one who becomes differentiated from others in the group in terms of the amount and quality of influence he/she exerts on the accomplishment of shared goals or activities of the group.

Further explanation of the leadership role in terms of influence is offered by Hollander (1964) who indicates that, since interaction can be evaluated through interpersonal assessments made up of task-related behaviors (measured against some expectation standards), an individual member who adheres to group expectations and conditions of competence over a significant period of time accumulates influence credits that permit innovation in the group. Consequently, this task-competent follower, at one stage of the group's interaction, may emerge as a leader in another stage. Subsequently, however, the leader who does not continue to fulfill the expectations of the group which are associated with his/her position may lose influence credits. The achievement and maintenance of the leadership role also depend upon the perceptions of others in the ongoing social interaction. In other words, the leader achieves only when he/she is in a perceived situation where he/she *can* achieve, and this situation nurtures the maintenance of the leadership role.

The situationists insist that the group environment is paramount, implying that a good leader in one group may not be a good leader in another. Also, a leader in any group may not be adequate in all instances even in that group. The situationists focus on specialized abilities rather than traits. For a leader to be effective, he/she is only as effective as perceived in his/her group, given associated factors, interpersonal interactions, and so forth. Situational studies reveal that certain leadership expectations are unique to particular group settings. For instance, Cartwright and Zander's (1960) work shows that while certain minimal abilities are required of all leaders, they are widely distributed among nonleaders as well, and that the optimal leadership abilities for one group may be quite different from those of another in a different setting. This means that just because a leader is suitable for one task, he/she may not be suitable for another (other) tasks; so, as tasks change, leadership changes.

LEADERSHIP STYLE

Three basic subconcepts provide a framework for describing the dynamics of the leadership role. *Influence* is one subconcept, and it can include virtually any psychological or behavioral effect or impact by one party on another in the process of interpersonal interaction. This impact may take the form of emulation, suggestion, persuasion, or coercion. *Emulation* denotes one's modeling of another's behavior, while *suggestion* refers to any attempt to influence another's behavior by advocating a particular course of action. *Persuasion* involves the use of some inducement in an attempt to evoke a desired response, while *coercion* involves the use of forcible constraints to achieve a desired response.

The second subconcept is *power,* defined as the ability to influence behavior. *Power* denotes the ability of a person or a group of persons to solicit prescribed behavior from others by means of superior formal or informal position (Bierstedt, 1950). Therefore, power can be understood as the capacity to affect behavior in a predetermined manner.

Another important subconcept of leadership dynamics is *authority,* which is defined as the institutionalized right to employ power (Bierstedt, 1950). In a sense, authority represents an artificial power structure. The three basic types of legitimate authority are rational legal, traditional, and charismatic. *Rational legal authority* is based on logical expedience, while *traditional authority* is based on custom and loyalty. *Charismatic authority* depends upon the qualities of the individual leader and is more illogical and emotionally based, because personal characteristics are more important than position. A charismatic leader is one who attracts members by means of his/her appealing personality.

These dynamics, when juxtaposed in a certain manner, allow a leader to influence the activities of a group in a certain fashion, and this comprises leadership style. There are four basic types of leadership styles: dictatorial, autocratic, democratic, and laissez-faire.

The *dictatorial* leader accomplishes tasks by instilling fear in the members-followers, usually in the form of threats of punishment.

216

This type of leader uses negative tactics based on the assumptions that people must be motivated to act, and that the best form of motivation is fear. The leader achieves results by threatening to remove the members' ability to attain their needs satisfactorily. This type of leader gets results, but the quality and quantity of achieved results are questionable in view of the fact that results are frequently accompanied by dissatisfaction among the members, since he/she *demands* rather than *commands* compliance.

Autocratic leadership is characterized by centralization of authority and decision making. This type of leader motivates members by forcing them to rely upon him/her for need satisfaction. The leader takes full responsibility for the work to be done, does not permit participation from members in decisionmaking, and does not tolerate deviation from predetermined rules. This leader gets results but suffers from the disadvantage that the group can be only as good as the leader. If the leader is weak and ineffectual, so will the members be.

Democratic leadership is based on decentralization of authority and decision making. This type of leader is characterized by the degree to which consultation with members on goals, problems, and tasks are shared with the group. The underlying assumption is that members are encouraged to function as a social unit utilizing the talents and abilities among them. This type of leadership motivates members to high levels of effectiveness because the process assures a large measure of belongingness and recognition.

Laissez-faire leadership exists when the leader provides no direction and allows the members to formulate their own goals and decisions. This lack of involvement by the leader frustrates the members who frequently flounder in search of common goals and purposes for the group, resulting in diffused action, disorganization, and confusion.

The pioneering efforts of Kurt Lewin and associates (1939) sparked numerous studies as a result of their initial comparison of autocratic and democratic boys' activity groups. These studies moved researchers toward the use of personality and behavior for comparing task-centered and person-centered styles of leadership: autocratic vs. democratic, structuring vs. considerate, directive vs. nondirective. The studies indicate that there are only a limited number of ways in which a person can get others to work together to accomplish a common task: (1) leaders can order, direct, guide, or get them involved in the task; (2) leaders can devote themselves to directing the task; or (3) they can set conditions so that members can become self-motivated and self-directed.

LEADERSHIP TRAITS

In the trait approach to studying leadership, extensive attempts have been made to enumerate the personality and special qualities essential for being a leader. Accordingly, some researchers have attempted to ascertain the following, mainly by experimental methods. (1) What specific innate traits of personality are responsible for the leadership role? (2) What traits are developed during the assumption of the leadership role? (3) What traits are specifically affected as the leader's tasks are accomplished? (Gibb, 1969).

The notion of cataloging personality traits of leaders commanded considerable attention during the early period of leadership inquiry. Bird, for example, culled a list of seventy-nine traits of leaders from approximately twenty inquiries which bore some resemblance to controlled investigation. He also focused on the exploration of leadership in terms of what leaders actually did rather than the prevailing notions about leaders.

Stogdill's (1974) herculean task of reviewing studies in over three thousand books and journal articles on leadership caused him to conclude that

> (Only a few) personality traits have been found to differentiate leaders from followers, successful from unsuccessful leaders, and high level from low level leaders. The traits with the highest overall average correlation with the leadership role are: originality, popularity, sociability, judgment, aggressiveness, desire to excel, humor, cooperativeness, liveliness, and athletic ability, in the approximate order of the magnitude of the average correlation coefficients (p. 91).

Stogdill's review of the literature allows one to conclude that the qualities, characteristics, and skills required in a leader are determined, to a large extent, by the demands of the situation in which he/she functions as a leader, although a few personality traits are more likely to be found among leaders than among followers. Contrary to Stogdill's original intention, his work moved thinking about leadership away from trait determinants toward an emphasis upon the times or situations as major determinants, for it is quite clear that, subsequent to his study, the view of leadership shifted toward interactions among members of a group and with the external environment (the situation). Shaw (1971) substantiates this notion by indicating that it is a mistake to think that the relationship between traits and the leadership role is universal, for a trait which is positively related to the leadership role in one situation may be either unrelated or even negatively related in another. This idea has resulted in substantial research which concludes that leadership roles are relative to situations.

Current formulations regarding leadership theory note that no single theory can account for the most relevant factors. Depending on the group purpose, content, internal and external constraints, various combinations of personality, function and situation are likely to be relevant. Research on professional leadership has not produced significant results. Lieberman (1976) states the problem succinctly in the following statement:

> A chain of events forms between leader behavior and social system characteristics, as well as member role within the social system, and particular events hypothesized to be therapeutic. To ignore the chain can only produce relatively weak relationships between leader behavior and outcome, no matter how elegant the measure of leadership (p. 236).

The ecological perspective provides a leader with knowledge about the members' functioning not only in the group context but also data pertaining to their home situation. As discussed in the earlier chapters, there are a number of key concepts from ecology that have a great deal of relevance for leadership interventions. However, it needs to be recognized that these concepts merely enhance one's understanding of where the members are coming from, that the group and the professional context of intervention is a temporary arena within which members have to learn, unlearn or relearn adaptive patterns which will be compatible with the environmental climate in their respective habitat. Furthermore ecological concepts provide a cognitive understanding of the members' functioning. In other words, this framework sheds light on the total situation of the members, their environments and the interplay between the two. In this context, ecological concepts discussed in the previous chapters having significance for leadership interventions are (1) habitat—natural surrounding; (2) adaptation—over time and at one point in time; (3) personal capacities—cognitive, affective, perceptual, interpersonal and social; (4) social environments—family, social networks, neighborhoods and institutions; (5) diversity and continuity—competing and complementary sentiments.

The ecological perspective for group work by itself does not provide the means for interventions. In this context, the formulations of Mead and Lewin are useful in charting pathways that lead to strategies for leader activity.

LEADERSHIP: ECOLOGY, MEAD AND LEWIN

Effective leadership interventions in social work groups have to take into account not only what is occurring in the group at a given moment, but also to conditions and occurrences in the members' and group's environments. In this context, ecological concepts as discussed in Chapter 2, complemented with Mead and Lewin's formulations, provide a direction and methodology for interventions.

Comprehensive leader interventions are influenced by member capacities, their environment and the transaction between the two. For example, a member with organic brain damage represents the person-capacity issue. The context or hospital may alleviate or exacerbate the members' capacities based on their expectations regarding the "patient-sick" role. The utilization or management of person-capacities in the hospital context represents the following transactional equation. Group leaders may intervene at any or all of the three locations outlined in the following diagram.

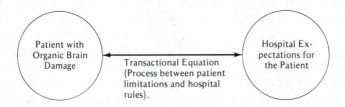

Both Lewin and Mead emphasized the active striving sentiments of human beings, the importance of interpersonal contexts, the direct relevance of the "present" as a powerful force manifested in and through a person's perceptual screen. Both also were influenced by Dewey to the extent that experiencing, continuity, and problem solving are interrelated, and that a person's assumptive world was continually being engaged in choices of actions in everyday life. Finally, both were concerned with rational, nonrational (characterological) and irrational processes, although the latter have been less well defined.

Each also had separate and distinctive contributions. Lewin borrowed from physics the notion of field theory which emphasized a field of forces by which a person is influenced. The gestalt of the group is a direct application of his interest in holism. Concepts such as climate, atmosphere, and group emotion describe this idea. The inextricable interrelationship between the person and the group direct the leader's attention to the question: to what problems in the group is this (member's) behavior relevant? The focus on goal orientation and aspiration among members emphasizes the purposive nature of groups. Conflict and tension are paramount. When felt needs are disturbed, conflict is a precursor to change in his scheme. Stability represents the congruence of ideas and feelings manifested in new concepts which need to be applied to be learned. Lewin's research also led him to consider the connection between leadership, group process and products and group climate, which altogether may be subsumed as alterations in part–whole relationships. The internalized frame of reference, or internal committee by which persons continually reassess memberships in other groups reflect his attempt to correlate the outside (the past) with the present. Questions relating to a person's past group memberships may be useful in assessing his/her capacities for groups, both in terms of strengths and weaknesses. These concepts are abundantly useful for group leaders in attempting to assess the laws or relationships which describe the reality of the group. When applied overtime, and in a person's natural field, one begins to see articulation between ecology and Lewin.

Mead was a social philosopher whose concern focused on meaning and the process by which meanings became internalized. Communicated meaning and words form acts such as body movements, facial expressions, tone of voice, appearance and so forth. The meaning of any act, as manifested in perception, values and feelings, and attitudes, becomes complete by the other person's response to the initiating act. It is by taking on the role of the other that one learns to anticipate the social effects of one's action. Society has stabilized meanings between acts in standardized sets of conducts which we learn to understand and expect, such as lawyer-client, teacher–student, clergyman–parishioner, policeofficer–citizen, parent–child, borrower–lender and so forth. When we learn to anticipate and respond accordingly to these sets in social interaction, then a process of socialization has taken place.

Significant others in a person's life also become anchor points from which one's personal identity is formed. The dynamic is role taking. The process includes active use of imagination and interior dialogue between the impulsive spontaneous "I" and the visualized "other" which frames a set of plans of action and guides behavior. This is also a continuous process of reflective thought. Hence our attention is directed to just what meaning a person ascribes to action which is to be found in subjective perceptions and statements. Mead's conception of self would transcend Lewin's notion of internalized committee to include a sense of self that emerges out of these other memberships.

Mead noted that roles are negotiated, recruited and affirmed through selective attention, responses and perception. Mead, then, directs our attention to processes which can inform the group leader, utilizing and developing concepts such as climate, leadership, role, goals and so forth.

In summary, ecology, Lewin and Mead, provide a set of reference points which inform each other and assist the leader in assessing and developing intervention sets. Publicly stated and developed criteria for change emerge out of role taking processes from which individual acts can be judged and accepted. Covert and overt aspects are negotiated and prioritized in an emergent culture which shifts to meet personal and group needs. Competing interests, exchanges, natural setting, the life arc and adaptation overtime are ecological additions. Principles of learning are drawn from these intersecting events and processes and become the base points that guide a leader's thinking and actions.

LEADERSHIP: STRUCTURE AND PROCESS

Group structure and process are interrelated concepts that are frequently applied in describing leader actions and events in groups. As described in earlier chapters, the relationship of group structure and group process is most crucial for the leader, because professional leadership can alter one or the other or both to influence or modify the behavior of group members as well as the other dynamics within the group. For our purpose, process refers to the ongoing relationships between and among members and the leader in a group. Structure is the term that is used to describe and analyze group events and happenings. When we attribute changes in the quality of the interactions, process is employed. When we refer to changes in patterns, then the term structure is used. Processes may be overt or covert and include thinking, talking, deciding, and evaluating and so forth. Structural concepts that capture stable and consistent patterns include goals, composition, size, contracting, norms, space, leadership, climate, and programming.

The effects of structure on process is evident when one or two members of a group fail to show up for a meeting in a group of eight members. In addition to issues of intimacy forced by unanticipated closeness, certain roles may be missing as well. Take for instance the case in which one active member who is excellent at initiating discussion is absent. Other members come to rely on this member and have difficulty in filling the missing role. Changes in process are also expected when newcomers enter a group. Changes are quite apparent when newcomers don't behave the way they are supposed to, which can alter members' perceptions quite sharply. It is not unusual in these circumstances that processes of exclusion and victimization occur. Other examples in which changes in structure are manifested in relationship changes within the membership would include the leader's actions that lead to an "authority vacuum" in the group, sometimes observed in a "conflict" culture. Different activities such as planning or sports can also influence processes and outcomes as well. Summer camps are an excellent example of process changes as a result of activities. Structural constraints are sometimes imposed by the environment in which the group is located. For example, in neighborhood centers it is not infrequent that social workers are charismatized whether they like it or not by powerful feelings of social hunger among residents. Process changes can alter structure as well. As members learn more about each other and begin to alter their expectations and response sets, hidden qualities of another member may emerge which is manifested in different role behaviors. A dramatic example is the movement of a member from scapegoat to valued membership.

Leadership is concerned with altering structure and/or process, sometimes referred to altering the conditions for purposes of individual and group development. Leader activities that attempt to bridge subgroup factions, confront an evasive member, or assist in reformulating group expectations for participation (frequency and quality), point to three interrelated targets for change: the individual, the subgroups and the group as a whole. Addressing institutional or neighborhood constraints adds the environmental aspect, as for example, in those situations in which a group of adolescent boys are continually stigmatized in a school setting by stereotyped hostile administrator behavior. Examples of facilitative leader role behaviors have been outlined by Underwood (1977) who organized a catalogue of appropriate interventions for purposes of integrating group task and maintenance roles toward optimal group development. These examples of leader role behaviors are consistent with Vinter's (1969) formulation concerning worker tasks regarding group development; namely, participant role patterns, activities, culture, and the external environment.

LEADERSHIP AND MEMBER ROLE INDUCTION

Structure and process variables are utilized by the leader at the initial stage of group formation. Members are introduced and prepared for the group through a process designated as role induction. The process by which a person is inducted in a group membership role can be perceived through a continuum of four basic phases. The first phase occurs when an individual is being considered as a potential member of a group. This can occur voluntarily, as is the case when an individual seeks group work services; or involuntarily when the individual is referred for such services. In this phase the person is ascribed the group member role. The next phase involves the individual becoming a participant in the group and hence achieves the role of a group member, which is based on learned past performance. These two phases are less complex than the next two. In the third phase the person is expected to go beyond involvement, which requires a commitment to change and use of the group. The last phase encompasses adaptation to other roles in the group context which includes behaviors such as receiving and giving help, disclosing personal content, reacting genuinely and spontaneously to other fellow members, and challenging one's own life situations. Clearly role induction is imbued with expectations and commitment.

In the broadest sense, the process of role induction begins at the onset of contact with the agency and continues through to termination. It is a definition of relationship which occurs at the interface of member-agency; member-leader; and member-member-group relations. These are the areas where stated and unstated expectations are defined and which hold potent implications for role behavior.

The member-leader relationship generates considerably more specific and identified expectations. The pre-group interview is generally structured around clarification of purpose, needs and goals of both member and leader. Additionally, an assessment of the member's desire to work and his/her abilities are discussed and reinforced. A leader may also verbalize reservations based on the "personal feel" of the member, if any, for appropriate placement. The subsequent contract has significant power for shaping future role taking.

Commitment to contract terms not only more specifically defines and represents an agreement of member behavior in a group but is a "visible landmark" for guiding behavior due to role shifts in the actual group experience.

The member-member-group interface is the arena in which role expectations are negotiated in a somewhat less official manner than those described above. "Psyching out" is a mutual sizing up process in role induction in which expectations are communicated on a variety of levels, both overt and covert. The important process is one where members come to follow role expectations through a mutual comparison of self and perceived views of others. Some situations may be more compelling than others for assuming a specific role. Pre-group interviews are one format for assessing the degree and quality of potentially marginal roles such as scapegoats.

These are the primary interfaces of relationship in which a member is inducted in assuming various roles in the context of a group; from the onset, a member's role becomes increasingly defined. Maintenance of the member through treatment is, then, accomplished through a direct communication of agency mandates and negotiated contract goals as they apply to the member role in the group. Optimally, skilled guidance by a leader through role induction processes in the various interfaces may in itself ultimately produce a desired change in otherwise dysfunctional social living.

The following case dramatizes the complex interrelationships between and among leadership, role induction, structure and process as they are manifested in the dynamics of a first group session.

Background Information

The group was sponsored in a human service agency to supplement a work incentive program designed to provide specific job slots to clients as preparation for entry into the labor market. Agency administrators decided to offer the group service as part of the overall program to (1) support and help members learn good work attitudes if necessary, and (2) to discuss and hopefully resolve any other problems that were being experienced in the program. Group leaders were recruited among agency staff who were available, interested, or had experience in working with groups. Individual members were informed of the group service through a letter of introduction which included the general purpose of the group as a forum in which problems with the training program could be discussed. Information on the time and place of the first meeting and the requirement for attendance of all trainees were also included. Individuals were randomly assigned to the groups that were limited to ten members.

Members Present: Alice Burke, Joan Bell, Freda Zelback, Murietta Lopez, Bill Anderson, Polly Whelan, Trudy Flynn, Georgette LaMer, Tina Rogaggio, Sophie Katz.

The members arrived at the set time, entered the room and sat around the table. Mr. Johnson, the leader, was standing

---

next to the coffee pot and nervously asked them if they wanted coffee and how they liked it. After he took the orders, he began to pour and serve. It was almost impossible to remember all the orders and seeing this, Mrs. Whelan got up to help. Mrs. Whelan's friend, Mrs. Flynn, helped also. Mrs. Lopez sat quietly, smoking her cigarette and just looking around. Bill turned to Mrs. Rogaggio on his left, and asked, "Where are all the men?" Alice Burke and Mrs. Bell were kibitzing about shopping; Freda Zelback sat quietly, puffing on a cigarette and fingering her pocketbook.

Mr. Johnson sat at the head of the table. He introduced himself, and looking at his notes said that they were there to talk about the work training program and any difficulties they might be having. Joan Bell asked him how long the program was going to go on and he replied that the programs varied depending upon the section. Mrs. Flynn wanted to know about her late welfare check, and was told she should check with the worker. Mrs. LaMer asked Mrs. Rogaggio what time it was, and then asked Mr. Johnson how long they would be here. He replied one hour—and looking at his watch said, laughingly, "only 45 minutes left." Mrs. Katz then walked into the room, sat down, apologized for being late, and added that she had to leave early because she had shopping to do in town and her baby-sitter had to leave early, too. In the silence which followed, everyone was staring at each other. Mrs. Katz asked what were they supposed to be doing here anyway. Mr. Johnson asked if she or any of the other members had questions to ask about the training program. Mrs. Whelan wanted to know what kind of jobs they would get after the training and Mr. Johnson explained it would depend on the program they were in. What was she in? She said cosmetology. Then she could work as a hairdresser. She asked if it would be far out of town, and Mr. Johnson didn't know. Well, she couldn't work if it was far out of town. Mr. Johnson asked her if she had always wanted to be a hairdresser and she continued nonstop "yes—for many years, ever since she was a little girl when her mother used to call her cutie and waved her hair." She always used to do her girl friends' hair, etc., etc. Meanwhile the others looked bored. Mr. Johnson tried to break in as Mrs. Whelan enveloped the whole group in her conversation. Finally he did say to her that maybe the others had the same experience—asking "What about you, Mrs. Lopez?" Mrs. Lopez was startled and not sure of what to say. She mumbled something about everything being all right. Mr. Johnson turned to Mr. Anderson and said jokingly,—"Bill, we're the only men here, we'd better stick together." Bill smiled and someone chimed in, that the men always stick together, and the group laughed.

Mrs. Rogaggio then popped up and said she was nervous about working because it had been such a long time since she had done so. Everything she did in training seemed to go wrong and she was going to fail for sure. Mrs. Flynn and Mrs. Zelbach then chimed in with their fears. Mrs. Flynn had seven children, and since she was past marrying age she had to pass—she had to make it. Mrs. Zelbach remarked that if they were going to fail people, she would have been out long ago, revealing that she never got out of the ninth grade. Mrs. LaMer added that she was looking forward to working because it would get her out of the house. "Anybody else?" asked Mr. Johnson— "What about you, Mrs. Burke, is this new for you, too?" Her answer—"Well I ain't been to school for a long time neither, but I hope I'm okay here." Mr. Johnson responded that she was doing very well, and none of them need to be nervous here, that we were all together. At this point, Mrs. Katz got up and said she had to leave. She put on her coat, and as she left, she snapped at Mr. Johnson "What kind of kid stuff is this anyway—I already know what I'm supposed to do." The group sat stunned.

Commentary

Approach-avoidance phenomenon are common in first meetings and the case example is no exception in that regard. Experiencing anxieties concerning who other members are, what they are like, and how each will "measure up" are part and parcel of the initial "psyching out" process. Personal discomfort among some of the members are registered in verbal and nonverbal ways. Examples include Bill's question regarding the absence of other men, and physical cues exhibited by Lopez and Zelbach. Uncertainties and ambivalences are also demonstrated by Mr. Johnson, the assigned group leader who concentrates his initial efforts on taking coffee orders.

The initial anxieties carry over and are tempered somewhat in the ensuing conversation prompted and structured into a question-answer format concerning program-relevant problems by the group leader. Both relevant (Bell) and irrelevant (Flynn) questions reflect not only ways of dealing with personal uneasiness, but with the group purpose as well. The uncertainty regarding purpose is reflected further, and temporarily contained (and avoided) when Mr. Johnson responds "only 45 minutes left," to a question concerning how much time was left.

The question-answer format is repeated as a response to a late member's question regarding group purpose. At this point, perhaps because the action in the field, influenced and blurred by the group leader's behavior, stimulates the outpouring of private sentiments by one member (Whelan) who envelops the group with her conversation. Sensing the discomfort, the group leader interrupts and directs a question to a startled silent member which appears to exacerbate the situation. The tension is eased when the group leader turns to the other male (Bill) and in a humorous aside, suggests that men ought to stick together.

To this point, the process clearly reflects the lack of clarity as to why members are there and what is expected. The group leader's attempts for structure through a question-answer format contribute to initiating feelings of safety (including his own), but these are controverted in the act of singling out a silent member for attention. When expectations are unclear, one can expect exploratory probes by individual members as well as defensive silences and expressions of exaggerated sentiments by individual members. Humor as a tension management device can be effective in relieving discomfort and supporting the potentially intimate relationship among members. Other tension management devices include rudimentary affiliation (Whelan–Flynn), and polite exchanges (Burke–Bell, Rogaggio–Anderson). These serve to contain the prevailing anxiety in the context of exploratory intermember engagements.

The stutter-step process appears to congeal in the last paragraph when, quite spontaneously, certain members begin to present their individual concerns and motivations for participating in the program. Their comments also signal a beginning commitment to engage in the group. The ensuing discussion reveals sharp differences among certain of the members' capacities, reasons for participating, and anticipated benefits both direct and indirect. A sense of purpose appears to emerge as manifested in the interactions between and among Rogaggio, Flynn, Zelback and LaMer. It is noteworthy that the emergent goals are different from both the agency-stated objectives and the group leader goals that are implied in his actions.

Ostensibly to encourage further participation after discussion has stopped, the group leader applies a favored technique by directing a question to another silent member. Perhaps sensing discomfort conveyed by the members' response, among other members or within himself, the group leader attempts to reassure the members that the group really is a safe haven. This action is subverted when one member takes abrupt leave following an angry outburst directed at the group leader but alluding to the members as well. Mrs. Katz, in no uncertain terms, states that the group is irrelevant for her.

The lesson to be drawn from the case excerpt clearly shows that group structure and process manifested in initial meetings is related to the extent of leader preparation in terms of assessment, composition, goal formulation, contracting, and agency policies. There is no substitute for thorough preparation in group work practice. Sound intake and role induction procedures which encompass the major ideas discussed in this chapter are essential for organizing and implementing professional service in groups. Skilled interviewing techniques with potential members can inform both the client and worker as to the wisdom of the choices and actions available. Assessing client capacities, strengths and weaknesses, and goals as they relate to the problem at hand can be integrated into an initial working agreement. In addition, potential members can be screened in or out depending on the evaluation of how much heterogeneity in terms of coping patterns and homogeneity in terms of problems are available. The group leader can also model, in the interviewing process, role behaviors that are analogous to those in groups. Cognitive and experiential structuring of anticipated client behavior can be provided through preparatory lectures, or excerpts of audio taped recordings of "good" member behavior, which have been shown to be correlated to positive outcomes (Bednar and Lawlis, 1971; Garfield, 1978). Anticipatory socialization procedures are worthy of careful attention and experimentation regardless of the group program offered. When they are completed with the practice principles cited in each of the structural properties, then the prospects of attainable outcomes for members the worker, and the group are enhanced.

CO-LEADERSHIP

In social group work, it has been a common practice for two leaders to assume and share the leadership functions. While there are a number of reasons for this practice, some of the more frequently mentioned are

1. When there are two leaders in a group setting, the chances of missing the subtle occurrences in the group process are minimized. Benjamin (1972) found that the eye contact utilized by co-leaders can be an effective technique to prompt each other to certain process material, such as significant affect being demonstrated by members of the group. One leader is generally more observant during the process time. Without the use of co-leaders, this display would perhaps have gone unobserved.

2. Two leaders, especially if they are of different sexes, provide an opportunity for members to experience and identify with "parental figures" of both sexes. Yalom (1970) proposed that co-leaders of different sexes have the special advantage of serving as models of a primary family to the group. Furthermore, he noted that the members of the group benefit by vicarious identification of the co-leaders' modeling of a heterosexual pair who demonstrate a mutual respect for one another. McGee and Schuman (1970) observed that a group conducted by two leaders came much closer to representing a family setting than did a group conducted by a single leader. It is also frequently suggested that the type and range of transference objects, (i.e., mother and father) are greatly enhanced by the use of two leaders in the group setting.

3. An experienced leader can groom and provide skills to a beginning leader within an actual group context. Anderson and his associates (1972) proposed that use of co-leaders can be made in training psychiatric residents in the process of group psychotherapy. They claimed that this practice can be an excellent learning tool as well as a method for proper continuous supervision of the beginning group worker. It was noted that while the term co-leaders implies that both workers are on an equal basis, this is not apparent at first. Co-leader equality grows with time and requires the maturation of the working relationship as well as increased skill attainment of the beginning leader. McGee and Schuman (1970) remarked on the senior-junior co-leadership which they felt can be used effectively for the purpose of training the group leader. Yalom (1970) noted that the more experienced leader can help the less experienced in understanding the dynamics and subsequent procedures when they are under attack by the group. In other words, the more experienced leader can serve as model for the beginning worker.

Whatever the reasons may be for the use of co-leadership, the practice is very likely here to stay. It has been observed to be a learning experience not only for the group members, but a growth process for the leaders as well. Co-leadership provides an opportunity to learn continually about oneself, one's blind spots as a leader in group situations, and one's total style of interaction in the group process. In this context, our contention is not to debate the virtues or limitations of co-leadership, but to suggest certain guidelines that can benefit the group work services for everyone, especially the members of co-led groups.

We want to reemphasize that co-leadership does not necessarily imply co-equal power. It is like saying that in a successful marriage the spouses always have equal power. In reality, this doesn't occur. There are situations in which one spouse or the other assumes more responsibility and/or has more power. Just as in marriage, co-leadership of a group is a partnership that can continue to function in any situation, even when one leader is absent for whatever reason. The leader that remains will take on the major responsibility for the functioning of the group. The secret of a successful marriage is demonstrated when the partners are accepting of each other's uniqueness, and are willing to let each other assume responsibility along their separate strengths. It is a shared partnership that involves mutual responsibility. Furthermore, the partners of a successful marriage are those who feel comfortable in being dependent on each other. In such marriages, there is sufficient freedom for both to develop their respective individuation without having to engage in open competition. As with a healthy marriage, a healthy co-leader relationship must be based on openness at all times. Co-leaders must work together to form a relationship emphasizing mutuality, support and respect for one another rather than competitiveness and divisiveness. When the partners or co-leaders in such relationships are able to operate with mutual respect and acceptance, the major beneficiaries are the children or members of the group.

In the process of working together, co-leaders need to be aware of the similarities and differences in their respective value systems as formed through different family roots and expressed in current lifestyles. The co-leaders need to be alert to the different opinions each may hold on a variety of societal issues that may confront them in the group process. If personal differences of opinion are not worked out in advance of group meetings, they will tend to creep back into the group process and create considerable discomfort in the group as a whole. On the other hand, when co-leaders can respect each other's opinions, and work together effectively despite differences, this experience can be therapeutic for the group members. So it is to the co-leaders' and group members' benefit that these different value structures are explored and accommodated. These authors have found that, as a general rule, the following areas are ones in which different values may influence the leaders' attitudes and opinions about subject matter that may come up in the group context.

1. *Family.* The whole area of family background and how the leaders were raised as children affects the values that each of them holds. Whether the leaders were exposed to a solid, steady, parental marriage or exposed to frequent fights and separations will determine their attitudes and feelings about marriage and if they accept divorce as an alternative to an unhappy marriage. For example, if one leader was raised in a family where divorce was not allowed and considered shameful and the other co-leader was raised in a family that had experienced divorce or was himself/herself divorced, then one can reasonably ask the question; how can these two leaders work together with a group of clients' whose marriages are foundering? Topical areas of sexuality such as sexual preferences, premarital, and extramarital relationships are often influenced by one's exposure to these differential life sytles both in the family of origin as well as in one's current environment.

The area of child rearing and discipline also affects leaders' values. One might expect differences if one was raised in an authoritarian household and the other in a household where children's opinions on family matters were actively sought. In the matter of discipline, if the leaders were never spanked as children, will they be able to accept that type of child rearing practice? The structure in their families of origin will affect how they see the male–female, husband–wife, superior–subordinate roles in a marriage. If, in the leaders' family, the male was the dominant figure, what impact will it have on their ability to understand a marriage in which the husband and wife both work and share money and power equally? Similarly, the leaders' attitude towards the use of alcohol and drugs might be influenced by the presence or absence of it in their own current families or families of origin.

2. *Work and Finances.* Leaders' work ethics can be very idiosyncratic. One leader may pride himself/herself on always being on time, working a full day and working overtime to prepare thoroughly for the challenge of his/her work. Another leader may be more lackadaisical and be involved only in satisfying the minimum requirements of the job. The leaders may also have very different ideas in the areas of spending and saving habits. One may value saving money for the future, the other may value spending for the here and now. When these two leaders are brought together to discuss budgeting we can see where conflicts may arise.

3. *Religious ideologies.* We believe the matter of religion is seldom discussed in group work, especially the leaders' position on this issue. The value that an individual leader places on his/her own religion will be another area of potential conflict between co-leaders. Religious stands on such areas as birth control and abortion will affect how a leader may react in a given group situation, for example, in group work with pregnant teenagers. Since there are such a variety of religions in our society and each of them espouses its own beliefs of what is morally acceptable and right, it is fair to assume that this could be a source of friction between otherwise compatible co-leaders.

4. *Social institutions.* The leaders' personal views and experiences with different social institutions affect their work with clients. For example the leaders' attitudes regarding institutional racism and sexism are all influenced by their values, which could be expressed both overtly and covertly.

5. *Political views.* Whether or not the leaders get involved in advocating for their client's rights is often determined by how successful they have been in such activities in the past and how deeply they feel their responsibility for doing so. Political views such as a leaders' stand on desegregation through busing can be an outgrowth of their value structure. Whether or not the leaders were exposed to overt racism and the discriminating forces at work in society will affect how they stand on such vital issues.

As discussed in earlier chapters, group members may bring conflicts which can be intrapsychic, interpersonal or allogenic in nature. These conflicts can fall under any of the five areas discussed earlier. Major discrepancies between co-leaders regarding personal sentiments in any of the five descriptive categories can distort an assessment of the members' struggles with respect to their sources and subsequent interventions.

From an ecological perspective, the concept of co-leadership would involve the following elements.

1. The two co-leaders should have complete clarity regarding their respective stands on the vital issues mentioned earlier.

2. They should understand that the environmental context of the group will have considerable impact on the group norms regarding the members' beliefs and attitudes in any of the five designated categories.

3. The co-leaders must recognize that participation in the group is only a temporary phenomena for the members, and ultimately they have to separate from the group. The co-leaders together need to facilitate this separation process. This is an arduous process, espe-

cially when the members and co-leaders share similar and profound sentiments about any of the five areas discussed earlier. To work effectively, co-leaders need to be compatible, flexible, know their own assets and limitations, be able to resolve issues of dominance and submission and interact with each other freely about their values, feelings and observations, before during and after the group sessions (Balgopal and Hull, 1973).

Direct application of the substantive issues between co-leaders are demonstrated in the following vignette. Two potential co-leaders approached one of the present writers for supervision of their work in a group. When they were asked how much they knew about each others' working style, both of them immediately responded, "not much." But, they did know each other personally and did not forsee any difficulty in working together. The writer suggested that before they embark on co-leading a group the two professionals should spend some time together and share opinions, feelings and values regarding each of the five areas discussed earlier. It was also suggested that their discussion should be held for at least ten hours, and divided into no more than three meetings. The rationale for this format was that adequate time for each meeting is essential before one can begin to share one's own beliefs and feelings freely. Both professionals readily accepted this suggestion and agreed to contact the writer again in two weeks' time. To the writer's surprise, the two potential co-leaders came to see him within three days, and informed him that they had abandoned the idea of working together. It seems they had gotten together the previous day and within two hours discovered that they were diametrically opposed on most of the five areas. To their credit, they realized that their intended collaboration would be a disservice to the clients.

9
Leadership:
Interventions

Leaders use group structure and process variables to describe and organize the reality of the group into a composite and a coherent pattern. Traditionally, identifiable recurrent patterns have been the basis for articulating a theory of group development. The purpose of discrete stages is to guide the leader in anticipating and using various roles and interventions. Rather than using this format, structure and process are used as the two key dimensions of group work to delineate specific intervention strategies. The rationale for this approach is to avoid the problem of overlapping interventions within and across stages, and at the same time to clearly distinguish the concrete applications of different strategies. Included in the following presentation of interventions is a discussion of purposes and intended effects, supported by relevant case illustrations. In many cases the intervention strategies are guided by the practice principles presented earlier.

Interventions refer to what the leader does in a planned and systematic way. The reason for professional intervention is to aid a group of persons to reach a set of realistic personal and group goals. Intervention also refers to entering into an "ongoing sytem of relationships, to come between or among persons, groups, or objectives for the purpose of helping them. There is an important implicit assumption in the definition . . . the system (group) exists independently of the intervenor" (Argyris, 1970, p. 15).

WARMTH, EMPATHY AND GENUINENESS

Empathy refers to taking on the role of the other. The important activity is for the leader to be able to "read" the person and to communicate that in a way that conveys understanding. Empathy deserves consideration because role taking is an important determinant in self-perception and behavior as noted in Mead's work. For example, it is hard to visualize an alteration in one's perception and behavior if the person cannot communicate with others except in a defensive and rigid manner. To accept the viewpoint of the other implies that one must have an adequate base of emotional flexibility, as well as the capacity for examining one's own feelings against the standards of trusted peers (significant others). Accurate perception of another's point of view is also an important determinant in deescalating conflict. It also enhances the range of options for continuity and variety of interpersonal responses. When there are accurate "readings" of other people, the options for helping and assisting others is also enhanced, an important principal in mutual aid. In ego psychological terms it refers to the defense of altruism, considered one of the most adaptive defenses by Vaillant (1977). For example, it is not uncommon for most members in the beginning phase of groups to feel skeptical about fellow members' potential in assisting them with their problems. This skepticism is further affirmed due to their own doubts about their respective roles as helpers. Empathy paves the way for their altruistic sentiments to emerge, facilitating improvement in their self-concept. Flexibility in role taking increases the sharing of a greater body of common experiences that in mutual aid, manifests itself in a greater number of coping patterns being shared as well.

In a group of parents of anorexic children, one of the group members is expressing her frustrations, anger, and guilt feelings over not knowing what to do when her child refuses to eat the food at the dinner table. The leader says that it must be difficult and asks how other fellow group members handle similar situations. One of the older members comments, "I know exactly how you feel because I go through the same thing. But now I have learned to accept it, and simply put the food away in the stove and tell my son that it will be there when he is ready to eat."

Accurate empathy may not be enough when a leader's personal life style, including value system, is quite different from that of members. For example in work with adolescent groups, substance abuse populations, and child abuse parents, the leader by virtue of his/her past experiences is not likely to be able to empathize with the members. In addition, value dilemmas may further block the perceptual screen. The task needed to be considered is that the leader take on the role of the learner so that he/she can begin to shape the correct use of his/her own professional skills. In such situations the leader may ask the members to assist him/her in helping the group by talking and sharing ideas and feelings.

In a parents group convened for the purpose of improving their relationship with children, a young, fairly well-to-do couple informed the group that they wanted to place their two natural children, ages seven and five, for adoption. The reason they cited is that their current life style is not conducive to raising their children in a healthy and acceptable environment. The leader had extreme difficulty in accepting the couple's desire to place their children for adoption, and, blocked by anger, could not explore the dynamics of the issue including options other than adoption for the couple. The air was cleared when another member pointed out to the leader his inability to recognize the anguish behind the couple's statement. At that juncture the mother said that do-gooder social workers would not waste a second in removing children from their home if they were physically abused. The couple continued to point out that they were fearful of abusing their children emotionally.

There are two important lessons to be drawn from this case. The first is that the leader clearly froze in terms of his own emotional sentiments and could not listen to what the couple were saying. The source of the discomfort was at the value level that is a profound aspect of personality. The other lesson to be learned is that the leader had established a climate where the members felt free to share some very important concerns that were shared by other members. The group member who intervened for the couple not only was empathetic with them, but also "bailed out" the leader on his insensitivity to the couple's plight. This is also an example of what Hollander (1964) refers to as leader's "idiosyncracy credits," which implies that the leadership mistakes are pardonable.

Empathic skills are enhanced when the leader attempts to understand, appreciate and work in the idiom of members whose life styles are very different from his/her own. This has particular significance in working with ethnic and minority populations. The leader does not have to hide behind his/her professional mask when members present a sharply divergent set of experiences which contradict the dominant societal norms. The leader simply has to accept his/her ignorance and ask for clarification of the members' point of view. A professional stance does not mean one has to impose egalitarian sentiments upon members who adhere to a strong patriarchal family structure, where, for example, mate selection for the children is determined by the father. Cultural norms become a powerful determinant in the members' and leader's field of action.

Use of empathy is important for assessment purposes in two other interrelated areas. The first is in assessing the value of empathy among deprived populations. It is likely in this situation that the skills, efforts, and patience needed to communicate with significant others may have become severely abridged by the members' self-oriented sentiments regarding survival. A common observation is that the extent of hostility and anger directed at neighbors may be a necessary distancing mechanism for not looking at oneself. Projecting blame and dissatisfaction toward others may serve to protect the ego at the time when a person is feeling most vulnerable. A related concern in this regard is that the relearning of empathic skills in a group may pose special problems for adoption in the members' home situations. This has been observed among children discharged from residential treatment centers and training schools, or adults reentering the community from a psychiatric hospital. The point is that the skills and behaviors to be learned and applied have to be judged for the utility and goodness of fit with the expectations and possible consequences back home. One method for dealing with this dilemma is for the leader to focus on anticipatory socialization problems regarding reentry into the members' home environments. For example group members may be asked to respond to a series of potential problems they might encounter as a first step in applying hard earned skills in what may be an unwelcome environment.

Warmth is the unsolicited expression of affection and concern that has also been referred to as unconditional acceptance. Warmth is often conveyed in nonverbal ways such as touching, facial expressions and gestures. Warmth is also a manifestation of caring which carries powerful meaning at those times that members feel most vulnerable, as for example, after poignant self-disclosures. In this regard warmth is related to one important item negotiated in the initial contract, whereby members are informed that group experience may be stressful. Member recognition of caring and concern expressed by the group leader leads them to anticipate a sense of safety and personal inviolability at times of anticipated uncertainty. Warmth, like empathy has the intended effect of helping a group maintain its momentum, fostering cohension and reducing defensiveness. The following example illustrates the expression of warmth by a group leader.

A group of senior citizens who reside in a housing project for the aged have agreed to meet together to discuss problems regarding relative isolation and feelings of loss. In the forthcoming meeting the topic under discussion focuses on the theme of loss and separation. In thinking about the recent loss of his wife, one man started crying softly, dabbing his eyes with a handkerchief. The other group members became silent and looked expectently first at their tearful colleague and then at the group leader. The group leader surveyed the situation, got up off his chair, approached the distressed member and with tears in his own eyes took and held the member's hands as an expression of comfort and concern. The tearful member after a few moments of silence looked up at the leader and nodded thank you. The other members then began to discuss how important it was to face the loss since they all had experienced it in one way or another. In a philosophical vein they agreed that they had to live with it and go on, as life must, to other things.

The expression of warmth was clearly and profoundly conveyed by the leader's simple act of physical contact. An important element in communicating warmth and concern is that it must not be exaggerated, overpowering, or patronizing. Excessive concern undercuts the respectful distance between the group members own individuality and the expression of assistance offered by others or the group leader.

Genuineness solidifies the act of caring in the spontaneity of its expression. For example if the leader in the earlier case of senior citizens had responded with a puzzled silence the incident may well have been perceived as embarrassing. Authenticity and genuineness are interchangable terms. Levitsky and Simkin (1972) described authenticity as a state of individuation, of truly being one's self. Gendlin (1973) discussed authenticity as a process, and according to him what makes the process authentic is not what is said, but the manner of the process.

Authenticity refers to a blending of a yet distinctive difference

239

between personal and professional closeness. When leaders are too objective—too preoccupied with maintaining their professional role—their human qualities such as sensitivity, concern for the members, and spontaneity are hampered. In their struggle to be ideal, leaders may fail to be human. Leaders can be concerned human beings without losing sight of their professional mission and commitment. To be genuine and authentic, a leader has to ensure that he/she does not project false images, nor hide behind a professional facade. The leader has to be himself/herself, but this does not mean he/she acts or behaves without consideration for the group members. Moreover the leader has to be sure that he/she does not use the group as a source to nurture own personal needs nor overwhelm the group with personal conflicts and struggles (Balgopal and Vassil, 1979). This ideology is based on the Eastern philosophy of Vedanta which emphasizes that selflessness and detachment leads to ultimate freedom. What this implies is that the leaders have to be cognizant that they do not deliberately or inadvertently impose their own personal agenda on the members. However it has to be recognized that detachment does not imply disinterest or lack of concern but simply emphasizes that this interest and concern has to be for the benefit of the receiver.

Genuineness or authenticity is not limited in its intent to simply honest expressions or feelings by the leader. Responsive feelings need to be purposive with respect to the focus and content of the group. In this regard genuineness can be applied in both positive and negative communications from the leader to the members. The negative responses need to be sensitively expressed in nonpunitive terms.

SELF-DISCLOSURE

Self-disclosure refers to the leader's expression of personal experiences that are purposively focused on the content and process of the group. Self-disclosure is manifested in sharing here-and-now feelings, and is interrelated to the broader process of making oneself known to other persons. The rationale for self-disclosure is based on the belief that the leader is not helpful when persons are treated as objects. Implied in the belief is the idea that common perceptions of fraternity shared between and among the group members provides a liberating and optimistic ideal.

Timing, content and the specific nature of the disclosure are all relevant variables. For example extensive disclosure about the leader's anxieties and feelings in the initial group sessions may very well induce a lack of self-confidence among members. In essence, too much self-disclosure can produce self-doubts, particularly as it relates to the leader's professional skills.

Leader self-disclosure can occur at either the content or the feeling levels. The danger of the leader's sharing personal material is that it can set a tone for the members who feel that they also have to follow the same pattern. A misperception in the leader's intent in self-disclosing may be manifested by members trying to out do each other by revealing more content than necessary from their past. Overproduction at either the content or feeling levels poses distinct limitations. At the content level the competition among members' ideas can degenerate into innocuous war stories. At the feeling level the danger is that the group members can drift into forming a mutual hand-holding society. Over disclosure by any one member can also intimidate other members who may not be as ready to share their intimate feelings.

Self-disclosure is not an end in itself. After an incident in which leader or members have appropriately shared their concerns, the leader must be attuned to the next steps which relate to the purpose and the intended effect of the self-disclosure. For example, the leader has to explore with the members the impact and relevance of the material to the significant problems which members have contracted to address. At this juncture it seems reasonable to state that self-disclosure is a complex intervention strategy that must be used in discriminating fashion. As with all interventions, the leader must be sensitive to not servicing personal needs in the process. The following example illustrates the leader's use of self-disclosure.

In a fourth meeting of a group organized to improve parenting skills, Mrs. Jones a shy, retiring middle-aged woman began to share her feelings of anger and humiliation regarding her fourteen-year-old son who was caught smoking marijuana on the school grounds. The leader commented that he knew what she felt because his thirteen-year-old daughter was dismissed from summer camp for similar reasons. The leader went on to say that incidents like this are bound to provoke strong feelings as experienced by Mrs. Jones. He then asked whether the members could direct their attention to specific ways for dealing with their children without alienating them.

The intent of the leaders self-disclosure was three-fold: (1) to support Mrs. Jones who had difficulty in revealing personal content; (2) to support self-disclosure as appropriate in the group; and (3) to use self-disclosure as a bridge to focus the discussion on specific parent-child issues consistent with the purposes of the group.

CONFRONTATION

Confrontation is a statement of the leader's perception which challenges the members or the group to recognize repeated occurrences of disabling behavior, to deal with dissimilarities between what is said and the consequent behavior, and/or to face the thoughts, feelings or actions which the members or the group deny or avoid. For example, a leader might respond to a member in the following way: "You say that you are not angry but your sarcastic comments and clenched fists suggest you are feeling angry towards Frank." The immediate effects of confrontation include preventing more clearly some aspect of the member or group process.

There are several types of confrontation possible. Experiential confrontation focuses on the here-and-now and is intended to dramatize the discrepancy between words and feelings. Confrontation can also be directed at a member's strength in the face of communicated feelings of weakness. For example, a member who is assertive on the job and relatively docile in a family situation can be challenged to examine his inability to generalize personal capacities for assuming his rights in the family. Action confrontation implies a challenge to act and the leader has a reason to believe that the means for assertion are presented. For instance the members in a marital couples group have been practicing skills for dealing with sexual stereotyping between partners through role play and role reversal exercises. However, the members were hesitant to incorporate this new awareness in their day to day relationships with their significant others. The leader challenged the members in the forthcoming week to be assertive at least in one incidence in their daily life and report the results at the next group meeting for evaluation and feedback.

Confrontation can occur at any point in the group's life. In the next example the leader presses for the members to make a commitment to the group.

In the first session the leader asked if each person in the room would introduce themselves. Some of the members were very hesitant and stared at each other or looked out into space. The implications of this hesitation to reveal personal identity had multiple reasons, such as, not wanting to go first, uncertainty regarding their presence, fear due to being in unfamiliar surroundings, and not knowing how much to share beyond their names. At this point the leader, rather than introducing them, indicated that this was their group and introducing themselves and sharing what they expect from each other would indicate their commitment to participate in the group. There was no response to this. The leader again suggested members speak up, and finally after a long pause one of the members introduced herself as Mrs. Gates and gave her reasons for being in the group. This prompted others to follow in sharing their reasons for coming to the meeting.

Confrontation as an intervention strategy is related to the leader's comfort and skill in dealing with conflictual situations. While leaders can prepare for anticipated and heated differences between and among members, sometimes confrontation can occur in a group without warning. Consummate skill is needed when this occurs, especially in deprived communities where direct hostility and interpersonal antagonisms are very much a part of their daily life. This point is illustrated in the following case:

The leader asked Al what it was like when he was working? Al didn't mind work except when somebody got on his neck. Once in a while the foreman would look at him like he was a dog or something. Joe exclaimed "they're always keeping you moving. The last job I had at Benson Beverages I got in a fight because the boss asked me to do something on my break and I told him to shove it." "Maybe he needed you just for a minute," countered the leader. "Naw, he was picking on me because I was the newest one, figuring he found a sucker." "What's a boss for Joe," asked the leader, "if not to see that things get done. What kind of boss would you like?" Rolly stated that he had an experience at a Chemical Co. on the platform which was pretty good. The boss was a nice guy and the crew was easy to get along with. You don't mind working in a place like that. Bob and Louis agreed. Ken joined in and said it was like that when he was working as a shipper for Fanny Farmer. "There were a lot of characters there and one of the guys used to be a boxer. Real tough. One joker was a wise guy and tried to throw his weight around and we got rid of him fast." The leader asked if getting along with others was important on the job. "Not if the boss gives you a lot of crap," said Joe. Paul noted that you can't have it one way. "You're not doing them a favor by working there. One guy can screw it up for the others. You ain't too easy to take sometimes Joe—always looking for a fight." "Are you looking," challenged Joe. The leader stood up immediately and demanded a stop right now.

In the above situation the leader was caught off guard and his own anxieties prompted him to act too fast. Experience in working with antagonistic members suggests that even in those situations in which physical violence is a real possibility, the confrontation does not last very long and other group members intercede very quickly. The leader in this situation might have waited a few seconds and then complimented both Joe and Paul for speaking their minds, for acting spontaneously, for holding on to their anger in words rather than resorting to physical fighting. Subsequently the leader could have explored how they could have used this experience and "made a win" out of it, thus reinforcing the incentive to work.

Confrontation can be effectively used when group members resist incorporating suggestions from earlier sessions and continue to dwell on their original plight. This is clearly illustrated in the next excerpt.

In the fourteenth session Mary began to narrate her sob story concerning her unhappy relationship with Joe. (Joe had mistreated and abused Mary, but she was unable to confront his meanness). The other members looked very bored over the prospect of listening to the same story. The leader looked at the group and said it looks like we are going to hear another heavy version of Mary's never-ending drama. The leader then looked at Mary and excused himself so that he could get properly settled. He got up and got pipes, tobacco and matches and returned to his seat. As Mary was ready to start with her story, the leader once again asked the other members if they wanted a drink of water or whatever. The leader also excused himself again and returned with a box of tissues and placed them next to Mary. At this point Mary exploded at the leader and shouted obscenities at him. The members were somewhat stunned by this outburst, but the leader calmly waited for Mary to finish. After the attack he noted that Mary was completely justified in being angry and wondered when she was going to express her anger towards Joe for treating her like "shit," to which she responded by attacking Joe in the same colorful language and manner. The members during this entire demonstration were very in tune, and applauded when Mary finished.

The effects of the confrontation in the above illustration were: (1) Mary shifted from feeling sorry for herself to directly expressing her pent-up anger towards Joe; (2) members' reaction shifted from being bored to being interested; (3) this led other members to consider how they set themselves up for failure; and (4) how the members' self-concepts were consistently being marred by "Joes" in their own lives. The leader's planned and conscious intervention, including the nondefensive response, set the stage for a shift in group norms from passively tolerating and reinforcing a victimization theme to examining and assuming their own responsibilities in setting themselves up as victims.

HUMOR

Humor can be used in a variety of situations. Vaillant (1977) describes humor in the following way: an "overt expression of ideas and feelings without individual discomfort or immobilization and without unpleasant effect on others" (p. 386). Humor serves the double purpose of helping people get close to one another as well as helping them get through difficult situations. The central dynamic in humor is that it relieves frustrations by minimizing anxieties between people. The use of humor to relieve group pressure as well as drive home a point is illustrated in the following case exerpt.

In a residential treatment center for addicts, someone "snitched" on another member who had smuggled in drugs and as a result was discharged. The group that followed was tense and divisive between those who approved of this action as in their best interests, and those who disapproved according to the street ethic that someone had "ratted." The leader pointed out that the treatment setting was not a prison, and concluded with "if you fly with crows, you're going to get buckshot in the ass." The group laughed and came to see the danger of harboring temptation in their midst.

Use of humor has applicability at all phases of group development. However, professionals are generally cautious in using humor in the beginning stage, particularly in a planned way. In the following example although the leader (therapist) is very caustic, his humor serves the purpose of bridging the hostile member's entry into the group.

A powerfully built man in his early 30s was referred to an all-male group. Brought recently to the hospital by the police, he evinced a barely controlled rage reaction and was considered potentially dangerous and unapproachable by staff. Entering the room after the session had started, he sat down opposite the therapist, breathing loudly through his nose, his teeth clenched, glowering fiercely.

T. (*Finishing with another G.M.'s issue, turning to new G.M.; casually*): Hi there, what's your name?

G.M.#1 (*Loudly, fiercely through clenched teeth*): Never mind!

T. (*Anxiously back pedaling*): O.K., you don't have to— (*Suddenly changing his mind; offhandedly puzzled*) Oh, 93, 322. Aren't—

G.M.#1 (*Frowning at T., then looking around the group; loudly and angrily interrupting.*): Who the fuck is this—

T. (*As several G.M.s look back and forth at G.M.#1 and T. and begin laughing; T. clapping his hand to forehead, then pointing at G.M.#1*): Wait, don't tell me. See if I can guess. Are you the guy whose wife sent him in here because he was out screwing the heifer, or—

(*G.M.s 2, 3, 4, and 5 burst out laughing; four others are watching therapist and G.M.#1 carefully*).

G.M.#6 (*Straightforwardly to G.M.#1*): This here is Frank Farelly and he conducts this group therapy class [sic] twice a week. You have to get used—

G.M.#1 (*Looking less fierce; interrupting G.M.#6, speaking to the group, some of whom continue to grin or chuckle; less loudly*): He sounds a little off himself—

T. (*Interrupting, in a chocked, hurt tone.*): Well, maybe you're right, 93,322, but I used . . . to be normal . . . as blueberry pie . . . before I started holding these meetings with this ding-bat crew here—

G.M.#1 (*Looking at therapist, elbows on knees, hands clasped in front of him; then lowers his head, turns it to the left, bites his lower left lip obviously trying to hide his efforts to keep from laughing, next shakes his head from side to side, snorting to himself in a soft tone.*): Shit!

G.M.#4 (*Leaning forward to speak to G.M.#1; grinning.*): We call this Weird Beard's Comedy Hour. It's the highlight of our—

(*Several G.M.s laugh, along with G.M.#1, who has ceased looking so angry and is openly grinning at the group*).

T. (*Looking at G.M.#1, smiling slightly; in a jocose tone.*): Well, ol' buddy, 93,322, you ready to tell us what you're so pissed off about?

G.M.#1 (*Frowning: in much better control.*): My name's Fred Blank, and you'd be pissed off, too, if your wife had you thrown in here by a bunch of cops the other night.

G.M.#3 (*Nodding agreement, looking at and addressing G.M.#1*): My wife did that to me a mongh ago, and I'm still angry at her in a way.

G.M.#1 (*Looking quickly at G.M.#3; firmly.*): I ain't staying in here for no month, that's for sure.

G.M.#4 (*Sitting back, watching interaction; to G.M.#1*): What was her beef with you?

G.M.#1 began explaining his situation to the therapist and the group and admitted he had a "hair-trigger temper." This cooperation was quite a change, enabling him to make use of the resources of the hospital to effect an early discharge.

(Farrelly & Bradsma, 1974).

The example points to an issue worth repeating, that a leader using any intervention has to have a sense of self-confidence and comfort in his/her applied strategies. Defensiveness or hesitancy will affect the leader's creative use of self. In the use of humor the leader was creative, but was also planned and confident in the way he reduced the distance between the new member and the group. The slightest manifestation of self-doubt could have led to an embarassing situation.

Humor can also be used by involving group members in confronting any one member's unrealistic expectations. This is well illustrated in an inpatient treatment group conducted in a psychiatric hospital.

A paranoid schizophrenic patient (G.M.#1), recently admitted to the hospital and a new member of an all-female group, has asked repeated (literally twenty times in the session) about going home: "Can't I go home? Please let me go home. Why can't I go home?" She interrupts continuously with her refrain, and is listening to neither other group members nor the therapist in their efforts to help her examine the behavior that led to her hospitalization and was keeping her there.

G.M.#2 (*A mentally retarded women, interposes.*): She's here for something, but she won't admit it.

G.M.s attempt to help **G.M.#1** repeatedly, but she consistently broadcasts the message, "I don't need to be here," and adds to **G.M.#3** (*Blandly*):

Don't think of me in your shoes. (*Turning to T., repetitiously*). Can't I go home?

At this juncture (three-fourths through the session) T. compares G.M.#1's behavior to the "Chinese water drop torture," (explaining it to the group in detail) and then begins saying, "Blip" each time G.M.#1 asks her question, responding in effect, "If you're not going to address yourself seriously to your problems, I'm not going to address myself seriously to your questions." Other G.M.s begin taking up the therapist's "Blip" refrain.

G.M.#1 (*Hesitating; attempts to rephrase*): I believe I'm well now . . . can I go home?
G.M.s (*Laughing; some shaking their heads in disbelief; as a chorus*): Blip!

G.M.#3 points out that G.M.#1 is not "consistent" enough yet to be discharged from the hospital.

G.M.#1 (*To G.M.#3; persisting.*): I'm consistent in wanting to go home.
G.M.#4 (*Laughing.*): Persistent is the word.
G.M.#2 (*Interposing*): I disagree on that. She's not strong enough. She's sick. She's not ready to go home.

248

> **T.** (*In a sing-song voice, wearily, to G.M.#1*): Annie, do you think that if you just keep it up and keep it up and keep it up that the staff will get worn down and finally say, "O.K., damnit, we give up, go home?"
>
> **G.M.#1** (*Smiling*): Well, I don't know, I might try it, if it'd work.
>
> (*G.M.s and T. laugh, provoking G.M.#1 to laugh along with them*). (Farrelly & Bradsma, 1974).

EXPLORATION

Exploration through the use of phrasing and directing general questions to members or the group can clarify the scope of the problem and stimulate communication and interactions among group participants. In early sessions or the beginning of a single session, social comparison processes and issues of personal vulnerability produce hesitant and cautious participation patterns. Although role distancing is an appropriate means for self protection, the group leader is faced with the problem of helping members in the transition from defensive involvement to judicious self-revelation. The use of general open-ended questions is common to good interviewing practices. Their purpose is to enhance self expression by minimizing emphasis on correct answers and maximizing flexibility in subjective and meaningful content. Responses to general questions also contribute to the individual member's commitment to the group simply because they talk more. Open-ended questions such as; "how does that make you feel?" or "could you expand on your concern to help us understand?" have the potential for enhancing other members' vicarious identification with the problem thus reinforcing the common purposes which bring them to the group. Exploratory questions that are under the control of the leader may vary in their ambiguity and structure. The type of response elicited depends on how much ambiguity the member or group can tolerate as well as on the problem specificity that is desired. A question such as "where shall we begin" is more open-ended than "what is it about your spouse that makes you angry?" The leader can further guide responses by emphasizing different words in the question itself. For example, in responding to a member or group's low keyed discussion on their frustrations with rambunctious children, the leader could ask "what sort of *feelings*

249

does this bring up in you?" or "what sort of feelings does this bring up in *you*?"

> During the meeting, Sue was discussing difficulties she was having with her boyfriend. "It's just like every other relationship I have—once I get too close, things stop working—so I guess I just have to quit getting close." The group members react with varied comments such as "don't do that, Sue," "there's got to be another way," "that doesn't work," etc. The leader intervenes with "Maybe it will help, Sue, if you tell us a little more about the situation—we could probably be more helpful if you could give us a clear idea of what's causing the problems."

Frequently, general exploratory questions are asked in the subjunctive which refers to starting questions with words such as "perhaps," "maybe," "might we," and so forth. The purpose of subjunctives is to provide a favorable and safe context for effective participation and learning. The implicit message is that the member or group has a right not to participate, thereby reaffirming the point of view that the member or group has a choice in the matter. It also conveys to the group that the leader may be asking an untimely question. The use of subjunctives is evident in the next illustration.

> A young boy is explaining in the group that he is unable to get his parents to listen to his side of any problem he gets into. The leader responds with "There might be some way that you could go about it differently. Perhaps someone in the group has some ideas of some way that's worked for them that might be helpful to Steve."

SUMMARIZING

Summarizing refers to a concise and coherent review of the main points covered in a group meeting. It may take place both during the session or at the end. When the leader chooses to summarize during the last few minutes before the group terminates, the condensed content can be evaluated for its accuracy and equally important, can set the agenda for the next meeting, thus providing continuity. Summaries can also include significant work that the group has produced. For the group, summarizing relevant content reinforces the group as a symbolic construct which has referent power.

Presenting a synopsis of events in the early part of a session is useful for helping absent members tune into current group process. During the course of a meeting and in keeping with the contract, the leader may choose to summarize as a way of bringing the group on track at those times when members seem to be going off on a tangent. In phrasing the content, the leader can raise questions about the next steps to get an initial commitment about where to begin next time, or to reflect on perceived ambivalences which implies residual issues that warrant further attention. Often the content can be useful as a reminder to the group that there are precedents which can guide their immediate concerns. In committee work, recorded minutes are a formal means for noting specific actions that the group has taken. As pertinent history, the minutes provide a basis for developing agenda in the future. For the leader, written summaries are a means for evaluating, approximating, and mapping the overall work of the group and its members in terms of immediate, short-term, and long-term goals.

Example

The single-parent woman's group began with a spirited discussion about their failed marriages, and in particular about the type of men they had chosen for partners. Specific complaints included the hard life they all had, particularly in raising children without help from their husbands, the wear and tear of constant irritations and chronic arguments, and the constant struggle of maintaining a facade of a happy marriage to their family and friends.

After twenty minutes of highly charged discussion, their emotional energies waned and the group drifted into what seemed to be a reflective and sorrowful silence. One of the members began to talk about a recent movie she had seen. Others joined in and conversations developed and shifted onto topics such as shopping, current popular songs, and other seemingly irrelevant concerns. The leader commented that the group had shared pertinent and powerful feelings

---

about their marriages, relationships with their partners, and frustrations they lived with. In order to get them back on track the leader asked if some of their frustrations were cleared up or if there were other unstated and leftover feelings which needed to be expressed.

In this illustration, the leader's summarization included a question designed to help the group move along to further consideration of derivative feelings and thoughts which had been sidetracked to avoid the underlying theme of loneliness and isolation. This example also demonstrates that interventions are often times combined, such as summarizing and exploring to assist the members in their work.

SUPPORT

Support is a general psychological strategy that is used to restore or strengthen a member or group's capacities. Among the various forms it can take are encouraging members to talk, or to continue in their deliberations either through verbal or nonverbal means. A nod of the head, a short praiseworthy comment, expressing acceptance of feelings or confidence in one's comments represent some of the more usual ways. Support can decrease feelings of tension, or guilt, or of uncertainty as in the case when members may feel self-conscious about self-disclosing too much. Too much support can become counterproductive and encourage excessive dependence on the "kindly, good parent" role. Attention to purpose dictates the use of this strategy as in all others, as for example, whether thoughts, feelings or specific actions are to be supported. Members may support each other in between group meetings through telephone contact, or by offering to share transportation. In a group of parents of developmentally disabled children, several of the parents had formed a car pool which reinforced group attendance and cohesion. In a residential family camp setting, members would volunteer to do the wash for those who were having trouble with organizing routines. In another dramatic example, three women in a family life education group took turns teaching a functionally illiterate member to read. Leader's support to reentry of psychiatric patients to community life is illustrated in the following example.

Example

An after-care group of "psychiatric patients" had planned to visit a coffee house in the city to see what it was like and to enjoy the music. The evening of the event, the group was quite anxious and hesitant about their trip, since it was a different experience, and they weren't sure what others would think when they walked into the coffee house. Their ambivalences showed residual fears that somehow they could be spotted right away as mental patients. The leader noted that these were reasonable doubts but pointed out that they had been meeting in the agency for several weeks, using public transportation and no one had complained of feeling different. Also trips to bowling alleys and movies had proved successful and enjoyable. The leader pointed out that they had worked very hard to get to where they were and while this event was somewhat different, they really had demonstrated that they were like a lot of other people who wanted to enjoy themselves. The leader suggested that the group get started but that if there were any strong feelings on any one's part, the group could decide; (1) to ride by the coffee house, but postpone going in for another time; (2) to drop in and leave early; (3) or to stay for one show. The members agreed to at least go to the coffee house and decide what to do from there.

In this illustration the leader reviews and encourages the initiative and "normalcy" of the members, the satisfactions they had gained in other group-sponsored activities and their successful struggle to recapture a meaningful life piece by piece.

COGNITIVE RESTRUCTURING

It is not uncommon in group work that members can get stuck in a groove unable to figure out what to do next. Sometimes the affective investment in a problem blurs their perceptual set and it appears that the group is expending energy without being able to move ahead. Cognitive restructuring refers to a complex strategy for changing perceptions or emotional sets which seem to impede the group members' abilities to change or view behavior of themselves or others as constructive or understandable. Cognitive

253

restructuring is synonymous with a perceptual reordering and the purpose is to break a log jam by inducing another perceptual orientation.

Example

The parents who were frightened of reprimanding their sons for their behavior seemed more responsive when the leader suggested that setting limits was like holding the child close, which helps him feel secure and safe.

In this illustration, a different perception for the use of limits was introduced to assist the parents in reframing their view and hopefully providing a rationale for and acceptance of limit setting.

It is important to note that the leader must enjoy a high level of credibility for members to accept suggestions that literally can turn them around. While the suggestion can alter their perceptions for the moment, they are still a step away from relatively comfortable feelings about implementing the actions. In this sense, restructuring is a liberating procedure that is a precursor to altered behavior.

Restructuring is a common tool used with youth groups because the leader is continually attempting to reorder ways of dealing with provocative events. For example, a suggestion to adolescent groups that walking away from or avoiding a fight is as "strong" as simply fighting is indeed difficult to accept even when it is clear that the consequences of responding physically to real or imagined challenges may lead to chronic trouble. It is true that choices are left to the group members but paradoxical sentiments need to be introduced.

Example

Roger, an 18-year-old adolescent and esteemed member of the Cobras, announced on the street corner one night that he was planning to marry Rose, a 45-year-old woman with whom he had been living for several months. The other members offered congratulations in a rather subdued way but privately commented aside to the leader, asking if he couldn't approach Roger and point out the tremendous mistake he was making.

Roger's status preempted the group members from challenging his decision. The task for the leader, who had a good relationship with the group and occasionally helped them with job seeking, getting driving licenses, and "personal" problems, was to try and reframe the situation to clarify for Roger some of the hidden consequences. The leader congratulated Roger warmly, wished him and his future wife good luck, and hoped that he would be invited to the wedding. The leader said he'd be happy to take a wedding picture so that 15 years later, when Roger was in his early 30s and his wife about 60, they could look back and see how they had changed. Roger smiled, said thanks and invited the leader for a cup of coffee in the donut shop. Roger seemed to drift into a silence while drinking coffee and the leader asked if anything was the matter. Roger looked at the leader and said, "You know I was thinking about those pictures—in 15 years Rose will look like my grandmother and I'll still be young." The leader remarked that sometimes love cancels those differences but it sure pays to think about it ahead of time. Roger finished his coffee and quickly left. Two days later, one of the group members told the leader that Roger and Rose had postponed their wedding for awhile.

In this illustration, the leader successfully induced another look at a situation that was loaded with problems. Yet, it had to be done in a way that would leave the choice in Roger's hands, and not violate his esteemed position in the group. This time it worked.

Restructuring is an imaginative act, sometimes taking the form of an odd intrusion that runs counter to the perceptions and expectations of the group or some members. An earlier example that illustrated the use of humor to help introduce a new member to a group is a case in point.

Sometimes restructuring can be used to provide the opposite side of a situation and to legitimatize that perception. In a marital counseling group, the group members are elaborating on what their partners do that they don't like. The leader suggests that the group think of caring acts that they would like to receive from their partners such as (taking trash out, making a special meal). The point of this strategy is to shift the group climate from defensive and destructive to nurturant and generative.

In general, restructuring is related to the broader area of problem solving. Scheerer (1963) noted that more than trial and error thinking was required for intelligent problem solving and suggested that sharp shifts in the way problems are viewed are often accompanied by insight. The issue that restructuring attempts to deal with is the functional fixedness that polarizes and frustrates solutions to problems. Among constraining factors are a person's incorrect premise that is embedded in a supportive climate. For example, incorrect assumptions between and among residents in a housing project are altered in a different setting (Vassil, 1978). Sometimes the problem is one of excessive zeal whereby a crusader attitude seals off other options that are perhaps less destructive. Habitual patterns of relationships, oftentimes nonrational (as in ethnic idiosyncratic behavior) are quite likely the hardest to unfreeze. The leaders tasks are to create conditions for loosening the habitual strongholds. The structuring in group developmental terms is more likely to occur as events become more complex. This means that greater amounts of differences are introduced into the group thereby forcing greater choices. In a group's life, the leader's retreat from authoritarian position to that of guide facilitator and resource, signals a major perceptual shift among the membership.

ROLE PLAYING

Role playing is a flexible intervention strategy which enables participants to acquire an understanding of their own roles, and those of others, and to develop a new role as participants and/or observers. The "as-if" characteristic of role playing allows an actor to break character, review and recast his/her thoughts/feelings/actions in the light of others' perceptions. The "as-if" quality not only protects the actor but also enhances creativity and sensitivity to the particular situation. Roles may vary from an external manifestation of inner personal tensions and images (psychodrama) to specific and carefully scripted behavior patterns. Role complexes are used to simulate real life situations, either as presently constituted or anticipated, in the context of the group—a safe audience. The focus may be on the cognitive, affective, or behavioral aspects, depending on the purposes and readiness of the group and members. Whether the structure of the role is ambiguous or specific, residual and uncomfortable thoughts, feelings, and actions may occur. For this reason, it is wise to debrief actors after an exercise and to reinforce the "as-if" dimensions. The practical benefits of role playing are the potential that the strategy holds for incorporating and applying new constellations of thought-feeling or actions in relevant problematic situations. In terms of leadership function, the tasks of the leader are to design and comment on specific roles-in-relationship (between and among members), thus modifying the process (what and how something is said) which then alters the group structure. Maier (1976) succinctly summarized the major features associated with role playing in the following way.

> Role playing is being applied more frequently as a viable social work intervention tool. Yet role playing is only a collective term for a wide range of specific interventive techniques. More explicitly, role playing as a technique for assistance with behavioral training requires a simulation of genuine life situations so that the learner can practice the behaviors to be mastered. Practice of behavior, repetition of practice, and intermittent feedback are the focal points of role playing exercised for behavioral acquisition. The model ideal might be ballet practice where training in skill development is important.
>
> In contrast, if affect issues are at stake the efforts are directed toward emotional expressions while behavioral manifestations are secondary. Role-playing structure serves as a point of departure. Roles can be reversed, interchanged, and altered while role playing continues. Departure from the script and normative interactions are fostered. A genuine Halloween party is the ideal model. To act as one feels—to trick or to treat as one fancies, and to have the facility to switch roles interchangeably for one's response to the occasion is the object of role playing for this dimension.
>
> Role playing with a cognitive emphasis demands special attention to timing—interspersing the role-playing experience with review and reflection. The accent shifts from participation (involvement) to participant-observation (involvement with ongoing review). Role playing then becomes an alternation of "play" and "cut." Role assumption and role reversal are chosen for observational input rather than for stimulation and reactive behavior. Role playing aimed at enhancing cognitive processes, including focusing on informational input, has its ideal model in the coffee house where each idea or comment is "chewed over" for its proper fit (p. 68).

Example

A group of eight tenants residing in a housing project agreed to meet with the leader in order to improve the quality of life in their stairwell. Harassment and punitive measures by the maintenance men regarding replacing lost keys, fixing plumbing, dispensing paint and trash collection were the priority issues.

For the first meeting, the irate tenants demanded, as a first order of business, to "straighten out" the maintenance boss. The leader suggested that the group "pretend" for the next few moments that he (the leader) was the maintenance boss who had accepted an invitation to appear before the group. To lend an air of reality to the task, the leader stepped outside, knocked on the door, reentered and sat down, and said in a gruff voice. "What's going on—I understand you got business with me." Madge started by asking in an angry voice, what business he had refusing to replace her lost key. He was supposed to provide service and that's what he was getting paid for. The "boss" responded stiffly that if she didn't give her keys to her kid, she wouldn't lose them. Betty charged saying in a loud voice, that it isn't his job to ask how keys were used, only to supply them. He had no right to keep people locked out of their homes. Furthermore, he was mean to the kids and was always reporting families to the housing authority for things that never happened. Several others in the group continued the tirade as the session was becoming steamy. The leader got up, commenting, "let's cut," and take time out for coffee. As he moved to the coffee pot, he overheard one of the members saying "we really fixed that boss."

The leader commented humorously that they really had a lot of energy invested and he could appreciate how frustrated they were. When he sat down, he asked the group to take a few minutes to examine what had happened. He noted how he felt being under attack, and stating that very quickly he was being pushed into a corner. Also in the process, he felt that the only option he had left was to counter attack. The response from the members was that the "boss" deserved it. The leader surmising that their destructive energies had been relieved for the moment, asked what they might expect to get out of the confrontation. Fran said, "more trouble." Several others nodded assent. The leader said if that was their goal, they could probably suceed but it didn't seem in line with improving life in the stairwell. The group them began to discuss just what avenues were open to them and what ways to deal with the condition they wanted to improve.

The use of role play clearly demonstrated very powerful feelings of frustration which had to be diffused so that a more realistic stance toward their goals could be investigated. An early meeting with the maintenance boss by a group that was relatively inexperienced in working together would have proven disasterous, both for the maintenance foreman, the group members, and perhaps other tenants as well. The members' appreciation of the likely outcome was a positive sign that they had capacities for realistic appraisal and that they had to devote more thought to the problem than was anticipated. The leader purposively focused on the action and its relevance to the group's goals, keeping it on the cognitive level. The emotionality served to bind the group and foster cohesion against a perceived common enemy. In later meetings, role play might be used again as a methodology for examining and anticipating the relationship of defensive responses to potentially provocative behavior, real or imagined, in meetings with the maintenance foreman or other housing project officials.

The leader may take a more active instructional stance with regard to the teaching of role behaviors. In this situation, sometimes referred to as coaching, the leader may stop the role play action in process, suggest a different response or perception, and then replay the situation. A variation in this approach is to invite other members to demonstrate or to suggest other methods for dealing with the events. When other members are invited to assume the role of constructive critic, then the adequacy of the actors actions, thoughts, and feelings can be agreed upon by group consensus. For example, in the previous situation, the leader could have asked several members to take turns in role playing the maintenance foreman with instructions to subtly provoke the members through expressions of disdain such as looking away when the member is making a point. The action could be stopped after the members anticipated angry and sarcastic response. At this point the leader would ask for a discussion of other types of reactions to subtle provocation such as asking the maintenance foreman what seemed to be bugging him, and how they could continue to work together, also highlighting the importance of listening and controlling one's feelings—two aspects of successful conflict resolution (Deutsch, 1973). Each cluster of responses needs to be evaluated to the outcome desired in the meeting. A new response set could be practiced until members agreed on its appropriateness. It needs to be mentioned that in practicing relational changes, it is not likely that memorization of any single act will provide the final safe and automatic answer. Instead, when the actions are discussed, feelings shared, and goals clarified, then it is anticipated that a certain gestalt has been internalized which serves as a frame of reference for continuing relationships which are expected to change over time as a natural part of interpersonal exchanges.

The teaching-learning format in educating members to examine, suggest, and demonstrate reaction to actors representing constituted authority can be generalized beyond any two actors in a role play situation. For example, the leader could suggest that the group members divide into training pairs and roles of tenant-maintenance boss be practiced and reversed. If the roles proved to be too difficult to master, then discussion could be centered on readiness for action. For example, tenant groups need to consider the risk of facing eviction before taking on community officials. One way to prepare a group for role playing anxious situations is simply to have them imagine it first, and deal with the images and with presenting anxieties before moving to a more concrete and rehearsed situation. Techniques such as these have been used in such situations as keeping delinquent youth groups secure, maintaining employment, applying for driving privileges, avoiding provocative situations (stealing) and so on.

Role structuring as an intervention strategy is intimately connected to the symbolic interactionist perspective, which guides the leader's focus to ongoing process details between and among participants. Assimilating increased capacities for discriminating one's own views and the views and intentions of others through perceptual-affective processes increases anticipatory power. For members in the group, this leads to the next step for reorganizing stereotype conduct. Symbolic incorporation of roles is enhanced when "bits and pieces" of relationships and the consequent gestalt are magnified for inspection. Subjective processes are paramount and in this context perfect correspondence between and among group members is not likely because most situations present a mixed reality. The aim of the leader is to provide conditions that can generate a methodology which can be learned and applied for managing mixed reality. The leader has to be cognizant however, that the process of role exchange has to be implemented within broader societal context. This methodology has to be able to bridge change in the group and member expectations with those in the immediate environments of the members. Mead's concept of significant others provides this needed connection.

USE OF PROGRAMMING

The use of role playing as a strategy is not limited to applications in an "as-if" format. The use of program activities to create, develop and implement new roles or reinforce current patterns of behavior is a skill that has been an important part of social work with groups since the inception of the profession (Middleman, 1980). While "pretend" activities with children can have considerable benefit as, for example, in assisting children to come to grips with fears and doubts regarding surgery, or with acting out youth in camp settings (Pawlak and Vassil, 1980). In the latter case, a treasure hunt was designed to foster cooperation among antagonistic juveniles and, indeed, to incrementally reorganize role relationships in a triad. It is essential to note that the doing aspect of any activity needs to be combined with the thinking and feeling as well.

Activities can be used profitably with adults in a real-life situation. In a family camp setting, a father-son tag football game brought out not only admired and hidden skills among the participants, but also reinforced the concept of teams, organized play and complementary positions that were not part of the ordinary activities back home in a housing project. On the negative side, the investment in the activity blurred the parent-child, and adult-youth distinctions between the participants so that winning or losing became a paramount goal in spite of the differences in size, experience, and know how between fathers on the one side, and young adolescent children on the other.

Strong feelings on both sides were manifested in less than gentle "tagging." Later that day, discussions about the intensity were conducted with both parties to sort out responsibilities and relationships between fathers and sons, adults and children, mentor to pupil, and coach to players. Hence what had emerged as adversarial relationships, was differentiated into realistic and complementary roles. Attention to the potential teaching-learning aspects of a simple contest can be organized around the conept of roles and role behaviors between and among the participants (Vinter, 1974, Whittaker, 1974).

Structuring program activities to advance group member role repertoires has implications for group process and development over time. In formed treatment groups of children, activities can be designed to induce and support individual capacities and abilities at the beginning stage, and move to more complex processes of sharing and contributing to group planned projects that serve the purpose of reinforcing a sense of identity and accomplishment. The time spent for planning (a complex activity) can be slowly increased over a time while parallel activities that reinforce stability and individual competence can be decreased. In activity group therapy with a group of thirteen-year-old boys, the most popular and desirable program was roller skating. Unfortunately, the differences in skills were used by some of the members to scapegoat one boy who was slightly built, shy and not very athletically inclined. The leader had to organize and create "on the spot" games which altered the destructive pattern and which could increase member satisfaction and cohesion. Variations such as individual and paired speed racing, were structured so that no one "lost" or won all the time. For example, faster skaters were asked to race several times around the oval floor and each time around had to catch a flag thrown by the slower skaters who were scored on a point system. Both slower and faster skaters were placed on different teams so that sides were equal. The number of feet that each team, as a team, could coast after a one lap start also served to generate meaningful participation at various skill levels. Both winners and losers were awarded soft drinks and cookies for their efforts. Time was allotted for both teams to practice scheme ways to outdo the others, a procedure that induced the more skilled to assist and include the less skilled. The excitement generated by the activity carried over into the boys' relationships back at the treatment center which reinforced the group spirit as well as individual status in the group.

In a disintegrated neighborhood, relationships among a natural group of juveniles were characterized by fairly rigid and antagonistic transactions that were manifested in a curious blend of chronic patterns of hostility mixed with cohesion. Differences between the boys were based on size and strength. A series of activities was suggested and developed by the leader and designated as indoor olympics. Five different events were structured in a small room, and the boys were asked to try each event, first as individuals and then in pairs that were roughly equal in size, strength and skills. For example, smaller boys were more adept at sliding under a low rope fastened to two chairs, while larger boys were better at broad jumping. A duck walk from one end of the room to the other favored neither large nor small boys because it had to be done backwards and without falling. In this type of activity, the usual member roles and positions of status were reorganized based on other criteria inherent in the game itself. This program can serve as a springboard for setting precedents that each member has something to offer. Over time and through other activities, it is not hard to visualize that role differentiation can be reinforced and extended into more complex patterns such as planning and implementing a group overnight in a camp setting. Activities may be used both for developmental growth as well as neutralizing chronic tendencies toward destructive behavior. (Refer to Chapter 5 for a more inclusive discussion of practice principles related to use of programs).

A number of strategies can be identified and extracted from these brief examples regarding the use of program and role differentiation.

SEQUENCING

Sequencing may be defined as a successive ordering of units along a continuum and carries with it a sense of progression. In terms of activities, it means that the leader may have to conceptualize how any single activity is related to future activities and inevitably to the goals of individual members and the group. It is also necessary to consider the capacities, skills and interest of the participants. In the process of utilizing and designing activities, the leader's role in the group is to assist the members in planning and implementing the activities, including the critical task of offering realistic choices. It is extremely difficult for an uninitiated group to deal with a question such as "what do you want to do" because the inevitable response will likely include too many and varied suggestions. A major leadership function is to establish a sense of continuity that is in agreement with immediate, short term and long term goals which also implies increasing complexity over time. Nor should it be assumed that progression can be controlled so minutely as to guarantee certainty in the next steps. Any time choices by members are to be honored and valued, one can expect unforseen complications and unplanned events. Complexity and organization are both related to role differentiation and the designing of activities needs to be centered on this point. An example would be a member's role transition from timekeeper in a tag team wrestling program, to referee, and to active participant. In one group of fifteen-year-old boys referred for service by the juvenile courts for their unacceptable behavior, the leader instituted in the eight weeks a simple craft's activity for making candlestick holders out of cardboard. The activity grew out of the group's expressed interest in purchasing jackets with group emblems. Once the mechanics for production were learned, the boys proceeded to sell the candlestick holders as Christmas ornaments and over a period of six weeks, accumulated enough money for the purchase. This long-term project required patience, perseverance, detailed planning for marketing the product, sales techniques and so forth. It was a remarkable display of self-discipline for a group of boys that had been and had earned the label of "losers." The project also affirms the potency of activities when a group is willing to invest in them. It is worth noting that when the group wore their jackets to school, they were dismissed immediately for setting a bad influence, which affirms the need for the leader to continually attend to the group's environmental context.

TIMING

Timing refers to a leader's execution of an action at the appropriate moment so as to achieve a maximized or desirable result. For example, pressing members for self disclosure too early or shifting discussion onto sensitive topics such as mourning or loss point to errors in judgment and timing. It is difficult for leaders to pinpoint exactly the "right" moment for a comment. Preparation and reflective meditation between group meetings can increase the likelihood for success but there re no guarantees. Perhaps the best that can be expected is that the leader has to take chances. There is comfort in knowing, however, that a lack of response to the leader's action does not diminish credibility because of the degree of flexibility inherent in the role. Feedback and recapitulation of events with the group is a practical safeguard.

Moving with the Situation

Calculated interventions that are considered timely but do not work, at least raise the general question of what the leader does next when faced with the unknown. The ability to flow with the events and keep tuned in and help a group move along is a critical skill which tests even the most experienced leaders. There are several possibilities that can be considered under slippery group conditions.

Silence One way to manage "dead spots" is to simply wait and listen attentively. The use of silence implies to the group that the next step is up to them. Undue silence can induce a general tuning out in adult groups, and chaos in children's groups; and in both cases, the momentum may have been lost. In the event of a nonverbal response, the leader is well advised to ask what it is that is holding the group back, or stating simply that he/she is not sure of what is happening and ask members for their insights. The use of summarizing after a "dead" moment is another possibility. Leader's revelation of his/her own discomfort can be facilitative in moving the group along.

Altering Group Patterns in Process Group members have a way of complicating even the best-intentioned and well-laid plans, and it is not infrequent that unplanned events turn an organized activity to chaos. The danger to participants is that while there may be a sense of euphoria and excitement in "letting go," their sense of responsibility and judgment slips and someone may get hurt in the process.

Example

In a previous illustration, one of the group members, John, the scapegoated child, became a target for several of the other boys to pick on, even though there was a good bit of organization in this activity. Speed skating races in the roller skating oval seemed to disintegrate right in front of the leader's eyes as three of the other group members began to tug and push at John as they skated by. The leader had to act fast to help regroup and reorganize the activity. The leader skated toward John, took hold of his arm and said, "Let's race and see how long it takes the others to catch us." After being caught, the leader suggested inventing a new game called "the chase." To make it consistent the leader volunteered to start by taking the hand of each boy and inviting the others to chase. The ones who managed to "escape" the longest would receive a free coke. The activity took the greater part of the session. After the game the leader commented that we could all have a lot of fun together.

Moving with the situation means that the leader can reorganize a disintegrating event in process and must be prepared to do it. This spontaneous strategy can also be referred to as experimentation which means the leader uses himself/herself creatively to link an unplanned event with the group's current processes.

Containment (Setting Limits) In group sessions which have deteriorated into steamy and sarcastic exchanges between members or factions, a practical device may be to simply stop the process and take a break—"time-out"—so that the antagonists can cool off. If the issues do not seem capable of at least temporary and partial resolution, the next step might be to ask for group members to volunteer to play out the parts of the members involved in the conflict based on their own perceptions. Subsequent to this, the leader can involve the total group in examining the original conflict, the role play by the volunteer members, and possible solutions in resolving the friction.

A variation of the strategy can be effective in those situations where group members begin to actually start fighting. The usual procedures with children is to let the participants tangle for a few minutes. By that time they are usually worn out and welcome someone interrupting the action and the leader's physical intrusion is a welcome face-saving device. Immediately following the act of setting limits to the action, the leader needs to invite the group to discuss what happened and what set it off, and ask how each of the participants views the situation and what can be done to negotiate a reasonable settlement. In setting limits to physical violence, the leader must be comfortable with using his hands to separate the combatants.

Examples

In a group of married couples having problems with interpersonal intimacy one of the male members continued to be verbally abusive towards his wife. When this behavior was pointed out by fellow group members it seemed to increase his anger to the point that he struck his wife. The leader immediately stepped in and took charge of the situation firmly, forbidding any future demonstration of physical abuse and threatening exclusion from the group.

A group of adults having difficulty with their drinking habits were meeting weekly for about two months. The original contract was that no member will attend a group session while under the influence of alcohol. At the ninth session a member arrived quite intoxicated and was incoherent. The leader had to suggest that the member go home and come to the next session "sober." Similar action is warranted in the area of substance abuse. For any flagrant violation of the contract, it is imperative that the leader set limits and contain the behavior.

On occasion the leader as a community representative has to set limits for the member's antisocial behavior that affects the environment. The following example clearly expresses this point.

The worker arrived on the street corner where the group was located. During a conversation with Jackie, he noted that Louie, who was standing nearby, darted suddenly into one of the store alcoves. It was late in the evening, and most of the stores, including this one, were closed. The worker suspected that Louie was going to make a nuisance of himself, and called him over. Louie paid no heed. The worker then walked over to Louie and saw him urinating.

Worker: "Gee whiz, Louie, why don't you go to your apartment across the street?"

Louie: "Everybody does it."

Worker: "That's not true, everybody does not do it. The police officers who were here earlier this afternoon don't do it. I don't do it."

Louie: "There are others who do."

Worker: "The people who do it are wrong. Your sister or mother could have been passing by, and they would have seen you. Wouldn't you have been ashamed?"

Louie: "What's wrong?"

Worker: "Do you bathe?"

Louie: "Yes."

Worker: "Why?"

Louie: "To clean myself.

Worker: "That's right. Does your mother clean her home?"

Louie: "She does."

Worker: "Now if you keep yourself clean and your home is clean, why do you want to make this place filthy? What you do is indecent—unlawful, too. The people who do it are slobs. You don't want to follow the example of slobs, do you?"

Louie appeared quiet and repentant for the rest of the evening. The worker was reserved, and let him feel the burden of his reproof. (Spergel, 1966, p. 130).

Although setting limits might produce discomfort for the leader, as illustrated in the following example, it is an unavoidable part of professional practice.

In a group of juvenile probationees one of the members bragged about his recent adventure of breaking and entering into a home to steal a gun which he later sold. The group members did not make a big issue of this incident. However, the leader intervened by stating in clear and affirmative terms that either the group member would have to inform his probation officer of the incident, or the leader himself would have to report it. The group was furious at the leader, called him "stoolie," and shouted obscenities for being a fink. The loyalty code of the group was broken in their eyes. The leader stood fast and in unequivocal terms stated their purpose for meeting, including the original contract and their probation regulation.

The intervention strategies such as sequencing, timing, setting limits and moving with the situation have been presented in conjunction with programming. It needs to be noted that each of these can stand on their own as separate strategies.

PARTIALIZING

Partializing refers to a breaking down of the problem or concern into component parts which are more easily addressed and able to be worked on. The intent of this intervention is to help the group move more easily and freely into the actual work of the matter without being overwhelmed. It is also helpful as a means of instructing the group in a skill of problem-solving.

Example

At a weekly meeting with a group of adolescent boys in a shelter home, the meeting started very lively. There had been a crackdown on rules in the home the previous week and the boys were verbal about problems that had arisen. The first five to ten minutes were spent with everyone complaining, how unfair it was, and that they were being set up to get into trouble. The leader called a halt and said, "It's real clear that you guys are upset and from what I'm hearing, you might have a right to be. But it also sounds pretty heavy, so how about if we make a list and then talk about each item on the list to see what the concerns are about each item."

Partializing as a sorting and itemizing activity conveys a number of important ideas to the members. First, there is the indication that the tasks faced by the group are manageable. A second aspect is the confidence that the clients can deal with the problem when it is broken down into smaller segments. Third, partializing assists the group in concentrating its energies on the purposes that brought the members together. Finally, the act of specification sets the stage for evaluating the individual members and group productivity.

CLARIFICATION

Clarification refers to keeping communication messages clear. It entails focusing on key underlying issues and sorting out confusing and conflicting feelings. The intent of clarification is to facilitate movement towards the goal, aid members in satisfying needs (healing agent), and combat resistance in cases where members use confusion to avoid specific issues or feelings. Example: A member might have conflicting feelings about getting a divorce. On one hand she is afraid of her husband and is miserable at home, but on the other hand she fears living alone. Other members remain silent as the woman rambles on and on in a confused manner. The leader could interject, "You are feeling as though you would like some help or advice from the group. You're afraid of your husband and you're afraid of living alone and can't seem to make a rational decision about what to do."

Clarification as an intervention strategy is also effective in assisting a member to become aware of his/her dysfunctional behavior which might be similar to their behavior outside the group. For example, a member who complains that he has a hard time making friends and that people do not show interest in him, also has a habit of not listening to his fellow members, rudely interrupts them, and always likes to keep the focus of attention on himself. The leader using clarification can point out to this member how his behavior is alienating him from other group members, and if his behavior is the same outside the group it is bound to affect his interpersonal relationships in general.

UNIVERSALIZATION

A common experience in the early formative stage of a group is that members perceive that their problem is unique and unlike any other persons'. Disconfirmation of this feeling and the attendant isolation that it carries can be a welcome source of relief. Universalization is the generalization from one member's experience to the group as a whole. When members gingerly begin to talk about their problems, usually in low-voiced tones and brief sentences, comments by the leader that many others are in the same boat is both supportive of the person's identity and reduces the group's tendencies toward inhibition.

Example

For several minutes, Mary talked about her ambivalence in presenting well-rehearsed material on a topic in front of her colleagues and staff in an agency. She stated that typically she would start sweating and begin stuttering a few words, which only made her more self-conscious and nervous. John was nodding his head and said that he also experienced stage fright. The leader looked at both Mary and John and then to the other group members noting that Mary and John experienced what all of us go through when we stand up in front of our audience. We get anxious, block out small portions of material, expect the audience to wait for us to stumble so they can laugh and so forth. The leader asked if other members could share their experiences and think of ways in which each of us struggled through the anxiety and carried out the task.

Universalization can be used to extend, apply, and integrate a specific learning issue for the member to more general considerations outside of the group, either in between meetings or in preparation for termination. It must be remembered that while a group is a microcosm of society it is not the same, otherwise there would be no need for the group. The quality that makes the group unique is that members can alter and examine troublesome patterns in a safe and secure protective envelope. Transferring the group-induced specific change to broader application in other social contexts is a major objective that the leader and the members work on together. When patients are ready to be discharged from a psychiatric hospital the assumption is that they have learned to manage their specific problems well enough to warrant confidence that these learnings can help them deal with more general problems likely to be encountered in their daily lives. Universalization can assist in developing this confidence through recurrent expression and testing of the member's bothersome pattern in events inside and outside the group. For example, a shy fearful member who has learned to assert himself in the context of the goup has to be able to extend and apply it outside the group. Disagreeing with fellow members or learning to offer an individual opinion in a protective setting is not the same as resisting intimidation and asserting oneself to a work associate or a superior on the job, in a doctor's office, or to family and friends who are continually looking over his shoulder. The leader can present group comments regarding other situations such as the above to help generalize the learning from a specific instance to other social contexts.

MODELING

Modeling is an intervention strategy which may be employed by a leader whereby he/she behaves in a certain way or even shows how to do certain things in an effort to encourage that same behavior by group members. Perceiving the leader engaging in certain behavior freely and without adverse effects induces the group members to risk trying the new behavior themselves within the context of the group. Bandura has demonstrated in many well controlled experiments that individuals may be influenced toward more adaptive behavior through observing and assuming the therapist's behavior (Yalom, p. 112).

If, for example, a leader wishes to encourage empathy in the group, he could frequently use highly empathic responses to members' sharing of experiences that related to the group purpose—and even those that did not.

> **Ms. G.:** . . . and when I realized that I had Huntington's Disease, I was so upset. All I could think of was my children.
> **Leader:** Because it is a genetically passed disease, you are feeling really concerned about them possibly contracting H.D., too. That must have been a very traumatic moment for you.

Hopefully, this would encourage similar behavior by other group members such as the following:

> **Mrs. A.:** Just finding out like that, after you have had children . . . how terrible for you. It must have been so frightening.

Modeling is not a simple task. It requires as most interventions do, a leader who can perform as a professional comfortable with his/her identity so that his/her behaviors are neither overly desirable nor detestable. The leader must consistently employ and foster those characteristics conducive to change in group members in such a way that they are worthy of imitation.

How the leader operationalizes this modeling intervention in the group will have a profound influence on its structure. If it is employed in a very rigid and didactic manner that is inappropriate to the group population they are likely to hold him/her as the individual in control, taking no responsibility for their own actions and relying on the leader to show them how to do those things they cannot. If, in contrast, the leader is too casual about the use of modeling, and more invested in sharing personal experiences with the group, he/she is liable to lose status as a professional and take on the role of group member. In either situation the learning and growth of the group is inhibited by ineffective use of the intervention strategy. Consistent and judicious use of modeling by the leader can encourage desired behavior by group members and aid them in enlarging their experiences in the group context for practicing their newly acquired skills in the "real world." Not only is the leader a model for group members, but so are members models for each other. Focusing on desired behaviors in individuals in the group by designating their strengths, aptitudes or skills can be an equally effective use of modeling.

The leader's demonstration of thoughts-feelings-actions that are conducive to creating a climate for change are powerful examples for vicarious learning by group members. Demonstrating principles in action enhances their value. In work with children, the leader's direct and enthusiastic involvement in an activity can set the tone for enjoyment and encourage participation.

Example

In a group of shy eight-year-old-girls fearful of water, the leader invented the game of "Whee." The leader started by running up to the water, dipping in her toe and shouting "whee" at the moment that her foot touched the water. She then took the hand of one girl who expressed delight at the leader's actions, and proceeded to repeat the activity with her. Next two more responsive members were included until all eight girls had joined in, each time shouting "whee." After several more repetitions in which the girls were led through snake dance motions and other variation of line and circle patterns, they were ready to begin the swim lesson.

While it is important for the leader to be skilled in the activity or action that is being undertaken, enthusiastic participation is more relevant. Modeling adult roles for delinquent youth is one of the most relevant social work roles in street work. The vulnerability and limitations that are related to being an adult are powerful antidotes to processes of hero worship that adolescents are prone to bestow on their leader. For example, in one group of sixteen-year-old boys, the leader cueing into what appeared to be a raucous meeting, began by inviting each of the boys to various forms of Indian wrestling matches. In several instances the leader was soundly beaten but continued to play, taking the loss in stride. The group began to joke about how weak the leader (who was physically smaller than some of the members) was and several beat their chests at their strength. The leader went along with the group's good humor for several minutes and then said, "OK. Can we get down to business and talk about how we're going to manage the camping trip?"

WORK WITH INDIVIDUALS, GROUPS, AND ENVIRONMENT

The group is the central focus vehicle for mediating between the person and the environment. However, each of these three inter-dependent entities require adequate attention and at times, empha-sis, in order to meet the goals for change. The rationale for this approach is that individual member's behavior in a group may be greatly influenced by an external source such as family events or misfortunes and pressure from social institutions. Secondly, the group itself may pose unique choices for members and as in the case of scapegoating, providing feedback for solving problems, or sup-port for new activities in the member's natural environment. The third influencing element consists of the effects of the environment on the group itself as for example, groups in hospitals, residential treatment centers, or neighborhoods. Discussion of pertinent issues in each of these three interacting facets can further extend and elaborate the leadership role.

Work With Individuals

As discussed in Chapter 2 the resources available for a group through its internal supply is often times insufficient which requires that the leader generate additional help from a number of outside resources. The leader's solicitation of specific assistance outside of the group has been designated as involving collateral contacts. The ecological perspective of group work which emphasizes the holistic approach

273

prompts the leader to be aware of the various influential networks which have a bearing on the individual's current functioning. A clear understanding and assessment of interlocking social elements guides the leader's activity in working with individual members through their significant others. Involving important persons outside of the group on behalf of individual members can facilitate the transition of group members to their natural environment. This approach also broadens and deepens the leader's understanding and knowledge of the total gestalt of the individuals, their current life functioning and struggles, and anticipated contingencies in the future. Attention to factors outside of the group has been actively implemented by group workers in community centers and settlement houses. Unfortunately as group work began to shape itself more "therapeutically" the leader's involvement with significant others was deemphasized.

Leadership interventions with individual members can be implemented through various strategies. Two major facets in this context are: a) indirect interventions with individual members which include soliciting help from significant others (collaterals) outside the group membership; and b) direct interventions with individual members which involves working with members both in and outside the group context.

Indirect Interventions On occasion leaders are called upon to provide services for short term committees as a natural outgrowth for group concerns and change. To improve the quality of life in stairwells, a group of families can focus on their own personal relationships as well as negotiate as a committee with responsible officials. Work with children can lead to the development of a parents group which may choose to deal with shool-child relationships as a committee. In these examples direct leadership of the group may evolve into a staff function, whereby the leader helps the group organize into a committee. In this instance the leader's role and duties would shift to include work with the elected chairperson and representative of the committee. In assisting the chairperson, the leader can provide help with preparing agendas, organizing the structure of the meetings, offering opinions with regard to group dynamics that may impede or support the specific tasks, and informally perform as a consultant or teacher to the chairperson regarding his/her strengths and limitations. In addition, the leader can function in the role of historian or record keeper which serves the purpose of referencing precedents and actions that can guide the group in their future efforts. From this base the elected chairperson can be assisted in developing summaries of rationales, pro and con, regarding action under consideration. Often the elected chairperson is overwhelmed with specific events that occur in committee meetings, or with issues that come to their attention in between meetings. This is likely to occur because committee members may voice strong disagreements about other members outside of the meeting. In these situations, the leader as staff person needs to be around to defuse personal anxieties that the chairperson may be facing as part of the job.

Another category of work with individuals who are leaders in groups involves the principle of working through others. In community centers and settlement houses the use of volunteers for direct leadership is a common phenomenon. This practice has been extended in health and correctional settings. In health settings, nursing staff are increasingly using small groups as a method of orienting patients to hospital routines, allaying personal anxieties regarding medical treatment, maintaining control of their own lives and facilitating recovery and return to their homes. In the juvenile justice system community-based group homes are also incorporating similar strategies. In other cases, indigenious leadership may be recruited from the community for volunteer work with groups. The leader's task is to train and supervise the volunteers in their group work. In a sense Leader A helps Leader B to help the client, C. The use of volunteers is a means for extending the social group-work service which has been a part of group work since its early beginning.

Direct Interventions   Direct interventions attending to the needs of individual members may take place both within and outside the group. Within the group, the leader may direct specific inquiries or comments to one member when the group topic is pertinent.

Work with individual members in the context of a group can range from special attention to a withdrawn and consistently silent member, a scapegoat, a member in crisis and an absent member. While the usual practice dictates that the leader utilize the group as a major source of help in working with these unique situations, there are occasions when the leader may resort to time limited individual centered interventions.

Member silence is a common phenomena in groups, but persistent silence is another matter. Significant reasons might include: a means for getting attention and arousing concern; feeling intimidated by the robust participation by fellow members; fear that breaking silence may lead to exposing vulnerable content and feelings that the person is not ready to deal with yet; anger towards the leader and other group members that cannot be comfortably expressed because of excessive fears of counterattack; and distinctions arising due to minority status. As a general rule the leader cannot be oblivious to this behavior and has to initiate contact, not to probe into the silence but to convey and reaffirm interest in the person's presence and right to full membership in the group. Some of the techniques that are helpful in this regard are; humor, support, exploration and confrontation. Sometimes unanticipated absences of individual members may require the leader to communicate with the absent member first, to maintain and reinforce the importance of attending as well as supporting the importance of the member in the group. For example, children may miss field trips because they lack money or appropriate clothes. At other times, outside events may interfere with a member's performance and leaders have to be sensitive to unique and unanticipated occurrences. For example, a youth may be suspended from school, may violate probation rules, may have extreme problems with parents or siblings and so on. While each of these situations may be relevant for the work of the group, the members may not feel that this is the proper forum, at least for the moment. Yet the pressures demand attention. In these situations as illustrated in the following example, the leader may reach out to the member and offer help in alleviating the circumstances.

In a group of older adolescents, Bob was considered the clown as well as the drinker, two roles that gave him a lot of satisfaction. He also was the group's timekeeper when they played basketball in an informal city league. Before one game, Bob showed up with heavy bandages wrapped around his right hand, the result of being drunk the night before and putting his hand through a plate glass window. The leader, also the coach for the team, asked what happened and Bob responded with a shy smile. Later that evening, Bob approached the leader and asked if they could talk. The drunken episode turned out to be an attempt at self-destruction since Bob had deliberately put his fist through the window with the expressed purpose of cutting his wrists. Further conversations revealed a profound undercurrent of depression and anger triggered by the fact that his father, separated from the family for several months, would have nothing to do with him. Bob was understandably too embarrassed to bring this out in front of his peers, yet it was important for him to maintain the group membership for invisible support, as it were.

Work with individual members outside the group may be of direct benefit to the other members. This is particularly true when the leader assists one member in getting a job, who, in turn might recruit others for employment. In another instance, helping one member secure a driving license can provide a resource in expanding the opportunities for trips and outings for the other group members.

On occasion the leader in work with groups will sense that there is a particularly stubborn and guarded member. Sometimes this occurs when there is a transfer of leadership. At any rate the leader has to make a conscious attempt to reach this person in the time and opportunities alloted in the service. Since a relationship of trust is essential between the individual members and the leader, it is in the leader's interest to initiate contacts slowly but surely and in small doses, between, slightly before, and after a group meeting. This may be done verbally through pleasant greetings, or through nonverbal acknowledgements. In some situations the pathway for relationship building may be through a friend who is also a group member. The skill is not to force the contact but let it develop vicariously and incidentally through interaction with the member's colleague.

Work with the Group

The group is a symbolic construct which has referent power for the members. There are a number of ways in which prevailing conditions in the group can be altered, and indeed must be, for change to take place. Altering the structure of the group can affect the process, particularly role relationships. The use of program has been discussed as an important tool for that purpose. Structure and process are also realigned when the existing organization of the group is challenged by creating an "authority vacuum" which refers to the leader's withdrawal from direct guidance to a facilitative position. One of the ways this can be done is through the use of leader silence or planned uninvolvement. While the transition should not be manifested as a crises, elements of doubt and uncertainty are likely to be induced. The result is a realignment of expectations and norms. Structure and process are altered slowly and purposively when the leader models and supports, verbally and nonverbally, specific member actions which are then "copied" vicariously and expressed in action by other members. Attentive listening, reflection, and self-disclosure are some of the modeling acts that the leader presents. Asking exploratory questions that enhance either divergent or convergent thinking, or offering facts and summarized content are instructive in helping the group's problem solving and partially cognitive efforts. Listing consequences to parents groups regarding excessive monitoring of children's behavior is a case in point. Supporting the group's stated and public concern regarding excessive interruptions or tardiness in deviant members is a way to bring pressure for conformity.

This brief discussion points to the fact that most, if not all, of the intervention strategies have impact for the group when they are purposively directed at the totality. It is also possible through the leader's attention and general support of certain group members who manifest publicly the desired characteristics of "good" group membership, to enhance the qualities necessary for mutual aid. There is one caution to these considerations. In discussing and developing group conditions, an "ideal" model or group may be envisaged. However, in actual practice this is hardly ever the case. It is more realistic to assert that different expectations or norms serve some members better that others, and the leader has to continually be aware of these conditions and it is not easy to do so if one is preoccupied with an ideal. The situation is well illustrated in cabin groups of children in summer residential camps. Both dependent and active children may be present in any one live-in group. Dependent children may need a protective climate, while activists need more freedom and challenge. The leader's mediation of structure and process must serve these two entities and herein lies the challenge of professional practice. Developing conditions whereby each of these two role types affirm and inform the others is a tedious and painstaking task that is likely to include slippage as well as forward movement. Contracting, guiding planning, use of programming, facilitating and supporting decision making and so on are means toward the end of peer learning and role changes at expressive, action, and perceptual-reasoning levels.

It is also important to note that the group can change itself. That is to say, in some groups, depending on purpose, a major task may be to assist members in identifying and examining the group processes in order to highlight their self-evaluation and observation in that process, as well as to assume constructive group roles for maintaining the process. An example would be the taking on of counselor roles when other members are working their way through a difficult aspect of their lives. Counselor roles might be modeled from the leader's performance.

Work with the Environment

The social context may encompass organizations, families or neighborhoods and their relevance and influence on individuals and/or the group. The direct and indirect influences of the social environment are an important characteristic of the ecological perspective. Detailed attention and observations of the specific reinforcing or potentiating transactions between individuals and groups are necessary for purposes of altering group structures and processes toward the end of achieving a satisfactory adaptation. Several examples of the influence of schools and families have been cited which point to the individual-social context interaction. In institutional settings, staff such as nurses, teachers, child-care workers, and other personnel can be trained to develop and implement expectational sets that promote, modify, or support adaptive behavior for constituent members. The purpose is to collectively alter, specific relational exchanges and induce expectations for adaptive patient or client, performance in an institutional setting. The leader as trainer or consultant can perform this task using individual, group, or workshop designs for training purposes. These are not the only models. In certain direct practice situations, the leader may work collaboratively as part of a team within an institution or in the context of inter-agency teams to develop and implement rehabilitative programs for clients. One of the most important and neglected aspects of any team work is that all team members accept that two of the necessary group roles are follower and learner.

Another modality for intervening between the individual and the environment can be implemented through advocacy proceedings. A case in point is youth workers who appear on behalf of clients in court proceedings, and present a realistic description of client competencies and a potential program that could include the efforts of the court, the agency, the family, and the client in restoring acceptable youth behaviors.

The relationship of the social context to group has been well cited in the delinquency literature by Spergel (1966). To alter group behavior and norms among street groups, one must necessarily pay attention to neighborhood norms as well. When one alters the structure and process of neighborhood networks through the use of small group methodology, then the social context and the potential for altering norms and processes in youth groups changes as well. A bifurcated approach such as this is the basis for multiskilled leaders, a point noted in earlier discussions concerning agency functioning. Other examples of the powerful influence of social contexts was noted in the illustration whereby the school principal quickly dismissed a group of "losers" who had spent considerable time and effort in earning money to purchase jackets with group emblems. It is not hard to visualize the utter frustration and reinforcement in the youth about the sense of abandonment and lack of belonging in the school system. The same illustration indicates dramatically the necessity for the leader to undertake measured actions to redress the imbalance and expectations between the school, youth and families. Indeed, to support the hard won gains by the youth in self-discipline, pride, collective problem solving and so forth a series of steps to involve parents and to engage the school system are reasonable objectives that are within the domains of the group leader. The specific leader strategies are combinations of those already cited. The general skill is effecting the environment.

Skill in mediating conflict situations require the use of bargaining and negotiating roles. One practical technique is the use of "supposals" which refer to conceptualization of potential offers or procedures and their exchange value to either or both of the parties in conflict. For example, the mediator may ask of party A, if party B were to make this offer, would you do so and so? A similar approach would be repeated with party B. The intent is to "float" possible compromises and points to test their acceptability, with the end in mind of a reasonable negotiated settlement that both parties can live with. The leader may be called upon to provide services as a neutral third party in cases of tenant-landlord disputes, between and within families, between competing groups in the neighborhood, and among departments and team members in large multidisciplinary institutions. Mediator skills are also useful in anchoring and implementing after-care programs with other professionals for purposes of reintegrating discharge patients into designated catchment areas.

In summary, the leader is in a position to influence group structure and process. Interventions can be directed to alter the group conditions, to alter specific individuals within and outside of meetings, or to alter contributing elements in the environment. Further refinements in the types and combinations of interventions depend on the assessment of the group state at any one point in time. The repertoire of strategies can be complemented by the structural components of group work. The leader is also in a position to influence the social context through training and supervision, as for example in the use of volunteers. The judicious application of combinations of intervention strategies must be governed by the guiding principle of purpose.

10
Education for Competence for Social Group Work

A profession's identity, apart from but related to its societal mandate, becomes operationalized in the teaching content and methods that are utilized in various aspects of the curriculum. The Committee on Practice of the National Group Work Section of NASW in 1964 (Hartford, 1964) stated the objectives of practice for social group work as encompassing promotion of well-being and citizenship, prevention of illness, restoration and rehabilitation. Agreement among social work educators, however, has not precluded differences in the purposes, form, functions and knowledge base necessary to carry out these objectives (Papell and Rothman, 1966). Hence the teaching of work with groups depends on a frame of reference and notion of professional function which underpins the content and the method.

Ecology as a metaphor provides an analytical context for practice. The major outline of the perspective includes concepts such as mutual aid, interdependence, development, resource cycling, and adaptation (Kelly, 1968; Germain, 1977). The absence of these processes in a person's social network is likely to produce a downward spiral of frustration and disappointment. Social group work can provide an effective antidote to despair and disparagement only

281

if the web of both social and personality processes are engaged. The ecologic perspective directs us to understand the complex disabling processes in the individual's natural surroundings. It leads to a conception of practice that Bennis and Slater (1968) have stated in the following way: "an active method for producing conditions where people and ideas and resources can be cultivated to optimal effectiveness and growth" (p. 119).

As presented in the earlier chapters, the interface between persons and environment is mediated by a variety of small group encounters. In essence, the small face-to-face system or group is a basic implementing component for what may be termed life in the homestead. Consequently, it would seem that small face-to-face groups are an important mediating vehicle in assisting the adaptive process between persons and environment, indeed many types of environments. The simpler structure and intimacy inherent in small groups provides a powerful reference group by which development or incapacity may take place.

It is impossible to present enough concepts and information necessary for a practitioner for all he/she has to know if one accepts the ecological perspective. But it is possible to develop a toughminded practitioner who seeks in his/her work, not a fixed reality, but approaches tasks in a context of the discipline and art of practice. Practitioners have to be people who can deal with the tensions between what they know and don't know in a time-limited, task-specific world. The theoretical stance demands an eclectic approach. It also demands a blend of three roles that are necessary components for competent, professional activity: namely, theoretic, practice, and empiric. It is the empiric role which maintains an open system, and also provides a quasi-neutral ground which ties together theory and practice (Argyris and Schon, 1975). Furthermore it is the empiric role that reduces the chances of flabby eclecticism. The formidable task is to develop a classroom culture which permits and encourages the utilization of practice and empiric roles within a broad theoretical perspective.

The import of the foregoing discussion is that the principles of process, cycling of resources, mutual aid and adaptation (learning) may be applied as guidelines to develop an educative culture in the classroom, which would utilize temporary systems such as small groups for learning and teaching material in theory, process and methods. By educative culture, we mean a set of expectations and agreements consistent with temporary systems whereby class members can feel secure, express differences, take chances, put up with discomfort, experience with new ways of thinking, doing and feeling and so forth. An educative culture also requires the demand for work which stretches the limits of tolerance for dependability and uncertainty in thought, feeling, action levels for students. In many ways a teacher has to develop the educative culture as a tension management system to use Glidewell's designation, which refers to the norms that encompass and permit bipolarities such as conflict or peace, security or uncertainty, foresight or spontaniety, control or support, to be worked out (Glidewell, 1975). These contradictions must be exposed for work to take place. In more abstract terms, the educative culture must permit the expression of thought-feeling actions encompassed in the dialectic between innovator and defender roles, and explicated further in responses to superior, subordinate and egalitarian sentiments that emerge in the class and small groups.

To summarize, the following aspects are essential guidelines in the teaching of group work.

1. The ecological metaphor provides a broad framework by which professional function is directed at the person-environment interface.
2. Various small face-to-face systems are present at the interface, and knowledge of group dynamics provides a powerful interventive tool.
3. Professional activity requires a blending of the empiric with the theoretic and practice roles which together prevent flabby eclecticism, as well as sharpen and hone knowledge and action.
4. The fullest expression of the integration of these roles is to be found in an educative culture that enhances resource exchanges (thoughts, feelings, actions) and work among constituent members.
5. Participation in the small group, as a temporary system is a powerful tool for individual learning, as well as providing principles by which teaching may be enhanced.

These guidelines form the basis for designing and implementing courses in the teaching of small group theory, process and practice.

An educational design requires an accommodation regarding the best mix between the didactic and experiential material. This decision will guide and structure the roles of teacher and student, participation patterns, the knowledge content to be developed and discussed. Two complementary and unique approaches are presented that are consistent with the ecological perspective. They emphasize different teaching-learning formats for group work education. In educating students for creative group work practice, the emphasis is on the experiential end of the continuum, and focuses on the teacher as one role model for learning. The structural approach for teaching centers on the didactic end of the continuum, and relies on limited use of the experiential format to support specific content.

EDUCATING STUDENTS FOR THE PRACTICE OF CREATIVE GROUPWORK[1]

A theory of instruction seeks to take account of the fact that a curriculum reflects not only the nature of knowledge itself but also the nature of the knower and of the knowledge-getting process. It is the enterprise par excellence where the line between subject matter and method grows necessarily indistinct. A body of knowledge, enshrined in a university faculty and embodied in a series of authoritative volumes, is the result of much prior intellectual activity. To instruct someone in these disciplines is not a matter of getting him to commit results to mind. Rather, it is to teach him to participate in the process that makes possible the establishment of knowledge. We teach a subject not to produce little living libraries on that subject but rather to get a student to think mathematically for himself, to consider matters as a historian does, to take part in the process of knowledge-getting. Knowing is a process, not a product (Bruner, 1966, p. 72).

Let us begin with two premises that grow both from accumulating perspectives of twentieth century social and behavioral science and from not-so-easily accumulated practical wisdom about social work with groups. The first is that the group worker enjoys a distinct advantage denied the one-to-one caseworker or therapist, since a group is a process-conducting entity, whether or not a worker, therapist, or facilitator is present. The worker in a group is not faced with responsibility for initiating and keeping alive a process. Rather, the group members initiate the process when they enter—some would say before they enter—a group (Garland et. al., 1965). They carry on a complex interpersonal process, acting, making decisions, and doing a variety of other things. The group worker does indeed seek to influence the group's processes, but does so within the framework of an ongoing series of social events that have their own viability, rhythm, and raisons d'être. This fact, which should be of

[1] Paul H. Ephross and Pallassana R. Balgopal, *Journal of Educations for Social Work*, Vol. 14, No. 3, Fall 1978, pp. 42–48. In this paper only slight revisions are made in keeping with the format of this volume. Published with the permission of the *Journal of Education for Social Work*.

great comfort to students of social work with groups, instead is often a source of apprehension, for reasons that will be discussed later.

All groups have their own lives. This applies to the classroom, in-service training workshop, field seminar, or other learning-teaching settings. The learning process exists within the class, among its members, just as the group process exists among the individuals who comprise it. As in a group setting, a classroom teacher seeks to influence the learning process, to affect its qualities. To pretend that a teacher does not affect what students learn is as frivolous as pretending that a worker does not affect what goes on in a group.

However, the learning process has its locus in and among the learners, just as any group process has its locus in and among the members. This fact should be a source of comfort to teachers, a way of freeing themselves from the frightful sense that they carry the entire responsibility for students' learning. Instead, the natural-ness of the learning phenomenon often inspires an interesting form of academic self-delusion: that one can or should be able to specify and control with precision what a student will learn in a particular class or course.

A second premise, which flows from the first, is that work with groups is a major preoccupation of a wide range of professions and organizations, the vast majority of them outside the often arbitrary boundaries of social work. The second edition of Hare's *Handbook of Small Group Research* lists in its bibliography 6,037 items, omitting virtually all the social work literature on work with groups (Hare, 1976). Medicine, psychiatry, policy sciences, business and public administration, education, educational, industrial and clinical psychology, and many other disciplines and professions are deeply committed to the study of small groups and techniques for influencing group processes. Theories—or, better, pieces of theories and promising concepts—have been drawn from sociology, develop-mental psychology, political science, and increasingly from mathe-matics and computer science and applied to the study of groups.

The proliferation of interest in group phenomena and techniques for influence can be viewed as a comfort and support, or as a threat. Widespread interest in influencing groups can lead to sterile jurisdic-tional petulance and to a misdrawn cognitive map so that one pretends that there is something unique about the groups with which social workers are concerned. As we have suggested else-where, a false, scholastic search for uniqueness can lead to over-looking the truly unique heritage of social work with groups, our historical primacy in recognizing the importance of both the individual and the social, both the member and the group (Ephross and Balgopal, 1975).

Alternatively, the panoply of group research and group work can serve as a resource providing a stream of basic knowledge on which social work practice with groups can be based, relieving the profession of the pressure of supporting both basic and applied research as well as educating practitioners. Recognizing the importance of the contributions that have been made outside of social work to the development of concepts and techniques of group work, perhaps social work educators can proceed to infuse into the group world some of social work's own learning. Some of our value base, our concern with the oppressed and the nonpowerful, and our focus on life's realities characterize the best in social work's heritage and can be infused into the group world. Social work does not have to bear the responsibility of maintaining interest in group processes. We are free to interact productively with all the research and practice around us.

But there is a potential problem when one seeks such interaction. There is the danger that one will excerpt from other fields not the concepts which can be carried over, nor the findings which can lead us to accumulate understanding of groups and how to affect them, nor even the concern with issues of proof which characterize good group dynamics research, but rather that one will identify with the technology of the researcher or practitioner of other disciplines and professions. One can become infatuated with a particular worker role definition, personal style, or even theoretical base, attribute group life phenomena to the effects of one of those variables, and forget that all of these have been introduced into group processes that are self-generating. If we permit ourselves such infatuations, or if we teach so that students do, we will have misunderstood both the nature of group phenomena and the mission of the social work profession.

These observations, it seems to us, have particular meaning for the process of educating social workers who will have creativity and skill in working with groups. Failure to apply the implications of these premises, when combined with technique worship and a lack of understanding of basic group phenomena such as conflict, can lead to ineffective teaching of groupwork and to producing graduates who lack the commitment to a career-long process of expanding and refining their skills, which is necessary for advanced levels of practice.

How can we educate students in such a way as to help them lay the groundwork for creative and skillful practice with groups?

What needs to be transmitted in the classroom and in the field setting? To attempt a comprehensive answer seems presumptuous, but we can sketch some guidelines.

Education for Creative Group Work

Because group processes are naturally occurring phenomena, it has been relatively easy for group workers to be seduced into a cool, detached, reflective mode of operation. Minimalist patterns of worker behavior seem to be given validity by the reflected light of prestigious therapeutic modes and also by T-group technology, though the latter is less extreme. After all, the cool, seemingly passive workers still find that the group members interact. Often unaware of the force of control that their passivity exerts, these reflective, purely reactive workers can convince themselves that by withdrawing they truly turn over the group to its members. Certainly there are groups for which this role is appropriate. Both therapy and T-groups have demonstrated the power of creating a vacuum to be filled by the group members' needs, fantasies, and expressions. The danger is that a student exposed only to this mode of worker behavior will develop a set of expectations that defines cool reflecting as the way a professional should act in a group, rather than as one of a great many appropriate ways.

Like other methods of helping processes, group work has been quite concerned with the concept of professional objectivity. Group work has been greatly influenced by the psychoanalytic school of thought, as have other methods. Often, psychoanalytic theory has been misinterpreted and the maintenance of perspective has been viewed as synonymous with a detached, aloof role definition for the therapist. Students, often quite anxious in their learning processes, easily resort to this style and justify it as the shibboleth of a "competent professional."

In some instances, a few students may go to the other extreme and feel that they need to be "humanistic" and become involved in their group to such an extent that it becomes difficult to distinguish them from their group members. The debate over whether the worker should be a participant, participant-observer, or merely an observer needs to be discussed, and clarity regarding these differential roles needs to be injected. Rather than being exposed to discussing the issue of objectivity and subjectivity from a purely theoretical perspective, students need to be assisted in assuming a knowledge that could help them become authentic persons and workers.

The authors are aware that the concept of authenticity has been receiving increasing attention by social and behavioral scientists. Many suggest that authenticity is both style and substance. Authenticity is an appropriate blending of professional knowledge and skills with personal attributes, characteristics, and style. The classroom instructor teaching group work courses needs to reinforce the concept of authenticity by being as genuine, human, and nondefensive as possible. One should be able to provide a nonthreatening, safe, trusting atmosphere through one's own acceptance of, positive regard for, and nonpossessive warmth toward all students. Further, the teacher should be able to identify and have a high degree of empathic understanding for students' struggles with working out personal and professional concerns (Truax and Mitchell, 1971).

Field instruction needs to complement what is being done in the classroom, by providing optimal opportunities for students to test our creative modes of interventions and encouraging them to use their own styles and to use themselves creatively. Students need to be encouraged to see their clients first and foremost as individuals who have life struggles similar to all other human beings, including themselves, and not merely as clients or patients. This will prevent them from needing to magnify pathology, deviance, or variant behaviors as central concepts in understanding the behavior of groups and their members.

A cursory survey of catalogues of schools of social work reveals an upsurge of newer models of practice in groups. Restricting ourselves for the moment to groupwork for clinical purposes, we note such models as gestalt therapy, transactional analysis, rational-emotive therapy, existentially based approaches, behavior modification-based approaches, and the application of group techniques drawn from non-Western religious roots including various forms of meditation. Other approaches, including movement therapies and art therapy, draw upon knowledge that has been available to social groupworkers for a long time, some of it overlooked in recent years. As an example, newer group approaches have rediscovered that talking is only one medium and not necessarily the most effective one through which people relate and by means of which relationships can be developed.

The Dangers of Technology

The danger in the explosion of technologies lies in the possibility that students will become committed to technology rather than to the welfare, enhancement, and growth of the persons who comprise a group. Power to bring about growth and change and healthy inter-personal behavior can be attributed wrongfully to a technique rather than to basic group processes. Thus instead of producing workers skilled in applying a range of group technologies based on mutual exploration, mutual assessment, and clarity of goals, a course sometimes misleads students so that they view applying a particular technology as the end product of their efforts.

It seems to us that technology worship is a danger to be avoided. This is not to say that a student may not grow into a worker who is a specialist in a particular modality of work with groups. It is to say that a sound foundation needs to be laid before such specialization can take place within a sense of perspective and appreciation for the complexity of group phenomena.

How can one avoid technology worship? We suggest that both the conceptual content of courses in social work with groups and the teaching methods employed need to be designed with the objective of producing a worker capable of creative eclecticism. Students need to be taught the basic assumptions on which groupwork is based. Emphasis needs to be given to basic issues of philosophy and value. In this context certain philosophical issues need to be dealt with: Is a human to be viewed as basically good or evil? lackadaisical or industrious? dependent, independent, or interdependent? capable of assuming responsibility for one's own behavior? These issues often are discussed within the human potential movement but seldom within the social work curriculum.

To educate students for the practice of creative group work, the emphasis first has to be on philosophy and assumptions. A second area of emphasis should be a knowledge base in small group theory and relevant concepts of group dynamics. Only then can a typology of strategies for intervention be taught and learned in perspective. Students who have a solid foundation in this context then will be able to comprehend the different modalities and apply them on a differential basis.

Conceptually, one needs a base of knowledge of group processes and phenomena—what is loosely referred to as "group dynamics." We are now far enough from our origins to be able to point out the seminal concepts that underlie creative group practice. These are the concepts to be found in the early writings of Cooley and Simmel, and in the sharply perceptive observations of the relation-ships between the social and the personal in groups which run through the writings of Mary Parker Follett and Kurt Lewin, who to this day affect discussion of group phenomena by forcing even opponents of their position to use their concepts when arguing.

Important concepts and demonstrations of ways of learning about groups are to be found among the symbolists and the symbolic interactionists, including writers like Morton Deutsch, Lewis Coser, Erving Goffman, and Herbert Blumer. One needs to be exposed to Mead and Dewey, who connect group processes with individual development and societal evolution. Then one can proceed from a conceptual framework to assessment to choice of technique, and group technologies become a rich and fruitful storehouse rather than a series of stultifying straightjackets or a series of fads to be followed slavishly until a new one appears on the scene.

One may note an interesting aspect of the technology worship that has crept into the group field. As students become infatuated with a technology, their identity with the profession of social work becomes attenuated. The processes that accompany the development of a "true believer" operate to split, rather than join. One begins to see the development of a series of subprofessions and the abandonment of the basic values and social purposes of the social work profession. An overcommitment to any particular modality or technology will make a student a technician—and given faddishness, a technician seriatim, a person whose career will be spent moving from one technique to another rather than as a participant in a badly needed knowledge-building and skill-building process.

Educational Approach

If one is to prevent an infatuation with technology on the part of students, how should one teach? In order for a student to learn that a particular group technology should be applied flexibly to a particular group, bearing in mind its needs, composition, particular configuration, and relationship to other groups and external environments, it seems to us that the student needs to experience a similar process of matching technology to needs in the classroom. A teacher who applies an identical, pre-cast educational technology to each class is in the long run teaching the opposite point of view from the one propounded here. If all groupwork classes are lectures-cum-discussion, are seminars, or are experiential, and this decision is made before the engagement between teacher and students, then students may be forgiven for deciding on a similar pre-casting in their work with groups.

Just as important, if the role-patterning in a class makes the teacher all-powerful as a source of learning and views students as consumers, students may be expected to introduce a similar set of expectations into their work with groups. If the communication and relationship pattern in class is one which puts the teacher out of real reach, untouchable in any genuine way by students, why shouldn't students think this is the preferred "professional" stance to take as a worker influencing groups? Finally, if interpersonal conflict is taboo in the classroom, if the risks of engaging in conflict outweigh the potential learnings and benefits, why should students be taught to carry a different set of expectations into a practice career?

In short, if one pretends that the learning-teaching situation is anything other than a collectivity of persons—one of those persons with a specialized role and a particular responsibility, but all of them persons nonetheless—then students will be tempted to behave in such a manner as to misperceive the nature of the groups with which they work and their own participation in those groups.

With some hesitance, because this term has acquired a variety of meanings over the years, we suggest that the classroom is indeed a laboratory experience, a chance to experience the complexities of interpersonal and group process in an atmosphere of some, though not total, safety. As one of the authors has suggested elsewhere, a clear focus on the validity, importance, and growth potential of allogenic conflict needs to be as much a part of the classroom experience as of the student's own practice in groups (Balgopal & Vassil, 1979). Allogenic conflict implies friction or discomfort as experienced by individuals due to significant differences among them. These differences may be on either implicit or explicit levels, or both. Differences may be physical, psychological, racial, ethnic, economic, or others. Because of numerous variables, most of which they have no control over, individuals experience alienation, stigmatization, and victimization. Such differences often add a burden to the daily life struggle. Not only conflicts that are on intrapsychic or interpersonal levels, but also allogenic conflicts, fall within the domain of social group work. For students to be aware of this level of conflict, they need to be aware of racism, sexism, and other blocking attitudes and feelings that lie within them.

One should consider the risks of the educational approach being sketched. Such an approach makes each learning-teaching situation somewhat of a risk for the teacher. In fact, each one is, as experienced teachers know. We maintain that legitimating the fact that both students and teachers risk themselves in the classroom simply gives visibility to a part of social work education that has remained in the doorway, if not in the actual closet. Some mechanical changes may be necessary, such as developing a course outline

after, rather than before a first encounter and preliminary negotiating session with students. Believers in the ultimate truth of one or
another of the group technologies will see the possibility that students may learn heresy. If one seeks the comforts of orthodoxy,
social work with groups is probably an unrewarding arena at best.

Conclusion

The potential gains of the approaches sketched here are great. They
center around the education of professionals who respect groups
and their members as the sources of life-affirming strengths, who
regard themselves as contributors and influences but not as origins
of group processes, and who regard method and technology as
servants rather than as determinants of the goals of individuals,
groups, the social work profession, and the struggling society of
which we are all a part.

STRUCTURAL APPROACH FOR TEACHING
SOCIAL GROUP WORK

The structural approach is based on utilizing interrelated segments
of knowledge in group dynamics, and group work by involving students in selected participant learning experiences.

The course is divided roughly into four unequal units that are
designed in sequence to provide increasing complexity over the
semester. The first four sessions encompass major concepts describing the ecological perspective, followed by discussions of
significant works in social group work which represent historic
shifts leading to correspondence with the ecological perspective.
Theoretical social science models that emphasize the group as a
mediating vehicle between person and environment are considered
next and include the works of Lewin, Mead, Thelen, Bales and
Glidewell.

The next unit encompasses the major content with respect to
group theory, methods and process. Each of six sessions is clustered
around topical areas such as group composition, goals, contract and
membership; group structure, programming, and roles; leadership;
decision making and conflict; values, norms, and controls; and
phases of development. Students are required to choose one of
the six areas of interest to them, and are to work in small, three to
five person groups to develop and organize theoretical, empirical,
and practice issues and strategies which are then to be presented in

one of the class sessions. Each of the student groups is charged to take a theoretical perspective related to the topic, review empirical data, and develop a presentation which attempts to link theoretical and empirical data to practice intervention. In addition, and to reinforce the empiric role, each group may utilize, modify or develop an instrument related to the topic, apply it by way of an exercise (film, role play, case study), and interpret the results. Their final task is to prepare a five to eight page summary of their work, which is handed out to class members.

The third unit includes several sessions which the teacher uses for both review and further discussion of interventive strategies such as support, modeling, confrontation, clarification, summarizing, and so forth. The last and final unit consists of utilizing and applying the knowledge of groups to the dynamics of the classroom as a large group.

The class materials are reinforced, expanded and integrated by two examination methods. Each group is required to do an inter-generational study of one recent article referring to their topic. For example, one can take several key citations of a recent article on group roles and trace back through two generations of citations specific articles and in each case assess the most relevant citations. This would provide a twenty to thirty year review of a line of inquiry leading to current knowledge of group roles. Implications for practice completes the assignment. The final examination re-quires each class member to observe two continuous sessions of an ongoing group in the field and analyze it with respect to each of the major topical areas. In addition they are charged with selecting a critical incident that had meaning for the group members, analyze dynamics of the incident, identify the factors that contributed to or inhibited change, and discuss the implications of the analysis for practice.

TEACHING TECHNOLOGIES

Developing an Educative Class Culture

Three techniques are used to develop a class culture which will enhance experimentation, give and take, support, discussion, and participation.

1. In the first unit the different readings are parceled out to randomly selected groups of three to five members each. The readings are presented in class at the next session after time is

allotted for each of the particular groups to organize their materials. The process is repeated another time within the first four session unit with other randomly selected groups of three to five members. The purpose is to enhance the class formation and cohesion process as well as helping students learn from each other. One of the main advantages of this particular process is that it permits a wide variety of readings to be done by various members of the class and also allows integration of these readings within the context of the particular class.

2. Class time is set aside to form and develop student presenting groups in one of the six topical areas. This is important fairly early so that the work groups can begin their preparation. The teacher meets with each of these groups the first time in order to help with the formation of goals, procedures, and so forth. In addition, the teacher will meet with each group prior to the presentation for purposes of developing a suitable teaching role based on the organization of the material.

3. The teacher models an exemplar for the class presentation that illustrates the requirements for student groups. For example, the class may be divided into five person groups, sex specific where possible, which are then required to perfom two tasks, one unstructured and one structured. Several observers are chosen and given an instrument by which certain aspects of the ensuing processes of their working groups can be assessed simply by using check marks. The data is analyzed on the basis on types of tasks, types of groups, along five or six dimensions (atmosphere, clarity of goals, satisfaction, products, and so on). Connections between and among the variables are posited from the data and are discussed for their relevance to practice. Next, members' feelings corresponding to types of tasks are discussed and interventions that would have facilitated more productive interchanges are considered. Suggestions from class members are followed with invitations to demonstrate the strategy or interventive technique by replaying the group exercise and asking either the designated leader of the small group or the class member who suggested the alteration or procedure to perform the task.

Developing Work Groups

The teacher meets with each working group as has been mentioned, once in the beginning and once prior to presentation. One of the more important considerations during this early session is to alert the group members that it is important to try and develop a presentation format different from the group that precedes it. The point of this is that, for example, if two or three groups use role playing simulations as the major presentation format, it is quite likely the third time around that such presentations will' be boring. It is recommended that each particular group wait until the week prior to the presentation before making a final decision about organization of material and format. This creates uncertainty and anxiety and raises important issues that the group must work through. Hence the process of differentiation begins as members must learn not only to accomplish a time-specific task, but to deal with each other as well, and to begin the experience of what it means to be a member in a particular group. The extent to which these purposes are accomplished feeds into the educative dynamics of the class as well. Not infrequently, membership problems crop up as students work together and the teacher is called upon to deal with and model ways of developing a tension management system. Student leadership roles developed in the working groups carry over into the class as well.

Integrating the Sessions

One of the more difficult tasks for the teacher is intergrating material between and among sessions. The use of instrumentation is helpful because it helps flesh out ideas into more meaningful material. It is very difficult to include highly complex devices simply because they are time-consuming and laborious in scoring and analyzing. An example for integrating concepts utilizing instruments is as follows. The FIRO—B instrument is quite helpful in delineating personality patterns that dramatize issues related to group formation and membership patterns. The role perception instrument developed along the lines of the Benne and Sheats (1948) formulation, and including members' perceptions of how often certain role behaviors occur for themselves, the group leader, and typical members provides a pattern that can be induced from a complex of twenty-seven to thirty-six role behaviors. The instrument is useful in the group structure and role topical area. A simple Q sort may be utilized to assess the culture or gestalt of a group in action, which is related to a topical area of group cultures, norms and values. These three instruments provide the data pool for connecting the gestalt of a group, the role perception patterns, and personality patterns. Implications for practice and interventions at three levels are fairly clear. To make the connection, one has to begin with the FIRO—B instrument and include the material on the group role presentation, and then combine these two with the group culture Q sort which is introduced at a following class session. Since it is not possible to utilize all three instruments at the same time, several mock problems or patterns have to be developed for teaching purposes. But the idea of personality, role perception, and culture are brought together in meaningful ways. Another integrating theme is to highlight the practice connections between, let us say, group formation and purpose with structure and process. A major teaching principle in work with groups is how structure and process are closely related to clarity of purpose. Unclear expectations and poor contracting lead to role ambiguity and fragile interpersonal relationships, which together heighten member anxiety. In addition the member transitions from wishing to engage, wishing to continue, and wishing to change are blocked and diffused. These sorts of connections clarify one of the roles of the teacher as integrative person. Additional aspects of the instructional effort take place during the review sessions after unit one and two are completed.

Practice Interventions

A practical procedure for assisting students to try practice skills is to replay a role simulation after discussion of the dynamics of the various factors inherent in the group presentation. The gist of the technique is to ask the student who offers an alternative strategy to assume the leadership role in the scripted situation and demonstrate how it should be done. A few minutes later, the student group leader may ask for assistance with another unique group event and another student would be asked to lead the group in demonstrating the intervention. The replaying of scripted situations with facilitative strategies offered by students provides an experiential situation for learning by doing. The use of role play, of course, offers the opportunities for developing interventive options at cognitive, behavior, or affective levels. In addition, students in the class may also coach the role players, both leaders and members, in situation-specific responses. A time-out period is necessary to rehearse the new strategies. The action may be repeated until the performance is considered adequate by the class and the teacher.

Integrating Settings and Other Environments

The notion of person–group–environmental interdependence means that the environment in which the group is situated affects what occurs in the group itself. It is quite easy for scripted groups to get stuck in a groove of thinking only about the internal dynamics of the group and class setting, partifularly considering the artificiality of the exercises. An experienced teacher will find examples from practice experience, or those of the students, helpful for introducing the effects of outside forces. For example, the effects of bureaucracy on staff performance in simulated agency staff meetings can highlight the influence of organizational factors. Simulations of group therapy sessions in hospitals can dramatize the inconsistencies and double-binds placed on patients and the effects on group function of the competing interests of discipline-specific care-givers. Issues of racism, sexism, and empowerment are common emergents in scripted groups, whether they be therapy, tenant councils, and so forth. Another approach to introducing "outside material" is to consider the effects of overlapping group membership in external groups on membership in current groups. If one accepts the principles of change inherent in a systems approach, then alteration of one part (the group) leads to pushes and pulls in some other part (the "other environments"). These considerations are to the point when the relationship between educative class culture and member (student) learning are discussed in a latter part of the course. In many ways, of course, this hits close to home and has more meaning. An example of the latter point would be to examine characteristics of the educative culture and member participation in that culture vis à vis the culture of other classes in the particular curriculum or the school in general.

Discussion

Ecology as an idea involves the person in the natural habitat. The ecology of a classroom situation contains a number of complex interrelationships which encompass the learner, the teacher, and the class as a formal system. The purpose of an educative culture is to create conditions whereby the three components can interrelate in such a way as to produce opportunities for exchanges in thought-feeling-action levels related to the dynamics and processes of stability and change in small groups. The blending of three problem solving roles, for lack of a better term, namely theoretic, empiric, and practice constitute the organizing principle for various process and content issues.

The utilization of small groups is an important organizing methodology by which learning is enhanced. The informal (psyche) and formal (socio) aspects of small groups are harnessed to produce what may be called a work (productivity) group that is essentially a balance of the other two. The product of the work group or working team includes an intermix of member feelings, group or task demands, which together must be faced to produce some sort of educative outcome. There are various ways that the small group can induce learning. Among these are providing support which helps students open themselves to learning; dealing with disorder and uncertainty; supplying correctives in knowledge; feelings, and actions; and counteracting the anxieties that are attendant on new situations such as loss, failure and dependency.

Experience shows that the following types of learnings take place as reported by students.

1. Concepts are fleshed out by use of instrumentation as the assumptive world of the student is opened up.
2. Students experience various roles not only as subjects in exercises but as members of small groups, as observers and as members in the class. Students vary in their ability to perform comfortably in all of these three areas but the greater options for participation also reveal their own particular tendencies which are learnings in and of themselves.
3. The practice interventions for learning by doing provide them with a set of rudimentary skills which are helpful in preparation for field entry. Appreciation of the effects of role rehearsing, modeling and so forth may be later utilized in their own particular work under "live conditions."
4. A sense of confidence is attained in understanding the connections between theory, practice and research.
5. A variety of exercises provide students with a repertoire of training techniques which may be useful in their own work as professionals.
6. Students developed that personal anxiety can be used in constructive ways.

A variety of teacher roles are fairly obvious in this methodology. A teacher functions as an expert in designated areas, as a facilitator for the class process and small group processes, as a catalyst for integrating diverse material, and as a role model. In addition, in those situations for which there are no answers, he/she can serve as a member of a class which requires sharing vulnerabilities as well as knowledge.

The integration of multitheoretical points of view is, of course, an extremely difficult task, and one is required to express limitations in this area. However, it is possible to elucidate a multilevel approach in viewing small group theory and processes and entertain the idea that several different approaches may enhance explanation and understanding of an event (Bales, 1979; Pawlak & Vassil, 1980).

Behavioral manifestations of events are continually related to thoughts and feelings and in this sense the importance for integration and enhanced comprehension is valuable.

It is possible from the above to sketch out the dynamics of change. Cohesion and conflict are ever-present in the educative culture as thought-feelings-actions of class members are stretched. New concepts and perceptions emerge, together with a recognition that some changes have to be taken, followed by trial and error actions. It is very difficult to express differences and be close at the same time. Learnings that take place have to be undertaken in small doses, encouraged by the teacher and peers. There are two shifts evident in the learning paradigm. The shift to cohesion is important because it offers predictability in the face of uncertainty. The shift to conflict is necessary because uncertainty generates a greater stream of resources and ideas that can be synthesized to adaptive action (Vassil, 1978). The educative culture provides the context for these processes to take place. The learning signifies a change from context to content and reaches its peak in a culture where interdependence is greatest. It is in the experiences of dealing with opposites or contradictions, as mentioned earlier, such as control or support, conflict or peace, and so on that individuals confront their opportunities and limitations. The context in which some of these contradictions are resolved is in the small work groups as well as in the total class.

In many ways, the classroom culture demonstrates phases of development as well. Between initial exploration, hesitancy, and cohesion, one often encounters resistance, anxiety and counterdependency among students as they attempt to deal with a different teaching-learning format. When students can build on each others' ideas, or express differences without defensiveness, or expose vulnerabilities without fears of ridicule or embarrassment, then a work phase appears to be evident. Termination and evaluation, synonymous with the ending of class, are often memorialized through some sort of congenial get-together during the last session.

There are limitations to this approach to teaching. Class sizes have to be fairly large in order to have adequate membership in small groups. The development and organization of the class is very time-consuming. In between classes, meetings with the student work groups take still more time and energy. The wealth of material to be understood poses special strains on the teacher for comprehension and integration. The transfer of learnings from class to field, of course, are unknown. Concurrent experiences in the field are essential to reduce the artificiality of the classroom. In addition, not all students are willing to invest the time and energy necessary for maximum use of the course structure. Some students prefer to be dependent learners and it is difficult for them to participate beyond their means. As a result, some work groups develop skewed patterns of effectiveness and discussion. Hence, it is not unlikely in some groups that members may be blocked because of their dependent learnings and therefore tend to be singled out as members with low motivation. Sometimes the class meetings provide more honesty than is tolerable, with the result that exaggerated behaviors produce feelings that may enhance embarrassment and guilt.

The sources of information for learning require a good deal of planning and preparation of course content. Consequently there are limits to what the students can produce out of their own imperatives. Also, the student resistance to research produces blocks in the use of instrumentation and scoring although simple procedures do tend to allay these anxieties to some extent.

Nonetheless, experiences with this methodology are sufficiently positive to warrant further experimentation and use as a unique situation in which to teach the dynamics of small group theory and process and its relationship to practice. The sketch of the change process suggests a model of competency that is based on learning by doing that enhances and incorporates thoughts-feelings-actions, and that welcomes novelty and diversity. The emphasis on description and measurement is intended to complement learning, not substitute for it. In the final analysis, the gestalt is more significant than a cataloging of measurable behavioral skills.

COMPLEMENTARITY BETWEEN EXPERIENTIAL AND STRUCTURAL APPROACHES

While experiential and structural approaches differ in emphasis regarding process and structure, there is complementarity between the two in certain overlapping areas. Among the most significant is the primary focus on interdependencies among social context, groups, and individual learning styles. Salient learning principles that can be derived include the following.

1. Students begin to appreciate how different learning styles emerge in different context. For example, the informal groups that form during class breaks meet needs for spontaneity and intimate interactions. This is in contrast to fears of failure and embarrassment when students are called upon to perform in front of an audience. In the small working groups, students are less inhibited in expressing assertive sentiments.

2. Students learn that despite sharp differences among them, their class requirements foster closeness at two different levels. The first is closeness for security and safety, and as an antidote for anxiety. The second is intimacy that is formed on the basis of sharing and pooling skills to achieve a goal. Students also learn that, in completing a task, small groups have the means for manufacturing the necessary roles, such as receiver, giver, expert, catalyst of ideas and feelings.

3. Initial anxieties produce defensiveness, competitive, and self-protective responses which dampen learning opportunities. In this instance, the students realize that competition weakens the needed exchange of resources. In addition, safety in small and informal groups alleviates the excessive anxiety but does not eliminate it. Students learn that "worry work" increases search behavior and enhances striving, demonstrating the constructive use of anxiety.

4. Individual and group needs are influenced by the demands of the institution through academic requirements such as examinations, assignments and grading criteria. In evaluating class dynamics, students begin to perceive how academic pressures freeze them into conformity, competition and punitive exchanges, which become evident in their small working groups, and in the total class.

5. Attention to subtle processes in the class and small working groups regarding members' respective perceptions, the meanings attributed to nonverbal cues, the communication patterns, all demonstrate how relationships can reinforce and sometimes rigidify interpersonal transactions.

In essence, both approaches foster an appreciation of the classroom as a small community, which increases the students' readiness to perceive the community as a complex of interacting forces. The use of small groups and the focus on the processes enhance the creation of benign cycles for defensive strategies through support, and upward spirals toward change rather than self-defeating patterns. These teaching points affirm the principle of interdependence between individual learning styles, small groups and the social context which is inherent in the ecological perspective.

CURRICULUM DEVELOPMENT IN GROUP WORK

Examination of the state of the art of any component of social work curriculum and practice is an essential but an arduous task. Social group work is no exception to this. In light of the numerous

changes and developments occurring within and outside of the profession, any discussion of the relevant curriculum content and
appropriate teaching methodologies of social group work needs to
include an examination of the philosophy, goals, and mission of
this method. In this context, the poignant concerns raised by
Maier (1964) have great significance.

- Our perception of the client to be served.
- Our understanding of the impact of the application of the
  social group work method.
- Our image of the student as a learner, particularly as a social
  group worker in-the-becoming.
- Our stance as social group work method teachers.

Using Maier's concerns as a base, the following list of issues and
concerns often encounterd by faculty members teaching social
group work courses is developed. This list is by no means exhaustive
nor does it reflect degrees of importance or priority. Curriculum
planners have to contend with the following five themes.

1. Mission and goals of social group work.
2. Curriculum content.
3. Curriculum format.
4. Teaching-learning format.
5. Faculty resources.

Mission and Goals

Mission and goals, broadly speaking, refer to the philosophy and
objectives that guide social work practice with groups. Tracing the
evolution of group work from its historical moorings in late nineteenth century intellectual and social thought to objectives as expressed in the 1964 working statement enrich and reinforce the
beginning students' appreciation of the uses and potential of the
group work method. At the same time that an historical review is
enlightening, it can also produce discomfort in the dilemmas which
have been generated along the way. Competing "truths" about the
nature of practice are manifested in views about pathology or
deviance; prevention, remediation, and/or restoration. For example,
is work with oppressed and deprived clientele "treatment"? Is
group "therapy" more valued than group "work?" Articulation
among competing truths is extremely difficult and one has to
decide whether eclecticism has advantages over more unitary
approaches.

The definition of the client to be served is related to agency auspices. Settlement houses and other community agencies may define the client as the neighborhood, while specialized agencies may focus their services on the person or the group. Although all formulations on group work emphasize the interdependence between the person, the group, and the environment, leadership functions may be directed to different combinations of these three units. The meaning of this to private practitioners may be quite different based on their argument that clients have a right to choose the form of service. These considerations have curriculum implications in determining professional competency for group work.

Course syllabi reflect the educators' position and intellectual stance regarding group work. The appearance of texts by nonsocial workers such as Yalom, Lieberman, Corey and Corey and others raises the question of identity for the student. There is an uneasy feeling that the value of borrowing and using knowledge from well-referenced non-social work texts may also weaken the intellectual and moral authority of the profession.

A related issue is whether or not volunteerism and self-help groups constitute an objective for social group work. The use of volunteers extends social group work values and objectives to more and more people, and has always been a part of the services offered through community-based agencies. Volunteerism has taken on a new form in self-help groups. Do professional associations with self-help groups begin to interfere with their efficacy by simply moving the professional leader from inside the group, to outside in the form of consultation?

Although issues of sexism, racism, cultural diversity and such fall within the domain of social work, the issue of the place of social group work in preparing students to practice within a pluralistic content needs to be addressed.

Curriculum Content

Derived from concerns with mission and goals, issues regarding group dynamics and their application to specialized settings and target populations need to be reviewed. A cluster of concepts that illustrates group processes can be presented, but their application to different client groups and settings may vary. Closeness or cohesion does not have quite the same meaning to adolescents in a neighborhood setting as it does to the psychiatric patients in a discharge planning group. The implication for practice of guest–host relationships in different complex settings need to be explored if the goal for education is to prepare students to be competent for work with interdisciplinary teams. If children constitute an important segment for teaching, it is will advised to consider the use of programming, because "talking" as an activity has its limitations. The teachers' frame of reference is a crucial element because students tend to identify with what the teacher knows best. As has been mentioned, including other competing truths may often confuse the students who require a good deal of certainty at the beginning stage of their professional development. On the other hand, introducing comparative models of group work broadens the students' educational base. In large part, the teachers' theoretical stance is reflected in the definition of client, derivitive definitions and applications of interventions, values regarding cultural pluralism with supportive content, importance of self-disclosure and authenticity, and teacher as expert or facilitator. An example of a current practice issue is co-leadership or co-therapy. The teacher will need to clarify his/her stance on the advantages or disadvantages regarding its use by the beginning practitioner.

Curriculum Format

The place of group work in the curriculum depends on where and how much content on group work is introduced initially. Other related issues are the number of group work courses, whether they are electives or required, and whether or not concurrent field experiences for working with groups are available. Curricula that emphasize a generalist orientation taught through mandatory core courses may include group dynamic content in human behavior courses and methods content in core practice courses. Variation in the expertise of different teachers in basic courses taught in multiple sections may require creative adaptations for students in subsequent group work courses. Mandatory requirements for group work courses can mean that all students regardless of specialization may be included in the classroom, resulting in a cursory overview of this content.

Concurrent field experiences incorporated in the classroom enrich course content with "live" situations, although close correspondence between classroom content and field learning is difficult to maintain. Carefully designed laboratory experiences in the classroom can be helpful when students do not have opportunity for group experiences in the field. Creative use of experiential learning augmented with audio-video resources can enhance student competencies in assessing subtle processes including one's own role.

Teaching-Learning Format

Teachers' orientation towards practice is intimately related to the teaching-learning format. Decisions regarding the methodology for teaching depends upon the teachers'· comfort, creativity, and preferred mode of introducing and delivering content. Experiential and didactic modes of teaching place different expectations both on teachers and students. The former involves students and teachers in developing knowledge through a shared process. The latter requires that the students master and apply predetermined content.

Clearly formulated contracts between the students and teachers have bearing on the quality of participation in the experiential format. For example, when the participants are assured that self-revelations will not go beyond the class context, they are freer in open participation. Similarly, other structural components of group work such as size, duration of class period, and the physical set-up of the classroom affects the quality of exchanges among the participants.

Other means are available in a didactic format. Mastery of group content and disciplined analysis can be enhanced through short biweekly examinations to assure minimum performances. A case method of study accompanied by written analysis can reinforce and extend recognition and understanding of group dynamics in action. Video-taped student skill exercise sessions in assessing performance levels through instrumentation can also be an effective means for competence acquisition in both cognitive and affective domains.

Faculty Resources

Faculty training, past and current experiences in group work practice and commitment to research are relevant concerns and raise other issues. The development of a body of knowledge depends on consistent and timely efforts and thinking regarding current and promising concepts, their testing and practical application. Continual shifting of teachers in group work courses preclude the continuity necessary to develop a program for reporting and advancing current knowledge in groups.

Maintaining current practice generates a rich body of experiences for teachers to incorporate and update their knowledge base. Preferences only for private practice tend to be narrow with regard to the types of experiences social work students are likely to encounter. Ways in which teachers can maintain and enhance theory and practice skills necessary for teaching competence include consultation, workshops, and involvement with field agencies. A commitment to research is well advised whatever the intellectual stance of the teacher, because it models the role of knowledge producer for students. Regular contacts among a cadre of group work teachers to share their concerns and ideas regarding group work curriculum and research can enhance the quality of instruction.

INQUIRY AND GROUP WORK PRACTICE

The ecological perspective is applicable to the study of human behavior throughout the life cycle. Particular emphasis is placed on the location of the client in time and the network of relationships present in groups, settings and neighborhoods that affirm or disconfirm one's identity maintaining and building processes. Developmental and contemporaneous events, personal and social, are viewed through many lenses (disciplines) which provide substantive content and concepts that are assembled to produce an integrative and qualitatively more complete picture of the client. The study of groups is a selective aspect of human behavior and it is assumed that broader social influences are asserted in and among a group of peers. The nature of the interpersonal relationships are posited to be a reflection of the level of integration or disintegration of the social systems within which the group exists. Symbolic interaction emphasizes the process of social perception in which a person checks out and orients himself/herself to another's expectation and reacts accordingly. In this manner, meaning is imputed to the situation (Chaiklin, 1978). Lewin's field theory stresses group relevant aspects of personality and behavior which are considered in the light of stable and shifting group states that define the context for action.

Considerable thought and effort are necessary to formulate propositions that seek to explain the connection among persons and environment, as they are manifested in the small group. Sorting out the complexities of group dynamics in terms of group and human behavior requires an eclectic stance simply because of the myriad of possibilities that one is confronted with. As mentioned earlier, to reduce the dangers inherent in a flabby eclecticism requires professional activity in the empiric role. In effect, practitioners need to complement a "warm" heart with a "cold" head. The method of inquiry is a necessary function for purposes of testing and clarifying the fit between understanding and intervention.

The purpose of the empiric role is to maintain an open system. Hence, to the extent that the if-then propositions which underpin the practice intervention are examined in the light of some sort of evidence (clinical or otherwise), then the connections between theory (understanding) and practice may be refined to the problem may be reconceptualized (the evidence leads to new questions). Hence, the empiric role functions as a relatively neutral procedure to both enhance and fortify the practitioners' work. In another sense, one might compare it to the positive use of the defender role in that ideas and experience are filtered through a set of procedures labeled "inquiry" which are the best that we have in order to arrive at an approximation of the truth or reality.

Two other comments need to be made at this juncture with respect to the empiric role. We do not suggest that workers need to be professional researchers with all the rigor that the term implies. We are, rather, suggesting a method of inquiry of a more intermediary sort. The point has been explicated by Argyris and Schon, (1975) who suggest that intermediate rigor would include at least the following.

1. Inquiry into the situation. The situation (problem) is taken seriously as a source of knowledge.
2. Form a perspective on the data (explanation or story), including a conceptualization. The perspective must be faithful to the data.
3. Maintain an apparently contradictory attitude toward the perspective on the data. One must be committed to act on it, but also prepared to accept a negative evaluation. Therefore, the stance must include a commitment to the perspective and a readiness to abandon it.
4. The perspective should yield sequencies of actions and consequences such that one finding will then lead to a revision in the perspective, a revision that makes sense of the outcome observed. Hence, the method of inquiry acts as a confirmatory and "open" mechanism to keeping practitioners honest (p. 160).

There is one other important point. Others may come to the same situations with different assumptions and perceive a different configuration on the data (behavioral vs. ego psychological orientation) and emerge with a different confirmed perspective. While it is not our purpose to compare and analyze two different theoretical and/ or ideologic perspectives, suffice it to say that whatever the orientation, there is an abundance of agreement that a data-based approach is necessary in order to maintain and enhance the intellectual and professional authority of the profession.

Central to the empiric role is the concept of patterning, which defines a characteristic arrangement of events in an objective way. Examples of patterns include a hen pecking, a mouse pressing a treadle bar, the number of cigarettes an instructor smokes in one hour, and so forth. Group interaction patterns, of course, are more complicated phenomena, and are encompassed in such terms as "passive-aggressive," "counterdependent" and so forth. The purpose of the empiric role is to externalize the worker's mental picture of just what terms such as the above mean. In more technical terms, behavioral patterns can be defined as a segment of behavior that is a suitable target for research. Properties attributed to behavioral patterns include that they can be identified and observed, occur with sufficient frequency, and can be classified and enumerated.

This volume has described and presented a variety of concepts and issues which continually confront practitioners in assessing groups. Following is an overview of relevant variables across phases of group development.

Group Phases

	Beginning	Middle	End
Group Variables			
Goals			
Roles			
Climate			
Leadership			
Subgroups			
Decisions			
Conflicts			
Change Mechanism			

To further complicate the picture, one could add comparisons with regard to types of groups, clients, settings, neighborhoods and so forth. Interventions are based on an assessment of the structure and process that defines each working moment of the group, which in abstract terms refers to part-whole (member–group) relationship. The empirical evidence regarding just what group components produce specific individual changes in specific situations is underdeveloped and remains a challenge for the future (Lieberman, 1974). Problems with leadership orientations and transfer of learning are but two of the thorny issues that need clarification in order to develop an empirically grounded theory of practice. These considerations lead to the conclusion that practitioners have to engage in research activities in order to inform practice outcomes.

There are several approaches available to practitioners that could be utilized for improving practice. Lieberman and Borman (1979) in a recent volume have attempted to sort out consistent processes and activities that occur in self-help groups. Using a "grounded theory" approach, which emphasizes discovery rather than verification, the researchers used participant and nonparticipant observation and interview methodologies to derive a series of inferred helping processes. Content analysis of narratives of meetings provided the basis for describing and categorizing help-giving activities, which are assumed to be related to processes. Two types of processes were noted. Behavioral processes included "modeling of methods of coping with stresses and changing behavior" (p. 247). Cognitively oriented processes were demonstrated by "support for changes in attitudes toward oneself, one's own behavior, and society" (p. 253). Emotional content, while pervasive and charged, appeared to be related to and inherent in the other processes. Examples of help-giving activities included empathy, mutual affirmation, encouragement and so forth.

Practitioners could use this approach to discover processes and helpful activities in their own practice. Workers could compile a data base by writing narrative reports after each session including their own participation and then subjecting the material to content analysis. Audio- and videotaping group sessions would remove worker biases that are inherent in report writing, and would also provide a more complete picture. By focusing on selected time segments of a meeting, the burden of analyzing a wealth of data could be reduced. In both situations, inspection and conceptualization of themes present in a single meeting, or over a series of meetings, would provide a beginning step in identifying processes and changes in the group that would inform practice.

Content analysis refers to a systematic ordering of descriptive accounts of recorded communication. Key words, sentences and larger narrative segments can be categorized and assembled as a basis for deriving inferences about the data (Marsden, 1971). Content analysis of group narratives can lead the practitioner toward the development of "sensitizing" concepts that can be refined into more rigorous instruments for further testing and evaluation.

The critical incident technique could be used singly or to supplement the above procedures. The concept of critical incident is defined as

> the confrontation of a group leader by one or more members, in which an explicit or implicit opinion, decision, or action is demanded of him. It may also be an observed conversation, a confrontation among mem-

bers, an event taking place, or a period of silence in which are expectations or demand is made of the leader. The essential property of a critical incident is that it is judged important enough for a group leader to consciously and explicitly consider whether to act in a specific way that is assumed to have an important impact on the group. (Cohen and Smith, 1976; p. 114).

According to Cohen and Smith (1976), the use of critical incident recording is enhanced when the following conditions are met: (1) when the context is specified (beginning, middle or end of a session and/or phase; group climate; persons involved; (2) specifying the behavior and/or conversation that led up to and preceded the event; (3) describing the event and including both surface and inferred underlying issues; (4) specifying the interventions, and its target (group, interpersonal, individual); and (5) specifying the results (pp. 124–125). Analysis of an accumulated set of critical incidents in conjunction with a group narrative can provide valuable information regarding structure and process components in a group, and emergent worker interventions. As elaborated in the following example, the advantage of this methodology is that it is simple to implement.

CRITICAL INCIDENT:
AVOIDANCE OF FEELINGS

Context of Incident

In the fourth session of the group, the members were continuing to ignore emotional content. As in earlier meetings, discussion was centered on innocuous topics such as current events, somebody else's (outside the group) tribulations and so forth. On several occasions during the early stages of the group, the group leader had attempted to explore the avoidance pattern of gentle comments and observations regarding feelings between and among members. No one in the group followed up on the group leader's comments. In the current meeting, the group leader addressed the issue more directly, asking if dealing with feelings was too threatening. One member, Joe, who has been alternately irritable, bombastic, and withdrawn, confronts the group leader in a voice filled with sarcasm and anger.

Event Preceding Choice Point

> **Joe:** I don't know why you're deliberately trying to needle us but I know it's on purpose since you keep on doing it, and I think you owe us an explanation. Every time things are going smoothly in there, you keep provoking us with comments about feelings as if we're doing something wrong.

The group is stunned by the attack and sits silently, awaiting the group leader's response.

Choice Point

Several issues may be considered with regard to the member's comments. On the surface, it appears to be a request for an explanation. The anger associated with the comments, the group's pattern of avoidance of feeling-oriented content, and the group's expectant silence suggest other dynamics are involved in this tense moment. The member's pointed and charged comments goes beyond a simple request and suggest a challenge to authority as well as a bid for control of the group. Concurrent guilt feelings and sensitivity to being infantilized are also intimated within the communication which may be a manifestation of a counterdependent need by the member, or represent the group's resistance to dealing with their own emotions and feelings toward the group leader.

Suggested Intervention

A direct and forceful response to Joe is likely to threaten the other members and exacerbate the group's resistance to emotional content. In addition, the group leader would present the model of an authoritative and omnipotent expert, thus significantly reducing the chances of the group working toward responsible autonomy and its own unique identity for resolving interpersonal problems.

The desired intervention should transform the emotional issue to one of group relevance. At the same time, the intervention to Joe should be calculated to avoid an emotional counter attack. To reduce the super-charged atmosphere, the group leader should strive to convey a calm and reasoned manner in his/her comments.

To accomplish these goals, the group leader should

1. Frame comments at a low intensity level to reduce further intensification of emotion and allay members' fears of omnipotence.
2. Address Joe at a conceptual level but not disregard emotional undertones.
3. Focus on the relevance of emotional content to the group as a whole.

To Joe:

"I hear your request and at the same time sense the strong feelings behind it. If you're asking me or the group to ignore feelings, we couldn't even if we tried. I also sense that there are unstated agreements in here against recognizing feelings and wonder how we got to this point."

To Group:

"How do the rest of you feel about Joe's comments and my observations?"

Intervention Outcome

The intervention is designed to recognize and legitimate the expression and recognition of feelings by group members. By opening up the issue in a way that involves group members as resources, the work of the group is supported.

The use of instruments such as questionnaires is another method by which practitioners can gauge group events and outcomes. Silbergeld et. al., (1975) developed and tested a questionnaire to assess the group atmosphere or psychosocial environment of a group, based on the earlier work of Moos and Houts (1968). The underlying assumption is that different psychosocial environments engender different member behavioral patterns. Members and worker are asked to check true or false on one hundred and twenty statements that define various aspects of the group atmosphere. Ten items in each of twelve subscales encompass the body of the questionnaire. Examples of subscales and defining items are (1) support—the stronger members of the group help the less strong; (2) spontaneity—group members are encouraged to share their feelings. Averages of members' and therapist's scores on each of the twelve dimensions can be computed and depicted in graph form. Each score on the graph would represent one subscale (horizontal axis) and a corresponding average score for members or therapist (vertical axis). Similarities and discrepancies can be gauged by visual inspection. Comparisons of scores could serve as the basis for assessment and evaluation of where the group is at one point in time. Agreements and disagreements between members and therapists could produce significant corrections in terms of the reality of the group as well as shedding light on member performances. Abbreviated versions of the instrument could be obtained by using only one half of the items which could increase its utility for practice. The disadvantage of the instrument is that it is not suitable for groups that have not been meeting regularly.

Interpersonal structures in groups can be elicited by using sociometric questionnaires. By asking individual members to rate how often (high, medium, low) they perceive the frequency of certain role behaviors with regard to themselves, the group leader, and a typical member, it is possible to construct role perception profiles that provide a descriptive account of interpersonal patterns. Role behavior can be categorized as group task, group maintenance and personal. Examples of role behaviors in each of the three categories would include group task—initiates ideas, gives opinions; group maintenance—shares feelings, expresses approval of others' ideas; personal—ignores others, gets upset at others' questions. Depending on the number of items chosen for each role category, fairly complete descriptions of role perception patterns can be developed.

Each pattern is likely to yield a unique theme that can be used to assess the group dynamics. Concentrating on either perceptions of the leader or a typical member would present information regarding leader styles and group norms. The presence or absence of certain roles could also serve as a guide for assessing leadership behaviors.

Cohen (1979) has developed a two-part sociometric instrument that provides information regarding significant relationships to individual members and the group as a whole. In part one, members are asked to think of relationships in the present group which have created a high degree of emotional involvement on their past.

Feelings regarding involvement may be cooperative or conflictual. Members jot the names of a person or persons (subgroups), along with brief comments specifying the nature of the relationship (friendly, ambivalent, and so on). As many as four designated significant relationships may be requested.

In part two, members are asked to repeat the exercise, except that significant relations to the group as a whole are requested. The advantage of the instrument is that relationships significant to members may not be the same as those important to the group as a whole. The results of the questionnaire can be reported back to the group for discussion and evaluation of the central events and relationships, and to see whether cooperative, conflictual or egalitarian sentiments are perceived. Caution must be exercised in reporting member's choices regarding significant others back to the individual because the experience can be upsetting. Assessment of the therapeutic uses for this information is required. Regarding instrumentation in general, the relationship of the activity to group and individual goals must be clearly indicated.

Individual members in groups can be assessed and evaluated over time as well. Hudson (1977) has developed a clinical package of instruments measuring marital satisfaction, generalized contentment, self-concept, sexual satisfaction, parental attitudes and family relations.

Members could be asked to take the appropriate instrument in the pre-group stage to establish a beginning reference point and later, at other regularly scheduled times during the course of the group. Average scores on the instrument can be charted and compared over time through simple graphing procedures. In addition, critical incidents and interventions could be described and recorded week by week so that connections between member performance, interventions and other group factors could be postulated. Numerous instruments for a variety of purposes applicable to individual and group assessment and evaluation have been compiled in a volume by Pfeiffer and Heslin (1973).

It is worth noting that skill in implementing the research role is developmental, just as in sound practice. Patience, perseverance and thoughfulness, which characterize competent practice, can be applied to enhance knowledge building and knowledge utilization. Submitting the results of empirical practice to public scrutiny and debate affirms the principle of collaborative effort among practitioners of similar and different persuasions for enhancing the moral authority of the profession.

Bibliography

Ackerman, N.W. *Treating the Troubled Family*. New York: Basic Books, 1966.

Addams, J. *Twenty Years at Hull House*. New York: Macmillan, 1910.

Alissi, A.S. "Social Influences on Group Value." *Social Work,* vol. 10, No. 1, January 1965.

Anderson, B.N. et al. "Resident Training in Co-Therapy Groups." *International Journal of Group Psychotherapy,* vol. 22, No. 2, 1972.

Anderson, J.P. "Social Work Status and Trends." *Social Work Year Book.* National Association of Social Work, 1960.

Argyris, C. *Intervention Theory and Method*. Reading, MA: Addison-Wesley, 1970.

Argyris, C., and Schon, D.A. *Theory in Practice: Increasing Professional Effectiveness*. San Francisco: Jossey Bass Publications, 1975.

Asch, S. "Opinions in Social Pressure." *Scientific American,* 1955.

Attneave, C.L., and Speck, R.V. "Social Network Intervention in Time and Space," In A. Jacobs and W. Spradlin, eds. *The Group as Agent of Change*. New York: Behavioral Publication, 1974.

Auerswald, E.H. "Interdisciplinary Versus Ecological Approach." *Family Process,* vol. 7, No. 2, September 1968.

Bach, G. *Intensive Group Psychotherapy*. New York: Ronald Press Company, 1954.

Bales, R.F. *Interaction Process Analysis*. Reading, MA: Addison-Wesley, 1950.

Bales, R.F. "The Equilibrium Problem in Small Groups." In E. Borgatta and R.F. Bales, eds. *Small Groups: Studies in Social Interaction*. New York: Alfred A. Knopf. 1955. Also in T. Parsons, R.F. Bales, and E.A. Shils, eds. *Working Papers in the Theory of Action*. Glencoe, IL: The Free Press, 1953.

Bales, R.F. and Cohen, S.P. *Symlog*. New York: The Free Press, 1979.

Bales, R.F. and Strodtbeck, F.L. "Phases in Group Problem Solving." In D. Cartwright and A. Zander, Eds. *Group Dynamics,* 2d ed. Evanston, IL: Row, Peterson, 1956.

Balgopal, P.R. "Social Groupwork: From Here into the 1980s, Where It Is, Where It's Going." *Indian Journal of Social Work,* vol. 40 No. 4, January 1980.

Balgopal, P.R., and Hull, R.F. "Keeping Secrets: Group Resistance for Patients and Therapists." *Psychotherapy Theory, Research and Practice,* vol. 10, No. 4, Winter 1973.

Balgopal, P.R.; Munson, C.E.; and Vassil, T.V. "Developmental Theory: A Yardstick for Ethnic Minority Content." *Journal of Education for Social Work,* vol. 15, No. 3, 1979.

Balgopal, P.R. and Vassil, T.V. "Group Psychotherapist: The New Breed." *Perspectives in Psychiatric Care,* vol. 17, No. 3, 1979.

Bard, M. "The Use of Dependence for Predicting Psychogenic Invalidism Following Radical Mastectomy." *Journal of Nervous and Mental Disease,* vol. 122, 1955.

Bard, M. and Sutherland, A.M. "Adpatation of Radical Mastectomy." *Cancer,* vol. 8, 1955.

Barker, R. And Gump, P. *Big School, Small School.* Stanford, CA: Stanford University Press, 1964.

Bartlett, H.M. *The Common Base of Social Work Practice.* New York: National Association of Social Workers, 1970.

Beall, L. "Corrupt Contract: Problems in Conjoint Therapy with Parents and Children." *American Journal of Orthopsychiatry,* vol. 42, January 1972.

Beck, A.P. "Phases in the Development of Structure in Therapy and Encounter Groups." In D.A. Wexler and L.N. Rice, eds. *Innovations in Client-Centered Therapy.* New York: John Wiley, 1974.

Bednar, R.L. and Kaul, R.J. "Experiential Group Research: Current Perspectives." In S.E. Garfield and A.E. Bergin, eds. *Handbook of Psychotherapy and Behavior Change: An Empirical Analysis,* 2d ed. New York: John Wiley, 1978.

Bednar, R.L. and Lawlis, G.F. "Empirical Research in Group Psychotherapy." in A.E. Bergin and S.L. Garfield, eds. *Handbook of Psychotherapy and Behavior Change: An Empirical Analysis.* New York: John Wiley, 1971.

Beiser, M. "Components and Correlates of Mental Wellbeing." *Journal of Health and Social Behavior,* vol. 15, No. 4, 1974.

Beiser, M. and Leighton, A.H. "Personality Assets and Mental Health." B.H. Kaplan, R.N. Wilson, and A.H. Leighton, eds. *Further Explorations in Social Psychiatry.* New York: Basic Books, 1976.

Bell, N.W. and Vogel, E.F. *The Family.* New York: The Free Press, 1960.

Benjamin, S.E. "Co-therapy: A Growth Experience for Therapists." *International Journal of Group Psychotherapy.* vol. 22. No. 2. 1972.

Benne, K.D. "From Polarization to Paradox." In L.P. Bradford, J.R. Gibb, and K.D. Benne, eds. *T. Group Theory and Laboratory Method.* New York: John Wiley, 1964.

Benne, K.D. "The Process of Re-Education: An Assessment of Kurt Lewin's Views." In Bennis et al., eds. *Planning of Change.* New York: Holt, Rinehart and Winston, 1976.

Benne, K.D., and Sheats, P. "Functional Roles of Group Members." *Journal of Social Issues,* vol. 4, No. 2, 1948.

Bennis, W.G., and Shepard, H.A. "A Theory of Group Development." *Human Relations,* vol. 9, No. 4, November 1956.

Bennis, W.G., and Slater, P.E. *The Temporary Society.* New York: Harper & Row, 1964 and 1968.

Berne, E. *Transactional Analysis in Psychotherapy.* New York: Grove Press, 1961.

Berne, E. *Games People Play.* New York: Grove Press, 1964.

Berne, E. *Principles of Group Treatment.* New York: Grove Press, 1966.

Bernstein, S. "Conflict and Group Work." In S. Bernstein, ed. *Explorations in Group Work*. Boston: Boston University School of Social Work, 1965.

Bernstein, S. Ed. *Explorations in Group Work*. Boston: Boston University School of Social Work, 1965.

Bernstein, S. Ed. *Further Explorations in Groupwork,* Boston: Boston University School of Social Work, 1973.

Bertcher, H., and Maple, F. in P. Glasser, R. Sarri, and R. Vinter, eds. *Individual Change Through Small Groups*. New York: The Free Press, 1974.

Biddle, B., and Thomas, E.J. *Role Theory: Concepts and Research*. New York: John Wiley, 1966.

Bierstedt, R. "An Analysis of Social Process." *American Sociological Review,* vol. 15, December 1950.

Bion, W.R. *Experiences in Groups*. New York: Basic Books, 1961.

Bion, W.R. *Attention and Interpretation*. New York: Basic Books, 1970.

Bird, C. *Social Psychology*. New York: Appleton-Century-Crofts, 1940.

Birnbaum, M. "The Clarification Group." In K.D. Benne et al., eds. *The Laboratory Method of Change and Learning*. Palo Alto, CA: Science and Behavior Books, 1975.

Blumer, H. *Symbolic Interactionism: Perspective and Method*. Englewood Cliffs, NJ: Prentice-Hall, 1969.

Blumer, H. "Society as Symbolic Interaction." In J.G. Manis and B.N. Meltzer, eds. *Symbolic Interaction: A Reader in Social Psychology*. Boston: Allyn and Bacon, 1978.

Bonner, H. "Group Dynamics: Its Origins and Influences." In *Group Dynamics*. New York: Ronald Press, 1959.

Bott, E. *Family and Social Network*. New York: The Free Press, 1971.

Bradburn, N.S. *The Structue of Psychological Well-Being*. Chicago: University of Chicago Press, 1969.

Brenner, C. *An Elementary Textbook of Psychoanalysis*. New York: Anchor Books, 1974.

Briar, S. "Social Casework and Social Groupwork: Historical and Social Science Foundations." In *The Encyclopedia of Social Work*, vol. 2, New York: National Association of Social Workers, 1971.

Briar, S. and Miller, H. *Problems and Issues in Social Casework*. New York: Columbia University Press, 1971.

Bruner, J.S. *Toward a Theory of Instruction*. Cambridge, MA: Harvard University Press, 1966.

Bruner, J.S. *On Knowing*. New York: Atheneum Press, 1969.

Cartwright, D. "Lewinian Field Theory as a Complementary Systematic Framework." In S. Koch, ed. *Psychology: A Study of a Science,* vol. 2, New York: McGraw-Hill, 1959.

Cartwright, D. "The Nature of Group Cohesiveness." In D. Cartwright and A. Zander, eds. *Group Dynamics*. New York: Harper & Row, 1968.

Cartwright, D., and Zander, A., eds. *Group Dynamics: Research and Theory*. Evanston, IL: Row Peterson, 1960.

Chaiklin, H. "Social Aspects of Behavior." In G.U. Balis et. al., eds. *The Psychiatric Foundations of Medicine,* vol. 2. Boston: Butterworth Publishers, 1978.

Cloward, R., and Ohlin, L.E. "Illegitimate Means, Differential Opportunity and Delinquent Subcultures." In R. Giallombardo, ed. *Juvenile Delinquency.* New York: John Wiley, 1976.

Cohen, A.M., and Smith, R.D. *The Critical Incident in Growth Groups: A Manual for Group Leaders.* LaJolla, CA: University Associates, 1976.

Cohen, S.P. "The Significant Relationships Form." In Bales, R.F. and Cohen, S.P. *Symlog.* New York: The Free Press, 1979.

Compton, B.R., and Galaway, B. *Social Work Processes.* Homewood, IL: Dorsey Press, 1979.

Conover, M.B. "Group Services." In *The Encyclopedia of Social Work.* New York: National Association of Social Workers, 1965.

Cooley, C.H. *Social Process.* New York: Scribner, 1918. As quoted by L. Coser in *Functions of Social Conflict.* New York: The Free Press, 1956.

Cooper, G.B., and McGaugh, G.R. *Leadership Integrating Principles of Social Psychology.* Cambridge: Schenkman, 1963.

Corbin, A.L. *Corbin on Contracts.* Vol. 1. St. Paul: West Publishing, 1963 (as quoted by Croxton, 1974).

Corey, Y., and Corey, M.C. *Groups Process and Practice.* Monterey, California: Brooks/Cole Publishing, 1977.

Coser, L.A. *The Functions of Social Conflict.* Glencoe, IL: The Free Press, 1956.

Cottrell, L.S. "The Competent Community." In B.H. Kaplan et al., eds. *Further Explorations in Social Psychiatry.* New York: Basic Books, 1976.

Coyle, G.L. "Social Groupwork." *Social Work Year Book.* New York: American Association of Social Workers, 1951.

Croog, S., Lipson, A., and Levine, S. "Help Patterns in Severe Illness: The Roles of Kin Network, Non-Family Resources, and Institution." *Journal of Marriage and the Family,* vol. 34, February, 1972.

Croxton, T.A. "The Therapeutic Contract is Social Treatment," in P. Glasser, R. Sarri and R. Vinter (eds.), *Individual Change Through Small Groups.* New York: The Free Press, 1974.

Deutsch, M. "Field Theory in Social Psychology." In G. Lindzey and E. Aronson, eds. *Handbook of Social Psychology,* vol. 1, Reading MA: Addison-Wesley, 1968.

Deutsch, M. *The Resolution of Conflict.* New Haven: Yale University Press, 1973.

Deutsch, M. and Krauss, R.M. *Theories in Social Psychology.* New York: Basic Books, 1965.

Dewey, J. *How to Think.* Boston: Health, 1933.

Dinoff, M. et. al. "Weight Reduction Through Successive Contracts." *American Journal of Orthopsychiatry,* 1972.

Duncan, S.D., Jr. "Some Signals and Rules for Speaking Turns in Conversations." *Journal of Personality and Social Psychology,* vol. 23, 1972.

Dunphy, D.C. "Social Change in Self-Analytic Groups," Unpublished Ph.D Dissertation, Harvard University, 1964.

Dunphy, D.C. *The Primary Group.* New York: Appleton-Century-Crofts, 1972.

Durkin, H.E. *The Group in Depth.* New York: International Universities Press, 1964.

Ephross, P.H., and Balgopal, P.R. "Group Work for the Seventies and Beyond." (mimeographed) Baltimore, MD: School of Social Work and Community Planning, University of Maryland at Baltimore, 1975.

Ephross, P.H., and Balgopal, P.R. "Educating Students for the Practice of Creative Group Work." *Journal of Education for Social Work*, vol. 14, No. 3, 1978.

Etzioni, A. *A Comparative Analysis of Complex Organizations.* New York: The Free Press, 1961.

Fagen, J. and Shepard, I.L., eds. *Gestalt Therapy Now.* New York: Harper & Row, Colophon Books, 1971.

Farrelly, F., and Bradsma, J. *Provocative Therapy.* San Francisco: Shields Publishing Co., 1974.

Feldman, R. "Modes of Integration and Conformity Behavior: Implications for Social Group Work Intervention." In P. Glasser et al., eds. *Individual Change Through Small Groups.* New York: The Free Press, 1974.

Feldman, R.A., and Wodarski, J.S. *Contemporary Approaches to Group Treatment.* San Francisco: Jossey Bass Publishers, 1975.

Fiedler, F.E. "Leadership: A New Model." *Discovery* 26, April, 1965.

Follett, M.P. *Dynamic Administration, The Collected Papers of Mary Parker Follet.* Ed. by H.C. Metcalf and L. Urwick. New York: Harper & Row, 1942.

Frank, J.D., and Powdermaker, F.B. *Group Psychotherapy.* Cambridge, MA: Harvard University Press, 1953.

Freud, A. *The Ego and the Mechanism of Defense.* New York: International Universities Press, 1936.

Fromm, E. "The Present Human Condition." In *The Dogma of Christ and Others on Religion, Psychology and Culture.* New York: Holt, Rinehart and Winston, 1963.

Gans, H.J. *The Urban Villagers.* New York: The Free Press, 1962.

Garfield, S.L. "Research on Client Variables in Psychotherapy." In S.L. Garfield and A.E. Bergin, eds. *Handbook of Psychotherapy and Behavior Change: An Empirical Analysis.* New York: John Wiley, 1978.

Garland, J.A., Jones, H.E., and Kolodny, R. "A Model for Stages of Development in Social Work Group." In S. Bernstein, ed. *Exploration in Group Work.* Boston: Boston University School of Social Work, 1965.

Garland, J.A., and Kolodny, R.L. "Characteristics and Resolution of Scapegoating." In S. Bernstein, ed. *Further Explorations in Group Work.* Boston: Milford House, 1973.

Gendlin, E.T. "Experiential Psychotherapy." In R. Corstni, ed. *Current Psychotherapies.* Itasca. IL: F.E. Peacock, 1973.

Germain, C.G. "Teaching an Ecological Approach to Social Work Practice." In *Teaching for Competence in the Delivery of Direct Service.* New York: Council of Social Work Education, 1977.

Germain C.G. "An Ecological Perspective in Casework Practice." *Social Casework*, vol. 54, No. 6, 1973.

Germain, C.G. "Ecology and Social Work." In C.B. Germain, ed. *Social Work Practice: People and Environment.* New York: Columbia University Press, 1979.

Getzels, J.W., and Thelen, H.A. "The Class Room Group as a Unique Social System." In *The Dynamics of Instructional Groups.* Chicago: NSSE, 1960.

Getzels, J.W., et al. *Educational Administration as a Social Process.* New York: Harper & Row, 1968.

Gibb, C.A. "An Interactional View of the Emergence of Leadership." *Australian Journal of Psychology,* vol. 10, 1958.

Gibb, C.A. *Leadership: Selected Readings.* Baltimore: Penguin Books, 1969.

Glaser, J.S. "The Stairwell Society of Public Housing: From Small Groups to Social Organizations." *Comparative Group Studies,* vol. 3, No. 3, August 1972.

Glasser, P.H, Sarri, R., and Vinter, R., eds. *Individual Change Through Small Groups.* New York: The Free Press, 1974.

Glasser, P.H., and Gravin, C.D. "An Organizational Model." In R.W. Roberts and H. Northen, eds. *Theories of Social Work with Groups.* New York: Columbia University Press, 1976.

Glidewell, J.C. "A Social Psychology of Mental Health." In S.E. Golann and C. Eisdorfer, eds. *Handbook of Community Mental Health.* New York: Appleton-Century-Crofts, 1972.

Glidewell, J.C. "A Social Psychology of Laboratory Training." In K.D. Benne et al., eds. *The Laboratory Method of Changing and Learning.* Palo Alto, CA: Science and Behavior Books, 1975.

Goffman, E. *Stigma.* Englewood Cliffs, NJ: Prentice-Hall, 1963.

Goffman, E. "Role Distance." In D. Brissett and C. Edgley, *Life as a Theatre: A Dramaturgical Sourcebook.* Chicago: Aldine Press, 1975.

Goldschmidt, W. Quoted in "Cultural Adaptation and Ecological Analogies: Analysis of Three Mexican Villages" by R.C. Mills and J.G. Kelley, p. 167. In S.E. Goalann and C.E. Eicdorfer, eds. *Handbook of Community Mental Health.* New York: Appleton-Century-Crofts, 1972.

Goldstein, H. *Social Work Practice: A Unitary Approach.* Columbia SC: University of South Carolina Press, 1973.

Golembiewski, R. *The Small Group.* Chicago: University of Chicago Press, 1962.

Gordon, W.E. "The Working Definition of Social Work Practice: The Interface Between Man and Environment." Paper presented at the Council on Social Work Education Annual Program Meeting, Boston, 1979.

Greene, G. "An Analysis of Problematic Situations in Psychotherapy Groups." Unpublished Case Study, School of Social Work, University of Illinois, Urbana, IL, 1979.

Genther, B. *What to Do Till the Messiah Comes.* New York: Collier Books, 1971.

Hambruger, H. et al. "Group Size and Cooperation." *Journal of Conflict Resolution,* vol. 19, September 1975.

Handlin, O. *The Uprooted.* Boston: Little, Brown, 1951.

Hare, A.P. *Handbook of Small Group Research.* New York: The Free Press, 1962 and 1976 editions.

Hartford, M.E., ed. *Working Papers Toward a Frame Reference For Social Group Work.* New York: National Association of Social Workers, 1964.

Hartford, M.E. *Groups in Social Work.* New York: Columbia University Press, 1972.

Hartman, A. "The Extended Family as a Resource for Change: An Ecological Approach to Family Centered Practice." In C.B. Germain, ed. *Social Work Practice: People and Environment.* New York: Columbia University Press, 1979.

Hearn, G. *Theory Building in Social Work.* Toronto: University of Toronto Press, 1958.

Hilgard, E. "The Place of Gestalt Psychology and Field Theories in Contemporary Learning Theory." In E. Hilgard, ed. *Theories of Learning and Instruction,* Chicago: University of Chicago Press, 1964.

Hoffman, L. "Deviation—Amplifying Processes in Natural Groups." In J. Haley, ed. *Changing Families: A Family Therapy Reader.* New York: Grune and Stratton, 1971.

Hollander, E.P. *Leadership, Groups and Influence.* New York: Oxford University Press, 1964.

Homans, G. *The Human Group.* New York: Harcourt Brace Jovanovich, 1950.

Hopper, E., and Weyman, A. "A Sociological View of Large Groups." In L. Kreeger, ed. *The Large Group: Dynamics and Therapy.* Itasca, IL: F.E. Peacock, 1975.

Hudson, W.W. "A Measurement Package for Clinical Workers." Paper presented at the council on Social Work Education 23rd Annual Program Meeting, Pheonix, AZ: March 1, 1977.

Inkeles, A. As quoted in G.V. Coelho et al., eds. *Coping and Adaptation.* New York: Basic Books, 1974.

Jaques, E. *Work, Creativity and Social Justice.* New York: International Universities Press, 1970.

Kalson, L. "Group Therapy with the Aged." In M. Seligman, ed. *Group Counseling and Group Psychotherapy with Rehabilitation Clients.* Springfield, IL: Charles C. Thomas, 1977.

Kelly, J. "Toward an Ecological Conception of Preventive Interventions." In J.W. Carter, ed. *Research Contributions from Psychology to Community Mental Health.* New York: Behavioral Publications, 1968. Also in D. Adelson and B.L. Kalis, eds. *Community Psychology and Mental Health: Perspectives and Challenges.* Scranton, PA: Chandler Publishing Co., 1970.

Kernberg, P.F., and Ware, L.M. "Understanding Child Development Through Group Techniques and Play." *Bulletin of the Menninger Clinic,* vol. 39, 1975.

Klein, A.F. *Social Work Through Group Process.* Albany: State University of New York, 1970.

Klein, A.F. *Effective Group Work.* New York: Association Press, 1972.

Klein, D.C. *Community Dynamics and Mental Health.* New York: John Wiley, 1968.

Knight, C.B. *Basic Concepts of Ecology.* New York: Macmillan, 1965.

Kluckhohn, C. As quoted in D. Leighton et al., eds. *The Character of Danger.* New York: Basic Books, 1963.

Konopka, G. *Social Group Work: A Helping Process.* Englewood Cliffs, NJ: Prentice-Hall, 1963.

Krill, D.F. "Existentialism: A Philosophy for Our Current Resolutions." *Social Service Review*, vol. 40, September 1966.

Kroeber, A.L., and Kluckhohn, C. *Culture: A Critical Review of Concepts and Definitions.* Cambridge: Harvard University 1952.

Leighton, A.H. *My Name is Legion.* New York: Basic Books, 1959 and 1968 editions.

Levinson, D. *The Seasons of a Man's Life.* New York: Basic Books, 1978.

Levitsky, A., and Perls, F. "The Rules and Games of Gestalt Therapy." In J. Fagen and I.L. Shepard, eds. *Gestalt Therapy Now.* New York: Harper & Row, 1970.

Levitsky, A., and Simkin, J.S. "Gestalt Therapy." In L.N. Solomon and B. Berzon, eds. *New Perspectives in Encounter Groups.* San Francisco: Jossey Bass Publishers, 1972.

Lewin, K. *Principles of Topological Psychology.* New York: McGraw, 1936.

Lewin, K. "The Conceptual Representation and Measurement of Psychological Forces." *Contributions to Psychology Theory*, vol. 1, 1938.

Lewin, K. Lippitt, R. and White, R.K. "Patterns of Aggressive Behavior in Experimentally Created "Social Climates", *Journal of Psychology*, vol. 10, 1939.

Lewin, K. *Resolving Social Conflicts: Selected Papers on Group Dynamics.* G.W. Lewin, ed. New York: Harper, 1948.

Lewin, K. *Field Theory in Social Science: Selected Theoretical Papers.* D. Cartwright, ed. New York: Harper, 1951.

Lieberman, M.A. "Up the Right Mountain, Down the Wrong Path: Theory Development for People Changing Groups." *Journal of Applied Behavioral Science*, vol. 10, No. 2, 1974.

Lieberman, M.A. "Change Induction in Small Groups." *Annual Review of Psychology*, vol. 27, 1976.

Lieberman, M.A.; Borman, L.D. and Associates. *Self-Help Groups for Coping with Crisis.* San Francisco, CA: Jossey-Bass Publishers, 1979.

Lieberman, M.A.; Yalom, I.D.; and Miles, M.B. *Encounter Groups: First Facts.* New York: Basic Books, 1973.

Linton, R. *The Study of Man.* New York: Appleton-Century-Crofts, 1938.

Litwin, G.H., and Stringer, R.A., Jr. *Motivation and Organizational Climate.* Boston: Harvard University, 1968.

Lloyd, G.A. *The Culture and Politics of Social Work.* San Jose: San Jose State University, 1978.

Lothstein, L.M. "The Group Psychotherapy Dropout Phenomena Revisited." *American Journal of Psychiatry*, vol. 13, No. 12, 1978.

Lowly, L. "Decision-Making and Group Work." In S. Bernstein, ed. *Explorations in Group Work.* Boston: Boston University School of Social Work, 1965.

Lowy, L. "Goal Formulation in Social Work Groups." In S. Bernstein, ed. *Further Explorations in Group Work.* Boston: Boston University School of Social Work, 1970.

Luft, J. *Group Process.* Palo Alto, CA: National Press Books, 1963.

Lurie, W. "Intergroup Relations." in *The Encyclopedia of Social Work.* New York: National Association of Social Workers, 1965.

322

Maier, H.W. "Some Reflections on Three Papers." In *A Conceptual Framework for Teaching of the Social Group Work Method in the Classroom.* New York: Council on Social Work Education, 1964.

Maier, H.W. "Human Functioning as an Interpersonal Whole: The Dimensions of Affect, Behavior, and Cognition." In *Teaching for Competence in the Delivery of Social Services.* New York: Council on Social Work Education, 1976.

Maluccio, A.N., and Marlow, W.D. "The Case for Contract." *Social Work,* vol. 19, January 1974.

Manis, J.G., and Meltzer, B.N., eds. *Symbolic Interaction: A Reader in Social Psychology.* Boston: Allyn and Bacon, 1978.

Mann, R. *Interpersonal Styles and Group Development.* New York: John Wiley, 1967.

Marrow, A.J. *The Practical Theorist.* New York: Basic Books, 1969.

Marsden, G. "Content Analysis Studies of Psychotherapy: 1954 through 1968." In A.E. Bergin and S.L. Garfield, eds. *Handbook of Psychotherapy and Behavior Change: An Empirical Analysis.* New York: John Wiley, 1971.

McDaniel, C.O., and Balgopal, P.R. *A Three-Dimensional Analysis of Black Leadership.* Houston: University of Houston, Graduate School of Social Work, 1978.

McGee, T.F., and Shuman, B.N. "The Nature of Co-therapy Relationship." *International Journal of Group Psychotherapy,* vol. 20, No. 1., 1970.

Mead, G.H. *Mind, Self and Society.* Chicago: University of Chicago Press, 1934.

Meltzer, B.N. "Mead's Social Psychology." In J.G. Manis and B.N. Meltzer, eds. *Symbolic Interaction: A Reader in Social Psychology.* Boston: Allyn and Bacon, 1978.

Meltzoff, J.E., and Kornreich, M. *Research in Psychotherapy.* New York: Atherton Press, 1970.

Merten, D., and Schwartz, G. "The Language of Adolescence: An Anthropological Approach to Youth Culture." *American Journal of Sociology,* vol. 72, March 1967.

Merton, R.K. *Social Theory and Social Structure.* Rev. Ed. New York: The Free Press, 1966.

Meyer, C. "What Directions for Direct Practice." *Social Work,* vol. 24, No. 4, July 1979.

Middleman, R.R. *The Non-Verbal Method in Working with Groups.* New York: Association Press, 1968.

Middleman R.R. "The Use of Program." *Social Work with Groups,* vol. 3, No. 3, Fall 1980.

Miles, M., ed. "On Temporary Systems." In *Innovation in Education.* New York: Columbia University Press, 1964 and 1968.

Miller, W.B. "Lower Class Culture as a Generating Milieu of Gang Delinquency." *The Journal of Social Issues,* vol. 14, No. 3, 1958.

Mills, T.M. *Group Transformation.* Englewood Cliffs, NJ: Prentice-Hall, 1964.

Mills, T.M. *The Sociology of Small Groups.* Englewood Cliffs, NJ: Prentice-Hall, 1967.

Miyamoto, F.S., and Dornbusgh, S.M. "A Test of Interactionist Hypothesis of Self Conception." *American Journal of Sociology,* vol. 61, March 1956.

Moos, R. *Evaluating Treatment Environments*. New York: John Wiley, 1974.

Moos, R., and Houts, P.S. "Assessment of Social Atmospheres of Psychiatric Wards." *Journal of Abnormal Psychology*, vol. 73, 1968.

Moos, R., and Houts, P. "Differential Effects of the Social Atmosphere of Psychiatric Wards." *Human Relations*, vol. 23, February 1970.

Munson, C.E., and Balgopal, P.R. "The Worker-Client Relationship: Relevant Role Theory." *Journal of Sociology and Social Welfare*, vol. 5, No. 3, May 1978.

Murphy, M. "Social Causes: The Independent Variables." in Kaplan, B. et. al., eds. *Further Exploration in Social Psychiatry*. New York: Basic Books, 1976.

National Association of Social Workers. *Proposal for the Future Delivery of Social Services: Position of the Western Coalition*. NASW Delegate Assembly 1971 (mimeo).

Neighbor, J.E. et. al. "An Approach to the Selection of Patients for Group Psychotherapy." In M. Rosenbaum; and M. Berger. *Group Psychotherapy and Group Function*. New York: Basic Books, 1975.

Northen, H. *Social Work with Groups*. New York: Columbia University Press, 1969.

Northen, H. "Psychosocial Practice in Small Groups." In R.W. Roberts and H. Northen, eds. *Theories of Social Work with Groups*. New York: Columbia University Press, 1976.

Northen, H., and Roberts, R.W. "Status of Theory." In R.W. Roberts and H. Northen, eds. *Theories of Social Work with Groups*. New York: Columbia University Press, 1976.

Odum, E.P. *Fundamentals of Ecology*. Philadelphia: W.B. Saunders, 1961.

Papell, C., and Rothman, B. "Social Group Work Models: Possession and Heritage." *Journal of Education for Social Work*, vol. 2, Fall 1966.

Park, R.E. As quoted in N.S. Timasheff. *Sociological Theory: Its Nature and Growth*. New York: Random House, 1961.

Parsons, T. *Essays in Sociological Theory, Pure and Applied*. Glencoe, IL: The Free Press, 1949.

Pawlak, E.J., and Vassil, T.V. "Prestructuring Cooperation Among Acting-Out Youth." *Social Work with Groups*, vol. 3, No. 1, Spring 1980.

Perls, F. *Ego, Hunger, and Aggression*. London: Allen and Unwin, 1947.

Perls, F. *Gestalt Therapy Verbatim*, Lafayette, CA: Real People Press, 1969.

Perls, F.; Hefferline, R.F.; and Goodman, P. *Gestalt Therapy*, New York: Delta Books, 1951.

Pfeiffer, J.W., and Heslin, R. *Instrumentation in Human Relations Training*. LaJolla, CA: University Associates, 1973.

Phillips, G. *Communication and the Small Group*. New York: Bobbs-Merrill, 1973.

Phillips, H.U. *Essentials of Social Group Work Skills*. New York: Association Press, 1957.

Polansky, N. et. al. "An Investigation of Behavior Contagion in Groups." *Human Relations*, vol. 3, 1950.

Polster, E., and Polster, M. *Gestalt Therapy Integrated*. New York: Brunner Mazel Publishers, 1973.

President's Commission on Mental Health. *Commission Report,* vol. 1. Washington D.C.: Government Printing Office, 1978.

Quinn, J. "Ecological Versus Social Interactions." *Sociology and Social Research,* vol. 18, 1933–1934.

Rappaport, J. *Community Psychology: Values, Research and Action,* New York: Holt, Rinehart and Winston, 1977.

Rausch, H.L. et. al. "The Interpersonal Behavior of Children in Residential Treatment." *Journal of Abnormal Psychology,* vol. 58 (1959).

Rayner, E. *Human Development.* 2d ed. London: George Allen and Unwin, 1978.

Redl, F. "The Phenomenon of Contagion and Shock Effect in Group Therapy." In W. Healy and A. Bronner, eds. *Searchlights on Delinquency.* New York: International Universities Press, 1949.

Redl, F. "The Art of Group Composition." In S. Schulze, ed. *Creative Group Living in a Children's Institution.* New York: Association Press, 1951.

Redl, F. "The Concept of the Therapeutic Milieu." In *When We Deal with Children.* New York: The Free Press, 1966.

Rioch, M.J. "The Work of Wilfred Bion on Groups." *Psychiatry,* vol. 33, 1970.

Ripple, L. *Motivation, Capacity and Opportunity.* Social Service Monographs, Second Series, Chicago: University of Chicago, School of Social Service Administration, 1964.

Roberts, R.W., and Northen, H., eds. *Theories of Social Work with Groups.* New York: Columbia University press, 1977.

Rogers, C. As quoted by D. Offer and M. Sabshin in *Normality.* New York: Basic Books, 1964.

Rogers, E.M. and Shoemaker, F.F. *Communication of Innovations.* 2d ed. New York: The Free Press, 1971.

Rose, A.M. "A Systematic Summary of Symbolic Interaction Theory." In A. Rose, ed. *Human Behavior and Social Process.* New York: Houghton-Mifflin, 1962.

Rose, A.M., ed. *Human Behavior and Social Processes.* Boston: Houghton-Mifflin, 1962.

Rose, S.D. *Group Therapy: A Behavioral Approach.* Englewood Cliffs, NJ: Prentice-Hall, 1977.

Ruesch, J. *Therapeutic Communications.* New York: W.W. Norton, 1961.

Russell, B. *The Impact of Science on Society.* New York: Columbia University Press, 1951. As quoted in H.L. Wilensky and C.N. Lebeaux. *Industrial Society and Social Welfare.* New York: The Free Press, 1965.

Sampson, E.E., and Marthas, M.S. *Group Process for the Health Professions.* New York: John Wiley, 1977.

Sarri, R.C., and Galinsky, M.J. "A Conceptual Framework for Group Development." In R.D. Vinter, ed. *Readings in Group Work Practice.* Ann Arbor: Campus Publishers, 1967.

Scheerer, M. "Problem Solving." *Scientific American.* March 1963.

Schniderman, L. "The Value Commitment of Social Work: Some Underlying Assumptions." In R. W. Klenk and R.M. Ryan, eds. *The Practice of Social Work.* Belmont, CA: Wadsworth Publishing Co., 1974.

Schonfield, J. "Psychological Factors Related to Delayed Return to an Earlier Life Style in Successfully Treated Cancer Patients." *Journal of Psychosamatic Research,* vol. 16, February 1972.

Schulman, I. "Delinquents." In S.R. Slavson, ed. *The Fields of Group Psychotherapy.* New York: International Universities Press, 1956.

Schutz, W.C. *The Interpersonal Underworld.* Palo Alto, CA: Science and Behavior Books, 1958.

Schutz, W.C. "On Group Composition." *Journal of Abnormal Social Psychology,* vol. 62, 1961.

Schutz, W.C. *Joy: Expanding Human Awareness.* New York: Grove Press, 1967.

Schutz, W.C., and Seashore, C. "Promoting Growth with Non-Verbal Exercises. In L.N. Solomon and B. Berzon, eds. *New Perspectives in Encounter Groups.* San Francisco: Jossey Bass Publishers, 1972.

Schwartz, W. "The Social Worker in the Group." In *New Perspectives to Groups: Theory Organization and Practice.* New York: National Association of Social Workers, 1961.

Schwartz, W. "On the Use of Groups in Social Work Practice." In W. Schwartz And S.R. Zalba, eds. *The Practice of Group Work.* New York: Columbia University Press, 1971.

Schwartz, W. "Between Client and System: The Mediating Function." In R.W. Roberts and H. Northen, eds. *Theories of Social Work with Groups.* New York: Columbia University Press, 1976.

Seabury, B.A. "The Arrangement of Physical Space in Social Work Settings." *Social Work,* vol. 16, No. 4, October 1971.

Seabury, B.A. "The Contract: Uses, Abuses, and Limitations." *Social Work,* vol. 21, January 1976.

Shaw, M.E., and Constanza, P. *Theories of Social Psychology.* New York: McGraw-Hill, 1970.

Shaw, M.E. *Group Dynamics: The Psychology of Small Group Behavior.* New York: McGraw-Hill, 1971.

Sherif, M. *The Psychology of Social Norm.* New York: Harper & Row, 1936.

Sherif, M. *Social Interaction.* Chicago: Aldine Publishing Co., 1967.

Shibutani, T. "Reference Groups as a Perspective." In J.G. Manis and B.N. Meltzer, eds. *Symbolic Interaction: A Reader in Social Psychology.* Boston: Allyn and Bacon, 1978.

Shostrom, E. "Group Therapy: Let the Buyer Be Aware." In Diedrich and Dye eds. *Group Procedures: Purposes and Processes.* New York: Houghton Mifflin, 1972.

Shulman, L. "Scapegoats, Group Workers and Pre-emptive Intervention." *Social Work,* vol. 12, April, 1967.

Shulman, L. "Program in Group Work: Another Look." In W. Schwartz and S.R. Zelba, eds. *The Practice of Group Work.* New York: Columbia University Press, 1971.

Shulman, L. *The Skills of Helping.* Itasca, IL: F.E. Peacock, 1979.

Silbergeld, S. et. al. "Assessment of Environment-Therapy Systems: The Group Atmosphere Scale." *Journal of Consulting and Clinical Psychology,* vol. 43, No. 4, 1975.

Silbergeld, S. et. al. "The Psychosocial Environment in Group Therapy Evaluation." *International Journal of Group Psychotherapy*, vol. 27, No. 2, April 1977.

Simkovitch, M.K. "The Settlement Primer." New York: National Federation of Settlements, 1936.

Simmel, G. *Conflict.* (1919) Translated K.H. Wolff, Glencoe, IL: The Free Press, 1955.

Siporin, M. "Ecological Systems Theory in Social Work." *Journal of Sociology and Social Welfare,* vol. 7 No. 4, 1980.

Slater, P.E. "Contrasting Correlates of Group Size." *Sociometry*, vol. 21, June 1958.

Slater, P.E. "Deification as an Antidote to Deprivation." In T. Mills and S. Rosenberg, eds. *Readings on the Sociology of Small Groups.* Englewood Cliffs, NJ: Prentice-Hall, 1970.

Somers, M.L. "Group Process in the Family Unit." Unpublished Paper, University of Chicago, 1976.

Somers, M.L. "Problem Solving in Small Groups." In R.W. Roberts and H. Northen, eds. *Theories of Social Work with Groups.* New York: Columbia University Press, 1976.

Sommer, R. "Studies in Personal Space." *Sociometry*, vol. 22, 1959.

Specht, H. "Social Trends." In H. Specht and A. Vickery, eds. *Integrating Social Work Methods.* London: George Allen and Unwin, 1977.

Spergel, I. *The Street Gang Work: Theory and Practice.* Reading, MA: Addison-Wesley, 1966.

Spergel, I. "Interactions Between Community Structure, Delinquency and Social Policy in the Inner City." In M.W. Klein, ed. *The Juvenile Justice System.* Beverly Hills, CA: Sage Publications, 1976.

Spiegel, J.P. *Transactions.* New York: Science House, 1971.

Stebbins, R. "Role Distance, Role Distance Behavior and Jazz Musicians." In D. Brissett and C. Edgley, eds. *Life as a Theatre: A Dramaturgical Sourcebook.* Chicago: Aldine Publishers, 1975.

Steiner, I.D. *Group Process and Productivity.* New York: Academic Press, 1972.

Stock, D., and Thelen, H.A. *Emotional Dynamics and Group Culture.* New York: National Training Laboratory, New York: University Press, 1958.

Stogdill, R.M. *Handbook of Leadership: A Survey of Theory and Research.* New York: The Free Press, 1974.

Stroup, H. "The Cultural Context of Social Work." In *The Social Work Yearbook.* New York: National Association of Social Workers, 1957.

Sullivan, H.S. *The Interpersonal Theory of Psychiatry.* New York: W.W. Norton, 1953.

Sulzer, E.S. "Reinforcement and the Therapeutic Contract." *Journal of Counselling Psychology,* vol. 9, Fall 1962.

Suttles, G.D. *The Social Order of the Slum.* Chicago: University of Chicago Press, 1968.

Thelen, H.A. "Human Dynamics: A Proposed Conceptual Framework." *Journal of Social Issues,* vol. 6, No. 2, 1950.

Thelen, H.A. *Dynamics of Group at Work.* Chicago: University of Chicago, 1954 and 1968.

Thelen, H.A. "Work—Emotionality Theory of the Group as Organism." In S. Koch, ed. *Psychology: A Study of Science,* vol. 3, 1959.

Thelen, H.A. "The Educational Ethos of the Midwestern High School." Unpublished Paper, Chicago: University of Chicago, 1974.

Thomas, C., and Garrison, V. "A General Systems View of Community Mental Health." in L. Bellak and H.H. Barten, eds. *Progress in Community Mental Health,* vol. 1, New York: Grune and Stratton, 1969.

Trecker, H. *Social Group Work.* New York: Whitside, 1955.

Tropp, E. *A Humanistic Foundation for Group Work Practice.* New York: Selected Academic Readings, 1972.

Truax, C.B., and Mitchell, K.M. "Research on Certain Therapist Interpersonal Skills in Relation to Process and Outcome." In A.E. Bergin and S.L. Garland, eds. *Handbook of Psychotherapy and Behavior Change.* New York: John Wiley, 1971.

Tuckman, B.W. "Development Sequences in Small Groups." *Psychological Bulletin,* vol. 63, 1965.

Turner, J.H. *The Structure of Sociological Theory.* Homewood, IL: The Dorsey Press, 1974.

Underwood, W. "Roles That Facilitate and Inhibit Group Development." In R.T. Golembiewski and A. Blumberg, eds. *Sensitivity Training and Laboratory Approach.* Itasca, IL: F.E. Peacock, 1977.

Vaillant, G. *Adaptation to Life.* Boston: Little, Brown, 1977.

Vassil, T.V. "Residential Family Camping: Altering Family Patterns." *Social Casework,* vol. 59, No. 10, December 1978.

Vinter, R.D. "Social Group Work." In H.L. Lurie, ed. *Encyclopedia of Social Work.* New York: National Association of Social Workers, 1965.

Vinter, R.D. "Program Activities: An Analysis of Their Effects on Participant Behavior." In R.D. Vinter, ed. *Readings in Group Work Practice.* Ann Arbor, MI: Campus Publishers, 1967.

Vinter, R.D. "The Essential Components of Social Group Work Practice." In R. D. Vinter, ed. *Reading in Group Work Practice.* Ann Arbor, MI: Campus Publishers, 1967.

Vinter, R.D. "An Approach to Group Work Practice." In P. Glasser; R. Sarri; and R. Vinter, eds. *Individual Change Through Small Groups.* New York. The Free Press, 1974.

Walberg, H. "Social Environments as Mediator of Classroom Learning." *Journal of Educational Psychology,* vol. 60, 1969.

Weiss, P. As quoted in D. Leighton et. al., eds. *Character of Danger.* New York: Basic Books, 1963.

White, R.W. *Ego and Reality in Psychoanalytic Theory.* New York: International Universities Press, 1963.

White, R.W. "Strategies of Adaptation: An Attempt at Systematic Description" in G.V. Coelho, D.A. Hamburg and J.E. Adams, eds. *Coping and Adaptation,* New York: Basic Books, 1974.

White, R., and Lippitt, R. "Leadership Behavior and Member Reaction in Three Social Climates." In D. Cartwright and A. Zander, eds. *Group Dynamics,* 2d ed. New York: Harper & Row, 1960.

Whitman, R.M. "Psychodynamics Principles Underlying T-Group Process." In L.P. Bradford; J.R. Gibb; and K.D. Benne, eds. *T-Group Theory and Laboratory Method.* New York: John Wiley, 1964.

Whittaker, J.K. "Program Activities: Their Selection and Use in Therapeutic Milieu." In P. Glasser, et. al. eds. *Individual Change Through Small Groups.* New York: The Free Press, 1974.

Whittaker, J.K. "Differential Use of Program Activities." *Child Welfare,* July/August 1975.

Wilson, G. "From Practice to Theory: A Personalized History." In R.W. Roberts and H. Northen, eds. *Theories of Social Work with Groups.* New York: Columbia University Press, 1976.

Wilson, G., and Ryland, G. *Social Group Work Practice.* Cambridge, MA: Houghton, Mifflin, 1948 and Cambridge, MA: Riverside Press, 1949.

Yalom, I.D. *The Theory and Practice of Group Psychotherapy.* New York: Basic Books, 1970 and 1975 editions.

Yelaja, S.A. *Authority and Social Work: Concepts and the Use.* Toronto: University of Toronto, 1971.

Index

A

Ackerman, N.W., 164, 165
Adaptation, 31–34, 45, 281, 282
Addams, J., 6
Alienation, 93
Alienative involvement, 80
Alissi, A.S., 40
Allogenic conflict, 47, 173–78, 291
Anderson, B.N., 230
Anderson, J.P., 5
Argyris, C., 235, 282, 307
Asch, S., 184, 185
Assessment, 119–30
Attneave, C. L., 39
Auerswald, E.H., 21, 30
Authenticity, 98–99, 176, 239–40, 288

B

Bach, G., 120–21
Bales, R.F., 57, 75, 83, 179, 180, 190, 194, 202, 298
Balgopal, P.R., 9, 47, 52, 71, 95, 97–98, 99, 159, 174, 214, 234, 240, 284, 286, 291
Bard, M., 34
Barker, R., 40
Bartlett, H.M., 100
Beall, L., 139
Beck, A.P., 165
Bednar, R.L., 199, 229
Behaviorism, 13, 15–16, 17
Beiser, M., 35–36, 87
Bell, N.W., 166, 167
Benjamin, S.E., 230
Benne, K.D., 68, 179, 202, 295
Bennis, W.G., 20, 157, 202, 282
Berne, E., 14, 15
Bernstein, S., 11, 169, 170, 171, 172
Bertcher, H., 121, 123
Biddle, B., 179
Bierstedt, R., 216
Bion, W.R., 163, 202

Bird, C., 218
Birnbaum, M., 174, 175
Blumer, H., 52
Bonner, H., 76, 179, 184
Borman, L.D., 309
Bott, E., 39
Bradburn, N.S., 34–35
Bradsma, J., 247, 249
Brenner, C., 163
Briar, S., 4, 80
Bruner, J.S., 84, 284

C

Calculative involvement, 80
Capacities, 113
    affective, 82–87
    cognitive, 83–85
    flexibility, 88
    individual, 81–83
    internal, 83
    interpersonal, 87–88
    perceptual, 85–86
    social functioning, 89–90
Cartwright, D., 74, 150, 185, 186, 215
Chaiklin, H., 306
Clarification, 269
Cloward, R., 40
Cognitive restructuring, 253–56
Cohen, A.M., 310
Cohen, S.P., 75, 83, 313
Cohesion, 198, 204, 206, 209. 211, 212, 299
Commensalism, 126–28
Communities, 40–42, 49
Competence, 34–36
Composition, 119–30, 161, 177
Compton, B.R., 140, 141
Conflict, 44, 45, 46, 47, 150, 166, 194, 198, 203, 204, 206, 209, 211, 212, 259, 280, 299
Confrontation, 242–45
Conover, M.B., 6
Constanza, P., 178

Contagion, 158
Containment, 265
Continuity, 26, 27
Contracting, 135–43, 160
  ecological perspective, 139–42
  group work, 136
  phases, 138–39
  practice principles, 142–43
  secondary contract, 139, 161
Cooley, C.H., 169
Cooper, G.B., 214
Corbin, A.L., 136
Coser, L.A., 162, 166, 169, 171, 172
Co-therapists (*See* Leadership)
Cottrell, L.S., 42
Coyle, G.L., 130
Croog, S., 38
Croxton, T.A., 135, 136, 137, 138
Cultural pluralism, 45

D

Deutsch, M., 66, 67, 169, 173, 204, 259
Developmental model, 11–12
Dewey, J., 4, 7, 12
Dinoff, M., 138
Diversity, 26–27, 125–26, 129
Dornbusgh, S.M., 190
Duncan, S.D., Jr., 86
Dunphy, D.C., 75, 207
Durkin, H. E., 173

E

Ecology, 20
Ecosystem, 25–26
Empathy, 236–38
Energy, 124–25, 129
Ephross, P.H., 9, 284, 286
Etzioni, A., 80
Exploration, 249–50

F

Fagan, J., 14
Family, 36–37
Farrelly, F., 247–49
Feldman, R., 15, 164, 165, 190
Fiedler, F.E., 214
Follett, M.P., 6, 12, 169, 170
Formed groups, 148, 149
Frank, J.D., 121
Freud, A., 163
Fromm, E., 51

G

Galinsky, M.J., 193, 198, 199, 203, 204, 205
Galaway, B., 140, 141
Gans, H.J., 40
Garfield, S.L., 229
Garland, J.A., 165, 193, 198, 199, 200, 202, 203, 204, 205, 209, 210, 211, 284
Garrison, V., 29–30
Garvin, C.D., 103
Gendlin, E.T., 239
Genuineness, 239–40
Germain, C.G., 21–22, 100, 281
Gestalt therapy, 13–14, 17
Getzels, J.W., 105, 109
Gibb, C.A., 214, 218
Glaser, J.S., 37, 38
Glasser, P.H., 10, 103
Glidewell, J.C., 47, 93, 198, 201, 203, 204, 205, 206, 283,
Goals, 2, 5, 130–35, 160, 178, 186
  avowed, 133–35
  long-term, 133–34
  short-term, 133–35
  unavowed, 133–35
Goffman, E., 97, 166
Goldschmidt, W., 92
Goldstein, H., 137
Golebiewski, R., 152, 195
Gordon, W. E., 2, 100
Greene, G., 59–65
Group boundaries, 44–45, 186
Group conflict, 168–78
  implication for practice, 173–78
  positive function, 169–73
Group culture, 188–90, 193–97
Group development, 157–59, 175, 193–212
  principles of, 211–12
  stages, 197–212
Group exchange, 46–47
Group habitat, 43–44
Group process, 118–19, 155–56, 176
Group resources, 45–46
Group structure, 118–19
Group worker, 47. (*See also* Leadership)
Gump, P., 40
Gunther, B., 145

H

Hambruger, H., 151
Handlin, O., 3
Hare, A.P., 148, 149–50, 151, 194, 285
Hartford, M.E., 4, 95, 119, 123, 132, 150, 151, 157, 158, 198, 199, 200, 203, 204, 205, 209, 210, 281
Hartman, A., 22

Hearn, G., 196
Heslin, R., 314
Heterogeneous groups, 123
Hilgard, E., 84
Hoffman, L., 164
Holism, 29–31
Holistic approach, 115, 116
Hollander, E.P., 215, 237
Homans, G., 185
Homogeneous groups, 123
Hopper, A., 151
Houts, P., 39, 312
Hudson,W. W., 314
Humor, 87, 245–49
Hull, R.F., 159, 234

I

Identification, 163
Impiric, 306–308
Inkeles, A., 29
Innovation, 105, 106–107
Interactions, 27–28, 46, 48, 49, 96
Interdependence, 126, 129
Introjection, 163
Involuntary status, 80

J

Jaques, E., 85, 207
Jones, H.E., 198

K

Kalson, L., 149
Kaul, R.J., 199
Kelly, J., 21, 25, 124, 281
Kernberg, P.F., 146
Klein, A.F., 101, 122, 137, 143, 164, 165, 170
Klein, D.C., 108, 151
Kluckhohn, C., 20–21, 189
Knight, C.B., 126
Kolodny, R.L., 165, 198
Konopka, G., 131, 146, 147
Kornreich, M., 199
Krauss, R.M., 67
Krill, D.F., 98
Kroeber, A.L., 189

L

Lawlis, G.F., 199, 229
Leadership
  co-leadership, 158, 229–34
ecology, 219–22
empathy, 236–38
genuineess, 239, 240
interventions, 235–80
Lewin, 219–22
Mead, 219–22
member induction, 223–29
roles, 213–16
self-disclosure, 176, 240–42
structure and process, 222–23
style, 216–17
warmth, 238–39
Leadership orientations, 105–6
Leighton, A.H., 29, 33, 35, 41–42, 84, 86
Levinson, D., 89
Levitsky, A., 98, 145, 239
Lewinian Change Principles, 68–71
Lewin, K., 49, 66, 92, 99, 166, 169, 189, 195, 217
Lewinian Field Theory, 66–73, 155
Lieberman, M.A., 219, 308, 309
Linton, R., 179
Lippitt, R., 166, 189
Litwin, G.H., 40
Lloyd, G.A., 100
Lowy, L., 11–12, 132
Luft, J., 155
Lurie, W., 5, 130

M

Maier, H.W., 257, 302
Maladaptation, 79
Maluccio, A.N., 135, 136, 137
Manis, J.G., 53–55, 73, 74
Mann, R., 198, 200, 201, 204, 206, 210
Maple, F., 121, 123
Marlow, W.D., 135, 136, 137
Marrow, A.J., 156
Marsden, G., 309
Marthas, M.S., 57, 58
McDaniel, C.O., 214
McGaugh, G.R., 214
McGee, T.F., 230
Mead, G.H., 49, 52, 53, 195
Mediating Model, 10–11
Meltzer, B.N., 52, 53–55, 73, 74
Meltzoff, J.E., 199
Merten, D., 93
Merton, R.K., 106
Meyer, C., 100, 111
Middleman, R.R., 143, 144, 146, 261
Miles, M., 70, 108, 189, 206
Miller, H., 80
Miller, W.B., 40
Mills, T.M., 56, 198, 201, 204, 206, 209, 210, 211

Mitchell, K.M., 288
Miyamoto, F.S., 190
Modeling, 271–73
Moos, R., 39, 110, 312
Moral involvement, 80–81
Munson, C.E., 52, 97–98, 99
Murphy, M., 38

N

N.A.S.W., 94, 100
Natural groups, 148, 149
Natural habitat, 25, 48, 94
Neighborhoods, 40–42, 49
Neutralism, 126–28
Nonobligatory mutualism, 126–28
Norms, 184–91
  culture, 188–90
  implications for practice, 190–191
Northen, H., 12–13, 17, 122, 132, 143, 144, 149, 150–51, 155, 164, 165, 170–71, 172, 186, 193, 197, 198, 199, 200, 201, 202, 203, 204, 205, 209, 210, 211

O

Objectivity, 97
Obligatory mutualism, 126–28
Odum, E.P., 25
Ohlin, L.E., 40
Organizations, 39–40

P

Papell, C., 9, 281
Parasitism, 126–28
Park, R.E., 21
Partializing, 268–69
Patterning, 307–308
Pawlak, E.J., 261, 298
Perls, F., 14, 145
Pfeiffer, J.W., 314
Phillips, G., 157
Phillips, H.U., 131
Polansky, N., 158
Polster, E., 14
Polster, M., 14
Powdermaker, F.B., 121, 122
President's Commission on Mental Health, 18
Programming, 143–48, 161, 260–63
  ecological perspective, 147–48
  practice principles, 148
  rationale, 146–47
Projection, 162–63

Q

Quinn, J., 25

R

Rappaport, J., 18, 21
Rayner, E., 88
Redl, F., 40, 120, 158, 189
Remedial model, 9–10
Resocialization, 103–104
Resources, 124–25, 129
Rioch, M.J., 163
Ripple, L., 82
Roberts, R.W., 12–13, 17
Rogers, C., 85
Rogers, E.M., 106
Role distance, 97–98
Role embracement, 97
Role play, 256–260
Roles, 178–184
  implications for practice, 182–84
Rose, A.M., 53
Rose, S.D., 15
Rothman, B., 9, 281
Ruesch, J., 93
Russell, B., 2
Ryland, G., 5, 7, 170, 172

S

Sampson, E.E., 57, 58
Sarri, R.C., 193, 198, 199, 203, 204, 205
Scapegoating, 162–68
  dynamics of, 162–64
  group process, 166–67
  implications for practice, 167–68
  victim, 164–65
Scheerer, M., 255
Schon, D.A., 282, 307
Schniderman, L., 141
Schonfield, J., 34
Schulman, I., 163
Schuman, B.N., 230
Schutz, W.C., 88, 121, 122, 145, 146, 295
Schwartz, G., 93
Schwartz W., 10–11, 17, 21, 132, 196, 206
Seabury, B.A., 40, 135, 138, 139
Seashore, C., 146
Self-disclosure, 176, 186, 204–42
Sensitivity training, 91
Sequencing, 263–64
Setting limits, 265–68
Shaw, M.E., 157, 178, 218
Sheats, P., 179, 295
Shepard, H.A., 157

Shepherd, I.L., 14
Sherif, M., 56, 184
Shibutani, T., 56
Shoemaker, F.F., 106
Shostrom, E., 151
Shulman, L., 144, 148, 164, 196, 203, 211
Silbergeld, S., 190, 312
Silence, 264
Simkin, J.S., 98, 239
Simkovitch, M.K., 6
Simmel, G., 169, 203
Siporin, M., 22, 26
Size, 148-53, 157, 161
Slater, P.E., 20, 150, 151, 152, 210, 282
Smith, R.D., 310
Social control, 81
Social environment, 36-43, 90-91
Socialization, 103-104
Social networks, 37-39
Somers, M.L., 4-5, 13, 37-38, 42
Sommer, R., 40
Specht, H., 99
Speck, R.V., 39
Spergel, I., 40, 42, 267, 279
Spiegel, J.P., 28
Spontaneity, 86-87
Steiner, I.D., 148, 150
Stock, D., 75, 190, 208
Stogdill, R.M., 218
Stoodtbeck, F.L., 194
Stringer, R.A., Jr., 40
Stroup, H., 6
Subgroups, 150, 156-62
  development, 156-58
  impact on group process, 159-60
  implications for practice, 160-62
Subjectivity, 97
Sullivan, H.S., 86
Sulzer, E.S., 138
Summarizing, 250-52
Support, 252-53
Sutherland, A.M., 34
Suttles, G.D., 40
Symbolic Interaction
  basic propositions, 53-55
  perspective, 52-53
  significance for group work, 55-66

T

Temporary Systems, 107-9, 111-12
T-groups, 91
Thelan, H.A., 40, 75, 96, 105, 109, 163, 166, 171, 175, 188, 190, 195, 208
Thomas, A.E.J., 179
Thomas, C., 29-30

Timing, 264-68
Transactional Analysis, 13-15, 17
Transactions, 27-28, 46, 48, 49
Trecker, H., 5, 131
Tropp, E., 6
Truax, C.B., 288
Turner, J.H., 75

U

Underwood, W., 223
Universalization, 169-71

V

Vaillant, G., 31-32, 87, 236, 245
Vassil, T.V., 9, 37, 38, 47, 52, 71, 95, 174, 240, 256, 261, 291, 298, 299
Vinter, R.D., 9, 10, 17, 132, 143-44, 147, 190, 223, 261
Vogel, E.F., 166, 167

W

Walberg, H., 40
Ware, L.M., 146
Warmth, 238-39
Weiss, P., 33
Well-being, 34-36
Weyman, E., 151
White, R., 166, 189
White, R.W., 33, 86, 88
Whitman, R.M., 155
Whittaker, J.K., 144, 147, 148, 261
Wilson, G., 3, 5, 7, 120, 131, 170, 172
Wodarski, J.S., 15, 164, 165
Working groups, 190-11
Work with individuals, 273-77
  direct inventions, 275-77
  indirect inventions, 274-75
Work with the environment, 278-80
Work with the groups, 277-78

Y

Yalom, I.D., 123, 152, 157, 159, 186, 189, 206, 230, 271
Yelaja, S.A., 80

Z

Zander, A., 185, 186, 215